LETTERS OF
HELENA ROERICH

1935 - 1939

II

Portrait of Helena Roerich (1937), by Svetoslav Roerich.

LETTERS
of
HELENA ROERICH

1935-1939

VOLUME II

AGNI YOGA SOCIETY
2017

Agni Yoga Society
319 West 107th Street
New York NY 10025
www.agniyoga.org

© 1967 by Agni Yoga Society.
Published 1967.
Reprinted 2017.

PART I

1935

1

16 July 1935

I read with deep emotion your letter with the description of the solemn day on which the Society was opened. Thus was inaugurated one more beautiful movement as a bulwark against warring darkness. I know how much of your heart's aspiration and self-sacrificing work went into the foundation of this pure nucleus of Light in the name of victorious culture! You are therefore the first to receive my ardent greetings and the joy of my spirit at this beautiful celebration of your achievements. Please give my heartiest greetings and best wishes to the Administration and all the founding members of the Society, who worked for this benevolent goal. May this stronghold grow in strength, and may it courageously, luminously, and joyously utilize its forces on the path of service for the General Good.

I was also touched by your reaction to the lofty idea of the Banner of Peace, and I would therefore like to ask if you would consider establishing within your Society a permanent committee for the promotion of the Pact and Banner of Peace? It should be possible to unite those groups already existing, thus achieving solidarity and accord in actions. Think it over.

I find your precautions for guarding the Society against the penetration of undesirable members extremely useful. It is indeed important to guard against the harmful element from the very beginning. Do not attempt to enlarge your activities too much. Primarily, the nucleus of the Society should be worked out and brought into harmony. Large numbers were never a guarantee of success.

I understand your complete joy in associating with flaming hearts. I knew and still know such joy. However, years of experience have taught me to be more reserved and not to trust impulses too easily, and especially of those who have just approached the Teaching. In the beginning, we all march like burning torches; but later, under the action of the unfailing occult laws, our true nature begins to reveal itself more rapidly, and certain characteristics, that we did not even suspect we had, come to the surface, qualities which otherwise perhaps would have remained unrevealed until the next incarnation. The Great Teacher says in *The Mahatma Letters*, "As the water develops the heat of caustic lime so does the teaching bring into fierce action every unsuspected potentiality latent in him [the aspirant]."

And now regarding your questions: One must bear in mind that during the whole expanse of their lives all the Great Teachers, and Mahatmas, or the White Brothers, were Bodhisattvas. Maha-Chohan, or Great Lord, is the title of the Lord of Shambhala. The duties connected with this appointment are undertaken alternately by the White Brothers, according to their individual tasks. The Seven Chohans correspond to the Seven Kumaras of *The Secret Doctrine*, but esoterically there are eight of them. All these Seven Kumaras were the Lords of Fire, who endowed humanity with Mind.

As for the brothers of darkness, these are certainly encountered within humanity itself. They are very numerous, and no wonder, for their path is the path of gratification of the base passions. The percentage of true workers of Light is very small; likewise, the percentage of "fireflies" is not large, the more so in that their ignorance and lukewarmness, or non-resistance to evil, work for the benefit of the brothers of darkness. It is difficult to imagine how skillful are the spirits of high degree among the brothers of darkness who consciously work for disunity. It is said that they love to use those who approach the Teaching of Light and who attach themselves to communities established for the Common Good, yet are not firm in devotion and convictions. Playing upon their waverings and by instilling doubt, they are able to bring on confusion and deterioration. That is why caution is advised with the new untested souls when they approach the Teaching. The brothers of darkness are very fond of brilliant intellects developed at the expense of heart, for through them they can act most subtly. Indeed, only the crudest spirits attack and make use of low consciousnesses. "If humans are threatened by devils, the Archangel is accosted by Satan himself! If small devils bother brothers—Satan himself besets hermits." And as it is said in the first volume of *Leaves of Morya's Garden:* "I know thee who scratches at the door. Thou hopest upon the shoulders of a guest to enter My House. I know thee. Thou hast become subtle and resourceful, even more resourceful than many of Mine. Thou has fastened thy clasps and prepared thy garments. Thou hast even *studied all My expressions**. I hear thee pronounce even

---

* Emphases added.

JOY. But here I shall stop thee. Thou dost not dare pronounce the joy of Love. Thy joy is the joy of hatred. But behind hatred is hovering the loathsome shadow of doubt. And doubt is not worthy of a shield. I will receive thy arrows in My Shield. But if thou wilt persist. I will send thee with a smile—but one." Thus, let us protect ourselves from all those who waver.

* * *

You ask when the brothers of darkness came into existence. Strictly speaking, they came at the same time as the Brothers of Light, from the moment that there appeared a spark of intelligence and of conscious, that is, free, will in man. With the first glimpse of discrimination comes the first concept of good and evil, and the already conscious will directs man hither or thither. But an entirely organized camp of the brothers of darkness began to function in Atlantis, during the Fourth Race. Their great battle with the Sons of Wisdom, or Light, ended in victory for the latter and in the destruction of Atlantis.

At the head of the Sons of Light stands the Archangel Michael. His adversary in the camp of darkness is Satan (who still bears the name, Lucifer, although he lost the right to this name long ago); at one time he was amongst the great Kumaras, who bestowed the light of Mind upon the poor Earth-dwellers, who lacked it. In connection with this, read the legend about Lucifer in *On Eastern Crossroads**. This legend is based on a *great Truth*. Thus, the Prince of the World is now fighting for his very existence. The predicted great Armageddon of our race is in full swing. And again the Archangel Michael, with his resplendent host, is fighting against Lucifer. Of course, victory is always with the Forces of Light, but dreadful cataclysms are unavoidable. That is why the strongholds of Light are so essential-during the approaching threatening time they can give shelter to all the Forces of Light. Although the decisive moment is behind you there is still time for many children to grow old. Thus the destiny of the world is in the hands of humanity. The planet can be saved only if there is a resurrection of the spirit, only if the consciousness is liberated from the phantoms of the past and directed toward the construction of the New World on the basis

---

*   *On Eastern Crossroads, Legends and Prophecies of Asia*, (New York, Frederick A. Stokes company, 1930).

of a new understanding of cooperation and knowledge. As I have already written on these themes, I will quote from one of my letters, it might be helpful to you:

Every great Teacher, speaking of the end of the world, could not have had in mind the *final completion* of the evolution of our planet. For if evolution were to follow its natural course of development, the planet would enter its seventh and last cycle and its humanity would enter the Seventh Race, with all its sub-races, so that at the crowning of such an evolution there could not be a Day of Judgment. For by that time humanity and the planet would have reached the condition of the higher worlds where there is no imperfection or conscious opposition to good by any evil force.

But of course, the Great Teachers knew the difficult karma of humanity and the planet. They knew of the threatening danger, and therefore They had in mind the approaching removal of the race, which is always followed by tremendous cosmic cataclysms and is foreshadowed by the great sorting in advance of the final Judgment. Being Initiates, They knew that this catastrophe could become the Last Day, owing to the terrible downfall of spirituality in the human race. Quite possibly, there may not be a sufficient amount of high counteracting, or rather, discharging energies to save the planet from the final gigantic explosion. To this explosion the Prince of the World is directing all his efforts, since he knows that in a purified atmosphere pierced by the new fiery rays, or energies, the spheres of Earth will become unbearable for him, and his continued presence here made impossible. Therefore, he strives for an explosion in order to float away on the wreck.

Remember, in the Teaching it is said that precisely the spirit of man can become the exploder of the planet. It is mentioned also that the number of dischargers is very small, and that They bear the whole burden of maintaining the planet's balance. A strong spirit can save a whole area from earthquake. Thus, in the ancient days, the Great Teachers sent their advanced disciples to places threatened by earthquakes.

Many naive people think that the dark ones act only through evil, corruption and crime. How wrong they are! Only crude and relatively insignificant forces act in this way. Much more dangerous are those who masquerade under the Light of the Teaching.

Ignorance and lack of intuition push many into the arms of darkness, and deprive them for a long time, if not forever, of the salutary influence and attraction of the rays of the great Stronghold of Light. Dreadful is Armageddon—the dark forces are struggling for their very existence. Despair unites them and makes them so persistent in trying to achieve their aim. The Prince of the World has very many talented collaborators—some conscious, some unconscious—and it is foolish to think that they do not know the ways of the most cunning subtlety. They are very shrewd and inventive, and they act according to the level of their victims. But all of them lack tolerance and warmth of heart. Thus intertwined is darkness with Light on our Earth.

The snare of darkness is woven by skillful hands.

Many terrifying things are now practiced in the world. A great deal of the most disgusting sorcery is spread all over Earth. Of course the biggest centers of population are usually chosen by the main dark forces and are used as their centers. And their best weapon is the ignorant masses. That is why the unity of all the white and near-white forces is so essential! But the latter so easily become greyish and fill the ranks of those of whom it is said in the Apocalypse, "because thou art lukewarm, and neither cold nor hot, I will spue thee out of my mouth." Only the power of devotion and the striving to serve the Great Hierarchy of Light can save from the widely spread snares of the Prince of the World.

Yes, the wave of evil is inundating Earth, and all the efforts of the self-denying workers of Light are needed in order to save the sinking vessel of humanity! That is why it is so extremely important to send out the sparks of Light, but at the same time to watch lest he who receives a spark, by lending it to one who does not merit it, set fire to the whole structure. The human soul is bottomless! And the most dreadful scourge of the soul is ambition; verily, there is not a worse foe, nor a more common one. If this viper is not checked immediately, it assumes the size of a boa constrictor. Ambition is a burning scourge for the stoutest hearts, and a terrible torture, which man cruelly prepares for himself.

Once more, I welcome you in your beautiful work. In spite of difficulties, treasure the higher joy of achievement. This joy of achievement must be cultivated in oneself as well as in others. This is most essential, since only in it lies the pledge of the salvation of humanity, the pledge for the approach of the New World! Great Spiritual Toilers and heroes are needed! Thus, create heroes! This was the farewell bidding of one of the Highest Spirits when he was leaving our planet. Let us become heroines and spiritual toilers, and we shall be taking the shortest path, until a joyous meeting.

The joy of the future is ordained, but, indeed, the period of waiting at the threshold is always wearisome.

2

22 July 1935

The Teaching of Living Ethics is by no means for the weak-hearted, and therefore only well-tested souls should be accepted into this group—it is quality, not quantity that counts. If there is a shortage of strong hearts, it is better not to start. One should not profane the Teaching of Light, and besides, we are not missionaries. It is said in the Teaching that anyone who is forcibly enticed would become a "millstone on the neck." We are searching for free souls, unfettered by any fears. "The Teaching is not sugar-coated nuts and it is not silver trinkets. The Teaching is rich silver ore." The books of the Teaching will spread, and, what is more important, they will get into the right hands. So many souls are looking for Light and for new values amidst the chaos of scorned and abased lofty concepts. From all corners of the world come enquiries and pleas for more knowledge about how to join the Army of Light. That is why it is so joyous for us to carry our lamp.

You write about caution, but who knows the need for it better than I? But I know also of courage, of creative daring, and first of all, of great balance. Therefore, caution should not turn into the fear that springs from persecution, neither should daring become senseless bravado. However, because of my very nature, I prefer the latter; I believe in the wise proverb, "God helps the brave," and also another, a more prosaic one, "To be afraid of wolves means not going to the woods, not picking mushrooms." Thus, let us say that caution must be combined with daring and should be applied in wise co-measurement with the circumstances and conditions. But the sparks of Light, which kindle the new consciousnesses, should be cast into space, for otherwise where would be the guiding Principle? Without these sparks of Light, all will sink into darkness and deterioration.

I know that extracts from my letter caused all sorts of comments, but what does it matter? Praise emanating from certain types can only result in humiliation and pollution; I would therefore prefer to be attacked by them. The ancient wisdom says, "Name your enemies, and I shall tell who you are." And the Teaching says, "Without slander grateful humanity would have interred the most vital manifestations." We should add to this the wisdom of Christ, "A prophet is not without honor, but in his own country, and among his own kin, and in his own house." (St. Mark 6:4). This truth has been repeated by all the hounded and persecuted benefactors of mankind, during all times and in all nations, but, alas, it will remain as strong as ever until humanity goes through the fiery baptism of the spirit. Thus, I am not afraid of anathema, and hardly anyone who is truly devoted to the Teaching and to the evolution of the spirit is afraid of it. Hence, I shall never renounce my convictions: I believe in the Unutterable Divine Principle, which abides in each human being, and I believe in the birth of Christ in the human soul on its way to perfection. Moreover, every educated man knows the significance of the terms *Krestos* or *Kristos* (Christ), and that they were taken from the pagan vocabulary. I wrote recently to one of my co-workers about the meaning of this term, and I will repeat it to you. Krestos was the designation given to a neophyte who was on probation as a candidate for the degree of Hierophant. Only after a disciple went through all the sufferings and passed all the tests, in the last ritual of initiation he was anointed and became according to the language of the Mysteries, Christ, "the purified." His finite personality was fused with his infinite individuality and he then became an immortal Ego. For the first Christians, the word *Christos* or Christ was synonymous with our higher Ego. In this sense, one should understand that Christ is the Redeemer of sins. Thus, the redemption of personal sins is performed by the soul—the conductor and the messenger of Christ—perpetually, during the long chain of earthly lives of our individual Ego. "The crucified Christ is represented in every human being, who, after the achievement of a certain degree of evolution, must descend into hell and bring back to the higher or normal state the soul fallen there through the lawless deeds of its lower ego. In other words, the Divine Love must reach the heart of a man and must conquer and regenerate him before he is able to realize the monstrosity of his transgressions against Divine Law and forgive himself for the sins committed against himself. This forgiveness can be achieved only through a complete fusion and unification with the higher Ego or with the Divine Law of Love."

In Christianity, I adhere to the faith of the first Christian Fathers, and I especially revere the great Origen and St. Anthony. I dream of a new ecumenical council, which would return to the pure foundations of the early centuries of Christianity. In the wonderful books of *Dobrotolubye** one can find beautiful thoughts. One even comes across praise for the enemies! Because no one but they can evoke so well our hidden abilities and qualities; and so they have been called "Christ's cauterizers," for in ancient days many diseases were treated by cauterization.

It is admirable that you plan to apply the Teaching in life. Verily, just as faith is dead without deeds, so the Teaching is useless without its application in life.

I understand what you mean in your letter and what you would like to learn. But I must warn you that I am against any kind of sentimentality and the rosy promises about the ease of attainments that abide in the late occult literature. Precisely they engender so many lukewarm, halfway aspirations which lead nowhere. Life has taught me how dangerous are all sorts of promises and encouragement of impossible hopes, how ruinous they can be, and how much betrayal they may cause. Therefore I do not like to conceal the reality if I see that the spirit is ready to accept it. I would rather keep silent than lull one with rosy promises.

And how can one promise anything when the key to all achievements is in man himself, and *without his participation no one else* can do anything for him? The Highest Teacher can help him only at a certain period when the spirit is ready to open the heart to the Call and to put into action his dormant divine forces. However, the strengthening of these forces is possible only if the disciple constantly continues to intensify his efforts to perfect and transfigure his inner being. Collaboration is a necessary condition in everything. Therefore, you should point out to all newcomers that there are endless degrees of disciples-

---

* Love of the good.

hip and of the approach to Light, and that each one can occupy only that degree which corresponds to his past accumulations; likewise, he can ascend the ladder only by his own intensive striving in the present.

But the path of Service is still more difficult, since this is the path of achievement, which requires complete self-denial. You may think that our life is easy, but if you knew the reality, your heart would speak differently. In order to bear the entire burden of the awesome responsibility and ever-growing difficulties, I affirm myself every day in joy and readiness to face the most difficult. Indeed, beauty is in self-denial. And now more than ever the world needs spiritual toilers and heroes, now, in the threatening days of Armageddon.

But, I do not summon anyone, and you should not call the spiritually immature, because an excessive burden is not useful. Great tempering of spirit and heart is necessary, for each day brings us all sorts of trials. The strain and tension of a bearer of the burden of the New World is awful! His work is performed on three planes; by his energies, he discharges the surrounding atmosphere, often preventing destructive earthquakes in his vicinity; he carries the burden of those who turn to him and is greatly responsible for all that is entrusted to him. Only very strong spirits can enter the Path of Service. Therefore one should never entice, or tempt by rosy promises.

Certainly, even the thorough reading of the books of the Teaching will invariably bring benefit through broadening the consciousness, thus affording a possibility for new flights of the spirit. But it is impossible to expect immediate fiery achievements and a fiery transmutation of the centers if the Teaching is applied spasmodically. The occult laws are exact and unfailing. The most exact correspondence prevails in the realm of the occult. Also, newcomers should be warned about one more occult law which is beautifully described by H. P. Blavatsky in an article called "Warning" in the third volume of *The Secret Doctrine*.

The coming year, 1936, which has already begun esoterically, will lay the foundation for many remarkable events. However, very few will be able to comprehend their significance. Just remember that everything happens in Inscrutable Ways; and therein is great wisdom, otherwise the dark forces would destroy all the best possibilities and beginnings. Thus, the proverb,

"Man proposes, and God disposes," is particularly true in decisive events.

I believe that you would fulfill a great task if you could take a stand for the defense of the Teaching. There are so many opportunities where you could say a good word, and one need not look for special occasions or deliver unusual speeches. An appropriate word, spoken at the right time, often leads to great deeds, or arrests ruinous results.

And so, please do not worry too much. Strive with your heart toward the Teaching, and much will be simplified and become clear. Each luminous undertaking is created in unexpected ways.

True, the volcano is raging, and much darkness is around, but those devoted to the service for the Common Good need not be alarmed. Calamities always happen to the lukewarm ones, those who follow half-ways and are fond of half-measures. We shall not err in saying that the peril to the world lies in half-measures and in non-resistance to evil. Verily, we live again in the times of Atlantis! Only now one should provide not an ark, but an airplane. And the best airplane is the wings of the spirit.

Courageously accept vigilance, and strong faith in the Leading Hand will carry you over any and all abysses. Courage, courage, and again courage—is today's dictum. The feathers of fear pull us down, whereas the wings of courage carry us over the abyss. Thus, let us be inspired by the beauty of courage and by the power of faith in the luminous future. I send joy to you, but this is a special joy, it is the joy of difficulties. When we shall learn not to be frightened by difficulties, we shall come close to the bearing of achievement.

3

30 July 1935

The definition of the Monad is correct. Thus, in *The Secret Doctrine* it is said that, "the Monad or Jiva *per se* cannot be even called spirit: it is a ray, a breath of the ABSOLUTE, or the Absoluteness rather... having no relations with the conditioned and relative finiteness, [Absoluteness] is unconscious on our plane. Therefore, besides the material which will be needed for its future human form, the monad requires *(a)* a spiritual model, or prototype, for that material to shape itself into; and *(b)* an intelligent consciousness to guide its evolution and progress, neither of which is possessed by the homogeneous monad, or by senseless though living matter. The Adam of dust requires the *Soul of Life* to be breathed into him: the two middle principles, which are the *sentient* life of the irrational animal and the Human Soul, for the former is irrational without the latter." Thus, "The Monad becomes a personal ego when it incarnates; and something remains of that [incarnate] personality through Manas, when the latter is perfect enough to assimilate Buddhi." Thus, individuality is built gradually, and can only be partially expressed on Earth.

More from *The Secret Doctrine*: "Metaphysically speaking, it is of course an absurdity to talk of the 'development' of a Monad, or to say that it becomes 'Man'... It stands to reason that a MONAD cannot either progress or develop, or even be affected by the changes of states it passes through. *It is not of this world or plane*, and may be compared only to an indestructible star of divine light and fire, thrown down on to our Earth as a plank of salvation for the personalities in which it indwells. It is for the latter to cling to it; and thus partaking of its divine nature, obtain immortality. Left to itself the Monad will cling to no one; but, like the 'plank,' be drifted away to another incarnation by the unresting current of evolution." It is also advisable to reread paragraph 275 in *Agni Yoga*.

And now with regard to Divine Love, what else can it be but the Great Principle, or the beginning of attraction, or affinity, or that very Fohat in its differentiation as Divine Love (Eros), the electric power of affinity and sympathy, allegorically manifested in the attempt to combine the pure spirit, which is a ray inseparable from the One or Absolute, with the soul. These two form the monad in man, whereas in nature it is the first link between *the eternally unconditional and the manifested.*

I am happy to tell you that I receive the most beautiful reports about your book. It is so pleasing to hear that, after having read your book, young souls are looking to you for leadership.

Work joyously, and bring light to the seeking souls.

4

30 August 1935

I received your letter a few days ago, and of course I would be very glad to help you. However, I think it is my duty to warn you that I do not agree with many of the statements in the books mentioned by you; moreover, I consider them to be even harmful. In life we come across bearers of various states of consciousness, and we must follow those responding most closely to our own spiritual and intellectual development. If, therefore, my words shall make you feel indignant, say so, and we shall send a friendly greeting to each other, while each follows his own path.

I am not familiar with the doctrine of the Liberal Catholic Church, and am therefore unable to say anything either for or against it. With regard to Donov, I have heard of him and have also read his good little book *Three Foundations of Life**. However, I must oppose your remark, and must state that there is only one Hierarchy of Light, which is of course, the Trans-Himalayan Hierarchy. Just as Light conquers darkness, so does the Hierarchy of Light battle against and defeat the hierarchy of darkness. The latter is very strong, since it acts through a multitude of followers. Not one teacher, living on Earth in ordinary earthly conditions, can be compared with the great Himalayan Masters. Those Masters are so lofty in their spiritual achievement that they are no longer able to accept the burden of purely earthly existence and of a personal, direct leadership of and contact with the masses. That would constitute an unproductive expenditure of forces. Their tasks are planetary-cosmic to such an extent that They can allocate only a portion of Their forces to the direct guidance of certain units of humanity, and therefore They use Their nearest trusted ones and disciples for the purpose of transmitting the spiritual Teaching. At the present time, Their main forces are concentrated on the gigantic battle with the destructive dark forces in the Subtle World and on Earth, on staying the clashing of the nations until a certain time, and on suppressing the subterranean fire which threatens to explode our planet. Verily, frightful is the tension of Their forces for the salvation of Earth; while humanity, in its madness, walls up dynamite everywhere. Thus, because of such small numbers of co-workers on Earth, these selfless Guardians of ungrateful and ignorant humanity have taken completely upon themselves the incredible burden of discharging destructive energies.

You write that you want knowledge, knowledge, and again knowledge! I presume you mean spiritual knowledge. If you have the fiery and constant striving toward the one chosen Image of

---

* Peter Donov (Riga, Gudkov, 1931)

the Hierarch of Light, you will achieve it. And the degree of this knowledge will depend wholly upon the accumulations of your own Chalice in previous lives, and on the power and ardor of your strivings in this life.

If you are to succeed you must remember constantly and ardently with your heart the One Chosen Image. Also, if you wish to practice self-discipline, choose one or two of your worst qualities or habits and try to rid yourself of them. This discipline seems very simple, but in reality is extremely complex and difficult; still it is certainly the most fundamental method.

You say that the counsels in Agni Yoga are so scattered that it is difficult to combine them into a system. However, to this I will say that this is the Teaching of Life in all its complexity, and the counsels were given to the disciples precisely on examples from life, when the circumstances which caused them arose; in this way they could be more easily assimilated. Indeed, the whole of nature demonstrates how a perfect organism develops its organs simultaneously, and not successively. Thus, the Teaching of Life is so constructed that on each new step the consciousness is able to embrace the greatest possible periphery and thus enter life, yet not be withdrawn from it.

Have you the first books, *Leaves of Morya's Garden I* and *II*? In a way, they are an introduction to the Agni Yoga Series, but in essence they actually deal with the majority of questions and aspects of life which are treated in detail and elucidated from different angles in the next volumes of the Teaching.

You are right, the purer the conductor, the easier it is for the Forces of Light to operate through him—indeed, purity of soul is essential. As it is said, purified psychic energy is a panacea for all diseases.

5

3 September 1935

Your statement is correct: precisely, the Fire of Space, when realized is transmuted into psychic energy. The so-called principles in us (excluding the physical body and the etheric double, which dissipate after death) are only aspects, or conditions, of our consciousness. Indeed all sub-divisions (spirit, soul, higher or lower Manas) are in reality only various qualities of the same fundamental energy of fire, life or consciousness—the highest aspect of which is psychic energy. Therefore, in order to attain the Fiery World—the world of the higher spirituality—we have to transmute or sublimate the fires of our nerve centers up to their seventh state. Thus, the Fiery World is the world of sublimated feelings or consciousness. Verily not one human feeling disappears; it exists in its subtle condition in the Fiery World and responds to higher attractions and vibrations. The whole of Cosmos is built upon the septenary principle, therefore, each energy, each manifestation includes in itself its septenary scale of tension and refinement.

And now, concerning the Mother of the World, each concept should be considered in its various aspects. Each cosmic principle or manifestation has its reflections or embodiments on Earth. Thus, the Mother of the World, when considered in her cosmic aspect, is Mulaprakriti, the One, all-containing, all-conceiving. In the earthly reflection, however, She is the Great Spirit of the Feminine Principle. Behind each manifestation, each aspect, and each symbol stands the great Individuality. Thus, each high Individuality has its own substitutes or personifiers, the nearest to it by ray, and sometimes it appears personally in such incarnations. Hence the concept of Avatara. Thus, the high Spirit that was incarnated, let us say, as Isis, Ishtar, etc., did not necessarily have to be the spirit of the Mother of the World, but was impregnated by her Ray; and, indeed, because of this, in the later legends the image of Isis became fused with the Image of the Great Mother of the World.

Yes, the period of our planet is now passing through is very grave and tense. Frequent earthquakes have poisoned the atmosphere closest to Earth, and one can expect outbursts of new madnesses in human consciousness. That is why it is so important to spread the books of Living Ethics. It is excellent that you pay attention to various omens—you should write them down.

I do not agree with you that eloquence is so essential. It is not a bad asset, but that is all. Of most importance is the quality of one's aura. Often, an eloquent speaker leaves just a fleeting impression, that is, if the spiritual tension of his aura was insignificant. Whereas two or three words spoken from the heart by a bearer of a luminous aura may transform the one who comes into touch with him. Thus, the main influence comes not from words, but rather from the quality and the tension of our inner fire. The very presence of such fiery aura in a large and mixed gathering brings soothing accord. It can happen that a mediocre lecturer, for some reason, singularly kindles his audience, and he gives himself the credit for it; but in reality there may have been in the crowd one or two intense harmonious auras, which, by their powerful vibrations, created the atmosphere favorable for perception. Arhip Ivanovich Kuinji, the teacher of N.K. [Prof. Nicholas Roerich.], was quite devoid of the gift of words. With difficulty, and between lengthy pauses, he could combine only a few words, but by the power of his inner fire, he could make such a tremendous impression with those few words. This abrupt speech suited his powerful spirit—like the heavy blows of a sculptor's hammer, it could bring forth sparks from blocks of stone!

6

5 September 1935

One must not be disturbed by disagreements between representatives of the various religio-philosophical systems, for out of the friction of opinions fly sparks of one Truth! However, I would certainly advise you to become more fully acquainted with the Eastern thought; many problems will then be solved easily. The difficulty lies in the fact that the Western mind can hardly, if at all, accept contradictions, whereas this acceptance is considered by the East as precisely the foundation of its philosophical systems, beginning with cosmogony and cosmology and ending with the moral code. Thus, he who worships only the formless Aspect in the highest state of illumination exclaims, "Verily, Formless and Form are one. Brahman (the highest Reality) and Maya (illusion) are one!"

Also it is essential to explain what is Samadhi, or the highest spiritual illumination. So much is written about this state by people who have never experienced it, or who have just experienced it in its slightest form. But there are as many gradations of Samadhi as there are degrees of consciousness and cycles of spiritual perfectment. The degree of illumination obtained corresponds always with our spiritual accumulations. Hence the variety in the depth of these illuminations should be made clear. If the attainment of Samadhi could give us omniscience, then the idea of Infinity would have to be abandoned. Moreover, the consciousness immersed in Samadhi obtains illumination in accordance with its individual accumulations and the spheres accessible to it, and can transfer only a part of these experiences to the physical plane. For the physical organism is unable to respond for a long time to the highest vibrations and impress them upon the brain without ruinous effects. Science has already proven the destructive effect of discrepant vibrations. Thus, a man returning from Samadhi retains certain memories, but this does not imply that he becomes all-knowing and that henceforth he can penetrate into the essence of any event. He has seen or experienced a certain state of ecstasy or a higher tension of emotion, or he has gained insight into the essence of this or that manifestation. Thus he may have achieved the perception of eternal being, of the highest love, of the beauty of Be-ness, of the unity of all beings, or of his presence in everything and union with all and everything; nevertheless, he will not become omniscient in the earthly sense of the word. Perceptions in Samadhi are of a different nature; one may come close to the nuomena of things, but on returning to Earth one must study their effects by *earthly* methods. It is, of course, exceedingly difficult to describe in words the inexpressible. But still, "Thought reigns above all Samadhi. The higher, the more powerful. The more flaming the thought, the more useful the manifestation. Truly, thought is all-powerful and limitless." Moreover, on our planet the attainment of Samadhi is accessible only to a high Arhat who lives in completely different conditions. Certainly Vivekananda did not achieve complete Samadhi, but, not being sufficiently prepared for it physically, even the degree of Samadhi in which he was immersed brought its sad results. His earthly death was the result of this premature and forcible experience.

The human organism of our planetary cycle is still far from such perceptions, and therefore lengthy preparation is needed, not only for this kind of manifestation but also for lesser fiery ones. The very finest vibrations of the unregulated force of Kundalini may destroy a body which is not trained or tempered for its acceptance. Let us bear in mind that the so-called "yogi," Ramacharaka (an American by the name of Atkinson), certainly was never a yogi even if he was amongst the listeners of Vivekananda. Hence the freedom with which he writes about mechanical methods without clarifying all the dangers connected with such forcing.

Thousands of books dealing with easy mechanical methods of developing the hidden lower psychic powers are now thrown upon the world book market. In truth, these ignorant and irresponsible writers are collaborating with the forces of darkness. The latter want nothing so much as to open certain centers in people and thus get hold of them, and through them to join in earthly life in order to fulfill their dark plans. Indeed they are trying to retain around Earth an atmosphere polluted by the very low emanations necessary for their existence.

Without doubt, simple, rhythmic breathing is in itself quite beneficial. People forget not only the benefit to be derived from fresh air but precisely how to breathe correctly, which actually is the foundation of our health. However, the pranayama of Hatha Yoga has nothing to do with such rhythmic breathing. The pranayama employed by the Hatha Yogis has as its purpose, by means of suspension of breath, rotation and other gymnastics, the arousing and calling forth of an influx of blood to certain centers, thus causing their increased activity. But one can well imagine how harmful it can be for a man to arouse the centers that are in organs which, for some reason, are weakened or even diseased; certainly their diseased condition will only be intensified. That explains why there are so many unfortunate cases among those who practice pranayama under ignorant and irresponsible teachers. The opening of the centers can safely take place only under the guidance of a Great Teacher, who sees the true condition of one's organism in all its complexity, and who knows what can be applied or permitted, and when. Let us bear in mind that precisely during the transmutation of the centers a tremendous tension and influx of blood toward them take place. The Teacher must know how, at times, to transfer these tensions to a less dangerous place, or to divert the excess of blood, in order to avoid general conflagration and even fiery death. Believe me, the Teacher will not lose a single moment if a disciple is ready for such transmutation, and will provide whatever is necessary for his organism in accordance with his way of life.

I have written enough to my correspondents about the harm of mechanical ways, and about the danger of the development of mediumship. For true discipleship, it is essential to apply the strength of the spirit and to know the truth, rather than to be tempted by all sorts of tricks, accessible to any medium.

After my definition of Samadhi, you can see how relative are illuminations. The concept of Infinity excludes the possibility of ever achieving absolute knowledge, and therein lies the entire grandeur—this is LIFE. Each Manvantara, each cycle has its truth, and humanity is given that portion of it which can be assimilated during that particular cycle. Of course, the Arhats cannot disagree on fundamental principles, but even they are perpetually learning and deepening their knowledge. Is it possible to imagine complete cognition? Surely that would be equivalent to annihilation! Indeed, what then would happen with our consciousness, the very essence of which lies in perpetual motion and perception? Infinite is life, and infinite are its perceptions and possibilities. I will conclude my explanation, with joy in the Immeasurable and Unutterable Grandeur.

And now regarding the Voice of Silence, or the voice of the Invisible Teacher. Most certainly, this voice may not necessarily be the voice of our higher Ego, but precisely the voice of the Teacher; for these manifestations are almost indissolubly linked with each other. Is it possible to hear the voice of the Teacher if our higher Ego is in a "somnolent" state? In true spiritual development (and not in the case of a medium) our higher Ego is indeed receptive to the voice of the Invisible Teacher. Therefore, when we begin to hear the voice of the Teacher, we also hear the voice of our higher Ego.

Do not be distressed, and remember that "all is possible in the realm of the spirit." Think of the parable about Dgul Nor in the Teaching. Once this formula is firmly realized, the mysticism which attracts you cannot be lost. Truly, we live in Infinity, and one should never lose sight of the significance of this majestic concept. Thus, trust your heart more; this is the only measurement, always and in everything.

Regarding Mme. Kryjanovsky, for your information I may tell you that the best pages in her books are written, based, and compiled on automatic writings and also on the visions of her blind sister. I was told this by a friend of their family. Besides, she was undoubtedly well acquainted with many occult writings. She certainly read the works of H. P. Blavatsky, for there is a quotation from *The Secret Doctrine* in her series of books about the Magi. But it is quite possible that H. P. B. herself borrowed this particular passage from some travel books. At the end of the last century, Western literature, particularly that in English, was enriched by not a small quantity of so-called occult novels, which often testified to the considerable spiritual enlightenment of their authors. Along with some remarkable pages in Kryjanovsky's novels, one also finds a great deal of vulgarity. Nevertheless, I prefer her "Magi" series to many contemporary novels, for books of this kind always awaken the imagination of the reader and inspire him, over and above grey commonness, toward the unusual and beautiful.

Certain writers erroneously attempt to make a Celt and a western Initiate out of Rama, this purest Aryan, an Avatar of Vishnu, and the hero of the majestic epic poem the *Ramayana*. The Cycle of Rama definitely exists, because Rama is an Avatar of Vishnu, and consequently the energies of his spirit nourish the consciousness of humanity for a particular term, or cycle.

St. Yves d'Alveidre was a psychic and a medium; and toward the end of his life, he fell under the sway of his astral instructors to such an extent that his books are perhaps even more erroneous than the books of some other authors of occult novels. Of course, his Agarta and the Supreme Pontiff are his peculiar refraction of the great Shambhala and its Lord. It is amusing to see how he mixed existing exoteric legends with the astral accumulations and instructions received by him from astral impersonators. He is a victim of irresponsible astral instructors. Thus, the name Vatan, given for a secret language sounds strange to an Orientalist. According to him, he got this word from some initiated Brahmin, but in Arabic, Urdu, and Persian, vatan means motherland. Apparently, St. Yves d'Alveidre misunderstand the man with whom he was talking, and who was simply trying to tell him about his mother tongue.

I have read his biography, and it is obvious that he was not a bad person, but that his mediumistic nature and his interest in spiritualism enfeebled his weak organism, resulting in mental imbalance.

To show you to what extent the lofty concept of the Stronghold of the Great Brotherhood in its various aspects penetrates and lives in the consciousness of different nations, I will cite for you certain information about a presently existing society in the Far East. This society has many members and, as I understand, accepts even foreigners into its midst. It has its sacred army, which has nothing in common with a military organization. However, it adheres strictly to the established hierarchic principles. The main meeting place of this society, which is called "The Extraordinary Moment," is on one of the local "holy mountains." Now, this sacred army is preparing for an "Extraordinary Moment," which is understood in the broadest and, what is most important, in the spiritual sense. Thus, according to their teaching, the world is now facing a crisis, after which its spiritual regeneration, or rather new birth, may be expected. Thus, all sorts of conferences, conflicts, all sorts of attractions and repulsions are greatly on the increase. Humanity is suffering the pains of childbirth, but "the time will come when the gates of Heaven will open, and the earthly world will return to the heavenly world." Six stages, six steps lead to this moment:

1. The first period of the Omens—the end of the Great War.

2. The second period of the Omens—political and economic failures due to international psychology.

3. The first period of cataclysms (short)—unprecedented upheavals in the whole world.

4. The second period of cataclysms (short)—the appearance of Heavenly Forces in the arena.

5. The first period of constructiveness—the enlightened reign of the Heavenly Emperor in the world, governmental order marked by monism of the religious cult and of the affairs of state. This will be a hegemony of Light over the world, dispensed by the Heavenly Emperor through the establishment of inviolable institutions of power, which by that time will be in effect. This enlightened reign will be expressed by a special term. ...

6. The second period of constructiveness—the coming of divinely inspired rulers, representatives of science, technology, etc. At present, according to the members of this society, the world is in the second of the stages mentioned above. The prophets of this movement speak of the new world as the kingdom of Spirit, through direct communion of men with gods. This, they say, will be an earthly life without disease and hardships; life illumined by the light of Truth, Goodness, Beauty, Joy, and Love; life directed by the Heavenly Emperor on the principle of justice. In all this, the most remarkable thing is that this Great Plan was, they say, conceived many thousands of years ago and the Central World Encampment of the Great Gods upon the Sacred Mountain, where gods gather together, and its earthly projection is the mountain of this holy vicinity. So you can see how a great thought is refracted by all nations, and inevitably each one of them attributes the main role to its own people and country.

* * *

Do not blame T., he really did not know Russia. The deliberately distorted ideas regarding Russia held even today by foreigners only reveal their ignorance. For the majority of foreigners, Russia was and is a country of vandalism, all sorts of violations and license, and, above all, of profound ignorance. Even the best minds believe that Russia has not progressed very far since the times of Ivan the Terrible. Civilization has supplanted the meaning of culture, and many do not understand that one can be a civilized savage. People forget that the accumulations of culture are gathered over centuries, whereas civilization can be established in one decade.

* * *

It is true that there cannot be any disagreement among the Arhats, for the truth they know is the truth attainable by the spirit who has completed his self-perfectment not only for Earth but also for the highest planets of our solar system.

In *The Mahatma Letters to A. P. Sinnett* it is said regarding Buddha that his spirit had run so successfully through his previous incarnations that he "escaped further reincarnations, but only on this earth... he will have to get reincarnated on the next planet. Only, ... he will be re-born in the highest—the seventh ring of the upper planet." Infinite is life and infinite are its attainments and possibilities. And so I shall finish this letter rejoicing at the Immeasurable and Unutterable Grandeur.

7

24 September 1935

It is most essential to point out the difference between mediumship, psychism and true spiritual development. Much harm has been done by books about all kinds of Hatha Yoga exercises. What ignorance is displayed in thinking that the highest and subtlest can be achieved by purely mechanical methods! You are quite right when you say that people, in striving for spiritual development (which to them so often means the achievement of psychic powers), forget that without active service to the General Good this development will be one-sided and unstable. Our inner fires are kindled only through contact with people. Only thus can we test ourselves; only thus shall we be able to sharpen and temper the blade of our spirit. Undoubtedly, certain isolation and *periodic* retreat is essential for the restoration of our forces. However, constant seclusion will never provide that tension of our forces which alone can bring their refinement. Many statements in the Teaching confirm this. For example, in the second book of *Leaves of Morya's Garden,* on page 47, it is said: "Christ, Buddha, and their closest co-workers did not use magic formulae but acted and created in full blending with the spirit. Therefore, in the new evolution the former artificial methods must be *abandoned. ...The mechanics of yogism are no longer suitable for the regeneration of the world.*" And further on, "Many times have saints returned to Earth because they had conveyed to the crowd too much of their exaltation instead of the structure of life. We are absolutely averse to monasteries, for they are the antithesis of life. ... *Indeed, through life one must attain.*" Likewise in the book *Agni Yoga* it is said, in the middle of paragraph 161. "Raja Yoga, Jnana Yoga, Bhakti Yoga are all isolated from their surrounding reality [from active participation in life]; and because of this they cannot enter into the evolution of the future." And in paragraph 163, "This most unifying Yoga [Agni Yoga] exacts an obligation *to construc* the entire life in conformity with a discipline externally imperceptible." This means that while constructing and working, one should take certain precautions and should follow the indicated regimen for maintaining health. Thus, if we study the lives of the Great Teachers of humanity, we shall discover that none of them shut themselves off from life, but poured all their forces, spiritual and physical, into the service of the General Good. Thus, in everything let us follow these great examples in a lofty attainment of self-renunciation. The crown of self-renunciation is glorious!

You could in turn, ask your questioners, "Would your spiritual development be benefited by knowledge of the degree of the spiritual height of Christ and Buddha?" You can quote to them from paragraph 8, page 190 of the second book of *Leaves of Morya's Garden:* "People will ask: 'Who is greater, Christ or Buddha?' Answer: 'It is impossible to measure the far-off worlds. We can only be enraptured by their radiance.'" Verily, compared to us Earth-dwellers, Christ and Buddha are indeed far-off stars of the Spirit. Let us remember that They, and also the Lord Maitreya, came from Venus at the dawn of the formation of physical man, therefore They are our Divine Forefathers and Masters.

Now, about St. Yves d'Alveidre, he was a typical psychic, who practiced spiritualism and came under the control of astral impersonators. His books are a strange mixture of fragments of truth with errors.

Certainly, to those unacquainted with Eastern thought, and who are approaching the Teaching of Living Ethics for the first time, one must give only as much as their consciousness is ready to assimilate. As it is said, "We must not intercept someone's thought, but infuse the new blood of life by nurturing the nervous system. Each answering word must be *not the nail of a coffin but the physician's ray.* A deferred reply may come in the form of advice."

Disillusioning people or shattering their point of view is only permissible when great caution is used. We can do it gradually by suggesting fragments of new thought, by a gradual process of broadening the consciousness; but it is dangerous to make a too abrupt break. To be sure, for some people books like the novels of Kryjanovsky or the fantasies of St. Yves d'Alveidre are inspiring, so that a strong criticism of such books might extinguish the weak flame of their spirits. Only strong spirits, unattached to earthly things, are able to face the truth in all its superterrestrial beauty. But it is inadmissible to open the eyes by force.

And now something else. Suggestion, if applied with force for the purpose of gain, is not only interference in karma but is plainly criminal. Whereas if we inspire and call forth lofty thoughts in man and his finer essence, or if we can restrain him from vice, such action is, of course, benevolent.

If, while doing good, we take a certain part of karma upon ourselves, such karma surely does not encumber our *spiritual* progress. Only the Arhat knows where and when he must not help; as for ourselves, we should stretch forth a helping hand whenever our heart tells us to do so. While doing this, however, we must always remember the law of commensurability and goal-fitness, also, that spiritual help is the highest.

There are some people who think they should give everything away, thereby making themselves dependent upon others! To such people we might speak with these words of the Teaching, "Who hath said that one must renounce madly! Madness doth so remain." However, one must help, for who knows when we are paying our old debts! Thus, if we refuse to help, we might thereby increase the interest on our debt with accumulating interest. It is a great mistake to refuse to help one's near ones because of fear of complicating one's own karma. Will this not be an act of the greatest egoism or selfhood? But of course one must learn to discriminate at the same time, since often one may help the undeserving and refuse the one truly in need. Here, as well, the heart is the *only judge*. Thus, if the help required is within our power, we should render it.

Above all, we should remember that our karma is created, weighted, or eased mainly by THOUGHTS. Precisely, thought and inner motives weave our aura, which is a magnetic field that either attracts or repels possibilities. Indeed, thought-motive—this decisive factor of our karma—is often overlooked by those who discuss karma. But were it otherwise, it would be impossible to break the magic circle of causes and effects. For all is karma and all is held by karma. However, when we finish one round of karma for a certain cycle, we start a new round on other planes and worlds, and so unto Infinity. When the conclusion of karma is spoken of, it means that karma is ended only for a certain cycle or planet, etc. Thus, the conclusion of a man's karma on our planet means that his inner nature has purified and transmuted its energies to such an extent that further physical life on Earth can no longer give him anything; precisely, all the elements or energies which formed his being have reached that state of perfection which was the limit for this planet. Such a spirit, depending upon his mission, either stays in the higher spheres around Earth or leaves for the higher worlds. Thus, thought is the primary cause and the crown of all creation. Thoughts rule the world, consequently they rule karma.

* * *

Do not be unhappy because of the necessity for spending so much time earning your living. We must all earn our bread. Indeed, all should be accomplished without retiring from life and by earthly hands and feet. Therein lies great beauty. Is labor performed in comfort and prosperity of great value? And do we ever hear much about such labor? No, all the giants of thought created amidst most trying circumstances. The work performed in ease and affluence cannot bring about the necessary tension of all the centers.

Verily, material prosperity and ease are our most dangerous

enemies. Nothing extinguishes the inner fire so quickly as security for the morrow. We do not know such security, and we work on the border of exigency and possibilities. However, at a difficult moment, when all our forces are tensed, when we have applied all our resourcefulness, help comes, but at the last moment—such is the law. All earthly burdens are necessary for the growth of the spirit. Thus, the best flowers of joy grow beside thorny roads. In time, new conditions will come into existence and the tasks will become broader. Possibly there will no longer be worries about earning a living, but there will be new problems, far more complicated and difficult. But if the Image of the Teacher lives in our hearts, can we worry about tomorrow! That which is considered the worst, from a human point of view, sometimes becomes our salvation and a step toward new possibilities. Verily, if our service is unselfish, not one hair will fall from our heads without the knowledge of the Great Teacher. Unselfish service, sincere devotion, and gratitude weave a strong thread by which all that is needful comes to us.

Thus, let us courageously meet the inevitable trials, and let us nurture the spirit through communion with seekers of Light. Events are ripening, one may expect many changes. But if we serve the great Light, the most destructive wave can only bear us upwards. Let us, therefore, in complete confidence in the Leading Hand create the light-bearing work.

8

1 October 1935

I received your call and am ready to respond as far as is in my power. Spiritual help is indeed the highest, and I shall be happy if I can give you such help. However, a certain unification of consciousnesses and contact on the mental plane is quite essential. As it is said in the Teaching, "One may picture two conversationalists of approximately the same development who yet do not understand each other. Perhaps between their consciousnesses only a few small links are missing, yet this small difference forces the cogwheels of thinking to turn differently, with the result that altogether different levers are set in motion." [New Era Community] Thus, I await your questions, for without questions there can be no answers.

You say, "Having suffered a deep spiritual disillusionment on my path, I have lost will and faith. Nevertheless, I still wait for the Teacher!" But if you wait, that means you have hope; therefore, faith is not yet lost, and this is most essential. Thus, let us go over your disappointments together and transmute them into accumulation of the great life experience, in the furnace of which our spiritual essence is conceived and strengthened. No theoretical knowledge, no philosophy can give you spirituality; only by drinking the cup of life's poison, with all its illusions, can we accumulate the Chalice of Amrita.

And so, I would like you to establish a clear point of view toward all disappointments. Should one be terrified by the destruction of illusions? Each broken illusion is another step of knowledge. True knowledge is austere, as is the spiritual path, and only the spiritually strong can hope to approach the path of accelerated spiritual development. Moreover, this path can never be eased, since only suffering, only *personal* tension can transmute our energies and give them the necessary balance. But blessed is he whose heart is aflame with the exaltation of heroic achievement; supernal joy becomes his lot. Thus, kindle all the fires of your heart, and exaltation of the spirit will be yours.

9

1 October 1935

You are right, it is most essential at present to think about *podvig**—people should understand *podvig* in daily life. Life is meaningless without *podvig*. And how expressive is the Russian word *podvig*, indeed, it has no equivalent in European languages. In this word there is a whole sense, the whole quality of aspiring action forward toward self-sacrificing *podvig*, into the future, into evolution!

I am happy to hear so many good reports about your book. I definitely know that it gave joy to all those who read it. The only obstacle is that our Russian readers are so very poor! But let nothing disturb you; just go ahead with your useful activities.

* * *

Did you know that the year 1935 has been prolific in lunar

---

* The word *podvig* is untranslatable from the Russian. I means a great or heroic deed plus spiritual achievement.

and solar eclipses? Thus, the second half of June and the beginning of July brought three eclipses, and the last solar eclipse will take place in December, about Christmas time. Eclipses are always followed by cosmic perturbations and by all sorts of madnesses in the world. This explains the poor condition of my health during all of this year, although there have also been other weighty reasons for it. The true natures of people are now being revealed everywhere, and this could be called the purification of space. Of course, knowing the occult laws, in accordance with which our inner essence is revealed when we approach the Teaching and the Aura of the Great Teacher, and understanding the entire danger of infection by obsession, particularly in the case of inherent mediumship, we really should not be astonished. Nevertheless, great is our grief when we see how, under the dark hand of the obsessor, the flower of the spirit withers and terrible betrayal creeps into the very heart of the structure of Light. But we shall live through this also.

The year 1936 was mentioned in many prophecies as the year of the personal battle between the Archangel Michael and the Dragon. Thus, in spite of everything, courage and the joy of a new battle for Light abide in our hearts. And is *podvig* possible without difficulties? I am very fond of the words of the remarkable Tibetan sage, Milarepa, who practiced great austerities. When people begged him to have pity on himself and stop leading such a hard life, he said that as all of us are subject to death, he preferred to die in pursuit of a beautiful goal.

Verily, if even one hundred people could realize the wisdom of this formula and would apply it in life, the world could be transformed in the shortest time. Thus, we shall fight for Light to the last drop of our blood, to our last breath. And you also should not be disturbed by anything. With flaming joy, take advantage of every possibility of contributing your share to the purification and improvement of human thinking.

10

1 October 1935

Many miracles come into our life, many affirmations. Therefore even the darkest betrayals and attempts to ruin our works cannot frighten us. The years 1934 and especially 1935 with their seven lunar and solar eclipses were quite exceptional in the number of dark omens. Thus, betrayal crept into the very heart of a luminous structure with an attempt to destroy what had been built by such pure striving and such flaming spirit. The enemy took advantage of the absence of N. K. and thrust the dagger at his back. Now the masks have fallen and the true faces are revealed. Of course we should not be astonished, for we know the immutable occult laws, under which when we approach the Teaching of Light and turn to the Great Teachers, our whole inner nature is revealed with a special force. Likewise, we know how liable to the danger of obsession one becomes if one allows oneself to give in to dark thoughts and insincerity, particularly when there is inherent mediumship. And yet, the heart grieves when we encounter such actions after fourteen years of close collaboration. Of course, at the very beginning of our work we received many repeated warnings and hints about a betrayal that might come after the promotion of certain people. The promotion took place, and their spirit failed. Ambition and cupidity are dreadful scourges—even giants are cast down precipices by them.

And so, we drink the chalice of poison tendered by the hands of our former co-workers. But in spite of this, strength and courage live in our hearts. For what is achievement without betrayal? The symbol of Judas is eternal and is inevitably present at the consummation of a great achievement. But after Golgotha comes the resurrection and the great exaltation of the spirit. This was indicated in all the Mysteries, therefore, even joy is aflame in our hearts. We know the Great Pledge of the Stronghold of Light, we measure the signs of Trust, and we know the victorious Shield. Our spirit cannot be frightened by any battles; we even have learned to love them, because what else can so temper the spirit and test our abilities and bring us great experience for the crown of fulfillment? And so, we may once more say, "Blessed are the obstacles; by them we grow."

We can also recall the wise words of Nietzsche, "Thou goest beyond them; but the higher thou risest, the smaller doth the eye of envy see thee. Most of all, however, is the flying one hated." Yes, at the present time, people revolt particularly against everything lofty, and against the law of Hierarchy. Only the kings of the spirit are aware of all the grandeur and immutability of this cosmic law, the majority always rise against it.

Indeed, the refinement of the spirit is indicated precisely by its ability to revere lofty values.

And so, courageously and joyously we begin the new battle for the Light of the new consciousness in the coming era with complete confidence in the predestined final victory.

* * *

I received with joy the wonderful message of your heart, in which you expressed your devotion to the Great Teacher. Verily, devotion is a quality characteristic only of kings of the spirit. It is quite obvious that you have brought this rarest quality from your past. Where else but in the East, and possibly in blessed India, should one seek the inception of this highest of qualities! All the spiritual achievements, her spiritual education, and the most refined ethics of India are based on this fundamental quality. The entire literature of India is saturated by the spirit of heroism and devotion. Nowhere are the links between Guru and disciple more understood and sacredly revealed than in India. Even during the temporary decline of the country, this reverence was preserved in the very heart of the people, and it gives a particular ineradicable coating to the innate culture of the Indian spirit. Thus, blessed are you if your heart vibrates to this great feeling of sweet savor. Verily, the fires of gratitude and devotion rise higher than those of any other offerings.

I shall conclude with the words of the Teaching: "Swimmers, if you do everything possible within your strength, whither can the most destructive wave carry you? It can only bear you upwards." Thus we shall pass, under the Great Shield of the Hierarchy of Light.

11

8 October 1935

Here are the answers to your questions:

1. The non-consuming fire, the burning bush of Moses, is the so-called heavenly fire, which can be manifested only when there is contact with an aura of certain tension. N. K. and I witnessed such fire during our journeying in Tibet. Once, late in the evening, this fiery phenomenon occurred in our tent quite unexpectedly. My husband was already asleep. I came to

my bed and stretched out my arm to turn down the blanket, and suddenly there arose a pillar, or rather a fire of wonderful silvery-purple-rose-flame. At first I did not realize what was happening, and with an exclamation, "Fire! Fire!" attempted to beat it out with my hands. But the fire was not extinguished, nor did the tongues of flame burn my hands, and I felt only a pleasant living warmth. Hearing my voice, my husband awoke and saw me standing against the background of this flame. The whole incident did not last more than a quarter of a minute, perhaps less, and the flame disappeared just as suddenly as it appeared. After this manifestation I saw the crystals of *Materia Lucida* and spirals, and the sparks of Fohat. However, these latter experiences resulted in a slight singeing of the centers.

2. The seventh principle is the element of synthesis, but it is not the higher Ego of man.

The higher Ego consists of three principles; the seventh, the sixth, and the fifth. I am enclosing a short note that I wrote to one of my co-workers. Perhaps you will find it useful.

3. The moon is our mother—it took part in the formation of our Earth and in populating it with human beings. The Lunar Monads, or *pitris*—the ancestors, as they are called by the Hindus, became incarnated in our human kind. The moon will disappear or disintegrate before the seventh great Round of our planet.

4. Almost all of the sciences originated in India. Egypt, Greece, and ancient Chaldea borrowed their knowledge from India. Similarly, Osiris, Hermes, and Orpheus came from the East; also, Pythagoras received his initiation in India.

5. There is a complete correspondence between the subtle and physical bodies. Therefore, each physical center has its correspondence in the subtle body. Consequently, all the astral feelings and centers exist just as do the physical ones, but in their subtle radiations. Yet they should not be considered separately, because their unity reveals a strict correspondence. The outer world is a mere reflection of the inner one. And just as the external feelings and energies are manifested only when the necessary conditions exist, so also the inner, spiritual energies are manifested when the astral or spiritual conditions are created on the inner plane.

6. Christ always felt a loss of strength when purifying and healing the sick. Remember, when a sick woman in the

crowd touched the hem of His garment, He immediately felt a decrease of strength. A great spirit imparts part of his strength each time he heals, each time someone touches him. And no matter how great is the supply of psychic energy, it can be temporarily exhausted. These moments of exhaustion are full of danger, because the protective net of the aura, bereft of those radiations from the store of radiations which nourishes our centers, is disturbed, and infectious microbes are able to enter the weakest area of the organism. This explains why Agni Yoga is so full of indications regarding the preservation of the protective net. A disciple who has reached a certain degree of Yoga is unable to remain indefinitely in the polluted atmosphere of cities; he often has to leave to lead a more or less secluded life amidst nature.

Christ, like Buddha and all other Great Teachers, often went into the desert.

Also, in *The Mahatma Letters* we find mention of a serious illness of the Mahatma K. H., after having contacted the auras of people, during the time of the founding of the Theosophical Society in India. He was compelled to retire into complete seclusion for several weeks. Thus, each plane of consciousness, each plane of existence is subject to certain laws, which, if violated bring their own consequences.

* * *

If you wish, you could mention that the doctrine of reincarnation was repudiated only in A.D. 553, during the Second Council of Constantinople. Thus, the doctrine regarding the pre-existence of the soul and its continuous return to Earth was declared "heresy" by official Christendom only in the sixth century A.D. Until that time it was tolerated and accepted by those churchmen who were particularly close to the Gnostics.

* * *

And now, just for your information, I will tell you of an interesting case of a recollection from a previous life. It happened in the eighties of the last century and was *written down* from the narrative of one of the participants. A lady who lived on an estate in the province of Pskov, accompanied by her husband and son, went on a visit for the Christmas holidays to a distant estate, belonging to some friends. They started out on a wonderful sunny morning, hoping to arrive before dark. However, after midday the weather changed sharply; it became stormy, the snow fell heavily, visibility became difficult, and in about half an hour the road entirely disappeared under the heavy snow. It was already dark, but there was no sign of any habitation, in spite of the fact that normally they should have arrived long ago. The road became full of holes, and the carriage was in danger of overturning. It was obvious that they had lost their way. However, it would have been very unwise to stop and wait until the weather cleared up, because the storm was growing stronger and stronger, and the horses and carriage would have been buried under the heavy snowfall. It was therefore decided to continue the journey and to trust the horses to use their own instinct. The moment the clever animals were permitted freedom, they understood what was expected of them; they lifted their heads, sniffed the air, and increased speed. In an hour or less the distant barking of dogs could be heard, and soon they saw a few lights and the carriage reached the stone gates of a big estate. A servant, hearing the barking of the dogs, came out with a lantern. When asked whose estate it was, he gave the name and added that the owners were abroad at the time. The travelers found that they were in the opposite direction from their destination. As it was already late, they decided they must stay at the estate. They called for the major-domo and asked him to open the house in order that they might stay overnight. But when the lady alighted from the carriage and saw the house, dimly lit by the servants' lanterns, she began to tremble and exclaimed in terror. "Never will I set foot in that house. Dreadful things have happened there!" She begged her husband to immediately leave this unhappy place. The husband and son were astonished beyond measure, and thinking that over-fatigue was the cause of her nervousness tried to calm her and convince her that she was mistaken, since none of them had ever before been in these parts. However, the lady was insistent upon leaving, and in order to prove her reasons, she said, "I can describe to you the situation of the rooms and also the furniture. When you enter the circular red sitting room, you will see on the wall above a table a large portrait of a woman, in a white dress, with flowers in her hands. Well, that was my own portrait. And ... I was so terribly, terribly unhappy!" Of course, the husband and the son, accompanied by the major-domo, went immediately to check this statement. They returned greatly shaken, for the description was precisely correct. They did not insist further upon staying in the unfortunate house, and since the storm had abated, and the moon had come out, they asked for a guide, deciding to return home.

Such recollections are rather frequent in the East. Newspapers mention these cases, which are corroborated by numerous witnesses. We know a local family, a member of which, a boy five years old insists to his parents that he is not their son and that he was formerly a monk and lived in a monastery. He often runs away from the house and searches for this monastery. Sometimes he manages to travel far before his parents notice his absence. Invariably, he sets out for Little Tibet.

12

11 October 1935

1. In reality, man cannot rid himself completely of karma, for karma is life. But the fulfillment of a cycle of karma, of whatever duration, depends upon our spiritual growth, and also on the mission we have undertaken upon a certain planet. This means that, having acquired a certain knowledge of the Teaching, and after an interval of time (a vacation, so to say), we have to commence the next, higher degree, and so on ad infinitum. These "vacations" may be that very place of rest, where there are no "tears or sighs." But no vacation continues forever, though it may be prolonged for thousands of years, therefore there is no eternal "rest."

2. There is a continuous birth and disintegration of worlds in the Cosmos. Often, the worlds that are disintegrating are still far from the completion of their evolution, and there are many reasons for their destruction. One of the most deplorable reasons is the benumbed spirit of the humanity that inhabits a planet. And our Earth is in danger of destruction before completing its ordained evolution. The crimes of people and their numbness of spirit have created such emanations around our planet that the salutary rays are unable to reach it. Our planet may end its existence with a gigantic explosion. The final Day of Judgment is not far off, and many children may live to see that DAY. That is why the giving of the Teaching of Life has been so hastened,

and why so many unusual omens are being rained upon Earth. But people are blind and deaf!

It is essential to awaken the human spirit! Verily, the destiny of the planet is in the hands of humanity itself! If the resurrection of the spirit takes place within the next short decades, the inevitable catastrophe may be only partial, as it was in the times of Lemuria and Atlantis; otherwise, we shall have to move to another planet. But in accordance with the laws of correspondence and co-measurement the majority of mankind will not be admitted to the higher planets, which are already populated. They will have to adjust themselves to a new world, which is not yet inhabited. And how many thousands, nay, millions of years would have to elapse before the new forms and bodies suitable for a new world could be worked out. Only exceptional groups of earthly humanity could enter the higher planets to continue their evolution in new, beautiful conditions.

The Great Brotherhood is taking extraordinary measures to save our planet from premature destruction. But the subterranean fire is most active, and the forces that can be discharged to neutralize the dangerous energy are pitifully small! Of course, there is no such thing in the Cosmos as irrational destruction; everything is based on profound reasons. Great GOAL-FITNESS rules in the Cosmos; all that is unable to proceed with evolution is churned over as cosmic refuse. Thus, having free will man chooses this or that destiny. And still, man zealously piles up heaps of rubbish which will engulf him if a regeneration of his spirit does not take place in time.

* * *

3. It is useful to give certain hints regarding a new program for schools. Precisely, from childhood the consciousness should be trained to realize the unity of life, the unity in Cosmos. Let our planet not be some isolated world, but rather, one of *the halting places on the great Path* into Infinity. We must realize our place in Infinity, as well as our dependence upon the complete unity of life in Cosmos—and the sooner, the better. Remember how it is said in the Teaching, "Verily, a feather falling from the wing of a small bird produces a thunderclap in the far-off worlds." We must realize most intensely our *awesome dependence* and interrelation with everything in life. Thence should come a

sense of great responsibility for each thought, word and action. Cause and effect act continuously and infinitely.

Someday, the consciousness of mankind will reach the point where it realizes that it exists in a gigantic Universal Laboratory and is a reflection of it. *Truly, unity must be understood on a cosmic scale.*

Likewise, it is useful to direct thoughts into the future. This alone will give a great impetus to the consciousness and will liberate it from the dust of yesterday.

4. *Imperil* is the designation given by the Great Teachers to the poison of irritability, however in the Eastern tongues there is an entirely different word for this poison. The sacred Senzar language consists of the best definitives, adopted from all existing languages. Many words with a Latin root are used in this language. Thus, *imperil* has a definite Latin Root. There are some words which have no link with any language known to us. Often a single word expresses a complex idea or action.

5. No one, not even the Greatest Spirits, possess complete omnipotence. They are all subject to the cosmic laws; hence, They can apply Their great knowledge and power when the cosmic conditions are favorable. Each miracle performed without a fundamental reason is considered by the Arhats to be a violation. It is said, "Even an Arhat can descend, by misuse of miracle."

Of course, the conditions existing at the time of Christ (just as at the present time) rarely contributed toward the possibility of a miracle. Therefore even Christ was not always able to cure those who came to him for help. In the Gospel of St. Matthew (13:58) it is said, "And he did not many mighty works there because of their unbelief." Thus, that which is desired is given only to him who is able to accept it. In everything *cooperation and collaboration* are required.

6. I would like you even more strongly to emphasize work as the main factor in the education of the spirit. Point out that quality is the most essential in all work. Also mention that mental work is absolutely necessary; for if the sweat of physical labor nourishes the soil, the sweat of mental work is similarly transmuted by the rays of the sun into prana and gives life to all that exists. If the significance of mental work is realized, there will follow a proper respect for all thinkers, scientists, and other creators.

Only mental work broadens our consciousness, thereby linking us with the far-off worlds and the whole Cosmos, and turning us to the joy of infinite perfectment. Precisely, we should cultivate in ourselves the joy of endless perfectment.

Your chapter about striving is quite good. It would be useful to connect this striving still more closely with the concept of *podvig by introducing this idea as the sole meaning of life.* Much is said about *podvig* in the books of the Teaching. Indeed, only *podvig* can nourish our spirit and accelerate evolution. Indeed, achievement and heroism must be thoroughly taught in schools. "Let children call themselves heroes and apply to themselves the qualities of remarkable people. Let them be given books of clear account, wherein the faces of toil and of will have been depicted without any soft coatings. Even for medicinal purposes this valiant call of life is irreplaceable. Such material must be given without delay." [New Era Community]

Use more broadly the quotations from the books of the Teaching, it will give newness to the book.

7. One must not think that the next Great Teacher will appear in the flesh and will preach among us, as did Buddha and Christ. Each epoch requires its own manifestations. Therefore, the type of Teacher who walks with a group of disciples from village to village has sunk into oblivion. Some Elder Brothers still use the physical body for special purposes, but not for encountering crowds.

I had to write on this subject before, therefore I will quote from one of my previous letters: "The Great Advent cannot be manifested in an ordinary way, and it cannot take place in the physical body. One should understand that the Great Lords take on or maintain this or that Image, according to the needs of the world. Why is it so difficult to imagine that a Great Individuality does not require a physical body to manifest very close to us? Moreover, the facts of the past, with examples in modern times show how strangely the appearance of Great Spirits is taken by ignorant humans. At best they have been given the epithet of charlatan or spy, or both. Generally, people attribute their own vices to others. It would be most edifying to read the historical facts of the life of Saint-Germain, the envoy of the White Brotherhood."

We can also recall H. P. Blavatsky, and all the appearances of the Mahatmas. How skeptically and often scoffingly were their messages and manifestations received! But, as I have already written, "Even if Christ Himself appeared now among us, would He be able to escape imprisonment, or even execution? ... One must realize that the Greatest Individuality cannot be manifested now, in the midst of chaotic thinking and the vibrations of depraved crowds. The Great Lords apply in everything the great law of GOAL-FITNESS. Please realize that in view of the level of contemporary humanity, the Advent of the Highest Ego in a physical form is entirely impossible and would be disastrous for the whole of evolution. The Great Individuality—invisibly visible—will rule, and is *already ruling*, garbed in the Rays of the powerful but invisible LABORATORY." Soon, very soon, these Rays will be directed to the awakening of the spirit of humanity.

"According to the most ancient testaments, the Lord of Shambhala is fighting the Prince of Darkness (Satan) himself. This battle, first of all, takes place in the subtle spheres; whereas, here the Lord of Shambhala acts through his earthly warriors. As for Himself, He can be seen only in the most exceptional cases. As for His manifesting in a Fiery Image, this would be disastrous for all and everything, as His aura is charged with energies of extraordinary power. In the Gospel of St. Matthew (24:27-39) the Advent and Judgment Day awaiting our planet are described fairly accurately. However, you will have plenty of time to grow old before this event, but partial catastrophes may take place sooner."

We are witnessing a great world-reconstruction. New laws are already written into the Tables of Eternity, but the great Revelation is not yet accepted. Woe to those who reject the spirit and who prefer to vegetate in ignorance, in debility, and in moral mire! The New World comes in realization of human dignity, in austere understanding of duty and the responsibility of each one to humanity and the whole of Cosmos. Cooperation always and in everything must become the order of the Day.

13

15 October 1935

Probably, you too must have noticed at times that the gates of possibilities are often very narrow. Indeed, in many cases the difficulty is not so much in the shortage of funds as that the magnitude of the work outgrows the consciousness of the co-workers. Yes, everywhere there is a shortage of people. What we need is an increase of strong workers, who are not afraid of bold undertakings.

Let the fireflies glow, if they be not caught in the nets of paltry hunters and thus betray the work. Uttering lofty words is one thing, but applying them in life is something entirely different; usually *these two actions do not go together.* Furthermore, I greatly dislike it when someone says that he is ready to give his life for the Teaching! In most cases, almost invariably, this is *the greatest lie.*

During my whole life, I have met only two or three people who were really ready to sacrifice everything; but precisely they refrained from giving assurances—they acted. Others came and donated because they had a surplus, or for profit when they heard that each gift is returned a hundredfold. But when this "hundredfold" was not forthcoming as expected, or it was delayed because of their own fault, they turned into the worst enemies and betrayers of the work. Often they would turn away at the final boundary. There were also those who were ready to sacrifice just one half, even when events required that everything be laid at stake. But can one expect success from halfway decisions? Can one expect a cure from medicine given in half doses? Of course, success in these cases was also halved. However, the most remarkable is that the second half, held back because of petty fears, was later taken away either by karma or some unexpected circumstances. There is still a third and most prevalent kind of people, who imagine that their very approach to the Teaching is already the greatest favor on their part. In their conceit, they believe that the Mahatmas are ready to perform a *puja* to everyone who approaches or even has read their Teaching. Not so! The Great Teachers rejoice and render active help only to those who truly strive. They are sorry for the butterflies, for They know that these butterflies must pass through centuries of difficulties before they can hope to approach the Stronghold of Light. It would be useful for such people to read the following pages from the Teaching:

"Someone will say: 'Is vigilance, or co-measurement, or mobility, or devotion difficult? Here, I feel that I can contain all these conditions; will you not take me on the distant journey into the COMMUNITY?' But has this hasty traveler thought about a certain requisite in the qualities mentioned by him?

Steadfastness was forgotten. Little fires flickering only for an instant contain all the qualities of flame, but darkness engulfs them as swiftly as a brazier does a snowflake. One cannot trust an isolated moment of containment; only STEADFASTNESS, tempered by toil and by obstacles, results in a trustworthy containment. A true musician does not think about each finger's calling forth a sound; only a pupil considers which fingers are convenient to use. The true co-worker does not think about the intended application of the qualities of labor. The music of the spheres is blended with the song of progress of labor. Ponder how like a fiery ladder is STEADFASTNESS."

"Someone decides: 'I will cross upon the fiery ladder.' Do so, to each one the path is open. But remember, if fear comes the steps melt into liquid flame. Whither will you go, not having acquired the quality of labor? When We say it is better to sleep on cedar roots, the follower can carry out easily the advice. It is easy to sleep, and especially when so advised. But when one is told to take up constant watch, then the steps become burning hot. One thing must be repeated: not easy is the ladder. Poor is the leader who conceals real danger. It can be conquered only with the help of complete knowledge. I see approaching another unreasonable person—this one is still more imperfect. He censures: 'Of what use is a solemn prophecy?' We shall say, 'The solemnity of a forewarning is proportionate to the degradation of your squeaking at danger. O thou biped, how many times you have lost your face at the first difficulty! We have seen you blacker than charcoal, and your negation has filled you with stench. Badly do you fare, having burned your steps and now asking alms of the abyss.' A new interrogator: 'How to reconcile the Teaching with science?' If science teaches authentic knowledge, then the Teaching is science. What purpose can science achieve when it is swollen with prejudices? He who is perturbed by solemnity of affirmations views science from his den of vulgarity. He who thinks about the community is not harmed by crawling reptiles. I say to you that I know all the complexity of the construction. I do not conceal how far the stones must be carried nor how great is the aridity. Precisely this realization, precisely the countlessness of the stars, gives affirmation to the fiery steps." [New Era Community]

Difficult is the path of true discipleship. Indeed, there is no knowledge, no philosophy and, moreover, no violation by magic that can give us spirituality. For only by experiencing life, by drinking the poison of all life's illusions, by preserving ardent aspiration for the service of the General Good can we fill the CHALICE of AMRITA.

* * *

I was sorry to read that there is still someone who admires mediumistic faculties, calling them achievements. In the Teaching, and in the East generally, this condition is considered rather a misfortune; I have written in detail about the danger of it. Think of the definitions of mediumship given in the book *Agni Yoga*: "mediums are like rudderless boats. ... A medium is but the inn for disembodied liars." Indeed, it is not just any kind of clairvoyance that indicates the transmutation of the centers. Actually, high clairvoyance has nothing in common with mediumship. The very character of the visions described by Mrs. X testifies to her contact with the lower astral spheres. Genuine clairvoyance is accompanied by beauty, grandeur, and simplicity, but not by piles of rubbish. Also, the environment in which her abilities were developed proves that we are dealing precisely with mediumship and not with open centers. Believe me, open centers are rare indeed, and the Great Lords, who watch over the evolution of humanity, guard carefully from early childhood those individuals who have earned the right to possess open centers. They are placed by Them in favorable environments, where they can better develop and express their gifts. But the Great Teachers *will never approach a person who lives amidst the fumes of alcohol and charges money for telling fortunes.* This would be an outrageous profanation of sacred knowledge and of the hidden achievements of the spirit.

Therefore, the only help that can be given to Mrs. X is the advice to give up all books on magic and cease fortune-telling, etc. Let her work more, and read the books of the Teaching of Life, which should be explained to her. But most of all she should purify herself spiritually. She should forbid herself to pay attention to calls from the astral world, and instead focus her attention and heart on the Image of the chosen Teacher.

The present condition of the Great Teacher is such that He does not manifest himself to anyone. This condition may be compared to the tension of a dynamo of tremendous power. Yet His help may come in the most unexpected way "through human hands and feet." In the astral world there are plenty of impersonators and good actors, and this should always be remembered. Let Mrs. X read The Voice of Silence by H. P. Blavatsky. The dangers of the astral world are described there quite clearly.

Thus, the Great Teaching of Light has in view the correct growth of the human spirit, but not the development of mediumistic abilities, which *cannot lead to anything*, but can only retard the spiritual growth, and even become destructive. And as nothing mechanical can be built into the foundation of true evolution or progress, I once again advise Mrs. X to give up all books that deal with the development of clairvoyance, etc. In the near future, when humanity shall have advanced in the understanding of the still hidden laws of the subtle energies, the possibility will come of utilizing mediums for certain scientific researches. Such mediums will have to live a very pure life, and methods will be found for protecting them and also those who come in contact with them. But at present contact with a medium may even be dangerous for those who are near him if they possess unstable auras.

Explain to her how harmful is concentration upon one particular center, as recommended in books written by irresponsible authors. This concentration stimulates that center at the expense of all others, and thus casts the entire scheme of their polarization into chaos. This process is truly disastrous to the vibrations, since it violates the balance of the established vibratory scheme. Remember what is said in the Teaching regarding the work of the Teacher with the disciples on all centers and on all the seven circles of clairvoyance and clairaudience. The Teacher watches closely the condition of the pupil's organism, and never would He open one center at the expense of another. Correct development or evolution exists only in harmony or balance.

And now regarding automatic writing. This, too, is considered to be a certain degree of obsession, for in automatic writing there is usually an external influence upon the physical center of the hand, and even that of the brain, which is most harmful and, if practiced often, can end in paralysis.

I have never written automatically, but I had a chance to observe this phenomenon in America, where it is widespread. The process differs: Some declare that they are not aware of what is written by their hand, whereas others say that each word is clearly impressed upon their brain. Some write very quickly, even violently, others, very quietly, carefully drawing each word. Some write with sudden changes of language; some, without having the slightest technique for drawing a simple object, suddenly sketch complete pictures. There are also cases of people writing from right to left, in an unknown language. Of course, all these do not issue from the subconscious, but obviously result from *external* influence. And the degrees of the "Guardian Angels," who wish to guide and communicate, certainly vary in the Subtle World. Through those who are harmless and friendly to us, we may, quite unexpectedly, attract a hostile force and one of not a small caliber. Therefore, I advise that automatic writing be avoided until a heartfelt bond with the Teacher has been affirmed. We can never tell who may wish to use us as their tools! And besides we can attract a force which is later beyond our capacity to control. So let each one seriously ponder before opening the way to unknown forces. If there is devotion to the Teaching, and a talent for writing, what need is there of automatic writing? For the writer the Teaching provides an inexhaustible source of themes.

Only spirituality and *podvig* advance us toward the loftiest achievement, that of Arhatship. If Mrs. X would become firm on the right path, she would really be able to help people. But in her present condition she is able only to open the doors to the lower strata of the Subtle World and to involve unfortunate victims in the dangers of obsession. There is nothing more deceptive than the visions from the Subtle World. Verily, little knowledge and partial truth are more dangerous than complete ignorance. Therefore, be compassionate, but do not be enticed by mediums; and above all, try not to see them as privileged beings!

I shall quote a page from *The Occult Anatomy of Man* by Manly P. Hall, a talented American interpreter of occult knowledge: "It will probably be wise at this point to describe the difference between a medium and a clairvoyant. To the average person there is no difference, but to the mystic these two phases of spiritual sight are separated by the entire span of human evolution.

"A clairvoyant is one who has raised the spinal serpent [Kundalini] into the brain and by his growth earned the right of perceiving the invisible worlds with the aid of the third eye, or pineal gland. This organ of consciousness, which millions of years ago connected man with the invisible worlds, closed during the Lemurian period when the objective senses began to develop. The occultist, however, by the process of development hinted at before, may reopen this eye and by means of it explore the invisible worlds. Clairvoyants are not born; they are made. Mediums are not made; they are born. The clairvoyant can become such only after years, sometimes lives, of self-preparation; on the other hand, the medium... may secure results in a few days. [But it should be added that the medium can work only in a limited capacity, in the lower spheres of the supermundane world].

"Automatic writing is gained by permitting the etheric arm of an outside intelligence to control temporarily the physical arm of the medium. This is not possible until the medium removes his own etheric double from the arm, for two things cannot occupy the same space [at their particular level] at the same time. The process of periodically separating the life forces from the physical arm is very dangerous, often resulting in paralysis. Mediumship is unnatural to man, while clairvoyance is the natural result of growth and the unfolding of the spiritual nature. There are a hundred mediums to one clairvoyant, for the clairvoyant can become such only through self-mastery and the exertion of tremendous power; while the weaker, more sickly, and the more nervous an individual is, the better medium he makes. The clairvoyant is unfolding his mind by filling it with useful knowledge, while the first instruction given the would-be medium is, 'Make your mind a blank.'" * Mediumship arrests correct evolution, and should be considered as retrogression.

Therefore, it is the greatest mistake to regard mediumistic faculties as spiritual achievements. Verily, they are the opposite of spirituality. Spirituality lies in the highest triad, and is precisely absent in mediums. Do not degrade what is of the greatest value to the world. Spirituality is always accompanied by *balance* and inborn wisdom.

Try to discriminate among the manifestations of mediumship, which is most widely spread today. Indeed, lower psychism is not far from mediumship, and also represents not a small danger. That is why it is so important to use all efforts to direct huma-

---

* *The Occult Anatomy of Man*. (Los Angeles: The Philosophical Research Society, Inc, 1929) pp.16-17

nity toward true spirituality and the strengthening of character in the battles of life.

And so, it is impossible to approach the Stronghold of Light and to acquire true knowledge, without the purification of one's mind and the cleansing of one's heart in the sweat of complete self-denial. But again, all this is said for those who are strong in spirit. For the weak ones much benefit is already gained if, by merely reading the books of the Teaching, they feel a certain warmth of the heart or a heightened vibration, which if repeatedly practiced affirm, and considerably purify and strengthen their auras.

"It should always be remembered that Our Teaching does not force itself upon people, neither does it forbid coming and going freely. It is given broadly, and imposes no prohibitions. Of course, warnings are given, but *not* threats and everyone is left to act according to his will. And as that which is sacred is given only to those who have proved their devotion to the principles of the Teaching through many years and in many difficulties, prohibitions and barriers are not necessary. It is given to all—take as much as you are able. But, of course, little is taken, for people have not yet learned to take the highest."

I consider *The Call* an extremely useful book, and just as essential as the other books. It treats in short formulas that which in the other books is broadened and analyzed from other points of view. In the whole structure not one stone can be omitted. The first book is the foundation stone.

A certain scientist speaks of the mistakes in the books of H. P. Blavatsky. I would like to ask him whether he has calculated as accurately the mistakes in the books of the past and contemporary scientists. In *The Secret Doctrine* many pages are full of quotations of the contradictory opinions and conclusions of the scientists and all of their inflated theories and hypotheses. And as for the person who repeats verbatim the words of the scientist mentioned above, I feel like saying, "Do not be a parrot!" Check this yourself, and if you have a chance, compare with the true TEACHING; but it is not advisable to cast into space something not verified by one's consciousness. Likewise, the quoted words of Soloviev are not convincing. If we accept the word NON-EXISTENCE in the sense that the Hindus do, i.e., absolute BE-NESS—it, however, being inaccessible to the limited human mind—I quite agree. But if it is taken literally, it is depraved and unworthy of any thinking person. You may find my criticism severe, but I believe that people should be responsible for the words they utter and quote. It is time at last to realize one's responsibility for words. On each word may hang the destiny of a man.

I am sending you courage and vigor, for if friends are increasing, enemies follow close by. But a warrior of Light welcomes adverse manifestations. Thus, temper your spirit and sharpen your discrimination.

14

7 October 1935

Indeed, God is love, and the whole existence of the Universe is based on love and nothing else! But how ugly and sacrilegious is the understanding of this love! Truly the concept of love is very far from the understanding of our present humanity. Into this highest cosmic concept people inject their cannibalistic, or devouring ideas. And that is why it is so hard, and at times even shameful to utter the word *love*. This word, on the lips of many bipeds, has become the greatest profanation.

I cannot agree with you that no one can be blamed for anything. Indeed no, all are to blame, and for everything. Since the whole Universe is an endless chain of causes and effects, how can we, particles of this Universe, be excluded from this cosmic law? The predestination that you mention exists and materializes only because it is the result of causes. Therefore I cannot agree with the statement that after death and passing into the Subtle World people will immediately find their satisfaction, happiness, and the whole meaning of all they sought on Earth. This would be contradictory to the basic cosmic law just mentioned. Undoubtedly, those who sincerely seek for the meaning of earthly existence and who strive after the highest ideals will find them there, in full accordance with their striving and thoughts. There is no scale of justice more precise than that which man carries within himself; for his own aura, which is woven out of energies, motives, and thoughts, is that true scale. Precisely these energies carry his spirit to the level which he himself has built.

The Subtle, or astral world is the world of effects, therefore those thoughts and strivings that did not find application on Earth will do so there, because there the inner man lives and acts with all his feelings and strivings. But can one expect that a man sunk in crime and possessed of an animal mentality could find happiness and satisfaction there? Inasmuch as an effect is the exact development of a cause, how can an evil-minded murderer, a seducer, or an idiot experience a condition of well-being in the higher spheres, which would be unbearable for him owing to their subtle vibrations! And more than unbearable, for the very approach of a being from the higher spheres causes incredible pains to such as he; furthermore, from contact with the higher energies, he decomposes. Great GOAL-FITNESS and precise affinity of vibrations reign in the whole Universe. Indeed, we live in a Gigantic Laboratory, and we ourselves are kilns, as it were; therefore, it is easy to imagine how the energies or chemical ingredients that enter our aura act upon our environment and, in turn, absorb or repel the energies around us. Reciprocity is everywhere and in everything. The world is based on the principle of equilibrium, and this law runs like a thread through all the Teachings of antiquity. In achieving equilibrium man becomes free of the attraction of Earth, and is able to act consciously and simultaneously on three planes—earthly, subtle, and spiritual or mental. With such an expanded existence, with such an illumined consciousness, life becomes full of meaning, beauty, and a special joyous wisdom. A broadened consciousness points out to us the paths of evolution, the paths of the future, and our mind gives humble gratitude to the grandeur and wisdom of the One Law of Love, which is expressed on Earth as the law of karma. (I foresee the protest of many people regarding such a definition of karma.) Therefore, I may say, any and all violence is certainly against the laws of the Universe and inevitably must cause explosions and destructions.

In looking back, we will find deep reasons which caused the fall of the old world. Indeed, the stifling of thought and spirit that took place in some countries engendered all kinds of madness. The flood, long dammed up, broke through and swept away everything in its path. Thus, no one and nothing is able to arrest thought, this fiery energy and the crown of the Universe. Yes, a great shifting has taken place in the consciousness of the masses of all countries, but many people cannot, or rather do not want to admit it and still hope to return to the former irresponsible life—indeed, irresponsible, and this devastating disease has spread almost everywhere. Do not think, my dear, that I justify the recent events and all the ensuing destruction, or that I approve of the ignorant levelling of everything. No, nothing is more repulsive to me than the all-leveling principle. The principle of uniformity is primarily unnatural, since it contradicts all cosmic laws. Be-ness itself is based on infinite differentiation. The whole of nature exists in multiformity and struggle—hence, its vitality and beauty. Therefore, we may say: uniformity is death and multiformity is life. Furthermore, the law of Hierarchy reigns throughout the whole of Cosmos. Precisely, subordination of the lower to the higher exists in the Cosmos. And what can exist without the Leading Principle? On what is evolution based? The multiplicity of forms and manifestations along with the unity of the fiery essence, the struggle for harmony and attainment of perfection, and the leading Hierarchic principle—these are the foundations of existence. Nature itself is our sole, and greatest Teacher and Lawgiver.

And now, regarding predestination. We cannot separate the eternal from the transitory. Eternity is the warp on which is woven the entire phantasmagoria of the manifested and transitory world. Out of this transitory, and, at the same time, ceaseless motion is molded in our consciousness the concept of eternity.

This being so, predestination exists for the eternal as well as for the transitory. But for the eternal, predestination is truly expressed in the eternity of its motion; whereas for the transitory it exists in its eternally changing phases, which are constantly evoked or engendered by new causes and effects, which in turn become causes, and so on ad infinitum. In other words, predestination is a result of an underlying cause.

Our higher fiery substance is eternal and unchangeable, but the consciousness (or soul), which is built up from the energies accumulated around the fundamental fiery seed, grows and changes. Thus the fiery seed of the spirit is the eternal carrier of constantly changing forms and expressions. Passing through various spheres and worlds, it engenders continuous causes and effects which are molded into a definite form of predestination, or destiny.

Meanwhile, prophetic dreams, best of all, inform mankind about the future. Thus, the map of the world was already set a long while ago to such an extent that it can actually be perceived in prophetic dreams. I remember how, at the very beginning of the war, I saw the map of Europe and Asia exactly as it is now. However, a new destiny is already prepared by the engenderments of the old world. As for our motherland, let us not worry about it. Assuredly, not the various parties will save it, but verily the hundreds of thousands of Ivans. And these same Ivans will demand a new light, a new spiritual food, and those dogmas that are justified by reason and logic. Consequently, the vestments of the new spiritual teachers must truly become snow-white, and they will have to follow the path of the great Spiritual Toilers of humanity and not reflect the Great Images in a distorted mirror of ignorance and avarice. I read with great spiritual satisfaction the books of *Dobrotolubye* and Origen's work, *On the Elements*. In spite of the numerous alterations introduced by later zealots, it is astonishing how far our present churchmen have departed from the first pure covenants of Christianity! Just think! Only in the sixth century A.D. was the dogma of reincarnation rejected by the Second Council of Constantinople! Thus the contrivances of greedy and petty minds were stratified and became dogma for the following generations which did not yet dare to think independently, for time—this magician and sorcerer—transformed the opinions of those wavering, limited minds into immutable foundations almost equal to Divine Revelations.

And there are so many affirmations in the Gospel about reincarnation, actually in the words of Christ himself. The Fathers of the Church committed great sin by eliminating this law of the Highest Justice from the consciousness of the flocks entrusted to them. But we are no less sinful in our passive indulgence, and non-resistance to evil.

Thus, all of us are guilty for ourselves and others, for we cannot isolate ourselves from the rest of humanity and from the Cosmos. Verily, the Cosmos is in us and we are in it. But only the realization of this unity makes it possible for us to join in such an existence. The fundamental problems of the meaning of our existence were resolved long ago, but people do not wish to accept this, for no one wants to take RESPONSIBILITY for each thought, each word, and each deed. And we shall return to Earth until we fulfill this accepted responsibility—by perfecting ourselves, Earth, and also all its surrounding spheres. After concluding our earthly perfectment, we shall cross in a glorious radiance of manifold Beauty to the far-off worlds, the next step of evolution upon the ladder of infinite perfectment.

Quite correctly you write, "Where is justice, if we are without love?" Indeed, justice, without the higher knowledge that comes with the revelation of Diving Love in man, is only a distortion. True, the nearer to God, the fewer the condemnations. Still, we need not fall into the other extreme—non-resistance to evil. Non-resistance to evil causes even more harm than injustice committed in ignorance but in the ardor of the spirit; for the victim in the latter case will find compensation, if not in the earthly life, then in the Subtle World, where the harvest is gathered. But who will take into account the spheres where evil is spread, owing to non-resistance or pusillanimous, shortsighted sufferance? The forces of evil are active and hold together in all their undertakings, and they are vehement in their actions. But the fireflies and the "lukewarm" ones are unable to unite, for they are too busy devouring one another. Thus is manifested the end of our Fifth Race, and the incoming cycle of the Sixth Race brings into existence a renewed consciousness.

Your thought regarding a permanent council of the world patriarchate coincides in many ways with our old dream about a Council of Culture. But, of course, for any consciousness that is dying out this thought would seem utopian. Verily, this Council, or League, of Culture will be realized in the coming race, in which spirituality will be awakened. But even now not a few forerunners of the Sixth Race are already appearing on Earth. Indeed, their enlightened ideas cement the space for future incarnation on Earth. They are the ones who create and defend all pure movements, and are fighting against the hordes of darkness. By the way, I believe in the future of South America; her potentiality is great, and in the furnace of struggle her countries will acquire power and will find their own lofty path. Were they not the first to support the great idea of the Banner of Peace and the Pact for the preservation of the treasures of human genius? They understood the high educational significance of the Pact and Banner of Peace for the rising generations, whose consciousness must be prepared from childhood to understand the irreplaceable value of the treasures of human creativeness. Only with such understanding and care for the higher concepts and values can we conquer the animal in us and the coarseness which is inherent in this state.

15

4 November 1935

I was so very sorry that the teacher you mentioned did not express the tolerance and broadmindedness befitting such a great spirit as his disciples consider him to be. I mentioned this because I have heard that this teacher forbids his pupils to read the translation of the books of the *Agni Yoga series,* and altogether forbids to write anything about the books of Living Ethics. Equally curious is his thoughtless remark that the book *Agni Yoga* is dangerous! I wonder what danger was seen in that book by that teacher and by someone else who pronounced the same formula before? It appears as though these teachers have to outlive intolerance and, possibly, some degree of envy as well. But let them be. Everybody chooses and builds his own path. And only time—the great sifter—will show who is right.

As I frequently receive letters in which people inquire about whom of the contemporary spiritual leaders they should follow and whether it is possible to unite the followers of, let us say, Peter Donov or Krishnamurti with the followers of the Teaching of Living Ethics, I think it would be useful to quote for you my answer to one such questioner.

"Verily, different are these paths; some are easier and longer, others more difficult, but shorter. Freedom of belief is the first rule of each true Teaching. Therefore, if a teaching proclaims the betterment of life and self-perfectment, it is all well and good; let each such teaching have its followers. But why should they all be urged to sit at one table?

"People are so different. Therefore, is it not wiser to let them freely unite on that step of consciousness which is nearest to them? Why should they be dragged forcibly to one's own side? If even beautiful flowers should be selected and planted according to their occult properties, for otherwise they destroy each other; if even a motley bouquet of flowers, combined without this knowledge, may become explosive and disease-spreading in our hands, how much more should this apply to people! And how careful they should be when they approach the Source of the Teaching and when they form groups!

"Spiritual unity, first of all, implies the toleration of many and various degrees of consciousness, but never forcing one's own upon others. The desire for some sort of conciliation is already such importunity. The example of nature should be laid in every foundation, for nature contains all things, yet brings into close proximity only that which is harmonious. Therefore, let us accept the expression of life in all its multiformity, since therein is all power and beauty. Hence, whatever is nearest to our heart reveals our true degree. The time will come when our spirit will indicate the next step. My advice is not to attempt an artificial conciliation, but to practice benevolent toleration and follow sincerely what is closest to you."

And now I shall answer your questions:

1. On the astral plane there are many who impersonate the Great Teachers, and these irresponsible spirits lead a great number of neophytes into error. It is also necessary to remember that the Great Teachers not only do not encourage the practice of spiritualism and magic but continually emphasize the danger of such practices. There are at present so many people who are ardently and, I would say, even self-sacrificingly working in the pits of evil, often applying consciously or unconsciously the blackest magic. From the books of Living Ethics you can see how the Teacher warns against all magic, and what strong expressions are used against mediumship and any of the forcible, mechanical means for opening the centers that are recommended by the irresponsible pseudo-occult schools. Where the word of the Great Teacher sounds, there can be no mechanical means or magic signs.

Can there be place for magic, when one has in mind only the transformation of the inner man? All the Teachings of Light deal solely with the inner man, whose sphere is the realm of thought and heart.

2. The attempts of your friend to make you reject all forms and rituals are unsound; for are not the practice of *rhythmical* gymnastics, dancing, and singing also rituals or ceremonials of a kind? People like to call the same thing by different names. Unquestionably, the higher the consciousness, the less the necessity for earthly symbols; however, we cannot entirely give up all forms, for life is manifested through forms, and one form only replaces another. Primarily, we ourselves are bearers of form; and in each creation, in each manifestation and action, we are bound by form. Therefore, we should not seek to obliterate forms, but rather to renew and perfect them, adapting them to the demands of the time.

And so, you are quite right in saying that rituals are essential in religion and that they will never be discarded, but that one form will replace another. While worshipping God in spirit we may nevertheless have a desire of the heart to bring to him the best expressions of our lofty strivings. And should not these strivings be expressed in beautiful and versatile creations and manifestations of the human spirit? Assuredly, in the future, each form will be evaluated in accordance with fiery substance which it embodies. Therefore do not be perturbed, and express yourself in the way your heart prompts you. The beauty of existence is in the manifoldness of its manifestations. Let us hope that each new form will be more beautiful than the previous one.

3. And now, one should remember that many persons claim to be disciples of the Mahatmas. But the number of true disciples is very limited. Once, a Great Teacher was asked whether he had many close disciples, and he answered, "Less than the number of fingers on one hand."

Indeed, how can the Masters, who are on watch over the world and who lead the greatest Cosmic Battles, overburden themselves by accepting a great number of disciples? Considering *the present state of consciousness of humanity*, this would be an unproductive expenditure of the most precious energy, which is so essential for maintaining the equilibrium of our planet. There are many who read the books of the Teaching of the White Brotherhood and who mentally follow the indicated path, and because of this they consider themselves as disciples of this or that Great Teacher chosen by them. They are partly right, for if they continue to strive, and mainly if they try to apply the Teaching in life, they will enter the path of true discipleship, sooner or later, in this or another life. But ask yourself sincerely and seriously—have you met many such disciples, who even partially apply in life the foundations of the Living Ethics learned by them from the books of the Teaching? And without a complete application of the Teaching, or rather, without self-denial in carrying out life's achievement, is it possible to hope for a closer approach? Think of the burden of a Teacher who takes the responsibility for a disciple! I can say that his burden is terrible! The scope of this strain cannot even be imagined by one who is not familiar with the occult laws!

Of course, one should not attribute the visions of the psychics to clairvoyance. For "there is much conscious, and still more unconscious, deception in the visions of ... undisciplined psychics. The realm of psychism is so complex, so fearful and it conceals many surprises for the self-deluded 'adepts.'" As it is said in the Teaching, "Without the High Guidance, one cannot be safe in this sphere." Only a disciple who is under the direct Guidance of the Great Teachers can discriminate regarding these visions. In order to see and understand correctly one must learn to control the lower manas and not permit it to interfere. There are many examples of visions when the higher Manas manifested the truth, but the feeling of selfishness called out the lower aspect of it, which, by its interference, not only brought its own additions but distorted the whole sense of the manifested truth.

I shall quote a page from the Teaching: "The ability is given to a fiery spirit to receive subtle energies. Only the fiery consciousness is able to conduct a current of subtle energies. Therefore the records must be scrutinized with a great deal of discrimination. It is because humanity has become accustomed to visualizing the Highest on a low plane, that the Images of the Lords have acquired such distorted forms. Indeed, people have become used to the thought that the Higher should serve the lower, but they do not realize that only the understanding of Service gives one the right to a manifested link of the Chain. Thus it is the distorted understanding of Sendings that produces the results which litter the space. ... Therefore, We shall give a fair warning against all distortion and false records. ... But what does a medium or a recipient poisoned with imperil reveal? Thus, it is necessary to purify the profane human actions and to destroy these records in the future. In the Fiery World only the fiery consciousness can be a true recipient of Our Sendings.

"It is asked why We do not put a stop to the false sources. Why do We not expose those who distort the Sendings? If one were to stop by force the current in whose wake humanity is proceeding, fanaticism would turn into brutality. Thus, the evil free will flows like lava, engulfing also those who rise against the Good, as history reveals. Surely, violent manifestations of force cannot carve a righteous path for humanity. Hence, all the subtle energies can be accepted only by a fiery consciousness. Thus, tolerance is truly the lot of the fiery consciousness. Of course, one should purify wherever there are accumulations of filth, and the lot of the fiery consciousness is to purify the records of space. Among the accumulated pages of human writings there will have to be noted those pernicious records which have clouded the brains of even well-meaning people. Thus on the path to the Fiery World one should understand the great significance of receptivity of higher energies and of subtle sendings." [Fiery World III]

4. The whole East believes in the Advent of the Lord Maitreya, but there are some who are aware that the Lord Maitreya now dwells in the Image of the Lord of Shambhala. Certainly, His Advent must not be understood as an appearance in the flesh, amidst earthly conditions and Earth-dwellers. The Teaching of the Lord Maitreya will be spread all over the world and it will proclaim the New Era—the era of the awakening of the Spirit, which is also called the era of woman.

It is most curious to hear about the belief of some people that the Great Teachers are divided into two camps regarding the books of Agni Yoga. This point of view shows a purely earthly concept, for the Teachers who belong to the Hierarchy of Light can never be divided into two camps. Such action is characteristic only of the black brotherhood, whereas the decision of the Hierarchy of Light is always *monolithic*. It is thus that Light conquers darkness.

It is true, the practice of occultism in the way it is understood by the majority, that is, the performance of mechanical exercises, is most dangerous. But the path of Light, the path of selfless service to humanity, readiness of the spirit, constant striving toward the perfectment of the inner man, and steadfast devotion to the chosen Ideal, this path, although difficult, has its spiritual joys. On the last step, the Carrier of Light inevitably drinks the chalice of poison, the chalice of betrayal by the nearest ones. Thus it was, thus it will be. The brighter the Light, the denser the darkness. Moreover, each Carrier of Light has his own Judas or Devadatta—be it a false-hearted king, as in the case of Saint-Germain, or the Coulombs and Soloviev in the case of Blavatsky. In the history of each Carrier of Light there is a tragic page of black betrayal.

5. Each sincere knocking of the heart will be heard. Therefore, knock, and do not be downhearted if the answer does not come immediately. The answer always comes unexpectedly, and almost always not in the form which we envisage—there are many reasons for this. Therefore, be vigilant and know how to discriminate. Perfect yourself.

I welcome your desire to share the Teaching with your friends. We call it the Teaching of Living Ethics, for under this name people accept it more easily. Unfortunately, due to irresponsible interpreters of the Eastern teachings, the majority of readers associate the word *yoga* with magic or pitiful fakirism.

16

16 November 1935

Advice has come to finish the book with the following words: "Written upon the threshold of the destined date." You may also hint that the New World comes to replace the old one, and in the process of this replacement all the cosmic forces will participate. Even a little foresight should tell a man to what an extent the world is atremor and how all the spheres are tensed in preparation for the spatial and earthly battles. Even a small consciousness should be able to realize the reconstruction toward which the world is moving. Even those who are unwilling to understand where the engenderments of humanity lead, even they must realize that the karma which brings all paths to the great Reconstruction is inevitable. It is really astonishing to what an extent mankind dwells in self-created illusions.

"Certain perspicacious people speak about the approaching end of the world. In describing it they talk as they were taught to think in elementary schools. They are little to be blamed in this, since their heads have been filled from childhood with the most monstrous ideas. And yet, they do sense some sort of end of something. Though dimly seen, still their spirit has a presentiment of some kind of change. They are called false prophets, but such a judgment is not fair, for in their own way they sense the end of an obsolete world. Only, they are unable to distinguish the external signs. Indeed, near is the hour when superfluous scales begin to fall, and the World of Light begins to come into being in joy. The most important processes can be carried out visibly-invisibly."

"When forewarnings are given, it is easier to distinguish events. Already something is being born, but the crowds are occupied with amusements. Already an explosion is prepared, yet the crowds rush into the hippodromes. And ancient seers knew of many changes which are now clear to historians. But their contemporaries only knew how to stone all those who were far-seeing. Is it not thus also today?" [Fiery World III]

And now—your questions. I should like to make a few additions to the septenary division.

1. Physical body.

2. Etheric double (sometimes called the lower astral body). Many of the phenomena of spiritualistic seances take place with the help of the etheric double of the medium.

3. Prana—vital principle, inseparable from all manifestations in the Cosmos.

4. Kama—animal soul (or higher astral body) through which desire is expressed in two aspects:

(a) Kama-Manas—lower mind, or the intellect.

(b) Kama Rupa—form (the subjective form of mental and physical desires and thoughts, or the thinker in action.)

5. Manas—self-consciousness, or the thinker (higher intelligence.)

6. Buddhi—spirituality, the spiritual soul as distinct from the human-animal soul; the conductor through which Atma is manifested.

7. Atma—Spirit, or fiery element or energy, spread throughout the entire Cosmos.

However, now that we have accepted this septenary subdivision, let us practice generalization, for it is always necessary *to generalize*. Therefore, point out that the so-called principles in us (with the exception of the physical body and the etheric double, which disintegrate after death) are just aspects or conditions of our consciousness. Indeed, all the divisions into spirit, soul, Manas—higher and lower—are in reality only various qualities of one and the same fundamental energy of Fire, or of life or consciousness, of which the highest aspect is psychic energy. Therefore, for the achievement of the higher spirituality, we ought to transmute and sublimate the fires of our centers to their seventh state. Thus, the world of higher spirituality, the Fiery World, is the world of sublimated feelings, or consciousnesses. Not any one human feeling disappears, but it remains in the Fiery World in its sublimated or refined condition, responding to the higher attractions and vibrations. The whole Cosmos is built on a septenary foundation; therefore, each energy, each manifestation contains within itself its septenary scale of tension and refinement.

And now, regarding the question of such interest to you—the planetary chains and the Moon.

As I have already written to you, by the planetary chain one must understand a certain planet regarded in various phases of its development and accompanied by its invisible spheres. All in nature develops according to one eternal law on a septenary principle. Therefore, similar to man, each planet has its seven principles or seven spheres. Of these seven spheres, the lowest and most material one (in the earthly chain, our Earth) is entirely accessible to our knowledge, whereas the other six lie outside of it and are invisible to the earthly eye. And each such chain of worlds is, so to say, an incarnation or the progeny of another, lower and dead chain. These seven spheres correspond to the principles of man. Thus our earthly chain is an incarnation, or offspring, of the older, lunar chain.

Here is a diagram of the Planetary Chains and extracts from *The Secret Doctrine* pertaining to this diagram.

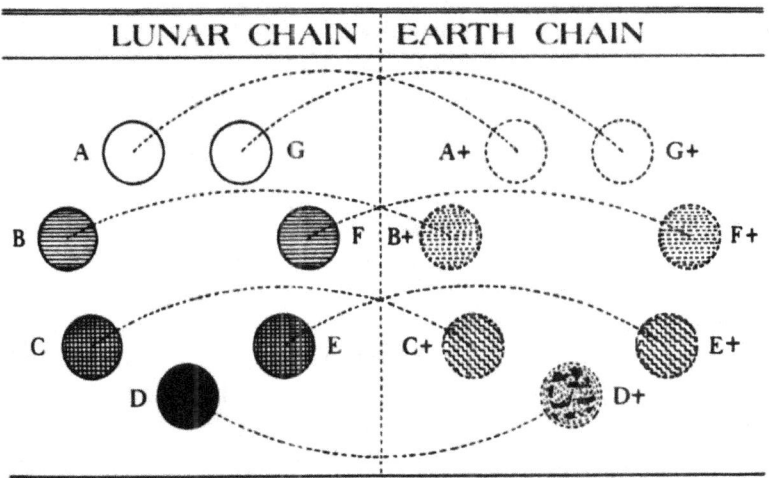

"When a planetary chain is in its last (seventh) Round, its Globe [sphere] ... A, before finally *dying out*, sends all its energy and 'principles' into a neutral center of latent force, a 'laya center' and thereby informs a new nucleus of undifferentiated substance or matter, *i.e.*, calls it into activity or gives it life. ... Imagine the six fellow-globes of the moon—aeons before the first globe of our seven was evolved—just in the same position in relation to each other as the fellow-globes of our chain in regard to our Earth now. And now it will be easy to imagine further Globe A of the lunar chain informing Globe A of the terrestrial chain, and—dying; Globe B of the former sending after that its energy into Globe B of the ... [earthly] chain;... then the Moon (our Satellite) pouring forth into the lowest globe of our planetary ring—Globe D, our Earth—all its life, energy and powers; ... [the moon] is the satellite undeniably [of our Earth], but this does not invalidate the theory that she had given to the Earth all but her corpse ...; and, [the Moon] having transferred them to a new center, becoming virtually *a dead planet*, in which rotation has almost ceased since the birth of our globe."

"Why should Venus and Mercury have no satellites, and by what, when they exist, were they formed? The Astronomers 'do not know.' Because, we say, science has only one key—the key of matter—to open the mysteries of nature withal, while occult philosophy has seven keys and explains that which science fails to see. Mercury and Venus have no satellites, but they had 'parents' just as the Earth had. Both are far older than the Earth, and, before the latter reaches her seventh Round, her mother Moon will have dissolved into thin air, as the 'Moons' of the other planets have, or have not, as the case may be, since there are planets which have *several* moons—a mystery again which no Oedipus of astronomy has solved.

"... The Moon is now the cold residual quantity, the shadow dragged after the new body, into which her living powers and 'principles' are transfused. She is now doomed for long ages to be ever pursuing the Earth, to be attracted by and to attract her progeny. Constantly *vampirized* by her child [Earth], she revenges herself on it by soaking it through and through with the nefarious, invisible, and poisoned influence which emanates from the occult side of her nature. For she is *dead*, yet a *living body*. The particles of her decaying corpse are full of active and destructive life, although the body which they had formed is soulless and lifeless. Therefore its emanations are at the same time beneficent and maleficent—this circumstance finding its parallel on Earth in the fact that the grass and plants are nowhere more juicy and thriving than on the graves; while at the same time it is the graveyard or corpse-emanations which kill... the nature and properties of the moon were known to every Occultist, but have remained a closed book for physicists."

"For the benefit of those who may not have read, or, if they have, may not have clearly understood ... the doctrine of the septenary chains of worlds in the Solar Kosmos, the teaching is briefly thus:

"1. Everything in the metaphysical as in the physical Universe is septenary. Hence every sidereal body, every planet, whether visible or invisible, is credited with six companion globes. The evolution of life proceeds on these seven globes or bodies from the 1st to the 7th in seven ROUNDS or Seven Cycles.

"2. These globes [or spheres] are formed by a process which the Occultists call the 'rebirth of planetary chains (or rings).' When the seventh and last Round of one of such rings has been entered upon, the higher or first globe 'A,' followed by all the others down to the last, instead of entering upon a certain time of rest—or 'obscuration,' as in their previous Rounds—begin to die out. The 'planetary' dissolution (*pralaya*) is at hand, and its hour has struck; each globe has to transfer its life and energy to another planet.

"3. Our Earth, as the visible representative of its invisible superior fellow globes, its 'lords' or 'principles,' has to live, as have the others, through seven Rounds. During the first three, it forms and consolidates; during the fourth it settles and hardens; during the last three it gradually returns to its first ... form: it is spiritualized, so to say.

"4. Its Humanity develops fully only in the Fourth—our Fourth—our present Round. Up to this fourth Life-Cycle, it is referred to as 'humanity' only for lack of a more appropriate term. Like the grub which becomes chrysalis and butterfly, Man, or rather that which becomes man, passes through all the forms and kingdoms during the first Round and through all the human shapes during the two following Rounds. Arrived on our Earth at the commencement of the Fourth in the present series of life-cycles and races, MAN is the first form that appears thereon, being preceded only by the mineral and vegetable kingdoms—even the latter *having to develop and continue its further evolution through man.* ...During the three Rounds to come, Humanity, like the globe [planet] on which it lives, will be ever tending to reassume its primeval form, that of a Dhyan-Chohanic Host. Man tends to become a God and then—GOD, like every other atom in the Universe. ...

"5. Every life-cycle on Globe D (our Earth) is composed of seven root-races. They commence with the Ethereal and end with the spiritual on the double line of physical and moral evolution—from the beginning of the terrestrial round to its close. (One is a 'planetary round' from Globe A to Globe G, the seventh, the other, the 'globe round,' or the *terrestrial.* [Cycle of seven races])..

"6. The first root-race, i.e., the first 'men' on earth (irrespective of form) were the progeny of the 'celestial men,' called rightly in Indian philosophy the 'Lunar Ancestors' or the Pitris, of which there are seven classes or Hierarchies. ..."

Take into consideration that: "... every 'Round' brings about a new development and even an entire change in the mental, psychic, spiritual and physical constitution of man, all these principles evoluting on an ever ascending scale. ..."

"... There must be a limited number of Monads evolving and growing more and more perfect through their assimilation of many successive personalities [or incarnations], in every new Manvantara. ... Thus, although the hosts of more or less progressed Monads are almost incalculable, they are still *finite,* as is everything in this Universe of differentiation and finiteness."

Thus, "... Our Moon was the fourth Globe [sphere in the Lunar Chain] of the series, and was on the same plane of perception as our Earth. ...

"Further, when globe A of the new chain is ready, the first class or Hierarchy of Monads from the Lunar Chain incarnate upon it in the lowest kingdom and so on successively. The result of this is, that it is only the first class of Monads which attains the human state of development during the first Round, since the second class, on each planet [globe-sphere], arriving later, has not time to reach that stage. Thus the Monads of Class 2 reach the incipient human stage only in the Second Round, and so on up to the middle of the Fourth Round. But at this point— and on this Fourth Round in which the human stage will be *fully* developed—the 'Door' into the human kingdom closes; and henceforward the number of 'human' Monads, i.e., Monads in the human stage of development, is *complete.* For the Monads which had not reached the human stage by this point will, owing to the evolution of humanity itself, find themselves so far behind that they will reach the human stage only at the close of the seventh and last Round. They will, therefore, not be men on this chain, but will form the humanity of a future Manvantara and be rewarded by becoming 'Men' on a higher chain altogether, thus receiving their Karmic compensation."

"The Monadic Host may be roughly divided into three great classes:

"1. The most developed Monads (the Lunar Gods or 'Spirits,' called, in India, the Pitris), whose function it is to pass in the first Round through the whole triple cycle of the mineral, vegetable, and animal kingdoms in their most ethereal, filmy, and rudimentary forms, in order to clothe themselves in, and assimilate, the nature of the newly formed chain. They are those who first reach the human form (if there can be any form in the realm of the almost subjective) on Globe A in the first Round. It is they, therefore, who lead and represent the human element during the second and third Rounds. ...

"2. Those Monads that are the first to reach the human stage during the three and a half Rounds, and to become men.

"3. The laggards; the Monads which are retarded, and which will not reach, by reason of Karmic impediments, the human stage at all during this cycle or Round. ...

"It stands to reason that a MONAD cannot either progress or develop, or even be affected by the changes of states it passes through. *It is not of this world or plane,* and may be compared only to an indestructible state of divine light and fire, thrown down on to our Earth as a plank of salvation for the personalities in which it indwells. It is for the latter to cling to it; and thus partaking of its divine nature, obtain immortality. Left to itself the Monad will cling to no one; but, like the 'plank,' be drifted away to another incarnation by the unresting current of evolution."

"Now the evolution of the *external* form or body round the astral is produced by the terrestrial forces, just as in the case of the lower kingdoms; but the evolution of the internal or real MAN is purely spiritual. It is now no more a passage of the impersonal Monad through many and various forms of matter—endowed at best with instinct and consciousness on quite a different plane—as in the case of external evolution, but a journey of the 'pilgrim-soul' through various *states* of *not only matter* but Self consciousness and self-perception, or of *perception* from apperception.

"The MONAD emerges from its state of spiritual and intellectual unconsciousness; and, skipping the first two planes—too near the ABSOLUTE to permit of any correlation with anything on a lower plane—it gets direct into the plane of Mentality. But there is no plane in the whole universe with a wider margin, or a wider field of action in its almost endless gradations of perceptive and apperceptive qualities, than this plane, which has in its turn an appropriate smaller plane for every 'form,' from the 'mineral' monad up to the time when that monad blossoms forth by evolution into the DIVINE MONAD. But all the time it is still one and the same Monad, differing only in its incarnations, throughout its ever succeeding cycles of partial or total obscuration of spirit, or the partial or total obscuration of matter—two polar antitheses—as it ascends into the realms of mental spirituality, or descends into the depths of materiality."

"What, it may be asked, are the 'Lunar Monads,' just spoken of? The description of the seven classes of Pitris will come later, but now some general explanations may be given. It must be plain to everyone that they are Monads, who, having ended their life-cycle on the lunar chain, which is inferior to the terrestrial chain, have incarnated on this one. But there are some further details which may be added, though they border too closely on forbidden ground to be treated of fully. The last word of the mystery is divulged only to the adepts, but it may be stated that our satellite is only the gross body of its invisible principles. Seeing then that there are 7 Earths, so there are 7 Moons, the last one alone being visible; the same for the Sun, whose visible body is called a Maya, a reflection, just as man's body is. 'The real Sun and the real Moon are as invisible as the real man,' says an occult maxim."

"In reality the Moon is only the satellite of the Earth in one respect, viz., that physically the Moon revolves round the Earth. ... Startling as the statement may seem it is not without confirmation from scientific knowledge. It is evidenced by the tides, by the cyclic changes in many forms of disease which coincide with the lunar phases; it can be traced in the growth of plants, and is very marked in the phenomena of human gestation and conception. The importance of the Moon and its influence on the Earth were recognized in every ancient religion, notably the Jewish, and have been remarked by many observers of psychic and physical phenomena. But, so far as Science knows, the Earth's action on the Moon is confined to the physical attraction, which causes her to circle in her orbit. And should an objector insist that this fact alone is sufficient evidence that the

Moon is truly the Earth's satellite on other planes of action, one may reply by asking whether a mother, who walks round and round by her child's cradle keeping watch over the infant, is subordinate of her child or dependent upon it; though in one sense she is its satellite, yet she is certainly older and more fully developed than the child she watches.

It is, then, the Moon that plays the largest and most important part, as well in the formation of the Earth itself, as in the peopling thereof with human beings. The 'Lunar Monads' or Pitris, the ancestors of man, become in reality man himself. They are the 'Monads' who enter on the cycle of evolution on Globe A, and who, passing round the chain of planets [globe-spheres], evolve the human form as has just been shown. ... These 'Monads' or 'divine sparks' are thus the 'Lunar' ancestors, the Pitris themselves. For these 'Lunar Spirits' have to become 'Men' in order that their 'Monads' may reach a higher plane of activity and self-consciousness, i.e., the plane of the Manasa-Putras, those who endow the 'senseless' shells, created and informed by the Pitris, with 'mind' in the latter part of the Third Root-Race [Fourth Round]." [Op. cit.]

1. They are called Manasa-Putras or Mind-born; the Sons of Light or solar Ancestors. Thus, our humanity owes them its accelerated evolution.

2. "In the same way the 'Monads' or Egos of the men of the seventh Round of our Earth, after our own Globes A, B, C, D, *et seq.*, parting with their life-energy, will have informed and thereby called to life other laya-centers destined to live and to act on a still higher plane of being—in the same way will the Terrene 'Ancestors' create those who will become their superiors." [*Ibid.*]

And now, I was happy to hear about your fiery signs. The vision of the flame of a candle is most characteristic for the kindling of the centers. Sometimes one may see such a flame over a luminous knot of, as it were, thick threads (nerves). The colored sparks also signify the awakening of the centers. The warmth of the heart is a beautiful sign.

Also, it is characteristic to see iridescent luminous zigzags. I have seen them several times during the last summer and they disturbed my work by thickly covering the sheets which I used for writing. They indicate the battles in the supermundane world. Continue your observations and write them down.

One must not neglect such observations of oneself. People lose the sense of observation, yet it is essential to know oneself.

17

18 November 1935

I was very pleased to see your subtle understanding of the legend about the Treasure of the World. Of course, each sign has many meanings. This Treasure is a fragment of the main body, guarded in the Stronghold of Light. The sending of this gift has signified, from immemorial times, an approaching era of predestined unification and power in the country where it appears. All the great unifiers and founders of nations have possessed it. The East especially is full of legends about this gift of Orion, and the peoples of Asia seek it everywhere. Ossendowski, the author of the book *Beasts, Men and Gods*, heard of these legends. There are many different versions of them which are more or less correct. Thus, the white horse, Erdeni Mori, of Tibet and Mongolia, who carries Chintamani (The Treasure of the World), is also connected with this occurrence. The legend recorded in *On Eastern Crossroads* is the truth. According to the legend, this Treasure brings with it a special Covenant which must be fulfilled. The casket mentioned in the legend belongs to the thirteenth century, and was said to have been made from leather which had been in the possession of Solomon himself. Many alchemic symbols are inscribed upon the leather. The famous Rabbi, Moses de Leon, who compiled the Zohar, was, during the persecution of the Jews in Spain, offered shelter by a German feudal noblewoman. She gave him and other persecuted Jews refuge on her estates, and as a token of gratitude he gave her a talisman and this precious piece of skin. The lady ordered a small casket to be made from this skin, and the talisman was preserved in it. The legend states that after a new power is established, the Treasure will return to the Stronghold of Light.

1936 was a year that was mentioned in predictions in all the ancient Scriptures, and the calculations of the events which coincide with that year were found in the Pyramid of Cheops. But who can understand and accept that event, which will be laid in the foundation of the New World? No doubt, much will come to pass during this year; not only in the higher supermundane spheres but also on Earth many omens will be manifested. I shall quote to you a page from the Teaching.

"A remarkable year draws near. But many do not grasp the significance of current events. Even those who have heard are wishing that events would be carried out according to their own imagination. Usually each one wishes according to his nature, but observes current events without prejudice. Fix your attention honestly, knowing that a great date is ensuing. Doves will bring you not only an olive branch but also a leaf of oak and laurel. Likewise Our sacrificial offerings are not a chance occurrence but are as steps of the future. Indeed, unalterable are the dates of great knowledge. Learn to love creative conflict. Know how to put your ear to the earth and to illumine your hearts in great expectancy. Let the ignorant desire evil, yet the dates weave the fabric of the world. Learn to discern. Learn to fly toward the ordained. Many are the garments and the veils, but the meaning is one. The preordained year draws near.

"Austerely and tensely, yet also joyfully, should this year be passed on Earth for those who are wise. I affirm a powerful rotation of energies, yet there too it is possible to awaken sleeping ones. Not obviously does the King of Glory arrive, but by the wise His step is heard. Leave the dead to bury the dead, and rejoice in the formation of life. ...

"Certain perspicacious people speak about the approaching end of the world. In describing it they talk as they were taught to think in elementary schools. They are little to be blamed in this, since their heads have been filled since childhood with the most monstrous ideas. And yet, they do sense some sort of end of something. Though dimly seen, still their spirit has a presentiment of some kind of change. They are called false prophets, but such a judgment is not fair, for in their own way they sense the end of an obsolete world. Only, they are unable to distinguish the eternal signs. Indeed, near is the hour when superfluous scales begin to fall, and the World of Light begins to come into being in joy. The most important processes can be carried out visibly-invisibly.

"When forewarnings are given, it is easier to distinguish events. Already something is being born, but the crowds are occupied with amusements. Already an explosion is prepared yet the crowds rush into the hippodromes. And ancient seers knew of many changes which are now clear to historians. But their contemporaries only knew how to stone all those who were far-seeing. Is it not thus also today?" [Fiery World III]

All the cosmic dates, all the combinations of the luminaries are approaching the consummation of the great Cycle, and humanity must be spiritually resurrected. The fiery energies are reaching Earth toward the appointed time, and we may expect great changes, which must bring the awakening of the spirit. The end of the reign of Lucifer approaches. The new race is being born.

Of course, Solomon was definitely a historical personage; likewise, the temple of Solomon is not a myth.

The great incarnations of the seven Kumaras, or the Sons of Reason—Sons of Light—were to be found in ancient times among the initiates of all countries and peoples, and later among the greatest minds of more recent epochs. Throughout the entire evolution of our planet, we owe to these greatest Spirits the progress of our consciousness. They incarnated in all races and nations on the threshold of a new shifting of consciousness and at each new turn in history. Verily, the greatest Images of antiquity are connected with these Sons of Light. The fall of Lucifer began from the time of Atlantis. Later he could be recognized in Ravana, the adversary of Rama, the hero of the epic poem, the *Mahabharata*. The Great Spirits tirelessly undertook the most difficult tasks of life, but few of their contemporaries understood even partially the grandeur and self-renunciation of these true Men-Gods. Hardly anyone can comprehend the entire significance of Their creativeness on the earthly plane and in the supermundane worlds. Many beautiful mysteries exist in the Cosmos, and when the spirit contacts them, the heart is filled with exaltation and with infinite gratitude to these spirits, the creators of our consciousness. During endless thousands of years, in self-sacrificing service for the good of humanity, They renounced the highest joys of the Fiery World and with bloody sweat stood on guard, accepting the wreaths of thorns and draining the cups of poison tendered by the hands of humanity, whose benefactors They were. When the veil is removed from the mystery, many hearts will tremble because of the crimes committed against these Saviors.

You are right, the study of the Teaching of Life requires a most careful attitude. One should approach the unprepared consciousness very carefully. Indeed, nothing develops as slowly as consciousness. "It is important to understand to what extent people's consciousness has become petrified. Therefore, do not give it food which it cannot assimilate. Side by side with the difficult give also the easy; otherwise people will not listen. The letters of the Teacher are inevitably diverse, because directed to different consciousnesses. This is not contradiction, but simply the best way. Thus, accustom yourselves to deal carefully with consciousnesses, as with fire."

We must practice great patience, and only by careful touches can we give a new direction to the thinking of people; not by breaking the old concepts, but by gradually broadening their meaning. Of course, each person requires an individual approach.

Last year was made especially eventful by the aggressions against enlightened undertakings. And yet, good omens were even more numerous. For the birth of new energies, these collisions of Light with darkness are necessary. For the purpose of healing, water has to be agitated; nothing is worse than stagnant water. We certainly know the source of support for the leaflets similar to the one you have mentioned. But then, such literature is popular only among people of a low mental level who are unable to discriminate independently and who are sunk in selfhood and self-destruction. Inapplicable to them are the wise words of Confucius who said that the one who does not react to slander, which is slowly absorbed by the brain, nor to insults, which, like sores, injure the body, that one verily can be called wise; he who takes no notice of either slander or insults can be called far-sighted. Precisely, far-sightedness points out the insignificance of all slanders before the face of historical truth when the Higher Justice pronounces its verdict on a world scale.

As for inner betrayal, here, of course, we deal with occult laws. There could not have been a pure structure of Light which was not betrayed in our age of Kali Yuga; and since we experience the most threatening time of Armageddon, the betrayals are even more numerous and intensive in their fury. As it is said, "Before the coming dates the dark ones are especially furious."

We were warned about the subtle betrayal, but we are hoping to be able to postpone it for as long as possible, i e., until a better combination of the luminaries. But the traitors could not hold back under the pressure of the black year with seven eclipses, and they threw off their masks. However, better aspects are not far off, and therefore we calmly watch the development of this madness. This betrayal, as I have already written you, was caused by cupidity and ambition. Someone decided to reap the laurels for himself only and to seize in his hands the fruits of the labors of all the other co-workers. N. K. was building everything upon the principle of common ownership, as well as upon broad social and public knowledge. But precisely this was not to someone's liking, and while N. K. was away the traitor, using favorable circumstances, started putting into practice his methods of usurpation, which had been thoroughly planned during fourteen years of collaboration. He was helped in this by unprincipled legal advisers. The microbe of dictatorship is infectious.

But we know how the Great Teachers look upon the betrayers. Indeed, "The Teacher permits the beginning of a new step. Betrayal is an attribute of such ascent. The Teacher considers the manifestation of abuse useful. The Teacher regards a dish of slander as a wonderful offering. The manifestation of slander brings tension of atmosphere, and each tension is already an ascent. Let the ignorant dance, they arouse the waves. The traitors will be overthrown." Thus, in full calmness and trust in the Guiding Hand we will continue to build.

True, someone will ask, How could such traitors be allowed to approach? But we should not forget Judas, Devadatta, Cassius, Brutus, and all murderers and betrayers, whose name is legion. Betrayal, like a shadow, follows a great achievement, and precisely by betrayal the greatness of an achievement can be measured. Many dark betrayers were known to H. P. Blavatsky and Comte Saint-Germain, and those Carriers of Light nearer to our own time, but their names became only greater because of this.

Prior to these two black years, a new sign of Great Trust was manifested, which, according to all the most ancient scriptures and prophecies, signifies the beginning of the New Epoch. Thus are the signs of Light and darkness intertwined. My letter is speckled with details, but so is life itself, in all its complexity. I would not like to end my letter negatively, therefore I shall conclude with the following:

"Let us rejoice at the manifestation of victory. People will still not see it for some time, but it is already here. Wait, impatient ones, not the eye but the heart determines victory. When a fiery structure is already realized in the Subtle World; then may the hearts of the builders rejoice. Those who sleep do not feel it if they are carried out of the house, but space is already singing." [Fiery World III]

18
26 November 1935

I quite agree that the crucified thief probably was no worse, and perhaps even better, than many of the respectable Pharisees and Sadducees. However, there are many steps between a thief and a high spirit. The assertion of Vivekananda which you have quoted remains in force; but, knowing the law of karma, we must understand that by liberation is meant the awakening of the spirit and its deliverance from the power of darkness. Indeed, we know that a sincere repentance before death, together with the last pure thought and powerful striving toward the Highest, carry the spirit into the spheres of the Subtle World in complete correspondence with this vibration, or striving. The words of Christ strengthened still more the striving of the thief, and his spirit was enabled to rise and ascend to a still higher level. Similarly, not only the sinless and the saints rest in Devachan. Each good deed performed by us receives its own reward.

Polarity cannot disappear, for all Existence is founded on polarity, and Fire—this life-creating element—is twofold in its Divine Origin.

Likewise, unity does not mean fusion into one form. Therefore, neither the ugly hermaphrodite, nor Siamese twins, nor people with double spines have a place in the evolution of the Beauty of Cosmos. Indeed the significance of Existence is in an infinite diversity of forms with one fundamental fiery unity.

And now, regarding blood and infection, I shall quote some paragraphs from the third volume of *Fiery World:*

"People inquire about the causes of infection, about the properties of blood and sperm, but they completely forget that at the base of these lies psychic energy. It preserves against infection; it is found in the properties of secretions. It is useless to take into consideration a mechanical summary of collected information if attention is not given to the participation of psychic energy. People call a certain immunity an influx of faith, but not without reason is a state of ecstasy called the radiance of the Fiery World. And such a radiance protects man against infection. It purifies the secretions, it is like a shield. Therefore a state of joy and exaltation is the best prophylaxis. Whoever knows rapture of spirit has already been cleansed against many dangers. Even ordinary physicians know how changeable is the condition of the blood and of secretions. But few connect this with the spiritual condition. One should not be enslaved by statistics; one can fall into error. It was not so long ago that the mental level was calculated according to the dimensions of the skull. Thus psychic energy has been largely forgotten."

I am adding another paragraph from the same book, which I believe will be of value to you:

"When we speak about Spirit and Matter, we should have in mind the higher meaning of Matter. But speaking about the liberation of the Spirit, we refer to those manifestations which can be called material life units. It must be known that in speaking about these unifications under various forms a downfall of the spirit is understood. For the spirit, being made manifest in matter, must aspire to the higher functions *together with matter*. Matter is impelled to creativeness which gives rise to forms of life. And the spirit must know specifically how sacred is the sojourn in matter. The cosmic concept of the Feminine Principle as Matter is so lofty—the Truth is so far above the worldly understanding! Only a pure and elevated consciousness can appreciate this comparison. It is difficult to dissociate Spirit from Matter." Without matter, spirit is naught.

From many sides come light-bearing news and omens about the approaching epoch. Each great epoch is accompanied by a special celestial omen, which inevitably appears through many centuries. The appearance of this omen took place in January, 1934. The stars were found in certain combinations. Let us be strong, solemn, and joyous. Continue your useful work!

19

7 December 1935

One may only regret that apparently the persons you have mentioned are familiar neither with the Eastern philosophical systems and teachings nor with *The Secret Doctrine* by H. P. Blavatsky. Therefore, they do not know who are the Kumaras, Sons of Light, Mind-born Sons, etc., mentioned there. And even if they have read *The Secret Doctrine*, they do not know how to make the next turn of the key. There is one Chain of the Hierarchy of Light, which continues into Infinity, and all the true Carriers of Light who appear and who are still on our Earth are links of it. Certainly, the Sons of Light, who came from the higher worlds (Venus and Jupiter) to our planet at the end of the Third Race of our Round for the hastening of the evolution of humanity, are the Greatest Spirits, who are at the head of the Hierarchy of Light that is the nearest and most accessible to us, owing to karma. They are the progenitors of our consciousness; to them, we owe our mental development. And, of course, They belong to the Chain of the Builders of the Cosmos. Each such Builder must pass through human evolution in order that later He may rise as the head of this or that planet. But as evolution is infinite, all these Builders, after completing one cycle of evolution, commence another and are born again, but on higher worlds. Ponder more deeply upon the concept of Infinity.

And regarding the statement of the person you mentioned, it would be interesting, first of all, to find out what he meant by saying that the Himalayan Mahatmas are born of Earth. For, strictly speaking, we can consider only the Prince of this world and all the Earth-dwellers who correspond to his ray as the Spirit and spirits born of Earth; for each seed of the spirit is conceived under a certain luminary, which, during a whole Manvantara, remains its leading star. Thus, the Prince of this world belongs to Earth, and owing to his previous achievements on another planet and because of a cosmic right he is the Host of Earth. Naturally, nearest to him are those spirits who are also born under the ray corresponding to his. But there are many spirits on our Earth who are already subject to higher vibrations because of their essence, or who possess the potentiality of the energies of other worlds that comprise our solar system, even those as distant as Uranus and Neptune. Moreover, let us bear in mind that the life of all the kingdoms of nature was transferred to our planet from the Moon. That is why in *The Secret Doctrine* the dual ancestors of humanity are pointed out—the Lunar and the Solar. The Lunar ancestors became in reality present humanity itself, or, rather, the majority of it, whereas the Solar ancestors are those Sons of Light who undertook the self-sacrificing work of creativeness for the benefit of the whole Cosmos. They came to our planet from the higher worlds, as has already been said, at the end of the Third Race of our Round. Since that time, They have continuously incarnated on the threshold of all Races and all great events, so that each time They could give a new impulse to the consciousness of humanity. Verily, Their lives are paved with self-sacrificing, heroic achievements. Verily, They have drained many chalices of poison. Thus, in the time of Atlantis they were the Founders of the Great Brotherhood on the Sacred Island. So also they are the Guardians of the Trans-Himalayan Stronghold during our Race.

Certainly the Mahatmas of the Himalayas are unable to contact the auras of Earth-dwellers for long. They cannot even remain in the atmosphere of the valleys, owing to the lack of correspondence in vibrations. Therefore a prolonged contact is mutually harmful; and in the case of Earth-dwellers it can be even dangerous. Thus, in the times of H. P. B. the Mahatma K. H., who contacted the aura of the valleys longer than the other Mahatmas, was recalled by his Hierarch into the Stronghold for recuperation. Likewise, we know that another Mahatma, when coming to see Blavatsky in the mountains of Sikkim, had to inhale a special preparation of ozone almost continuously. We also know that neither Buddha nor Christ were able to remain for long in the cities and amidst people and often had to retire into the desert.

The Himalayan Mahatmas live in complete solitude and admit into their Stronghold one or, at the most, two candidates in a century. Of course, there are exceptions. But They send their disciples and younger brothers to incarnate on Earth with a special mission; and from their very infancy They direct and watch over them. The occult bond established during many thousands of years makes the spiritual contact easy; and the accelerated opening of the centers and their fiery transmutation, which provides the fiery conduit for clairaudience and clairvoyance, becomes possible. But even with such readiness of spirit, the brother-disciple must manifest an absolute unwavering striving and great intensity in following the Leading Hand. Many tests must he endure, even on the last step. And the difficulties pile up and at times seem to be insurmountable. Even so, Judases are inevitable on the path in order that the path of Light may be inculcated more vividly. And the symbol of the draining of the chalice of poison remains inseparable from the Path of Service to humanity.

Sometimes the Mahatmas call their disciples into one of their Ashrams for a certain period; here They prepare their organisms for the sacred assimilation of subtle energies and give them instructions. So it was with H. P. B., who spent three years in Their Ashram before giving the world *The Secret Doctrine*. But you are quite right in saying that we ought not to be preoccupied with questions about which hierarchic degrees the Himalayan Brothers occupy in the chain of Infinity. We must work with the Great Teacher who called us, realizing that the degree of evolution of his Spirit is, for the present, inaccessible to us; and may God help us to be able to approach Him at the end of our planetary Manvantara.

And now, in a book of the Teaching there is a paragraph which might be applied to many earthly teachers. Here it is: "The Teacher who has not overcome intolerance cannot mold the future. The Teaching is given for the future. The spirit cannot advance without forging perfectment. Thus, it is possible to command the attention of listeners, but it is far more necessary to arouse a movement forward. The Teacher does not forbid reading different books. Everyone who fears puts limitations on himself, but the leader summons to a broad cognition. He will not restrain one from good in all its aspects. This liberality of spirit is indispensable. He who does not even wish to listen is already afraid of something. Thus, the fiery condition requires broad gates and the speediest of wings." [Fiery World III]

You are also right that expecting an evident sign from the Teacher to give us an impulse for intensified work would be considered as temptation and indicates weakness of striving. Thus, in the book *Agni Yoga* there is a beautiful paragraph: "To Him of the great Illumination there came a pupil seeking a miracle: 'After the miracle I shall have faith.' The Teacher sadly smiled and revealed to him a great miracle. 'Now,' exclaimed the pupil, 'I am ready to pass through the steps of the Teaching under your guidance.' But the Teacher, pointing to the door, said: 'Go, I no longer need you!'"

Verily, blessed are those who believe without having to see, for this proves that their spirit has brought this faith from previous lives, and the chalice of their achievements approaches its final accumulation.

I welcome your efforts toward self-improvement. I suggest that you keep daily notes regarding your progress. Put down how far you have succeeded in applying at least one of the advices chosen by you from the Teaching, or in eradicating some habit which hinders your progress. Such daily notes are very beneficial for a test or examination after a certain time has expired.

All your spiritual sendings are good, and of course you should continue them. This is a purely Eastern custom. As for accompanying these sendings by various positions of the hands and fingers, I can only say that if you feel that this helps you, you should continue to do so. The most important in all sendings is the sensation of warmth in the heart. No movements, or rhythms, or chants are of any help if the heart is frozen. The key to all achievements is in the heart, in its fiery energies.

Certainly each High Spirit is a reservoir of life-giving energies, which constantly irradiate the surroundings. A nucleus formed by three such spirits can create miracles. The Great Hierarchy of Light is the Cosmic Reservoir of such Forces.

Yes, any smoke is harmful, especially tobacco smoke.

And so, do not be discouraged, continue your work with a striving heart. Armageddon is in its full fury. Broad is the threshold of the year 1936. At the moment, we, too, are drinking of the chalice of poison; yet courage and striving do not leave us. We love battle, since in battle we temper our forces and refine our abilities. Knowing of the predestined victory of the Forces of Light, let us courageously oppose the dark ones.

Just before dawn, the sky from the valleys seems especially dark, but those who stand on the mountain already see the coming light.

20

7 December 1935

The approach to Light demands from us not only moral purity but also physical cleanliness. Precisely, on certain spiritual steps physical hygiene is absolutely essential. Thus no animal should be permitted in the living quarters, and even birds should not be permitted in bedrooms; for that which is low attracts the low.

In connection with this, I shall quote a paragraph from *Fiery World III*: "Manifestations can be either subtle or connected with the dense world. Not rarely do dark entities [from the Subtle World] strengthen themselves by the presence of creatures of

Earth which they attract. Thus, there may appear some stray dogs or cats or mice or annoying insects. Dark entities strengthen their substance from animals. Repeatedly has the Teaching pointed out the participation of the animal world in subtle and low manifestations. Sometimes they cannot manifest without the participation of animals. But for the courageous spirit all such manifestations are as nought... but it is very important for science to know these connections of animals with the Subtle World. I do not advise having animals in bedrooms. Certain people themselves sense the practicality of such vital precautions, but others, on the contrary, aspire, as it were, to attract invisible guests."

And if dogs and birds are so objected to, what can be said about cats, whose natures are definitely considered as belonging to the dark orders? One should be fond of animals, and should pity them, but it is disgusting to see the distorted sentimentality lavished upon them by certain types of people.

"Who hath said that one must renounce madly? Madness doth so remain." Is it not the madness of hypocrisy to give away everything and then to expect help from others? And if help is refused, to become full of hate, as usually happens. Unfortunately, a certain type of giving is often performed with the secret hope of receiving in return a hundredfold the amount given. But it is forgotten that only those receive a hundredfold who think least of all about receiving anything. Thus, he who does not understand the great law of balance, or co-measurement and goal-fitness cannot become a true follower of the Teaching of Light.

You write that the letter about God continues to make some people indignant. Verily, it is surprising how people do not understand and deny the concepts in even their own accepted scriptures and religions! Thus, the words "No man hath seen God at any time" and "God is a consuming fire" even now remain a dead letter for them.

* * *

The fiery conductor of clairaudience is considered the most direct one, the nearest, and the most sacred. Only one ignorant of occultism could think that the letters delivered, even by the so-called "occult mail," prove a closer contact than the direct fiery conductor of clairaudience, which is used by the entire

White Brotherhood among themselves. All the books of the Teaching point out this direct contact. Could the experiment of Agni Yoga be performed without a direct contact with the Great Teacher! Indeed, all the books were and are given by the Great Teacher on the basis of this experiment.

* * *

Intrigues are not far from betrayal, therefore let us practice caution. Discrimination is the first quality on the path of discipleship, and it does not come easily. The disciple must be armed against all the eventualities of life. How else can he fulfill his great mission as a co-worker of Cosmos?

* * *

I quite understand that the beauty and austere self-discipline and achievement in life that I affirm in my letters may be above the consciousness of many, and not to their liking. But I consider it sinful to advocate sentimentality, which is based on false concepts. I have tried my best to uplift their spirits, but I certainly cannot do it by offering tinseled visions in the style of L. Yes, the majority of people are great hypocrites when they insist on wishing to know the truth and only the truth. Indeed, they are afraid of the truth most of all, always and in everything.

Instead of an austere construction of life, people expect sweet dreams to comfort them, and easy achievements amidst an environment of the Magi of "occult" novels. But the crown of the Arhat is attained only by the strongest, in the severest tension of achievement, and through a powerful, unshakeable striving of the heart, purified by bloody tears of sufferings throughout many, many lives. The heart of the Arhat has to go through all the joys and also all the sufferings and the sorrows of the earthly path; he must drink the entire chalice of poison. Verily, hard is the path of ascent, and especially on the last steps. It can be compared to a climb in the darkness over steep basalt rocks when the hand searches in vain for a jut to get hold of. However, handrails are prepared for the striving spirit, and only at the last moment of complete exhaustion before a fall will the solicitous Hand give support. This was also my experience while my heart was almost breaking under the incredible tension felt during such an ascent. Yes, many symbols of the hard ascent were manifested. Moreover, the complete draining of the full chalice of poison is inevitable at the consummation of the path. Yet, with all that, when the spirit has known lofty joys, when the beauty of the higher worlds is cognized, all these difficulties do not frighten, but even bring their own joy, for they signify the approach of the end of the path. Thus, a Judas also must appear in order to throw into greater emphasis the light on the path.

And now to your questions:

1. Bear in mind that one should not rely upon all types of musk from various animals. Only the musk deer eats the beneficial food which produces in the male the equilibrating substance. Therefore, the musk of the civet is not so good, for it does not contain that equilibrating substance. It can excite, but it does not strengthen. The secretion of the beaver is somewhat better; however, it is not good for prolonged use. Musk is to be found in heath-cocks, but there is little use in trying to produce the substance from them, since they possess very little. The best thing is to breed the musk deer. Of course, all varieties of musk should be considered only from a medicinal point of view. For perfumery, a substitute has already been found, the so-called *muskon*. One may hope that, owing to this discovery, a most valuable animal will not be totally exterminated.

2. I consider all antiaphrodisiac preparations positively harmful. A powerful force exists in sexual energy, the basis of vitality and creativeness; therefore, one should try to balance it and direct it correctly, but any artificial suppression is impermissible. In some cases, intense physical labor gives excellent results. All the ancient Teachings indicate that we should not suppress our emotions, or what are usually called, passions, but balance them and refine their qualities. In connection with that you might reread paragraph 12 on page 209 in the second volume of *Leaves of Morya's Garden*.

3. The words of the Teaching "But I say, for your benefit, evoke My Name more often." certainly mean wise and heartfelt repetition, for how otherwise can the bond be established with the chosen Teacher? Such repetition or retention is always recommended in all Teachings; whereas the repetition of the Name IN VAIN is condemned, i.e., when people amidst most unsuitable surroundings idly use the sacred Names in their talk. The latter is usually done by beginners, or, in general, by those who do not realize the sacredness of holy things.

4. "For cosmic dates manifested 'vessels' are chosen" *Leaves of*

Morya's Garden II, p.121. And the answer is: The whole life is built precisely by cosmic dates. These dates are marked by the coincidence of the ripe karma of a certain nation, or even nations, with definite combinations of the luminaries, the results of which are new shifts in the historical movement of peoples or in the life of the planet.

5. "What vessels?" The answer: In all Teachings, precisely man is compared with a vessel containing the Divine Fire. For the fulfillment of a certain mission within the cosmic dates, the servants of Light or, as they are sometimes called, "the chosen vessels" are sent to Earth, after having been tested during thousands of years. They select co-workers brought to them by karma, but if eventually these co-workers prove to be unworthy, or harmful for the work, they can replace them by others. You, of course, know that lengthy collaboration creates a certain occult bond, which is not easy to break without painful consequences for both sides. In such cases of the substitution of co-workers (or the "manifested vessels") can appeal to the Teacher and ask him to liberate them from the effects of the aura of the departing ones.

6. "Thus, let us conclude about the vitality of dates and the mirrors of the future." (*Ibid.*, p.122.) The answer is: That which is mentioned above regarding the cosmic dates also explains their vitality. As for the mirrors—this concerns the prognosis of the future on the basis of existing data. And these mirrors, or visions, which are produced by a special process on a polished metallic surface, are true only from the moment they begin and so far as the spirit of the one who is connected with the prognosis is firm and unshaken in his striving. Whereas if he wavers, the mirror of the future will change in conformity with the waverings of the spirit. This is why all Teachings advocate *steadfastness* and *firmness* of spirit. Only by possessing such firmness can one build and be protected on all paths. The ray can protect only the one who firmly follows the indicated light and does not deviate from it. Therefore, for cosmic dates only those "vessels" are assigned and sent who have been thoroughly tested in firmness of aspiration.

I shall quote for you a passage from *New Era Community*: "Why is the discovery of signs of the future likened to weaving? In weaver's work the warp is of a definite hue, and groups of threads are divided according to color. It is easy to determine the warp and one can easily find the group of threads, but the design of this group permits different combinations, depending upon a thousand current details. Indeed, the inner relationship of the subject himself will be the principal condition. If his aura should be too unsteady, then the prognosis will be a relative one. Then it will resemble a certain game, wherein, being given a few scattered points, one must identify a definite figure.

"Where, then, is the best ferment with which to steady the wavering of the aura. The best ferment is striving. It is impossible to sting or to smash an impetuously directed body. Striving in motion attains validity, and becoming lawful it becomes irresistible, for it enters into the rhythm of the Cosmos.

"Thus proceed in the small and in the great, and your texture will be unmatched, crystal, cosmic; in brief—beautiful.

"Striving, nothing else, results in mastery over the elements, for the basic quality of the elements is striving. In this state you coordinate the elements with the higher creativeness of the spirit and become the keepers of the lightning. Man shall become keeper of the lightning. Believe it, by striving only will you conquer."

"Striving is the boat of the Arhat. Striving is the manifested unicorn. Striving is the key to all caves. Striving is the wing of the eagle. Striving is the ray of the sun. Striving is the book of the future. Striving is the world manifest. Striving is the multitude of stars."

Thus preserve striving for it propels all fields of knowledge. Striving is the key to the lock.

And now, regarding the mirror—the invention of the devil. It is spoken of in *On Eastern Crossroads*—of course, this should be understood allegorically. The mirror of the devil is a symbol of man's attachment to his personality or selfhood. The devil's mirror reflects just its own selfhood, whereas the divine microcosm reflects the Macrocosm.

I welcome your firmness. Do not be distressed by the uncovering of the true faces of people and by the unavoidable loneliness. This disclosure of the true faces of people is inseparable from the great school of life, and on the last step you encounter betrayals. In all the Teachings is engraved the symbol of the drinking of the chalice of poison by all Carriers of Light. The beauty of achievement is truly emphasized by these manifestations of darkness. The most significant events are followed by monstrous betrayals. And so you should be courageous and firm, and should not be perturbed by any monsters. As it is said—one should learn from the examples of aggression.

21

9 December 1935

I am delighted to learn about the formation of the section, "Unity of Women," and I welcome with all my heart the idea of organizing a children's theater. Indeed, the theater is a powerful, perhaps the most powerful means of building character in children and youth. Truly the theater, if the plays are well chosen, can inspire youth to emulate the great images and impel young souls toward achievement and heroism. Therefore, the greatest attention should be given to this project. For this purpose, the Mysteries from the lives of the great Spiritual Toilers for Good and the legends about national heroes are especially suitable. These enthralling, lofty, moral images can increase respect for the concepts of the honor and dignity of man—the qualities so easily lost today—and lacking them, the result is deterioration. And rightly, in order that the seeds might yield fruit, one should start precisely with the children.

You ask about "Unity of Women." I perceived in it an idea of universal unity for the upliftment of the level of women's consciousness in all countries and for the affirmation of women's rights, not through violence and ugly demonstrations after the manner of the suffragettes, but rather through self-perfectment and the development of one's potentialities. In the activity of "Unity of Women" should also be included the program of "the Communities of the Heroic Sisters," about which I have already written you. Certainly each program should vary in accordance with the local conditions and existing possibilities. Yes, women should actively rise to the defense of their rights and those of children, and by means of word and deed they should raise the moral and cultural level of their respective countries.

In America there are many useful organizations in which women play a most active part. Thus, among such movements we should point out the so-called Chautauqua. This organization aimed to give to the most remote localities in the country the possibility of becoming acquainted with current accomplishments in all fields of science, the arts, and social movements; and, parallel with this, to also give a review and evaluation of world events, of course taking into consideration the general level of the listeners. For this purpose, special lecturers and artists are invited, and usually, during the summer, they succeed in covering great distances. The people living in these localities are informed well in advance of their coming, and as a rule a special building is prepared or large tents are set up, which the troupe brings along with it. I heard from a lady who went on such a tour that all the tickets are generally sold well in advance. This organization is quite successful financially, and its activities are steadily growing. True, they have also to include circus performers in their program, for the latter still attract the biggest percentage of the public. And yet, owing to this added attraction, useful and educational numbers can also be heard. In such a way, this Chautauqua goes all over America. They travel mostly by cars.

Enclosed are *Diary Leaves* of N. K. in which he speaks of the women's movement in India. There you will find many beautiful and most useful ideas, many of which you could utilize. Of course, the condition of women in the West is much better than in the East; nevertheless, they are quite far from having equal rights. Only when women's equality of rights is accepted on a planetary scale shall we be able to say that our evolution has attained the status of humaneness. At the moment, in most cases we are but "bipeds," as the Great Buddha called the ignorant and evil-minded. The equilibrium of the twin Elements is the foundation of Life, and the violation of this law has placed our planet on the brink of destruction. But will many understand this?

What can one say about the progress of the Pact in Europe? There is plenty of talk and all sorts of promises, but it is difficult to know what may come out of them in the near future. At the moment Europe is busy with entirely different considerations, and she stands on the threshold of many events. I only know that in many countries the committees of the Pact began to function, but then some of them soon ceased to exist because of lack of initiative and constancy in their members. The main obstacle is in the shortage everywhere of right people. But if we recall that it took seventeen years before the idea of the Red Cross was carried out in life, our friends can be justly proud of the results already achieved, and should arm themselves with patience for further progress.

I am glad that you love our locality. The laboratories are still in the process of being built, and we still have not the means for equipping them and installing electricity. This requires a very large sum of money which we do not possess. We realize that we are passing through a most difficult period of time and that later it will be easier. When we meet I shall tell you of the extreme difficulties we continually have to overcome. But we learn to welcome every obstacle, since how otherwise can our firmness be tested, our abilities sharpened, and our devotion proven to the Great Teacher, who constantly watches over us and sends his Help at the last moment? Therefore, your words about the grave yet beautiful time which we are now experiencing are close to my heart. Precisely, grave and beautiful is our time, when the Hierarchy of Light for the first time pours so many signs on Earth; when so many Calls resound in space, and so much Light and Knowledge are given!

You act wisely by not immediately accepting newcomers as members of the Society. Much discrimination must be applied. Often the true faces of people are not quickly revealed. Therefore, all sorts of precautions are necessary. I rejoice with you at the spiritual progress of your friends, who are so dear to your heart. Yes, nothing will replace the warmth of the heart, and so I believe that wherever you keep watch, everything will turn out well.

Let us courageously and strivingly cross over the threshold to many events.

Who will dare to speak against the principles of the Living Ethics? Who can be against refinement and introducing into life a true understanding of culture? Would not such a protesting voice be raised against the very Foundations of Existence?

Let the wings of the spirit grow. They will carry you over all abysses, and your secret wish may be fulfilled.

22

12 December 1935

Many thanks for the interesting book about the little girl who is able to read thoughts. Such signs are now quite numerous everywhere, and it is advisable to assemble them. Thus, our local papers during the last few days write about a little girl who remembers her past life. I enclose the clipping and also the Russian translation summarizing it. I am also quoting some paragraphs from the books of Living Ethics about a little girl who can read thoughts.

"The ability of the child about whom you spoke is a direct proof of what was said earlier. When a child makes use of pure psychic energy, it knows that which is inaudible to others. But when the will of reason acts, then the current of basic energy is broken off. It has been prescribed—be simple in spirit, which means to allow pure energy to act. Do not impede its current; grasp the fact that violence by the reason only impoverishes one. Thus, a scientist knows which book he should take from the shelf not through reason but with straight-knowledge. People are right when they act by this unassailable straight-knowledge." And also:

"Why are people amazed at many cases of children who remember their past? Precisely nowadays are being born many such evident intermediaries between this and the Subtle World. They also remember about their sojourn between the earthly lives, but people do not know how to question them about this. The important thing is not that they remember about buried gold, but that they can tell about precious sensations. Thus takes place a *rapprochement* of the two worlds, and this circumstance precedes great events. But for a long time not many will apprehend to what an extent everything is changed around them. Remember the old tale, how the king was being taken to execution but he was so far removed from reality that on the way he was much concerned about the stone that fell out of his crown."

"It is true that mostly sick and so-called abnormal people are the ones who manifest a link with the Supermundane, and therein lies a great reproach to humanity. Indeed, the healthy people ought to sense the nearness of the Subtle World. But the distinction between the sick and the healthy has become confused. People have covered their reason with a crust which has given rise to prejudices. Behind this fence the Subtle World is not visible. So-called abnormal people are usually free from prejudices and because of this they do not lose contact with the Subtle World. Indeed, so often during illnesses do people see through both past and future; some have viewed their past lives and recovered forgotten aptitudes. A new boundary must be laid between the state of torpor and true health. New discoveries are of no help. People must receive such shocks that they are rendered able, without any fever, to preserve the memory about the past and that which is ordained.

"During extraordinary dangers clairvoyance flashes out, which means that it is possible for something to shake up the sediments of the consciousness. The same thing occurs during epilepsy when, in the words of the afflicted, the heavens are opened to him. It also means that clairvoyance is possible amidst earthly conditions. Indeed it is instantaneous, too quick to be marked off by earthly time. And also in this lightning-like timelessness there is apparent a quality of the Subtle World. Of course, dreams are also timeless, and yet they may contain a great number of events. By various examples we can recall that which formerly was quite known to every one." [Fiery World III]

People do not realize that the basis for great events lies in the shifting of the spatial rays, in the *rapprochement* of the worlds, and in the renewed consciousness which brings a new understanding of life. Much has already been manifested. So, let us meet the Unrepeatable Year.

23

14 December 1935

Devotion to the chosen Teacher was considered a necessary and fundamental quality of a disciple in all the Teachings of antiquity. Therefore, blessed are you if this quality is not alien to your spirit.

You expect tolerance toward all groups who follow their beloved Teaching (certainly the Teaching of Light), and of course you are right. But then you should be neither distressed nor indignant if someone is just as ardently devoted to the Lord M. as you are to your chosen Teacher. In connection with this, there are lines in the third volume of *Fiery World*, which I shall quote to you:

"The Teaching of Good must be the friend of Good in all its manifestations. This truth appears simple, yet evil intention continually tries to distort it. The Teacher of good must be grieved, seeing how the workers of Good become twisted and how they exclude each other. Such a mutilation of Good takes place when someone bears a burden of Good which is too much for him and someone else attempts to carry a double load. And if someone will dare to think about a triple load, he will not find many helpers. Millions of years have not been enough for humanity to learn to rejoice at Good, to grow to love it as something of the utmost utility. The Teaching must stimulate in all the bearers of Good a feeling of broad sympathy. Otherwise it will not be the Teaching of Good but a teaching of egoism." Thus, I welcome you as an apologist.

May you carry joyously your load of Good.

24

17 December 1935

Everything you write is most interesting. The suffering that comes from the realization of the dreadful catastrophe which awaits our planet if humanity refuses to come to its senses is very close to me. From early childhood, I myself was under the pressure of presentiment of impending catastrophe. Repeated dream-visions about the destruction of the planet left an indelible trace in my consciousness. Likewise, I shall not forget the days when, as an adult, I was told of the last period of testing for our planet and experienced the manifestation of suffocating, absolute darkness. For several days after this experience, I was in a terribly nervous state. It is said: "Not many can look upon this enemy of the planet [absolute darkness] without becoming ill." Now, of course, the dread and pressure are overcome, but still sadness remains at the thought of the possibility of such final destruction.

And now, regarding N. K. not speaking of present day Russia. It should be understandable for any sensitive spirit. N. K. deeply loves his country and is most devoted to it. This feeling is so sacred that to talk about it among those who do not understand or who are hostile would be simply sacrilegious. In the East it is customary not to talk of the most sacred, and in this respect N. K. belongs to the East. His heart sees and knows that which others are still unable to understand. Evolution creates its immutable cosmic course, and a great historical selection is taking place throughout the entire span of the planet. All who sincerely love their country understand how solicitously one must treat it during a difficult and painful period of transition toward a new construction after a gigantic explosion has shaken it to its very depths. Our country has already started on the road to recovery and is looking for a new, glorious path. The most joyous manifestation is that the masses have awakened to conscious life, to the understanding of general cooperation, and great is the thirst for knowledge among young people. Of course, countercurrents are inevitable, but a great shifting of the consciousness of the people is evident. Therefore, should we not practice special solicitude toward our country?

The renascence of Russia is a guarantee of thriving and peace for the whole world. The destruction of Russia is the destruction of the whole world. Some begin to realize this now. However, quite recently people thought the opposite, namely, that the destruction of Russia would be the salvation of the world, and they tried their utmost to destroy and disunite her. Great was the fear of the growth of Russia, and even if this fear had its reason, no one attributed it to the true cause. Thus, there was fear of all kinds of usurpation of power by Russia, but nobody could foresee and deduce the consequences of that explosion (which was greatly helped by many), which was to upset the world balance. Great are the consequences of that explosion in Russia! Purified and regenerated, Russia will become a bulwark of true peace on the new foundations of broad national collaboration and free cultural construction.

25

18 December 1935

Undoubtedly the sacrifice of Christ and his acceptance of crucifixion for the sake of bringing the Teaching of Light had tremendous significance for all humanity on all planes of existence. Sacrifices and great achievements were also performed by other Great Teachers for humanity's sake. And it is difficult to say whose sacrifice was greater—the sacrifice of Sri Krishna, the Spiritual Teacher and kingly builder of life, or the sacrifice of Guatama Buddha, who, during more than sixty years, bore the heavy burden of teaching for the affirmation of the great Law.

It is indeed correctly narrated in *On Eastern Crossroads* that the revolt of Lucifer brought Christ to the world. This revolt brought other Great Teachers also, who came before Christ as well as after him. Long is the list of the self-renouncing lives of the Highest Spirits who fought the dark forces. According to the traditions of the East, the revolt of Lucifer had already begun at the end of the Third Race. The great battle, which took place in the Fourth Race between the Sons of Light and the sons of darkness and which is mentioned in all the ancient traditions, strongly emphasized this great drama of our planet. The drama is that Lucifer, by cosmic right, is the true Host of our Earth. The seed of his spirit potentially possesses all the energies that are centered in the kernel of our planet. Therefore, it is easy to imagine how well acquainted is the Host of Earth with its interior, and how all its energies are subordinate to him, whereas the other Great sons of Light who arrived on our planet belong to the higher worlds. And the Greatest among Them accepted the responsibility for this planet. He remains on perpetual Watch, and according to all Scriptures He is the conqueror of the Dragon.

The Highest Spirits, who have accepted responsibility for the evolution of humanity, have incarnated continually on Earth in various great Images. Remember, it is said that all the Heavenly Forces cannot gather as much power as that collected by the performance of One great earthly achievement in combination with the Higher Forces. For Earth, all must be done by earthly means, in earthly conditions.

Certainly no one can be saved by the sacrifice of Christ from the trickeries and traps of the dark forces. For no one can save someone else. However, the Teaching or Christ once again reminded humanity of the threatening danger and indicated the path to spiritual redemption—to salvation. But the snares of the dark forces and the danger from them not only did not disappear but increased before the decisive battle. Therefore now, more than ever, the unification of all the forces of Light is essential in order to repel the hordes of darkness who in their fury and madness, attempt to explode the planet itself. But this unification, considering the present state of consciousness of the majority, has to be attempted with great caution, for often an approach only increases the discord. Thus, people often repeat the proverb, "One alone in the field is not a warrior," but the real, profound, and stern meaning of these words does not penetrate petrified hearts.

I suggest that you emphasize in your work the extent to which the esotericism in the Teaching of Christ is not understood and is passed over in silence, even in the Gospels. Also, you could mention that the first ray of the New Epoch will radiate a new understanding of the Teaching of Christ. "Thus, let us accept the appearance of Christ as a sacred sign, and let people revere all the signs of the Sublime Path."

Part II

1936

1

11 January 1936

I have read your letter very attentively and I must say that most of all I rejoiced to see that apparently you no longer belong to any pseudo-occult societies or organizations. Indeed, nowadays, such organizations are just as numerous as mushrooms after rain! And I know what a mixture they are! Some are insignificant, but there are others among them which are exceedingly dark and dangerous. You were right in being perturbed at seeing "revenge instead of fighting through love" in the "Order" described by you. Certainly there can be no hint of revenge in teachings of Light. Indeed, the first foundation of every Teaching of Light is the eradication of any possibility of the feeling of revenge. As for the resistance to evil indicated in them, this is not revenge, because it presupposes defense of the General Good, whereas revenge is based upon personal feeling. And you know that selfishness is the root of all misfortune. He who is capable of revenge can never become a disciple. One who is unable to practice discipline of thought and feelings cannot hope to progress speedily on the chosen path of Light.

You ask, "Why did the Teacher not come to me at that time? Why did He not lead me forward with a firm hand?" But the Teachers never come to anyone. We ourselves must reach out to them. And even if the Teacher had approached you at that time, are you sure that you would have accepted his firm Hand? Would you not have thought it unbearably heavy, and would you not have rejected it, perhaps even with worse blasphemy? Not easy is the path of discipleship. It has nothing in common with the descriptions of the life of the Magi and initiates in occult novels.

Further on, you ask, "Why was such an experiment necessary? Only to bring disappointment, to arouse my distrust in people and organizations?" But you must understand that an experiment is never forced upon us, we ourselves created and accept it, for karma puts us in those conditions in which we must learn a new lesson or repeat the previous one, not as yet learned. Perhaps you had to learn to discriminate regarding appearances and once again convince yourself of the failure of the pseudo-occult organizations, and also learn to outlive a partiality to rituals and forms. Many are still convinced that it is permissible to approach the higher Sources through dead rituals and repetitions of senseless mantrams, which have now lost their meaning, since their value lies only in rhythm, born in a flaming heart. Nothing external, without the inner striving, can be of real value. Rituals, if they are beautiful, can assist in creating a certain exalted mood, but it is impossible to look upon them as an independent, self-sufficient condition for spiritual ascent.

You write, "Where is the guarantee that the 'Order,' unknown to anybody, will not again attract me and compel me to commit the silliest acts, justified by higher, mysterious aims? How can one discern a pure movement?" But precisely a pure movement will never expect you "to commit the silliest acts, justified by higher, mysterious aims." Each Teaching of Light, first of all, insists upon *intelligence, rejects all forcing,* and expects only purity of thinking, intentions, words and deeds. Likewise, no masks are permissible. Masks are left to the agents of darkness, who have something to conceal, and you are right to beware of them. At the moment, they are very numerous, because of the approaching dates, which are critical for them; and they are extremely active on both planes recruiting assistants into their ranks. But how incredibly hard is the karma of those who are enticed by them!

I doubt that hunger can develop a magnetic power in you. Of course, continence is essential in everything, but hunger can intensify nothing. Great balance is ordained by all the teachings of Light. And if you realize the presence of this power in yourself, let it help you to develop persistence in striving toward the indicated benevolent aim.

All that you write has been taken into consideration, and my advice to you is to now become acquainted with the books of Living Ethics, at least with the two volumes of *Leaves of Morya's Garden* and with *Agni Yoga.* If your spirit resounds to them, do write to me after you have read them and give me your impressions, as well as your perplexities, and I shall answer you. Also, please let me know which particular expressions do not seem clear to you. There are expressions in Eastern languages that are difficult to translate into our crude European tongues. In conclusion, I may say, "All is revealed; all is attainable." It is for us alone to enter and accept. And the primary conditions for achievement are honesty, courage, fearlessness, invincible striving, great patience, and gratitude for each crumb. Certainly, betrayal, even in thoughts, is impermissible. But if there is sincerity and a flaming heart, everything becomes easy and joyous. Thus, love your chosen Teacher with all your heart, with all your being, and attainments will not be slow in coming.

2
17 January 1936

I quite agree that for some people the idea of cosmic consciousness is as frightening as brimstone. How can they think of cosmic consciousness if they are not yet able to completely comprehend the meaning of human consciousness? Even many "clever" people do not realize what cosmic consciousness actually is; hence, they think that by ignoring it they are able to protect themselves, and chiefly to save themselves from some danger. Moreover, they probably associate this cosmic consciousness with a particular kind of internationalism. Truly, it is difficult to know how certain things are refracted in ignorant minds.

There is much talk about the need for development of a national consciousness, and this is right, for love of one's country is a sacred feeling. Precisely, national consciousness is the expression of the character of a nation, and it is the quality of this character that is the most important in each manifestation. People and countries should safeguard the basis of their character and individuality by developing and enriching it with all the flowers that grow in their meadow, and with all the possibilities that are open to them. Precisely, the task of the national genius is to transform and allow to pass through the prism of its consciousness the achievements of all peoples and ages, and to present its own unrepeatable synthesis of this conglomeration of creative manifestations. But a small mentality understands national consciousness as something separate and therefore limited; whereas any separatism is unnatural and harmful, because it is against the law of the unity of Be-ness. And as the laws are uniform in everything, all separatism and constriction result in withering and eventual death. The Law of Be-ness indicates a constant expansion and endless unfoldment. Only in this unfoldment, in this perpetual containment of all possibilities is there eternal life. Sever this realization, and the life of such a man will become attached to only the fleeting consciousness of a single personality.

Eternal life is won precisely by cosmic consciousness, or the realization of one's own cosmic origin.

In our age, it is already realized that if humanity desires to evolve successfully, it must accept a certain international collaboration, although at the present stage, this collaboration is manifested more powerfully in mechanical and material achievements than in spiritual unity. However, science marches ahead with such gigantic strides that the next step will soon be realized, namely, that of collaboration with the Cosmos. Then cosmic consciousness will cease to frighten even obvious ignoramuses, and will become a normal factor; and no man, realizing his place in Cosmos, will remain in his own little coop. Only then will spiritual unity come into being.

* * *

All that you write about some persons who have left the Teaching of Living Ethics is not unusual. Indeed, if it were not so, the world would not be in a state that is without issue, and cosmic cataclysms would not threaten us. It is painful to hear such statements as "the idea of the General Good is just empty words." Certainly, for a heart reduced to ashes and for an ossified mind the General Good will be empty words. But an enlightened consciousness understands the *completeness* of its *dependence* on the General Good. The General Good was, and is the foundation of each Covenant. The Teaching of Christ is precisely the teaching of the General Good, and those who do not understand and who deny this principle, deny the Herald himself. It is better not to start any discussions with such consciousnesses. Yes, only the acceptance and assimilation of the law of reincarnation would have brought humanity to the correct understanding of the General Good. It is amazing how those who sneer at the concept of the General Good, nevertheless take advantage of all conveniences contrived for the General Good in the cities, such as the excellent means of transportation, etc.

* * *

And now to your questions. Paragraph 279, *Fiery World II*: Morua is a plant which grows in our region. It is a bushy plant, and its odor reminds one very much of verbena. I shall send you a few twigs, but not now, because it is winter. Through negligence I used a capital letter in writing the name of this plant, and it could indeed have brought confusion to many readers.

* * *

Certainly it is never and nowhere suggested that all should live in crowded communal quarters. This must be understood in a broader way. Assuredly, not in all working communities do people live together. They gather for common labor, but their personal lives and daily routine go on separately. The idea of common labor does not necessarily mean physical proximity. Precisely, there is no need to jostle one another physically. Each age dictates its own demands and conditions, and it is quite impossible to completely return to the old forms. Thus, the Lord Buddha also forbade physical crowding in his communities, and took care that each member had his own cell. In His communities, there was even no partaking of food in common. All *bhikshus* ate alone. They gathered together only for mutual labor and spiritual discussions. In fact, communities are possible only where the auras of the members are fully harmonized, but this is so rarely achieved. Therefore, if you are planning to establish a community, do it as simply as possible without binding yourself by any obligations, and mainly by practicing the most intensive labor—and arm yourself with infinite patience and tolerance. After all, in many instances the co-operative principle could be applied without insisting upon living together. It would be much easier to experiment with communal living for a short period of several weeks during the summer months.

You might like to copy the whole way of life accepted in the Stronghold of the White Brotherhood, but this is quite impossible for this life is so different from our conditions. The Brotherhood works in groups, and the growing problems harmoniously unite the Council for new combinations. The work is divided into three sections; first, search for means to ameliorate the conditions of the earthly plane; second, search for ways to convey to people the results obtained; third, search for means to communicate with the distant worlds. The first requires diligence and patience, and the third demands alertness and fearlessness, but the second demands such self-sacrifice that the most difficult flight would appear as a rest.

However, now is the time of the grave and decisive

Armageddon, and therefore all research and all scientific tasks are temporarily stopped; and all the Forces of Light are directed to repulsing on both planes the ceaseless attacks and terrible craftiness of the Black Brotherhood. Thus, on the Watchtower neither sleep nor rest is known. Who of the Earth-dwellers is able to imagine this condition of supreme tension? In addition, many Brothers spend most of their time in the Subtle World, for precisely there the Teraphim of victory are created. And so, in the Subtle World there now resounds the call and the victorious song of the Warriors of Shambhala. For thousands of years the great Stronghold of Light has prepared for this battle with the forces of darkness. The predicted Armageddon is dreadful; all the subterranean monsters take part in it, and the Forces of all planes are drawn into it. Does not the madness that is now taking place indicate the unprecedented times! Who ponders upon the menace to our planet? Do many know that the main concern of the Stronghold of Light is to save our planet from premature explosion? Indeed, the most awful outbreaks of subterranean fire threaten our planet. In many places on the ocean beds the earthly crust is very much eroded, but who thinks about these threatening signs?

No Earth-dweller could withstand that intensive labor which is now taking place in the Stronghold of Light. That is why humanity is so criminal when, in its madness, it commits blasphemy against its Saviors. They call to Christ while every moment betraying his Covenants and vilifying the Hierarchy of Light to which He belongs. But the disparagement of the smallest member in the Chain of this Hierarchy cannot find justification in Christ's eyes. "Many will say to me in that day, Lord, Lord, have we not prophesied in thy name? and in thy name have cast out devils? and in thy name done many wonderful works? And then will I profess unto them, I never knew you: depart from me, ye that work iniquity." (St. Matthew 7:22,23) Thus can one hope for happiness and for justification when saying, "the General Good is just empty words?" Such a man will be left empty, for, verily, emptiness is in his heart and head. Christ and the General Good are synonymous.

In connection with the idea of communal labor, I would like to quote for you paragraph 35 from *Fiery World III:* "So much is said about cooperation, but so little is comprehended! This is one of the most misconstrued concepts, because in a human community the idea of united labor is so distorted. Life in the community of co-workers has in view no forcing of feelings, of obligations, of constraints, but an affirmation of united work in the name of manifested Good. If the human community would accept the law of united labor as the law of life, to what an extent human consciousness could become purified! For the rhythm of a common task can unite various specialists and individuals who differ in their qualities. The Law is simple, but how many distortions surround it! The manifestation of the human nearness of the spirit is conditioned by many causes, spiritual as well as karmic, but under the ray of labor a community may be organized with the aid of the law of co-operation. Therefore, it is necessary to educate the co-workers through labor and by the affirmation that each co-worker is a part of the whole. However, one should exclude incorrect thinking about the personal. Such interpretation will not help a community to become affirmed as a single channel. So many sad happenings can be avoided through the expansion of consciousness and by the subtle understanding that it is inadmissible to encroach upon the heart of another being. Thus, on the path to the Fiery World the co-workers should understand that one may advance only through the law of Common Labor—there is no other measure! The subtle is attained only by the subtle; and the subtle threads of the heart resound only in a tension of many thousands of years. Therefore, let the co-workers especially realize this single path. Precisely, the law of united labor permits no infringement upon the heart of another."

And paragraph 36: " In the community one should remember about the sacredness of feelings. One should especially remember that it is inadmissible to evoke forcibly the subtle feeling in a fellow worker. One should not develop subtle vibrations in the heart by outside demands. Only an inner, merited action gives birth to a conformable vibration. Rarely is this life of spirit found amidst choking earthly vibrations. Yet this manifestation—when spirit resounds in harmony with spirit—is so beautiful! First of all, in the development of the consciousness of the community one should affirm the understanding of co-operation. In this understanding the community can become strengthened, and the worm of self-pity will vanish. Thus do We administer advice to the disciples, affirming the joy of labor without encroachment upon the heart of another. Long since was it said: "One cannot be dear by force!" This is also a cosmic formula. But one can greatly purify the path of concerted labor. Thus, let the disciples remember the manifestation of co-operation as an important step in the daily life of the community."

Yet so often the co-workers allow a cruel sense of jealousy to develop, which wrecks so many beautiful undertakings!

3

18 January 1936

Many thanks for your heartfelt letter and your photograph. I am gradually collecting a regular gallery of the portraits of friends, and I love to look at them and watch the change of expression on their faces. Have you noticed that the portraits of living people change their expressions? I was also very glad to hear about your activities. Sow the useful seeds as broadly as you can, but always bear in mind the level of the consciousness. Garb the great truths in the most acceptable garments. Great compassion is revealed in veiling the Light in order not to blind the weak-sighted. Always, and in everything, we should be guided by the heart. It is said that only a small consciousness proudly attempts to display all its imagined brilliance, but a great consciousness does not fear to conceal itself if it is obvious that many concepts cannot yet be absorbed.

Of course you are right that the Revelation of St. John should be commented upon cautiously. Indeed, each scripture, each legend from antiquity has seven keys or meanings. Regarding Revelation, many scholars have now come to the conclusion that it is another version of the Book of Enoch and of the Dragon legend of pagan antiquity. Therefore, Revelation should be considered of much greater antiquity than formerly was thought. Chapter XII has several meanings, and a great deal has already been found concerning the astronomical and numerological key to this universal myth. According to the Sacred Teaching, the "*war in heaven*" mentioned there, "refers to several events of that kind on various and different planes of being. The first is a purely astronomical and cosmical fact pertaining to cosmogony. ... If the sidereal prototype [of war] refers indeed to a *pre*-manvantaric period, and rests entirely on the Knowledge ... of the whole program and progress of cosmogony. ..." the knowledge of which is in possession of the Great Teachers, the second aspect of the war in heaven had its reflection on Earth, and the place of its action was not in the depths of interplanetary Space, but in the Himalayas.

"It is the record of the terrible strife between the 'Sons of God' [Sons of Light] and the 'Sons of the Shadow' of the Fourth and Fifth Races. It is on these two events, blended together by legends... that every subsequent... tradition on the subject has been built." But regardless of what the astronomical sense of this universally accepted legend of the battle in Heaven is about, the human phase of it is based upon true historical events which were distorted and debased into theological dogma (the Fall of the Angels) only for the purpose of fitting it in with the aims of the ecclesiastics.

In *The Secret Doctrine* there are further explanations of certain chapters and verses of Revelation. I shall again quote extracts which may interest you.

"In the *Introduction* to Archbishop Laurence's translation of it from an Ethiopic MS. in the Bodleian Library, ... author of the *Evolution of Christianity* remarks: 'In revising the proof-sheets of the Book of Enoch [we were still more astonished by the resemblance to the writings of the New Testament] the parable of the sheep, rescued by the good Shepherd from hireling guardians and ferocious wolves is *obviously borrowed by the fourth Evangelist* from *Enoch* lxxxix, in which the author depicts the shepherds as killing [and destroying] the sheep before the advent of their Lord, and thus discloses the true meaning of that hitherto mysterious passage in the Johannine parable—"All that ever came before me are thieves and robbers"—language in which we now detect an obvious reference to the allegorical shepherds of Enoch.' [Book of the Prophet Enoch, page XLVIII. Publ. 1883].

"It is too late in the day to claim that it is Enoch who borrowed from the New Testament, instead of *vice versa*. Jude (14, 15) quotes *verbatim* from Enoch a long passage about the coming of the Lord with his 10,000 saints, and naming specifically the prophet, *acknowledges* the source. This 'parallelism between prophet and apostle, has placed beyond controversy that, *in the eyes of the author of an Epistle accepted as divine revelation,* the Book of Enoch *was the inspired production of an antediluvian patriarch* ... the cumulative coincidence of language and ideas in Enoch and the authors of the N. T. Scripture, ... clearly indicates that the work of the Semitic Milton was the inexhaustible source from which Evangelists and Apostles, or the men who write in their names, borrowed their conceptions of the resurrection, judgment, immortality, perdition, and of the universal reign of righteousness under the eternal dominion of the Son of Man. This *Evangelical plagiarism* culminates in the Revelation of John, which adapts the visions of Enoch to Christianity, with modifications in which we miss the sublime simplicity of the great Master of apocalyptic prediction, who prophesied in the name of the antediluvian Patriarch.' (Introd., xxxv.)

"'Antediluvian,' truly; but if the phraseology of the text dates hardly a few centuries or even millenniums before the historical era, then it is no more the original *prediction* of the events to come, but, in its turn, a copy of some scripture of a prehistoric religion. ... 'In the Krita age, Vishnu, in the form of Kapila and other (inspired sages)... imparts... true wisdom [as Enoch did]. In the Treta age he restrains the wicked, in the form of a universal monarch [the Chakravartin or the "Everlasting King" of Enoch*] and protects the three worlds [or races]. In the Dvapara age, in the person of Veda-Vyasa, he divides the one Veda into four, and distributes it into hundreds (*Sata*) of branches' (Vishnu-Purana).

" *Saith Uriel (chapter xxvi, 3) in the *Book of Enoch* 'all those who have received mercy shall for ever bless God the *everlasting King*,' who will reign over them.

"Truly so; the *Veda* of the earliest Aryans, before it was writing, went forth into every nation of the Atlanto-Lemurians, and sowed the first seeds of all the now existing old religions. The offshoots of the never dying tree of wisdom have scattered their dead leaves even on Judaeo-Christianity. And at the end of the Kali, our present age, Vishnu, or the 'Everlasting King,' will appear as Kalki Avatar, and re-establish righteousness upon earth. The minds of those who will live at that time shall be awakened, and become as pellucid as crystal. 'The men who are thus changed by virtue of that peculiar time [the sixth race] *shall be as the seeds* of other human beings, and shall give birth to a race who shall follow the laws of the Krita age of purity'; i.e., it shall be the seventh race, the race of 'Buddhas,' the 'Sons of God,' born of *immaculate* parents." [*The Secret Doctrine*, vol.II, *On the Myth of the "Fallen Angel," in Its Various Aspects.*]

* * *

But what is, in reality, the *Book of Enoch*, from which the author of Revelation and even St. John, the author of the fourth Gospel, so largely draw in their writings? It is simply a book of Initiation, which, in allegorical and cautious phraseology, presented the outline of certain archaic Mysteries that took place in the inner temples. The so-called "Visions" of Enoch concern his (Enoch's) experiences during initiation and what he had learned in the Mysteries.

* * *

In all the remote legends, the description of the creation of our Earth concerns, of course, only the Fourth Round, following the pralaya, or obscuration which began after the Third Round. Of the first two races of this Round, we have a most limited knowledge, and as yet it has not been revealed by the Great Teachers, because it is difficult for our consciousness to comprehend that condition which has no present equivalent on Earth. But in the Fourth Round, man appeared earlier than the animals.

The prayer of Christ, which still remains unheeded, was the prayer of the heart for the welfare of all humanity. Each Great Spirit directs evolution *strictly in accordance* with the laws of the Cosmic Magnet or with the law of evolution. And therefore the will of such a spirit is so powerful, because it is identical with the Will of the Cosmos.

The fall of Lucifer actually came about as the result of his raising against the law of evolution or the Will of Cosmos. Reread the legend about Lucifer in *On Eastern Crossroads*—it is the truth.

Thus at the time when the Great Brothers of Lucifer, who came with him to our Earth, are building an eternal movement; at that time when They say, "Why have one Earth when all worlds are destined," and thus create the right path for humanity so that through a broad cooperation with the far-off worlds a true exchange shall be established, Lucifer prefers to fence himself off from the neighbors. But in the unity of Be-ness, in the law of interchange, any separateness results only in dissolution or death. However, Lucifer could only impede, not interrupt the current of life. Precisely His rebellion and the carrying out of His plan for the self-sufficiency of earthly matter brought forth a corrective from the body of the White Brotherhood, an organization unknown to other planets, because of its obligatory battle-readiness. As it is said, "The battle of desperation transformed the Bearer of Light; and the ruby aura became infused with the blood-red glow. His followers truly began to apply depraved means," which only delay the dates but do not exhaust the destiny. Therefore the armor and the swords of the Brotherhood could have been gladly reforged into the parts of the laboratory apparatuses much sooner, and the Ladder of Light, which is the link between Heaven and Earth, could have been set much closer. "How vivid the recollection that the last Great Teacher suffered an outrageous death for what would seem to have been already long since known to humanity!"

You may ask how this psychology of isolation was created. But in each big feudal lord you can see an identical example.

Lucifer is the Prince of this world(Earth) in the fullest meaning of the word. His spirit potentially possess all the same energies that belong to Earth.

In normal conditions, the Host of Earth would exalt matter by filling its particles with the idea of unity. The Spirit of the Lord of the planet goes through the human form as the *first teacher* of the mastery over matter, and therefore he becomes an expert in the properties of this matter. With a worthy attitude, he would be a valuable friend of all new formations; there would be no antagonistic actions, only a search for mutually beneficial ones. But the Host of Earth doesn't think so; he does not care for the friendship of spirit. You can well imagine how the Host of Earth knows all Earth's labyrinths! And a too great enlightenment interferes with his plans! His servants are not adverse to learning something useful for themselves; they even have their own gatherings where they discuss how to use the new discoveries to harm the growth of spirituality. But his difficulty is that the movements of spirit are very fast, and the reservoir of the Source of the White Brotherhood is great. Still, one cannot deny his inventiveness, and especially now when the dates have arrived. Now you realize how serious and threatening is the raging Armageddon—the battle of the Forces of Light with the hordes of Darkness!

* * *

You understand obsession quite correctly. Actually, while there is a struggle, there is no real obsession. An obsessed person no longer struggles, and even does not realize that he is obsessed. The pure heart need not fear obsession. Sincerity does not admit obsession.

4

21 January 1936

One should remember, or rather know, that there is not a single book that is free from mistakes or obscurities, or simply typographical errors and omissions. Even in the books and letters of the Adepts one meets so-called contradictions, but for those who know, these are not "contradictions," but simply the results of incomplete statements. The Universe is most complex, and it is impossible to put all its great diversity into a few formulae that can be applied to each particular case. Thus, regarding a concordant soul there is also much that cannot be adequately covered by words. It is impossible to use an apothecary's scale in ascertaining the degree of individualization that is achieved in each separate case in this or that group of the lower kingdoms; therefore, one must take the average degree of their condition. The group soul must be understood in this case as concordance in primal feelings, and precisely such concordance can be expressed by the term *common soul* or spiritual concordance. Even the Great Teachers often call their Group, One Ego.

* * *

Thus, you are astonished that the author of the book you have criticized called the law of karma "blind, yet intelligent"! But one must always remember the counterpositions in each cosmic law. This law is called "blind" by the author, because of its *immutability* and unwaveringness when it acts cosmically and inevitably. The law of karma becomes intelligent in the actions of a man with an awakened mind, but the lower kingdoms are subject to law which is "blind" for them.

The Lords of Karma, though directing the evolution of the world, are certainly governed primarily by cosmic laws, and they direct or adapt their will to the evolution of the Cosmos or great Goal-fitness. Therefore, your question, "Is it possible that the Lords of Karma are blind?" is simply out of place. Regarding the statement of the author that "karma does not act during the first and last quarter of the round of evolutionary development," here also is no error but simply the same inconclusive explanation. In all Teachings very little is said about the condition of man in the first three Rounds, or even about the first two races of our Round. Yet, from the hints one is able to conclude that in the first two races of the Fourth Round, men, though imbued with spirituality, did not possess what we call reason, and therefore we may assume that they blindly followed the inevitable law of karma. Whereas, in the last quarter of our Round when humanity shall become sufficiently refined and attains the densified astral state and its primordial spirituality through the opening of the higher centers—but with a developed and enlightened intelligence—it will conclude its earthly karma for that particular Cycle or Round and will leave Earth to begin a new cycle of existence on a different planet; or, after the period of Earth's obscuration, it may again continue its evolution in the new earthly Cycle, or the Fifth Round.

Likewise, in the pages of this book you find a statement about the number of incarnations which occur in sequence in the same sex; this categorical statement, being inconclusive, can also lead to misunderstandings. But if I were to deny it, I would have to reveal certain points that cannot yet be exposed to wide publicity.

Why does it seem to you unfair that "man can speed up his karma and then it will not overtake him"? It seems to me to be quite the contrary, since were it otherwise we would never be able to emerge from this magic circle. And now you may ask, "How can man speed up his karma?" I will answer, "By improving his thoughts and motives." It has been mentioned many times in the Teaching that precisely our motives and thoughts create our karma; deeds are secondary factors. Indeed, thoughts create our inner substance. Thoughts are accumulated as energies in our Chalice and aura, and if these energies are purified and refined, it is clear that they can harmonize with and attract only that which is equally pure; therefore, all that is wicked and base cannot affect us with its full force. Thus, if you meet a man to whom you did some harm in a past life, if your aura is sufficiently purified the actions of his evil energy will be unable to hurt you in full measure, even though he feels animosity toward you. And this malicious energy will then turn like a boomerang against himself. Therefore, the advice to purify, improve, and refine one's thoughts and motives is so practical. The spirit carries within itself its own achievement and armor. The purification and fiery transfiguration of our inner being make us the lords of karma. Indeed, the consummation of karma on one planet comes when all the elements, or energies, that enter our essence are harmoniously unified in one striving and have reached the perfection preordained for that particular planet.

And now regarding the Androgyne. Note that this statement is in quotation marks and is taken from my letter to the author of this book. As I have already written you, the third volume of *The Secret Doctrine* was compiled without being corrected by H. P. Blavatsky herself. Moreover, one cannot completely rely on the notes of her disciples, which often were not checked by H. P. B. From personal experience, I know what surprises one encounters in similar notes! Therefore, I intend to mention in my will that am not responsible for any notes that are claimed to have been taken from my statements, unless they bear the mark of my own corrections and a corresponding signature.

I wonder why it is not clear to you that Christ could call the Unknowable Primary Cause "His Father"? Regardless of how transcendental is the Primary Cause, it is verily the Father-Mother of all that exists.

In conclusion, I must remind you that criticism is easy, but art is difficult. And a disciple who has read the books of Living Ethics with his heart must realize how important it is to practice on his path the *benevolent eye*. Nothing is ever created by criticism alone.

The book of which you so disapprove brought joy to many searching hearts, and I heard many touching and excellent reports about it. As for the mistakes, or rather some inconclusive statements, there are not many more of them than in other writings, regardless of the realm to which they belong.

Before we are ready to move ahead, human consciousness must assimilate what has already been given. Indeed, humanity today is on the edge of an abyss—to be or not to be? Therefore, it is much more important to carry out in life the principles of Living Ethics, than to know the exact number of incarnations allowed in the same sex, or all the degrees of spiritual affinities in the lower kingdoms, or finally, whether the people of the seventh race will possess two spines or three nostrils, etc.!

And so, do not criticize, but instead analyze each question

from many angles, remembering all the multiformity and complexity of the Universe.

In your last letter you say, "You know that *regardless of what you may say to me I shall not be offended, but shall only be grateful.* These are not mere words, but truth. I often say it, for I have noticed that people like to say so, but nevertheless take offense at the first remark." The underlining is yours, I say, Blessings to you if you have attained this realization. Therefore this particular answer of mine "will not extinguish your flame," even if it be "smoky." There is not much honor in growing a garden of offenses. Taking offense is that very same selfhood which impedes our approach to Light.

5

25 January 1936

We welcome with all our heart your intention to write a book on the theme you have chosen. You are right, the question of religion is most important. One may say that it will be the cornerstone of the coming epoch of preordained spirituality. Therefore, without delay, we must build into the consciousness of the young generation the true understanding of this most essential concept. The very word *religion* is said to come from the Latin *religare* and means to bind, precisely a bond with the Higher World. By violating this bond, humanity deprives itself not only of true knowledge but of existence itself, for the life-giving Source of Benefaction nourishes all worlds. We also completely approve the plan of the work you have in mind, and we are sure that you will approach all the ideas you have mentioned with the utmost warmth and thoughtfulness.

If only the representatives of the churches could understand the time they face! The time of great purification and creativeness of the spirit when, if united, and with a new, evolved consciousness, they could examine the great Gospel of Christ, and in studying and comparing it with the most ancient religions, they could comprehend the profound esotericism of the Teaching of Christ, which is based entirely upon "Primary Revelation"—the source of all the teachings of all times. The church fathers should become the true spiritual pastors of the people, carrying into life the foundations of

Living Ethics encountered in each Teaching of Light. It is dangerous to remain behind the growing and evolving consciousness; it is dangerous to deny the discoveries and achievements of science, which, owing to accumulating events, still remain isolated manifestations. But the time is not far off when these manifestations will be unified, and will stand as indisputable facts.

Are we to follow the example of those ignorant cardinals who were ready to burn Galileo at the stake because of his declaration regarding the rotation of Earth? Therefore, it is necessary to be able to see in the Covenants exactly what harmonizes with the newest discoveries of science, and not to support that which has been distorted and adapted to different purposes. It is necessary to study the Covenants with the utmost honesty, sincerity, and enlightened consciousness, rejecting all the later interpretations, which have obscured the fundamentals to such an extent that "instead of beautiful Images there will remain only dust-covered mask." And that is why I particularly welcome your work and your activities, which are gradually and cautiously putting into the consciousness of the masses the purified foundations of the great covenants.

True, mistakes on the path of Light are inevitable, for who is perfect? But all depends upon the quality of these mistakes, as well as on our attitude toward them and on the strength of our bond with Hierarchy. Only the one who turns away from the Light, and thus cuts off the bonds with Hierarchy, falls into the abyss. Thus, dreadful is the path of betrayers.

In your previous letter, I overlooked your last important questions regarding the suffering of the heart, so I shall attend to it now.

Suffering in all cases may be considered a blessing, because it refines our feelings and teaches us great compassion. Joy alone cannot give depth to the feelings. Therefore, the combination of these two opposites is essential for the consummation of the path. A petrified heart is not worthy of the name, the "sun of suns." A petrified heart, not responding with all its fibers to the joy and sufferings of its surroundings, cannot belong to a disciple who walks on the path of Light. In fact, with perfectment the whole scale of feelings comes to such refinement that the heart of a high disciple on the last step at times appears to be an open would, as it were, and he often senses physically its burning pain. Yet this sensitivity is not so much linked with oneself as with others and the Common Good, which for certain kinds of people is empty words. Especially painful is any kind of coarseness.

I think that many people do not fully realize what is meant by a "petrified heart." Possibly they imagine that although we frequently encounter the blows of life, yet, having a broadened consciousness and a realization of our link with the Hierarchy of Light, we learn to accept these messengers calmly, because we realize that we either deserve them or they will be of help to us. This will be that very tempered spirit whom nothing can frighten, but whose heart strives more fierily toward Hierarchy and the service of the Common Good.

Truly, as it is said in the Teaching: "Tranquility of consciousness develops proportionately with the realization of the Higher World. There is no greater joy and beauty than affirmation of the existence of the Higher World. Prayer is the outcome of realization of the living bond with the Higher World. The very concept of such a bond makes a man strong and aspiring."

Thus, Vivekananda often used to ask his disciples if they could imagine all the softness and tenderness of heart of the Great Teachers. But the compassion and help of the Great Teachers, owning to their great knowledge, is often expressed in forms that do not correspond either with our own understanding or desires. Hence, the frequent remark which, alas, I have heard myself, "The Great Teacher is somewhere far off and does not hear the appeals addressed to him." There is no greater error than to think thus. However, in order to be heard one must apply sincerity and striving of the heart.

It is also possible that some mistake the achievement of the state of *vairagya* for a petrified heart. For them *vairagya* means precisely petrifaction, whereas in reality it is the renunciation of attraction to corporeal things, and such renunciation should take place mainly in thought. Detachment from base, carnal manifestations does not mean the absence of feelings. Thus, detachment from food does not mean that a man has lost the sense of hunger, etc. But when the state of *vairagya* has been achieved, man gives credit where credit is due and learns to discern where is the *most important* and the *guiding*.

"A petrified heart is no longer a heart, but a piece of rubbish."

* * *

One of my correspondents often encounters the most peculiar opinions regarding the Teaching of Living Ethics. These come from the so-called "Donovs." However, I always insist upon tolerance toward all spiritual movements, and I advise not to force the books of Living Ethics upon anyone and chiefly not to enter into arguments. With some people any exchange of opinion becomes an argument and a personal offense. True, the latter proves the possession of only a small degree of consciousness and knowledge. Buddha said, "Revere your own faith, but do not slander that of your brother." It is also said by the Brahmo Samaj that not a single religion should be slandered, ridiculed, or hatred. Therefore, a spiritual teacher, whose disciples attribute his origin to the Solar Hierarchy, should display great tolerance toward other Teachings. Our consciousness is measured by our tolerance.

6
4 February 1936

It is very good that you have pointed out the danger of obsession. You should also mention that often the majority of insane people are simply obsessed. Likewise, you might give a place to some hints regarding the harm of lower psychism, which can also lead to obsession. Much has been said against psychism in *Fiery World*. At the same time you should point out the higher paths, the paths of the heart, and the accumulation of spiritual synthesis. It can be pointed out that in the near future, when humanity advances in the understanding of the subtle energies, the problem of mediumship will be correctly solved. Conditions and methods will be found for the protection of mediums from outside influences, and they could then be attracted to cooperation for the purpose of scientific research.

* * *

It is very useful to reveal the facts about mediumship and psychism, for humanity in its search for the unusual and unusual experimentations has delved in its ignorance into the blackest magic and sorcery. I have written recently regarding a certain medium, and I quoted the words of Manly P. Hall, a talented

American lecturer and writer on occultism. I will quote them again for you: "It will probably be wise at this point to describe the difference between a medium and a clairvoyant. To the average persona there is no difference, but to the mystic these two phases of spiritual sight are separated by the entire span of human evolution.

"A clairvoyant is one who has raised the spinal serpent into the brain and by his growth earned the right of perceiving the invisible worlds with the aid of the third eye, or pineal gland. ... Clairvoyants are not born; they are made. Mediums are not made; they are born. The clairvoyant can become such only after years, sometimes lives, of self-preparation; on the other hand, the medium, ... may secure results in a few days." [Loc. cit.] But, of course, one should add here that the medium is limited to the lower strata of the Subtle World. Actually, the higher planes are not accessible to the medium, for his higher triad takes no part in his manifestations—mediumship arrests correct evolution, and should be considered as retrogression.

I have also written about the harm of concentrations on a particular center, as prescribed in the books of pseudo-occultists; for such concentration stimulates one center at the expense of others, throwing into chaos the whole scheme of their polarization. This process causes real harm in the sphere of vibrations, for it violates the equilibrium of the established vibratory scheme. Do you remember what is said in the Teaching about the work of the Master upon all the centers of the disciple, over all the seven circles of clairvoyance and clairaudience? The Great Teachers carefully watch the condition of the organism of the disciple, and they would never open one center at the expense of another. Correct development, or evolution, lies only in harmony or balance. The opening of one or two centers leads only to lower psychism or mediumship. Automatic writing would also be considered as a certain stage of obsession, for during the process of automatic writing, there is usually a stress on the physical center of the hand, and even on that of the brain. If practiced often, it becomes very harmful and could end in paralysis. Not one medium can be considered an Agni Yogi. Only spirituality and *podvig* carry us toward the acceptance of the fiery chalice. Mediumship is as a particle of impurity in the fiery chalice of an Agni Yogi.

Much is said about psychism in the Teaching. I do not know

how long it will be before you will be able to read it, therefore I will quote for you two very important Discourses:

"Verily, a medium has no open centers, and the psychovision, for contact with the higher worlds, also is unattainable for him. Man is in error about the power of the medium, and We are often distressed to see how enticing to people are physical manifestations. A materialization attracts them like a magnet. [We likewise have recourse to physical manifestations, but circumstances vary.] We prefer the channel of the spirit, and for sacred missions we use the channel of the spirit only. An Arhat sometimes waits for centuries to give a sacred mission. The manifestation of certain missions demands special combinations. We Arhats follow the principle of goal-fitness. The experiment of the Mother of Agni Yoga is distinguished not by brilliancy but by cosmic scope. The world knows about the White Fire. The world knows about the Invisible Light. Where We wish to reveal the subtlest energies, there We act only through subtlest energies. Where the Arhat must entrust the Sacred, there We manifest highest cautiousness. Where the Arhat knows the eternal Law, there He rejoices, and He sends the exultation into Infinity. Record My mission ... as the highest concordance on the planet. The concordance of Spirit and Matter is the rarest cosmic manifestation. Humanity might well say, 'We are deprived of the highest.' The most subtle energies should be treated with great caution." [Infinity I]

"The destruction of the contact with the higher energies actually isolates humanity from the Cosmos. How is it possible to exist in the Cosmos without any comprehension of world evolution? Thus, a conscious relationship to world evolution includes indirectly an understanding of Hierarchy as a life-giving Principle. Precisely, psychism and mediumism turn man away from the Higher Spheres, for the subtle body becomes thus so saturated with lower emanations that the entire being is altered. In reality a most difficult process is contained in purification of consciousness. Man does not precisely differentiate between the fiery state of spirituality and psychism. Thus, we must overcome the terrors of psychism. Actually, the ranks of those instruments are filled by the servants of darkness. Thus, on the path to the Fiery World one must contend with psychism."—*Fiery World III, 365*

"Indeed, the abyss of incomprehension is the path by which

humanity is now proceeding. Verily, contemporary thinking is the proscriber of psychic investigations. Yet, it is possible to go so much farther and deeper by knowing the division and the connection between the three bodies. Because, if the physical body is already formed, the astral body has been almost formed, and the most subtle, mental, body has been formed only by the chosen ones. But those who have been initiated into higher fiery energies, and who know the fiery transmutation of the centers, can affirm fiery manifestations. All other manifestations must be divided into two categories. The first, when the spirit cannot pass over the abyss because the mental body has not yet been sufficiently formed, so that the spirit cannot appear beyond the limits of the lower strata; the other category, when one center is manifested partially. It must also be remembered that the Fiery World is inaccessible to a spirit so long as the higher centers have not begun to be transmuted. But above all stands the spirit which kindles its own spiritual Fires, for its mental body creates correspondingly. On the path to the Fiery World one must sensitively discriminate in psychic manifestations."—*Ibid., 369*

I am glad that you, too, have been drawn into the correspondence concerning the Teaching. Bring Light—what can be more beautiful than such labor? Your answer ... is correct. Indeed, how else can we be saved from Spatial Fire? Moreover, during the cataclysms of the future, precisely the countries that are nearest to the volcanic belt and also some islands will suffer the most severely. Actually, the North is, in this respect, safer. In India, during the last two years, 200,000 people perished from earthquakes. All the time, we are aware of the subterranean movements around us. It is true that our only salvation and protection from all calamities and evil is the Hierarchy of Light. However, for this, an indestructible bond must be established. And, verily, words of reverence are not sufficient—the fire of the heart is needed.

7

18 February 1936

Every warrior of Light courageously accepts the accelerated payment of old accounts. The sufferings of those who have entered the Path of Light are transformed into wonderful flowers of the spirit. Certainly it is not easy to achieve spiritual liberation from earthly attachments. But when ahead of us lies the great goal of Service, and when the heart is aflame with devotion to the Great Teacher, then the most burdensome is transmuted into the joy of self-renunciation.

I can see that you are disturbed by the attempts of certain people to affirm only their own concept of the world. I advise you to accept such attempts with complete calmness. Let people discriminate for themselves. It is impossible to force the consciousness, therefore, manifest tolerance and restraint. Nothing grows as slowly as consciousness. For the assimilation of each new concept, it is necessary not only to throw light upon it from all angles but also to repeat it perpetually, precisely "until a design is fixed in the brain," as one Thinker put it. Those who are unable to appreciate all the depth and the cosmic scale of thought revealed in the Teaching of Life and who constantly shift their path are not ready to accept the Fiery Teaching. Therefore, not only would it be out of all proportion to waste time in trying to convince them but it would also be even wrong to violate an unstable consciousness. It is indicated in the Teaching that even with those who have agreed one should not waste much time. Indeed, first let them show that they have applied the first call. There is no point in repeatedly dipping a vessel into an empty well; but once a man proves to be valuable, one must apply toward him the maximum tolerance and patience, in order that, by careful touches, his consciousness may be prepared for collaboration. Consciousness should be broadened most cautiously. Only organic development and versatility of accumulations can assure the true growth of our treasury.

I entirely agree with you that the admittance of unstable elements into an esoteric group or a governing body presents a serious danger. Therefore, we must fight this evil, and tactfully eliminate the corrupting elements. Try to accept only those who are well tested; those who with all their hearts have assimilated the foundation of the Teaching, with truly a sincere devotion to the Hierarchy of Light. Without it, there can be no real understanding of the Teaching, for only this silver thread of the heart links our consciousness with the consciousness of the Teacher. Those who reject the necessity of understanding the leading concept of the Teacher should be told that the present day predominance of all-pervading corruption is the result of negation of authority in all spheres of life. But what can exist without the leading concept? I shall never tire of repeating the words of the Teaching: "The entire Universe is saturated with this principle." On what else can evolution be based? Therefore, each one who rejects Hierarchy, rejects evolution. Of all principles leading to the broadening of consciousness, the principle of Hierarchy is the most powerful.

Our black age is truly full of every kind of negation, and particularly negation of the foundations of Be-ness. The loss of understanding of the vital and leading concept of the Teacher has resulted in chaotic thinking and licentiousness on one side, and on the other it has allowed the fanatics to create idols out of the greatest Teachers, enclosing them behind a gilded barrier, and surrounding them with inaccessibility and paraphernalia that has become entirely meaningless. Thus, the living heartfelt bond with the Higher World was violated, owing to the increased ignorance of the later followers.

Of course, those who claim that "no Teachers can free you, only you yourself," are repeating one of many such formulas from the Eastern Teachings and the books of Living Ethics. Precisely, everything must be done "by human hands and human feet." No one can force our consciousness to accept a truth for which we are not yet ready. Only our inner striving can create the essential transmutation. The whole Eastern wisdom asserts that only by personal efforts and constant labor over self is the knowledge and possession of the truth achieved. However, that very same wisdom states that "The Teacher may be called a beacon of responsibility. The bonds of the Teaching are like a saving rope in the mountains." The one who has accepted the leadership of the Teacher hastens his path. And by easing and accelerating his own path, at the same time he eases the path of his near one. I shall quote my favorite paragraph (84) from the book, *Agni Yoga*: "I recall a Hindu boy who found the Teacher. We asked him, 'Is it possible that the sun would grow dark to you if you would not see it without the Teacher?' The boy smiled. 'The sun would remain as the sun, but in the presence of the Teacher twelve suns would shine to me.' India's sun of wisdom shall shine, because on the shore of a river there sits a boy who knows the Teacher." And we may add: "If a barbarian should make an attempt against the Teacher, tell him how humanity labels the destroyers of libraries."

And again it is said, "With whom may one fortify one's thoughts? Only with the Guru. He is as a rock, near which it is possible to be sheltered from the storm. Reverence for the Guru is the path to the Higher World. But chaos cannot tolerate construction. One should direct attention to the basis of thought in order not to be exposed to the whirlwind."

Our poor humanity, with its one-sided preoccupation with materialism (the church, too, serves materialistic bases and demands) needs more than ever before the realization of the Higher World and the leading concept of the Guru-Hierarch. Humanity's disease is chaotic thinking and lack of self-discipline. The slaves of yesterday revolt primarily against the leading concept, against discipline, and against cooperation. Only a king of the spirit realizes the significance of Hierarchy, for, in order to rule, one must first learn to obey. The principle of the leading concept must be affirmed in the consciousness of humanity if it wishes to progress. But, of course, all fanaticism is frightful, since it is the offspring of ignorance and ends in zealotry. It is actually the antipode of true devotion and reverence.

Every Hindu knows what devotion to the Guru means. And we know that all the majestic concepts and the whole beauty of Eastern thought evolved precisely from the sequence and succession in the infinite Hierarchic Chain, which consists of links formed by the limitless devotion of a disciple to his Guru. Thus, the East looks upon a Teacher who rejects the Hierarchic principle as upon a dry, rootless tree. To deprive the spirit of reverence for the great concept of the Teacher is equivalent to spiritual suicide. The Great Teachers provide our nurture; without it, not only would we die but so would the whole planet.

Actually, if the Great Teachers were to forcibly pour forth their rays, we would be burned to ashes unless we possessed the power of receptivity. Everything requires reciprocity, correspondence, and co-measurement. All of life is based on mutual exchange and cooperation. Therefore, an isolated man who limits himself to his own self is destined to death, both physically and spiritually. Thus, if someone affirms just one abutment, the structure will not be firm and will not withstand the stress of the approaching whirlwind.

Therefore, ask all those unsteady and disputing ones, Have they read all the books of the Teaching of Life? And if they say, "yes," examine them; many surprises may await you. Incredible is the ignorance and lack of understanding of the most simple foundations of spiritual development! And just think that through the ages the Founders of the religions of all the world have set the link with the Higher World as the basis of Existence! And our black age is ending with calls to violate this one salutary bond!

The rending of our planet from the Higher World has brought it to the brink of disaster. The most pressing measures must be applied in order that humanity may return to the understanding of the foundations of Be-ness and the grandeur of human destiny.

8

7 February 1936

You probably remember how Schure, in his book *The Great Initiates*, attempts to make a Celt and a Druid out of Rama, the purest Hindu hero of the *Ramayana*, from Ayodhya. The same author disguises the Jew, Moses, as an Egyptian! One must read Schure withdiscrimination.

The last mail brought me inquiries and criticism regarding the article "The Solar Path." The critic draws my attention to the fact that this article contradicts the Teaching of Living Ethics, that many statements in this essay are similar to the preachings of Krishnamurti, who denies Hierarchy, and that at times it contains an "almost exact repetition of the statements of the followers of Steiner." I shall have to answer this letter and advise this young critic to learn to read with his heart and mind, and not merely with his eyes, if he wishes to attain to true knowledge. He does not hesitate to attack Vivekananda, for he is very puzzled by Vivekananda's views on acquiring wealth, whereas the books of Living Ethics condemn the desire for personal possessions. However, the critic ignores the fact that Vivekananda in talking of the duty of a householder emphasizes first the acquiring of knowledge, and then, of wealth. And in this word *then* lies the true meaning. With knowledge, in the way it is understood by a Hindu, wealth becomes a blessing, because it then serves not personal ends but the General Good. Thus, people pay attention to the dead letter without thinking of the sense of what is written!

* * *

Why do you think that I might be against the publishing of the biography of V. I. Kryjanovsky? With regard to holiness, I have my own criterion, but undoubtedly she deserves respect, for her books brought a certain benefit as you justly write. It is also true that the "Magi" series is written with more talent and a greater wealth of correct information than the works of many later novelists who wrote on occult subjects.

* * *

I am glad that you have convinced yourself of the low quality of some mediums. I can confirm the correctness of the information given by Mr. L. People usually forbid to others those things in which they are particularly interested themselves. Today, more than ever, all kinds of sorcery and cheap spiritualism are wide spread. That is why it is so important to disseminate the books of Living Ethics, which point out the harm of such practices.

In one of your letters you write to me about a scientist who is experimenting with the transmission of thought. Such experiments are more than timely. I suggest that you familiarize yourself with these, and if they merit it, write an article for your magazine. Today, many progressive minds are working along these lines. Already for the last thirty years at Duke University in America, Professor Rhine has conducted similar experiments with his students and has achieved remarkable results. He recently published a book about his experiments and observations, and we sent for it. After we have finished reading it, and should we find things of interest, we will share our impressions with you.

You wrote that the scientist whom you mentioned approaches these experiments from a purely materially scientific point of view. I would not blame him for that. I would first consider the results of his experiments as he describes them; then, one could introduce the spiritual factor and the realization of psychic energy into similar experiments, and later compare the results of the two methods. Such comparison can be very edifying. It would be advisable in such an experiment to form a special group of mediums of a certain type, which is not so simple, for often mediumistic abilities are in a latent state and are revealed only after repeated impacts. By the way, the experiments of Professor Rhine have established the most interesting fact that mediums are far from being the best channels for thought-transmission at a distance.

Indeed, the time has now arrived for science to announce a new understanding of the spirit. The modern church has alienated us from the Higher World, but modern science will bring us nearer to it.

I shall quote for you a paragraph from one of the books of Living Ethics: "You know of many experiments in thought-reading. Western people, being told about it, have no idea how inherent to the East is this psychological quality. In their ignorance they even call it superstition. Whereas, if thought is an organic creation, then it can be laid open. Even meager physical apparatuses can catch the tension of thought. Even the thermometer and electrical apparatuses react to the rising of thought. Thought even changes the temperature of the body. To such an extent does the psychic apparatus dominate the physical that it is even correct to identify the psychic apparatus as a part of the physical. There exists an apparatus which writes down the flow of thoughts; this flow also is reflected in a radiation [the aura] and may be detailed by the comparative method. ... There are few attempts to connect mechanics with the psychic. Whereas, you know how a scientific attitude toward the psychic alleviates and transforms all existence. ... I reiterate that attention to the possibilities of the psychic apparatus is undeferrable." [New Era Community]

* * *

We received a letter from Harbin, telling us that it was forbidden there to celebrate the anniversary of Leo Tolstoy. Could one go further? Indeed, back to the Middle Ages!

9

18 February 1936

There are several interesting remarks about the blood in the little book I sent you, *The Occult Anatomy of Man* [Op. cit., p. 24], by Manly P. Hall. It proves scientifically that "the blood of every man is individual. When crystallizing, it forms into geometric patterns which differ with each person." As he puts it, "The story of man's soul is written in his blood. The position he occupies in evolution, his hopes and his fears, all are imprinted on the etheric forms which flow through his blood stream... so that by means of blood analysis a far surer system could be evolved for crime detection than any of the now existing methods. It is interesting to note that the coefficient of the blood of some nations is, according to a known tabulation, almost the same; whereas the comparison of the blood of other nations sharply differ, for example, the blood of the Russians and of the English, according to the same tabulation.

* * *

With regard to the question about the cult of the cat and of certain birds in Egypt, it is quite clear that the deification of animals was encouraged for the sake of the masses with a definite aim. For the most part, it was based on purely practical grounds and was for the purpose of protection. Thus, the killing of the sacred bird, the ibis was punished in Egypt by death. We know, however, that the Nile was full of crocodiles, and the valleys of Egypt abounded in many poisonous snakes, whose victims were numbered in thousands. And only this bird, the ibis, killed these snakes and destroyed the crocodile eggs, thus preventing the excessive breeding of these monsters.

Similarly, the worship of the cow in India and the forbiddance of killing it arose from the necessity of preventing the destruction of this most useful animal. It is known that in ancient times such deification did not exist, and the population of India lived on the meat of these animals.

In Egypt, cats were very useful against invasion by rats and mice. Moreover, the cat possesses a great deal of animal magnetism and was used for the lower evocations—also in Egypt there was not a little necromancy. The struggle between white and black magic has existed from times immemorial. These two opposite camps were already clearly defined in Atlantis.

You know that in the book of Living Ethics there is a paragraph about sacred animals: "It is rightly understood that so-called sacred animals were not deities, but were a natural consequence arising from local conditions. Even now people often speak about some sacred obligation meaning thereby, not a religious rite, but a useful moral action. The conditions of antiquity often required a special attention to certain animals, or trees and plants. Sacredness signified inviolability. Thus was preserved something rare and necessary. The very same protection contemporary people call 'preserves.' Thus, one should refer very carefully to concepts that are not clear. So much has been added to the province of religion that, because of its antiquity, superficial observers are completely unable to distinguish the fundamental from the stratifications around it. The temple even now is a gathering place where, along with ceremony, barter and sale take place, and local matters are discussed. The same piling up of confusion is still taking place. Therefore let us not be excessively harsh toward the term *sacred animals* and other long-forgotten archaic symbols." [Aum]

To these lines, as you can see, there is not much to add.

10
22 February 1936

"Can the High Spirits be ill and even become subject to infection?" Of course they can, if the conditions of their tasks require their constant communion with people. Remember that a High Spirit constantly gives part of his strength to those who come to him and who surround him, and no matter how great is his store of psychic energy, nevertheless it can be temporarily exhausted, owing to his excessive generosity of spirit. And such moments of exhaustion are full of danger; for the protective net of the aura, when deprived of the emanations coming from the store that nourishes our centers, is violated and laid open to infectious microbes, which can then penetrate into a weaker spot. That is why the books of Living Ethics so persistently emphasize the guarding of the protective net. A disciple who has reached a certain degree of spiritual development is unable to remain too long in the polluted atmosphere of cities and is obliged to retire into nature in order to accumulate prana and lead a more of less retired life. Christ, Buddha, and other great Teachers often used to retire to the desert, and never stayed long in one place. In the Gospel of St Mark (5:25-34) it is indicated that Christ, while purifying and healing the sick, suffered an expenditure of strength. When the sick woman touched the hem of his garment, Jesus knew in himself that the virtue had gone out of him.

Likewise, Bhagavan Sri Ramakrishna, a contemporary spiritual teacher of India, during his teachership was constantly surrounded by people and contacted many with malignant diseases, thus pouring out his forces beyond all co-measurement. Consequently, he became ill with a throat ailment, a form of cancer, which caused his death. It is important to mention that this disease created confusion in some weak minds, who began to doubt the degree of his spiritual stature. The ignorant think that a high spirit is protected from illness and danger regardless of circumstances; but we know that if the stone thrown by Devadatta from a high rock at the Buddha while he was passing below did not kill him, nevertheless it injured a toe of his foot. There are also indications that the Lord Buddha often experienced severe pains in his back. Likewise, in *The Mahatma Letters* we can find an account of how the Mahatma K. H., during the time of the founding of the Theosophical Society in India, was obliged to retire for several weeks into complete seclusion, after being in contact with the auras of people. Thus, each plane of existence is subject to its own laws, and the violation of them brings corresponding consequences.

* * *

And now regarding the fires of St. Elm. This is the glow that accompanies the discharges of atmospheric electricity; usually it appears during a thunderstorm, in the form of small lights that can be seen over sharp-pointed objects such as church spires, the masts of ships, etc. These little fires produce hissing sounds, a sort of crackling. The sailors of the Mediterranean regard St. Elm as their patron and consider these little fires to be a visible sign of his protection. Although the fires of St. Elm have cosmic electricity as a common basis with the manifestations of the so-called non-searing fire, the quality of the latter is entirely different.

There are plenty of proofs regarding such a non-searing fire, and I will give you the following story of an eye-witness of this. In 1933, a Tibetan lama, Karma-Dorje, paid us a visit. We discussed various spiritual matters, and he told us among other things about his meeting with the renowned hermit, Kshetrapa, who lives in a cave not far from the small village of Shasregtog in Eastern Tibet. According to local traditions, this hermit appeared in that cave at the time of their great-grandfathers, and since that time his outer appearance has not changed at all. Like all hermits of this kind, he never wears clothes; his hair covers him like a mantle from head to foot; his skin is dark; people say he is not a Tibetan, although he knows all the local dialects. The cave in which he dwells consists of several compartments. In the very last of these there stands a dry tree, and the floor is covered with something like soft ashes. The local people say that around his cave, even during the heaviest snowstorms, there is not a trace of snow. They also assert that he has saved their village many times from epidemics. Undoubtedly this hermit possesses many siddhis; he lives in austere solitude and allows only a few chosen ones to see him.

Lama Karma-Dorje, being present during the hermit's conversation with some visitors, noticed the following interesting detail. Before answering anyone's questions, Kshetrapa would whisper to some invisible higher Powers, as it were, as if he were consulting them, and then he would transmit their answer. Seated in his cave, he also could call forth a non-searing flame, which would first spread over the ground and then settle on the dry tree in the depth of the cave. Lama Karma-Dorje himself touched this flame, and had no burns on his hands; he felt only a pleasant warmth.

During his conversation with the hermit, the lama told him that he suffered from acute headaches and asked the hermit to give him one of his hairs as a protective talisman. Kshetrapa looked as if he were indignant, and thereupon quickly took a stick and s truck him strongly on the head. Under the impact of this blow, the lama was thrown from the cave and rolled down the hill. After he came to, he was, to his great astonishment, completely unscathed and there was not even a trace of the blow. As for his headaches, after this unusual treatment, they henceforth disappeared entirely.

The European traveler, Arnold Heim, visited this part of Tibet in 1933, and mentioned this very same hermit. He was also visited by the well-known traveler in Tibet, Mme. David-Neel, but he would not allow her to approach. Standing at the entrance to the cave, he threatened her sternly with his stick.

The lama who visited was certainly an exception among the so-called *sadhus*. After a short stay with us, he came one morning to say goodbye. He told us that he must hurry, since his Teacher, who lives in Tibet near the holy mountain, Kailas, called for him; he heard his voice. In six months he again came to us and told us that his Teacher had died, and that he had not arrived in time. Now the lama has retired into complete seclusion for ten years, after which he will return and teach.

Obeying his Teacher's biddance, Karma-Dorje never carries with him more than two pounds of food and two rupees in money, even on his longest marches. During his stay with us, he had many remarkable visions. My son painted his portrait, and I am enclosing a photograph of it. Those who are familiar with the type of Tibetan lamas will certainly admit that his face is unusual.

Also enclosed is a newspaper clipping about a fakir who remained buried for forty-two days without food. I personally do not approve of such practices. Today, we need positive human achievements on the earthly plane and not breaking away and leaving for heavenly spheres. Those who do escape are, in a way, deserters from the luminous host of Armageddon.

Can it be possible that you have never heard of Sophie Kovalevsky, a mathematical genius and our Russian pride? Years ago, I read her autobiography written in French, which covered only her childhood and youth. The later period of her short life was described by her best friend, a renowned Swedish author. As usual with us Russians, her genius in mathematics was first appreciated abroad. Only after her exceptional triumphs abroad, and just before (although it often happens even after) death, was she honored by being elected a member of the St. Petersburg Academy of Sciences! Thus, whenever a discrimination of real values was concerned, our country stubbornly continued during centuries to resemble. ... But the coming epoch will know how to safeguard the bearers of true values.

I shall quote briefly about Mme Kovalevsky from the *Encyclopedia Britannica*: "Sophie Kovalevsky (1850-1891), Russian mathematician... was born at Moscow on the 15th of January, 1850. ... In 1868 she ... [married a young student] Waldemar Kovalevsky, and the two went together to Germany to continue their studies [in mathematics]. In 1869 she went to Heidelberg, where she studied under H. von Helmholtz, G. K. Kirchoff, L. Konigsberger and P. du Bois-Reymond, and from 1871-1874 read privately with Karl Weierstrass at Berlin, as the public lectures [in universities] were not then open to women. In 1874 the University of Gottingen granted her doctor's degree *in absentia* ... on account of the remarkable excellence of the three dissertations sent in, one of which, on the theory of partial differential equations, is one of her most remarkable works."

After her lectures in the University of Stockholm, Madame Kovalevsky, in 1884, was appointed full Professor at the University at the request of Gustav Mittag Leffler, also a pupil of Weierstrass. And "this post she held till her death. ... In 1888 she achieved the greatest of her successes." The French Academy honored her with the Prix Bordin, which was competed for by all the outstanding mathematicians of the day. "The problem set was 'to perfect in one important point the theory of the movement of a solid body round an immovable point,'" the problem having been set for six years by the Berlin Academy without producing any results. Madame Kovalevsky's solution "was so remarkable that the value of the prize was doubled as a recognition of unusual merit.

"Unfortunately, Madame Kovalevsky did not live to reap the full reward of her labors, for she died [on February 10th, 1891] just as she had attained the height of her fame and had won recognition *even* in her own country by election to membership of the St. Petersburg Academy of Sciences." Note particularly the emphasis on "even."

* * *

You want to know how Madame Kovalevsky solved problems. Certainly with the aid of the fiery power. In her autobiography she says that in her childhood the answers to some of the most complicated problems were instantly pictured in her brain; likewise, she sometimes saw the figures and formulae as if they were inscribed before her. True, she worked hard, as is seen in her biography, but it is obvious that in her case the touch of the fiery ray, which awakened her Chalice and aroused the forgotten knowledge, was a frequent happening.

And now I shall tell you about an episode from my own life. In the days of my early youth I studied music, for which I had a special aptitude. Once I had to take a public examination, and I was expected to perform a few musical compositions, including a prelude and fugue by Bach. But the family circumstances were such that I was unable to learn the most difficult composition, namely, the Bach fugue. There was only one day left before the examination. In great despair, I went to the piano knowing beforehand that it was impossible to learn the Bach fugue by heart in one day. However, I decided to try my utmost. After going through the piece several times from music, I decided to check how much I remembered—and here came the miracle. The whole fugue came to my memory most clearly from beginning to end, and my fingers went over the keys as if by themselves without the slightest mistake; I played both the prelude and the fugue with unusual inspiration. But besides the unusualness of such instantaneous memorizing, when I played the fugue at the examination before a whole conclave of professors, I was again filled with a special inspiration and received an enthusiastic acclaim from them. This episode was also a manifestation of the fiery ray. The ray touched the Chalice and the long known, which had been submerged, came to the surface.

And now let us return to Madame Kovalevsky. She was not only a genius in mathematics but also an excellent writer. I still remember how brilliantly her autobiography is written. Her novels, *The Nihilist*, *Vera Vorontzoff*, *The Sisters Rajevski*, and the unfinished work *Vae victis* bear testimony to her great literary talent. Her father, a general in the Artillery, Corvin—Krukovsky, was a high landowner. In Kaluga Madame Kovalevsky had an older sister and a younger brother. Her sister was very beautiful and was also a gifted writer. Dostoevsky often paid visits to their family, and he greatly admired the literary talent of the elder sister. He was the object of childish adoration by Sophie, but, alas, his love belonged to her elder sister, who, in turn, did not share his feelings. In her autobiography Madame Kovalevsky touchingly describes the suffering and jealousy of the child's heart. She was quite unhappy in her private life. Her marriage to Kovalevsky was a nominal one; it was only to give her a certain freedom and a chance to go abroad to study. But her marriage ended dramatically.

* * *

I will answer your other questions at a later date. The battle between the forces of Light and darkness is growing and takes on dreadful dimensions.

11

17 March 1936

It is difficult to give even approximately the duration of the sojourn in the Subtle World between the incarnations of a person of average cultural development, because the cycles of evolution follow in accelerated progression, and therefore, if in the previous race and in the beginning of our Fifth Race the intervals between incarnations were great, now they are considerably reduced, and one may speak not of centuries, but of decades or even years. Similarly, during recent centuries, one could observe accelerated incarnations among the disciples of the Great Teachers, owing to some special reasons; the consciousness of humanity requires speedy shiftings. Therefore, it is advisable to point out even more emphatically the unusually threatening time which we are now experiencing, and also to mention the approach of the fiery energies to the earthly spheres for the purification of our planet of its dense atmospheres, engendered by human crimes. You can point out that this approach of the fiery energies undoubtedly will permit a new convergence of the worlds, and people will witness many unusual phenomena in nature. Parallel with this convergence, reincarnations will be accelerated, and more and more frequently children will be born who remember their previous lives, which could be easily checked, because witnesses will still be living. Likewise, phenomenal children will be born more frequently, and, too, science will be enriched by new remarkable discoveries. Precisely, the shifting of the spatial rays will bring about a regeneration of consciousness and will make possible new convergences of the worlds. Verily, the New World will come in the glory of the new rays.

If you are not too afraid of attacks, do mention Armageddon. It is absolutely essential to make people realize how serious and dangerous the present time is. Indeed, the majority of people even deny that such a battle is at all possible. There is much harm in such ignorance.

Verily, it is regrettable that so few people realize to the full the gravity of the present time, for dreadful indeed is the battle between the worlds of Light and darkness.

1. One should not claim that "... the astral light is weaker than sunlight," for there can be no comparison between the two. The earthly sunlight is strong and crude, but the radiance of the astral light in the higher spheres certainly surpasses our earthly concept of light. I shall quote the following lines from *Aum*:

"The light of the Subtle World has no relationship to the earthly understanding of solar light. In the lower strata, darkened consciousnesses create obscurity, but the higher the consciousness and thought, the more luminous is the miraculous radiance. Indeed, the dwellers of the Subtle World see both Earth and the luminaries, but the earthly lights are transmuted by their consciousness differently. Likewise with the thoughts of the Subtle World; though they are based on the same energy, their process is original. The law of equilibrium normalizes mental excesses."

Vague thoughts will leave nothing but trembling outlines. In everything, it is essential to apply clarity, power, and revivification by fire.

* * *

2. Everything is subject to its own laws and conditions. Thus, when the high Beings from other, higher planets come to Earth to help humanity, the cosmic conditions were favorable. One of those High spirits returned to his own planet in order to establish an exchange of communications with the earthly Stronghold of the Brotherhood and to find conditions for transmissions of thought and for sending new elements which are not yet to be found in the atmosphere of our planet, but which would help to discharge the accumulated darkness. All such possibilities are achieved by persistent experiments and research, and collaboration between the Greatest Spirits on both planets. Verily, infinite are the possibilities and discoveries!

Of course, the Planetary Spirits of our solar system act in complete concordance, for together they all create the will of the Cosmic Magnet and are in contact with each other. However, each possibility requires the existence of certain cosmic conditions. There is no doubt that, owing to special planetary combinations of cosmic dates, certain conditions for communications are facilitated. Thus, with the approach of the fiery energies to Earth, it is also possible to attract Lofty Visitors from the higher spheres of our planetary chain to the spheres close to Earth. In the battle of Armageddon the participation of all the forces of the invisible worlds is required. The greatest Spirits communicate between themselves and act in complete cooperation, without needing to be in any particular place for this purpose.

And now, regarding Jehovah. Jehovah does not always signify the Planetary Spirit of Saturn. All such symbols have many meanings, and often one name covers many concepts or substitutes. Esoterically, Jehovah means Elohim. It is also true that the

Jewish nation had its inception under the rays of Saturn, but, as yet, I cannot trust more than this to paper.

* * *

The battle is very menacing, and betrayals are numerous and varied. All betrayals only confirm the eternal law of the close manifestation of the dual origins. Where there is the highest light, there also is the highest measure of darkness. As it is said, " You pay attention to the world conflagration, but it is only the beginning. All the dark ones are attracted by darkness, but those who contain a spark of Light become aflame. The Time is great!"

In the Teaching of Life, it is said, "Victory will become evident within a certain time, but all the phases of the Battle should be accepted. Let us not forget that all the best Forces are gathered on Our side. Thus, it will be possible to approach the next step. The servants of darkness will themselves help to bring the success. It is necessary to understand how near are the dates, in order not to postpone the new possibilities. There can be no resistance to the Forces of Light. If the forces of darkness take upon themselves the foul work—let them perform it. The greatest names and concepts are already involved. Everything can proceed only through expansion. ... Certainly the Battle is terrifying. ... Certainly with each day the New Forces, the Invisible Ones, are evoked. From such approaches to the earthly spheres the most unexpected tensions can take place. Let us accept the Battle with the united force of all Our participants. Unity will be the unconquerable Banner. ... Who will understand the tension of the forces of Light? Who will fail to take into consideration the extent of the battlefield? The united ashrams, the strongholds of spirit, are now needed more than ever before. What is going on in a certain country ... can be called by two names: a crusade, for one side, and the diabolical fury, for the other side. Those who think this is accidental are mistaken. The Teaching never entered the world without struggle. Thus, let it enter as usual, otherwise people will forget it. But imagine the dimensions of the Battle, in which all the planets are involved. ... Thus, with all the strength of the spirit, and with all solemnity, let us participate in the Battle of Light against darkness." When the bond with the Hierarchy of Light is strong, all will be turned to good use. And in order to be able to ascend the new step, it is necessary to accept the battle and to overcome the difficulties. Draining the chalice of poison is inevitable on the last steps, and betrayal must emphasize the path of Light. Thus, let us accept this initiation also.

We know that "the betrayal deteriorates slowly." Owing to certain circumstances, this is indeed the wisest judgment. Life is so complex! People usually form their judgments only on evidence and circumstances known to them, and they entirely ignore a whole number of the most important factors, which either complicate or resolve the current of this or that task or event. But the consciousness of the Great Teachers, which operates on three planes or worlds, knows the origin of causes as well as their effects. Therefore, with complete confidence in the higher wisdom, we should calmly watch the various phases of all events. We also know that for many people and things danger is salvation; and regarding certain events, we may even say—the more dangerous, the better. Danger will help to outlive many things in the speediest way. But let us remember the benevolent signs over our country, and let us not be afraid. Many observers are liable to err greatly in their calculations, or, as the saying goes, "bet on the wrong horse."

Let us be on that side over which is extended the Shield of Light, and we shall not err.

12

19 March 1936

An Ashram means a sacred place, a temple, a monastery, a school of sacred wisdom. Therefore, the earthly Stronghold of the Great Brotherhood can be called an Ashram. In the Subtle World there are also ashrams of the White Brotherhood. Just as on Earth, they are not numerous, for there, also, great discipline and tense labor are demanded; and where are those who are willing to give themselves to greater labor instead of the promised "rest"?

Why think that the fiery rays can be only over an Ashram in the Subtle World? Verily, above each earthly Ashram or stronghold of spirit the rays arise, and under special conditions they can be seen.

* * *

Indeed, every opposition to the progress of thought or advance in any realm of knowledge should be considered as a manifestation of Armageddon. But so many foundations have deteriorated that we ought to face all the facts calmly. It is impossible to arrest the powerful march of events!

* * *

You mention your correspondence with S. I think it will not bring you much joy, judging by my own experience. It is not only useless to waste time on such correspondents, it is actually harmful. Long ago, such people found "truth" in earthly security, hence the concept of infinite perception and knowledge does not exist in their dictionary.

The task you have in mind will become a precious contribution, but you will have to work hard at it. It is very important to emphasize the difference between spiritualism, in the way it is practiced now, and a true scientific exploration and study of psychic and parapsychic phenomena. But be careful in your statements regarding the moon, because all that I have quoted from *The Secret Doctrine* about the lunar chain is not accepted by science, and even if a small number of unprejudiced minds are able to treat such theories with a certain degree of tolerance, the majority consider them to be the maximum of blasphemy. Therefore, I would not say too much about the moon in the work conceived by you. Moreover, the Great Teachers do not now reveal all the secrets connected with the moon. There is an accepted rule that people are given only that which their consciousness is ready to admit, even if dimly, and hints regarding what has already been met with in scientific works and research. *It is impermissible* to give people *something of which they have not the slightest idea,* or for which they have not even suitable words! Therefore, only that is given which the foremost minds of humanity are able to grasp. And we must say that it is being given generously, yet even a hundredth part of what has been offered is not yet assimilated. H. P. Blavatsky wrote that in her time the revelation regarding the lunar chain aroused among readers and disciples a whole storm of the wildest fantasies and contradictory opinions, some of which even appeared in print; but in spite of all the pleas for further information, the Mahatmas preserved complete silence.

* * *

You are right that the planetary chain, with all its globes, or spheres, or principles (call them what you please), is one complete whole. Actually, all the globes concentrically interpenetrate one another and represent definite planes of consciousness, or existence. True, a planet is a living organism, for in the Cosmos not a single atom is devoid of life, consciousness, or spirit, and in the ancient philosophical writings one encounters the comparison of Earth with a huge animal, having its own peculiar life and, therefore, its own consciousness, or revelation of spirit.

Properly speaking, there is no passive element in the Cosmos; everything exists through the interpenetration and interaction of spatial energies, which evolve from the infinite billions of focuses, or centers that fill the Cosmos and are ceaselessly being formed within it. Everything moves, everything changes; consequently, everything lives. Also, do bear in mind that the higher principles of the planet are contained in the human monads. Therefore we may say that the higher principles of the Moon left her when, during her final evolutionary consummation, the human monads abandoned her for the new planetary chain. The life of a planet can be understood as a combination of all the elements created with it. So much the more is the responsibility of all the thinking dwellers of the planet.

At present, the moon is a corpse, but a living corpse, because decomposition is nothing but lower life. Moreover, you must remember that, after the completion of evolution on one planetary chain and before the beginning of life on a new chain a pralaya or nirvana comes for all its beings and entities. All the principles of the lunar chain are carried over to the earthly one. Also, the lunar chain was lower than our earthly one. I shall quote a few more lines from *The Secret Doctrine*: "The [lunar] Monads which enter upon the evolutionary cycle [on the earthly chain] upon Globe A, in the first Round, are in *very different stages of development.*"

Therefore, only, "The most developed Monads ... reach the human germ-stage in the First Round; become terrestrial, though very ethereal human beings toward the end of the Third Round, remaining on it (the globe) through the 'obscuration' period as the seed for future mankind in the Fourth Round, and thus become the pioneers of Humanity at the beginning of this, the Fourth Round. Others [less developed] reach the human stage only during later Rounds, i.e., in the Second, Third, or first half of the Fourth Round. And finally the most retarded of all, *i.e.*—those still occupying animal forms after the middle turning point of the Fourth Round—will not become men at all during this Manvantara. They will reach to the verge of humanity only at the close of the Seventh Round, to be, in their turn, ushered into a new chain, after *pralaya*—by older pioneers, the progenitors of humanity, or the Seed-Humanity..., viz., the men who will be at the head of all at the end of these Rounds. "

Likewise, note that in the diagram attached to my earlier letter [16 November 1935], "Unlike the others, the Fourth [Globesphere] has no 'sister' Globe on the same plane as itself, and it thus forms the fulcrum of the 'balance' represented by the whole chain. It is the sphere of final evolutionary adjustments, the world of Karmic scales, the Hall of Justice, where the balance is struck which determines the future course of the Monad during the remainder of its incarnation in the Cycle. And therefore it is, that, after this central turning-point has been passed in the Great Cycle,—*i.e.*, after the middle point of the Fourth Race in the Fourth Round on our Globe—no more Monads can enter the human kingdom. The door is closed for this Cycle and the balance struck." Therefore, we should expect no more migrants from the Moon.

* * *

And now regarding the picturing, or the vision of the Image of the Teacher. True, at first it begins with a mental or intellectual image, which should reach the highest possible clarity, and after it has been clearly impressed upon the center of the third eye, you will be able to see it with eyes closed. At times, the Image may be surrounded by a luminous outline, as it were; at times, it may consist of light and shade without clearly defined lines. Also, in the beginning, some see the Image trembling and its outlines distorted. But gradually this trembling disappears, and the Image becomes settled. In order to stop this trembling Buddhist monks close their eyes and cross the currents of the eyes; that is, they concentrate their sight upon a focal point, which helps greatly. The crossing of the currents of the eyes became such a custom in all concentrations, that many Buddhas and Bodhisattvas are even pictured with the eyes crossed, and the glance directed to the tip of the nose. You may try this method, but, of course, without forcing and extreme crossing of the eyes. You should not allow any feeling of tension or discomfort to enter into it. Thus, I would never exceed five minutes of such exercise and would start with one; but above all, do not be discouraged if the results do not come as quickly as you would wish. All these achievements belong to the realm of higher psychism.

Read the biographies of the great Spiritual Toilers and you will realize with what difficulty they attained the opening of the centers and the Higher Communion. Even such a great saint as St. Anthony sometimes had to wait years for his questions to be answered. True, in our days, some human organisms have advanced so much in their refinement that many manifestations no longer require those tremendous efforts of strength, tension, and patience that were required in past centuries. Yet even now, only mediums achieve an easy penetration into the nearest layers of the Subtle World. However, we should not envy them, for verily the highest spheres are *inaccessible* to them, with some rare exceptions. And just as in the ancient days the Hierophants of Egypt would not accept mediums as disciples, so, also, present-day Brahmins, in their few remaining Ashrams, will not admit a single fakir.

But apart from all this, the conditions of Armageddon have a great influence over all manifestations, and while some phenomena even increase, other more subtle ones become more complex. Thus, when the waves of the Battle are strong, it is very difficult at times to hear the Communications, and afterwards an acute anguish of the heart is felt. So, instead of being saddened, you should rejoice at every little star you see, since, indeed, these signs are much more significant than all the vivid visions of the mediums, for they indicate the right development.

* * *

As regards karma, can we insist that a certain case or situation in which a man finds himself is entirely his karma? If we begin to think thus, we shall soon refuse to help each other, explaining our refusal as not desiring to interfere with an allied karma. There are even some deluded people who might refuse to help their fellow man, fearing to complicate their own karma.

But would this not be a sign of the greatest selfishness? Who, apart from an Arhat or a high Yogi, can know when and where one should not help? Often, an encounter with an overburdened man may verily be our karma, and in refusing to help him we put a burden on ourselves. We must stretch out a helping hand whenever our heart prompts us to do so, bearing in mind the law of co-measurement and remembering that spiritual help is the highest. *Quite correctly, your heart told you that we should not be dogmatic.* Life is so complicated! Therefore, always and in everything you should guide yourself first of all by GOAL-FITNESS.

* * *

In my last letter I mentioned that Lamaism bears much the same relation to true Buddhism as our church Christianity does in the Teaching of Christ. Some time ago, I was asked about the two main schools of Buddhism. I give here my answers with a few additional comments.

1. Mahayana and Hinayana are the two fundamental schools of Buddhism. The literal translation is "Great Vehicle" and "Small Vehicle." Mahayana, or "Great Vehicle" is spread all over the North—in Tibet, in Mongolia, among the Kalmucks and Buriats. There are also followers of this school in China and Japan. Hinayana exists mainly in the South—in Ceylon, in Indo-China, and there are also some divisions in China and Japan.

Mahayana originated in southwest India in the second Century B. C. The founder of Mahayana was the great Teacher, Nagarjuna. Almost simultaneously, perhaps even a little earlier, this Teaching was introduced by Asvaghosha in northwest India. He was a dramatist and a father of Sanskrit literature.

The main difference between the Mahayana and Hinayana is that the first, in addition to Guatama Buddha, recognizes the Hierarchy of Light, which is headed by many Bodhisattvas and Taras. Besides Maitreya, especially popular among these Bodhisattvas is the Bodhisattva Chenresi, the Tibetan Avalokiteshvara, (the Protector of Tibet) and the Bodhisattva Manjusri (the Protector of Buddhism). Of course, there are also many others. Among the Taras (Feminine divinities) the many-eyed and many-armed Dukkar is considered the highest. She is likened to the Mother of the World (the Lakshmi and Kali of India), and sometimes to the White Tara. Likewise worshipped are the Yellow Tara and Green Tara, so called because of the color of their rays.

The second difference between the two Teachings is that while the Arhat of the Hinayana aspires toward individual, personal salvation, the Bodhisattva of the Mahayana makes his aim the salvation of the world, for the sake of which he takes a vow not to enter Nirvana until this aim is achieved. The Teaching of the Paramitas, or the achievement of the Highest Virtue, is particularly characteristic of the Mahayana.

The followers of Hinayana do not recognize any Hierarchy other than the Buddha Guatama and his one successor, the Bodhisattva Maitreya. It is obvious that they do not accept the authority of either the Dalai Lama or Tashi Lama. There are other minor differences, but they are not so essential. It is also true that the Hinayana is an exoteric school, whereas the Mahayana is an esoteric Teaching. In Tibet Mahayana is divided into two multiple sects; the one of the Yellow Hats, or Gelugpa, is mostly known in Tibet and Mongolia, it was founded by the great reformer Tsong-Kha-pa in the fourteenth century. The other—the more ancient—is the sect of the Red Hats, or Nyingmapa; the Dugpa is one of its branches and is spread all over Sikkim and Little Tibet; its founder was a Hindu, the Teacher Padma Sambhava. Both the Dalai Lama and the Tashi Lama, and the entire government of Tibet, belong to the Gelugpa sect.

Apart from these two sects in Tibet, there is one very vital and the most ancient local creed, known by the name Bon. At the present time, this ancient creed has borrowed very much from Buddhism. However, the Bon lamas and also the majority of the lamas of the Red sect, are very much attached to sorcery, and to the crudest necromancy and Tantrism.

2. Are there religions and communities in the East which accept the Teaching about Maitreya? The Bodhisattva Maitreya was promised to the world as the coming Buddha by Gautama himself. This is the reason why the Hinayana also accepts this one Bodhisattva. Maitreya corresponds to the Kalki Avatar in Hinduism (the "White Horse Avatar"—see the Revelation of St. John), and to the Messiahs of all nations. All the Messiahs are inevitably Avatars of Vishnu; therefore, they belong to One Ego. In the exoteric legends the difference between Maitreya and the Kalki Avatar is that while the Kalki Avatar will appear at the

end of the present Kali Yuga for the final destruction of the wicked, the renovation of humanity and "the restoration of purity," Maitreya is expected earlier.

Statues in honor of the Bodhisattva Maitreya were erected in India and Tibet at the very beginning of our Christian Era, and there is not a single Buddhist temple where there is not now an Image of this Bodhisattva, be in on tankas or as a colossal figure sometimes occupying the height of three stories of a temple. Of course, all Buddhists believe that Maitreya will appear in Shambhala, and the most enlightened of them know that Maitreya and the present Lord of Shambhala are One and the Same Individuality.

I shall quote an interesting passage from *The Secret Doctrine* taken from the *Puranas*.

"As the '*Satya-yuga*' is always the first in the series of the four ages or Yugas, so the Kali ever comes the last. The *Kali-yuga* reigns now supreme in India, and it seems to coincide with that of the Western age. Anyhow, it is curious to see how prophetic in almost all things was the writer of Vishnu-Purana when foretelling ... some of the dark influences and sins of this Kali-Yuga. For after saying that the 'barbarians' will be masters of the banks of the Indus, of Chandrabhaga and Kasmira, he adds: 'There will be contemporary monarchs, reigning over the earth—kings of churlish spirit, violent temper, and ever addicted to falsehood and wickedness. They will inflict death on women, children, and cows; they will seize upon the property of their subjects, and *be intent upon the wives of others:* they will be of limited power, ... their lives will be short, their desires insatiable. ... People of various countries intermingling with them, will follow their example; and the barbarians being powerful (in India) in the patronage of the princes, while purer tribes are neglected, the people will perish. Wealth and piety will decrease ... [day by day] until the world will be wholly depraved. Property alone will confer rank; wealth will be the source of devotion; passion will be the sole bond of union between the sexes; falsehood will be the only means of success in litigation; and women will be objects merely of sensual gratification. ... *External types will be the only distinction of the several orders of life;* ... a man if rich will be reputed pure; dishonesty ... will be the universal means of subsistence, weakness the cause of dependence, menace and presumption will be substituted for learning; liberality will be devotion; mutual assent, [will replace] marriage; fine clothes [will be regarded as] dignity. ... He who is the strongest will reign... the people, unable to bear the heavy burden, *Kara-bhara* (the load of taxes) will take refuge among the valleys. ... Thus, in the Kali age will decay constantly proceed, until the human race approaches its annihilation (*pralaya*). ... When the close of the Kali age shall be nigh, a portion of that divine being which exists, if its own spiritual nature ... shall descend on Earth ... as *Kalki (-Avatara)* endowed with the eight superhuman faculties. ... He will re-establish righteousness on Earth, and the minds of those who live at the end of Kali-Yuga shall be awakened and become as pellucid as crystal. The men who are thus changed... *shall be the seeds of human beings*, and shall give birth to a race who shall follow the laws of the Krita age, (the age of purity).' As it is said, 'When the sun and moon and the lunar asterism Tishya and the planet Jupiter are in one mansion the Krita (or Satya) age shall return.'

"'... Two persons, Devapi, of the race of Kuru and Maru [Moru], of the family of Ikshvaku, continue alive throughout the four ages, residing at Kalapa [Shambhala]. They will return hither in the beginning of the Krita age ... Maru [Morya] the son of Sighra through the power of Yuga is still living ... and will be the restorer of the Kshatriya race of the Solar dynasty. ...'

"Whether right or wrong with regard to the latter prophecy, the *blessings* of Kali-Yuga are well described, and fit in admirably even with that which one sees and hears in Europe and other civilized and Christian lands in the full XIX-th and at the dawn of the XX-th century of our great era of ENLIGHTENMENT."

"... In *Matsya-Purana*, chapter cclxxii, the dynasty of ... Moryas (or Maureyas) is spoken of. In the same chapter. it is stated that the Moryas will one day reign over India, after restoring the Kshatriya race many thousand years hence. Only that reign will be purely Spiritual and 'not of this world.' It will be the kingdom of the next Avatara.'' [Op. cit.]

Thus, the initiated Hindus know much about their Mahatmas, who dwell in the Trans-Himalayas, but from the curious they guard well this sacred knowledge. In her time, many of them opposed H. P. Blavatsky, for she gave out to the world these sacred names. Indeed, in India there still exists a great reverence for everything sacred, and particularly for these Highest

Teachers of humanity. Not a single Hindu would pronounce the name of his Guru to an outsider, so sacred is it considered.

Now you will understand how sacredly rings the name of Maitreya or Kalki Avatar of Muntazar in the hearts of the East. Indeed, all religions rotate around this one concept of the Avatar and the coming Messiah. This faith, or rather straight-knowledge, is that fire which keeps and nourishes the spiritual life of our planet. Extinguish this fire, and the planet will sink into the darkness of destruction. Verily, there is nothing more vital, more powerful and beautiful than this concept of the Great Avatar. All the prophecies, all the visions, and all the most ancient and sacred legends of all nations hide under different symbols and allegories a great Book of Lives of the Greatest One, who fights with the apocalyptic Serpent.

* * *

And now regarding the "search for the living Buddha," indeed, at present it can evoke a smile. And certainly, only the ignorant believe literally that every Dalai Lama is an incarnation of Bodhisattva Avalokiteshvara, and every Tashi Lama, of Buddha. All this must be understood metaphysically. The incarnation of the great Spirits into this or that personality must be understood as a reinforced, or even constant sending of a ray of a High Spirit to a successor chosen by him. Precisely, at the birth of the one appointed to fulfill the mission, the High Spirit who is nearest to his karma sends His ray to him in order that it may follow him all his life. This ray is received by the newborn infant, even as the rays of the stars under which he is born. He grows under this ray, and in gradual development there comes about a complete assimilation of this ray by his organism. Over this conduit comes what we call the incarnation of the ray, or the highest Hiero-inspiration.

You should know that the matter or the energies that clothe a High Spirit are indestructible, and owing to the law of attraction, or affinity, may in certain cases enter the substance of the subtle body being formed around the lofty spirit who is ready for a new incarnation. Of course, the contemporary Dalai Lamas and Tashi Lamas are so far from a lofty concept of spiritual leaders that only the ignorant masses believe that they are high incarnations. But the tradition regarding the incarnation of one and the same Ego in these representatives of spiritual power is still strong. In connection with these searches for incarnations, many edifying things happen. Undoubtedly, the people very often come across the new incarnations of their own lamas. But there is nothing surprising in this, for these lamas were often the most ordinary people.

While traveling through Tibet, we encountered many interesting things. We had with us an ancient prophecy, and once we showed it to a very well educated Buriat, a graduate of the University of Petrograd. After he had read it, the man became very excited and told us that this was precisely the same prophecy that he had once heard from the lips of a small Mongolian boy. He told us that in a small village not far from Urga a boy was born who, when no older than a year, suddenly, in the presence of several people, uttered this very same prophecy. Of course, this boy came to be regarded as an incarnation. We know nothing further of his destiny.

One should not think that in the book, *Beasts, Men and Gods*, everything is based on the most unlikely fantasy. There is more truth in it than people think. For instance, the sorceress mentioned in this book was still living when we were in Mongolia. Likewise, the unexpected arrival of the Great Lord of Shambhala at Gompa is not an invention, we ourselves heard of a version of it. One can still come across such miracles in the East, but they are revealed only to those who are ready to give up everything in order to find them.

My letter has become much too long, therefore I shall finish it. Note and write down all your subtle reactions; you will thus sharpen your attention, and many things will become accessible.

13

30 March 1936

I was glad to hear about your friend's idea of establishing a cooperative publishing house. This work is certainly closer than anything to my heart. There is nothing higher and more beautiful than the uplifting and broadening of the consciousness of the reader. A publishing house can indeed become an instructor and awakener of the thought of the young generation. Of course, all literary, philosophical, scientific, and other humanitarian writings, as well as textbooks may be accepted by the publishers provided they are of high quality and usefulness. Plans must be laid in such a way as to not bring a loss. It is essential to make the price of a book accessible, and also to preserve its aesthetic appearance. I am quite sure that you will succeed in this, as well. I always think of the Teacher's concern about placing the needed book in the humblest hands, i.e., in the poorest household. Of course, all the income from the sale of the books of Living Ethics should be used by the publishers for further publications.

With deep joy I read your words: "I think, nay, I am convinced that the work entrusted to us is the main task of our life; in fact, it should be considered above life itself." Verily, with such consciousness one can move mountains! And when today we read the just received newspaper article by Sudrabkaln about the excellent Latvian writers and the growing interest in serious books, and also about the new wave of romanticism and heroism, which is not so noticeable in Latvia, our hearts were elated. Verily, a vast, sacred work has been started by the Latvian Society. Powerful are the seeds which are entrusted to us and to you for sowing. Wide is the field, and wider than the widest must be the sowing. Therefore, above all, guard unity and magnanimity among the members in performing your sacred task. I realize how hard it is, how one has often to crucify oneself; nevertheless, there can be no unity without tolerance and readiness to give in. I am aware that at times, even when we see that harm is being inflicted upon the work of Common Good, even then we have to give in, in order not to create still greater harm by our opposition. Life is very complex, and only a broadened consciousness allows us to build, over and above all difficulties and even betrayals.

And now, regarding Armageddon, you are quite right—Armageddon is symbolic of the last decisive battle between Light and darkness. But it should not be thought that this battle can soon be over. It will continue for a number of years, but the fury of it will differ in various parts of the planet. Where the human spirit awakens more quickly for the leadership of the spirit, there the great construction will begin. With each year the influence of the forces of Light will increase, but it is essential that the human spirit be able to accept the gifts that are sent. The greatest possibilities are knocking at humanity's door, but the choice is always free. Verily, the coming time will be the greatest test for all humanity.

The word *Armageddon* is the Greek equivalent of the Hebrew *har megiddon* (the mountain district of Megiddo). In the Hebrew writings, the final great battle between the Forces of Light and darkness was indicated by this name, and was foretold by all the ancient prophecies in the scriptures of all peoples as the "Great Day of God's Judgment." Much is said about it in the Apocalypse, and in the same book (chap. 16, vs. 16), this name is mentioned. Moreover, the dates of this battle and of the beginning of the New Epoch, or Cycle, can also be found in the most precise calculations of both the Egyptians and the Hindus.

The name of this battle is symbolic in memory of a terrible and actual battle which took place in Megiddo (an ancient city in Palestine), not far from which the Canaanites under the leadership of Sisera were entirely destroyed. This dreadful total destruction remained for a long time a terrible memory for the nations that witnessed it. According to all the Scriptures, the dates are now coming for the final destruction of the army of Gog upon the mountains of Israel. And Israel does not necessarily mean the Jews, it signifies precisely "the chosen." In a similar way, the mountains of Israel must be understood as other mountains, just as the New Jerusalem does not necessarily mean Jerusalem in Palestine. The sacred language always uses symbols. There is the Heavenly Jerusalem—the Abode of the Hierarchy of Light—and the earthly Jerusalem, which should be understood as that place which, throughout all the Earthly cataclysms, remained intact and inviolate.

* * *

You ask whether there could be an illumined obsession. Yes, but extremely rarely. Yet of course you are right in that the term *obsession* could hardly be applied to the exaltation of the spirit or to being imbued with Divine Bliss. Thus, in Russian literature one finds this term used for conditions which are completely opposite in sense. Indeed, the qualities of these states differ greatly. Thus, in obsession by the dark forces a possession of the lower centers occurs, whereas the assimilation of the forces of Bliss, or of Hiero-inspiration, can take place only with the opening of the higher centers, provided that there is complete spiritual and physical purity and an especially harmonious upliftment of the vibrations of the whole organism; otherwise, death is inevitable.

Thus, it is said in the Teaching that "The power of the higher energies may not be transmitted through fragile vehicles, yet by overcoming the usual state of disharmony one may render less dangerous the contacts of the higher wings. Again let us recall the various means for bringing oneself into an exalted state. From antiquity people have attempted by special means to shield themselves from danger in contacting the Higher Forces. But the best expedient will be constant thought about the Higher Forces. By such means psychic energy becomes accustomed to the possibility of reaction to the Higher Forces and, in order that it be not shaken, the nerve substance is reinforced accordingly. Of course even one's best friend can cause a shock if he enters unexpectedly." [Aum] All this mentioned above concerns the higher *Hiero-inspiration*. But in the rarest and most exceptional cases and under special conditions there were instances when a Higher Spirit entered into a perfectly pure body. Thus, in the ancient theurgy one can find hints that during the most sacred Mysteries a High Spirit entered temporarily the body of a priest of high degree, who had undergone a lengthy and special preparation for this event. However, this was the *rarest* of cases, and only for especially benevolent purposes.

There are many degrees of being imbued by the Diving Spirit, or Bliss. In fact, all these have the same basis, only there is an *endless difference in quality*. Thus, there is only one Fire, yet we know of the black fire and the silvery fire. The subterranean and supermundane fires are related, but are far apart in their actions. In like manner, the same psychic energy can raise the knife of a murderer, or direct the scalpel of a surgeon who saves the life of a patient. So, also, there can even be a conditional immortality of evil, but such immortality is worse than annihilation.

The real kingdom of evil is our earthly plane. In the supermundane spheres, evil can exist *only within its own limits*. The light in the supermundane spheres burns the darkness. There the dark entities are destroyed by contact with light. That explains why the dark ones try with all their might to extinguish all the inceptions of Light here on Earth and within the limits accessible to them in the lower strata of the Subtle World. Verily, Earth is the hall of justice and adjustment of the measures of the Cosmic Scales.

Obsession as something coercive, always pertains to darkness, whereas the Higher Forces infuse one with the spirit, or send the ray of Hiero-inspiration to him who is able to assimilate it. There is no higher achievement than the assimilation of the ray of the Fiery World.

"When a man realizes all surrounding influences, he is then able to begin self-activity. He learns to discern where is the higher Hiero-inspiration and where low destruction. It is not so easy to distinguish all the cunning wiles, but it is fortunate when the heart is atremor with realization of usefulness to the Higher World. Contacts with the Higher World are spread throughout life; even in small everyday matters the sparks of higher tension can be discerned. There are no actions which are not intensified if they touch the Higher World. One should love such tension, for without it there can be no Great Service!" [*Ibid.*]

* * *

The Book of Enoch in an English translation can be seen in the Bodleian Library at Oxford. I do not know whether or not it is translated into other languages. In their time, the representatives of the Church were very much against it. Yes, the dark clouds are gathering, but somewhere the dawn is already breaking. Therefore, the broadening of the consciousness through the assimilation of the foundations of Living Ethics is so urgent. And equally needed is an understanding of the unusual time through which we are passing, a time in which the destinies of many nations are being decided.

14

30 March 1936

In one of your precious letters you asked the meaning of the phrase, "data about Kalachakra are passed over in silence." Kalachakra (the Wheel of Time, or the Wheel of the Law) is the Teaching ascribed to the various Lords of Shambhala. Traces of this Teaching can be found in almost all the philosophical systems and teachings of India. At present, it is perhaps known particularly in Tibet. One can also find obscure hints concerning Shambhala in Western literature. After all, the legend of the Grail also originated in the East, and is actually one of the numerous versions of the very same Shambhala. The chronicles of the West have also recorded the receipt of news from "The Mysterious Abode" by Constantine the Great and also by the Byzantine Emperor Manuel. Likewise, Genghis Khan received messages from the Sage of the Great Mountain. In the twelfth and thirteenth centuries the Western Christian Church, through its Popes, was also aware of the existence of a Mysterious Spiritual Abode and Brotherhood in the heart of Asia, headed by the then famous Prester John, as this Great Spirit called himself. This Prester John, from time to time, sent admonishing and warning notes to the Popes and other heads of the Church. According to historical records, one of the Popes sent an embassy to Prester John in Central Asia. One can well imagine the purpose of such an embassy, and, of course, after divers misfortunes and vicissitudes, this embassy returned, unable to find the Spiritual Citadel. Yet Prester John continued to send his admonishing notes.

The Holy Grail is now guarded in the East. Recently there appeared quite a few investigators of the mysterious personality of Prester John, and also of the symbolism of the legend of the Grail. There is a theory that the Holy Chalice, or Grail, is the sacred Stone (read the legend about the "Stone" in *On Eastern Crossroads*), and such a version has its reason.

Many people have searched for and even today are still attempting to get to this Stronghold, but in vain, for only those who are summoned may reach it. History knows a number of outstanding individuals whose destiny it was to give a new impulse for advancing human evolution, who had previously visited this Stronghold of Great Knowledge. Thus, Paracelsus at one time spent several years in one of the Ashrams of the Trans-Himalayan Stronghold, obtaining the great knowledge expounded by him later in many volumes, often symbolically, for there was great persecution of these beacons of knowledge. All of his works are translated into German, English, and French. Many scientists and physicians gather their knowledge from his books, but, as usual, the source is often deliberately not mentioned. Thus, the Teaching of Kalachakra or the Teaching of Shambhala, is not only mentioned now but there are even certain "spiritual" persons who forbid their followers and friends to read these books.

Let us also not forget our own genius, H. P. Blavatsky, who was so slandered. She spent three years in one of the Ashrams of Tibet, and then returned to the world with great knowledge and an illumined message regarding the Mahatmas. Had there not been so much malice and envy on the part of her contemporaries, she would have written two more volumes of *The Secret Doctrine*, in which pages from the lives of the Great Teachers of humanity would have been included. But people preferred to kill her, and her work remained unfinished. History repeats itself, and again the dark forces creep out of their holes and try to suppress the resplendent Message, but Light conquers darkness!

The Teaching of Kalachakra is the Great Revelation brought to humanity at the dawn of its conscious evolution in the Third Race of the Fourth Round of Earth by the Lords of Fire, or the Sons of Reason (amongst whom were and are the Lords of Shambhala.)

Certainly Christian Science heals by means of psychic energy, and undoubtedly some of its followers succeed in performing remarkable healings. However, just as in everything else, there must be right discrimination and application; therefore, parallel with remarkable healings, there are also failures. All is good in its own place, but it is not always possible to avoid a surgical operation. Likewise, infectious diseases cannot be cured by suggestion. Everything requires correspondence and goal-fitness. Thus, some cases require homeopathic methods, whereas others must be treated by allopathic means. But the main condition is that the healer who acts through his psychic energy should be well informed and pure in heart.

Your inquirer wants to know "How to reconcile the use of musk by the yogis with the law of love and non-causation of harm preached by the occultists" and also another worry of his, "If musk is the product of an animal organism, it must be full of animal magnetism, and therefore, together with the benefit, animal magnetism enters the yogi's organism and pollutes it, etc. ..." We can reply that the very high Yogis, who live in different conditions created by them far from our earthly hustle and bustle, can make use of musk without the killing of animals. Precisely, this is emphasized in the books of Living Ethics. And as for the disciples who live in ordinary *earthly* conditions, to avoid animal magnetism they would have to become nudists and emigrate to warmer countries if they decided to adhere strictly to the law of not causing harm (in the sense in which your correspondent means it). Take wool, for instance—it would have to be rejected, because it contains too much animal magnetism. Or again, silk would also be excluded in order to save the silkworm. Even linen garments would have to be forbidden, for one should not subject the flax to those sufferings through which it passes during the refining process. Thus, the only alternative would be to cover oneself with dry leaves, since it would not be permissible to pluck them. Of course, one would have to forget about leather shoes, and even ones made of bast. The use of leather shoes would directly encourage the killing of animals, and procuring bark for bast shoes would be very painful to the tree. Similarly, food would have to be limited to milk (provided the cow had had enough for her calf), fruits, nuts, and seeds, of course, not taken from the tree or stalk, but only after they had become rotten, otherwise pain would be inflicted upon living organisms.

I remember a story about how Bernard Shaw once visited the famous Hindu scientist, Jagadis Bose, and began to boast of being a vegetarian and that this great sensitivity would not allow him to inflict pain even indirectly upon any living thing. Bose said nothing in reply, but then and there by an experiment demonstrated visually to the writer that pains are suffered by carrots and potatoes then they are cut, or chewed with relish by the jaws of such "sensitive" people.

But maybe all this would not be too terrible for a "sensitive" man, for perhaps he would accept the covering of dry leaves and the prescribed food. However, it would be far more difficult for him to refuse to breathe, or to cover his nose and mouth as do some fanatics of the Jain sect in India who are afraid that, by the very act of breathing, they might kill some tiny midge. Your inquirer surely must know that the space around him is full of living creatures, which he swallows every second and which he crushes with each step. The fanatical Jains, while walking with their eyes upon the ground, occasionally perform sudden and amusing leaps in order not to tread on the larva of an insect.

In conclusion, we may advise your inquirer to become better acquainted with the books of Living Ethics and to understand the spirit of the Teaching. Vegetarian food is advised, not just for sentimental reasons, but mainly because of its greater benefit for health; and furthermore, it is mentioned that some fish feel even less pain than plants. As for the fear of introducing animal magnetism into one's organism, one may answer with the words of Buddha—if high achievement could be attained only by abstaining from meat, the elephant and the cow would have reached it long ago. And again—asceticism has no value as a means of liberation from the bonds of Earth. It is more difficult to find a patient man than one who nurtures himself with air and roots, or garbs himself in bark and leaves.

And regarding karma, your inquirer will find in Buddhism many most valuable explanations. He will learn that karma is either purified or burdened primarily and mainly by our thoughts and motives; deeds are but a secondary factor—*precisely, thought creates karma.* Were it otherwise, man in his present conditions could never break out of the magic circle of karma. For a high Yogi no animal magnetism is to be feared, nothing can pollute him, for everything is consumed by his inner fire. But we, the humble Earth—dwellers, pollute ourselves immeasurably more by unfit thoughts than by swallowing a piece of meat or by using animal secretion for medical purposes.

Apparently your inquirer has forgotten the saying of Christ, "Not that which goeth into the mouth defileth a man; but that which cometh out of the mouth, this defileth a man." (St. Matthew 15:11)

Let us also remember that well-smoked meat contains far less animal magnetism than the aura of pet animals which we keep in our inner chambers. True achievement is not in artificially safeguarding oneself from harmful and impeding influences, but in rising above all obstacles by the *power of the spirit.* And only when this has been achieved has man the right to retire into better conditions, in order not to waste the high energy on self-defense but to give it fully to the service of humanity.

Thus, let us sagaciously observe the conditions in which we live, and without any false sentimentality let us realize the spirit of both the ancient covenants and the new, and in maintaining equilibrium we shall be able to apply the wise counsels in all their co-measurement and goal-fitness.

Unfortunately, I cannot trust to the mail the information which contradicts that which you have received; we must be very careful in dealing with these questions. Vast work is being done. A great reassessment of values is taking place. Intellectual work comes to the fore and begins to be appreciated above many other things. And so we shall live to see the illumined regeneration.

Therefore, let us not condemn too much the hundreds of thousands, who, in their own way, build the great country.

* * *

My heart rejoices at every understanding of the Foundations of the Teaching. Verily, only devotion together with constant striving leads us to the Abode.

But verily this is the rarest quality, and no wonder it is considered a sign of the most precious accumulations.

"He who is ashamed of devotion, who renounces the Hierarchy from fear of losing his individuality is poor, and empty is his Chalice." And also, "For him who wishes an easy life it is better not to live. Let him not think about the Higher World who willfully demands rewards for his merits. Whoever reckons wealth in the material world is a pauper in the Higher World." All these simple truths are not acceptable to faint hearts and shriveled brains. But the broadened consciousness and the flaming heart rejoice at each obstacle as the tempering of the blade of the spirit. It is not an easy life, but a life tensed and saturated with difficulties that brings achievement; therefore, it is so very important to learn to love obstacles and to find a special wise joy in the service of the Common Good.

* * *

I believe you will firmly follow the path you have chosen; therefore, I rejoice at your youth and your qualities. You will be able to bring much good to your motherland. You should never forget that everything is performed in Inscrutable Ways. Look vigilantly into events; the clouds are gathering, but somewhere there is the glow of the dawn.

15

15 April 1936

Your considerations about karma are quite correct. If people thought less about karma and more about the purity and perfecting of their feelings and thoughts, they would succeed more completely. The very fear of creating new karma is in itself harmful, for it paralyzes our energy, the accumulation of which is a guarantee of overcoming the very same karma. Many most monstrous distortions may be observed in connection with the understanding of karma. One meets some fanatics in the East who, from fear of complicating their own personal karma by interfering in the destiny of their fellow man, refuse to help him and sometimes even stand calmly down while someone drowns or perishes in fire, not realizing that precisely this refusal of help heavily encumbers their karma. Who can tell when and where we repay an old debt? Only an Arhat knows when and where not to interfere; as for ourselves, we should offer a helping hand whenever our heart prompts us. But, of course, in everything commensurability must be practiced. Therefore, it is not the engenderment of new karma that should be feared, but its quality should be of concern. *Insignificant* karma will bring *insignificant* possibilities, whereas karma of great responsibility, although very burdensome, alone brings great achievements in the future. Therefore, people must not avoid actions and responsibilities, but rather should think of how to perfect their motives and qualities.

* * *

One cycle is already ended. Let us strive into the future. A new and glorious page of history is now being written. Please realize with your heart that the nation's consciousness is awakening for labor in common, for participation in constructiveness, for new love of the motherland, and for ripened thirst for knowledge. There are many beautiful signs. Watch these signposts. Verily, a "Palace of Unparalleled Beauty" is promised, and the signs of prosperity remain constant over the country. Thus, amidst the chaos of destruction, the predestined is being safeguarded, and many things are already taking the right direction. Events are hastening. Be courageous and in love and trust direct your heart toward the Great Teacher. The Forces of Light will turn everything toward the Good. Inscrutable are the Ways.

* * *

You have pointed out beautifully that the improvement of the people's condition is not just because of changes in the norms of the government, but because of the changes (and I would call it perfectment) in the human thinking. Many old concepts are not suitable for the new national consciousness and are unfit to enter the dictionary of the future. The New World demands new concepts, new forms, and new definitions. All the events clearly indicate the direction of evolution. The epoch of work in common, cooperation in common, and collective solidarity of all workers without any class distinctions is now being created. And the most essential problem which humanity is now facing is precisely the synthesizing of the spiritual with the material, the individual with the universal, and the private with the public welfare. Only when the one-sidedness of the narrow, material, earthly experiments shall be realized, will the next step come—the striving to unify *the material world with the Subtle World*. And the new achievements in science, new explorations, and discoveries of the laws of psychic energy will demand from humanity not a renunciation of the "heavens," but a new revelation and understanding of them.

Indeed, the discovery of the laws of psychic energy will help to establish a new direction of life; then the unity of the worlds will become evident. Verily, the future world, the Higher World, will arrive in the accoutrements of the laboratory rays. Precisely, in the laboratories the advantages of the higher energy will be proven, and through this will come not only the confirmation of the superiority of the radiations of men compared to all other rays yet known but, parallel with it, the difference in the *quality* of such radiations will be clearly revealed; in this way the significance of spirituality will be fully demonstrated. Technique will be subordinated to the spirit, resulting in the perception of higher laws, and hence the attainment of higher aims, which will lead to the transformation of the whole of material nature. The transformed nature, and the transformed spirit of the people will in turn prompt the creation of new, better forms of the structure of life. And only then will the newly arisen striving toward the Hierarchic Principle be correctly understood, striving that now finds its expression in an infatuation with "leadership." However, "leadership"—the elected one and servant of the crowd, is usually deprived of synthesis, because the masses actually do not admit synthesis. Therefore, the fad of leadership is a caricature of true leadership. The leader, or he who leads, must be the bearer of spiritual synthesis.

Beautiful are the words you wrote, "not only subordination but also power and leadership should be considered as service, and only as such can they be justified." Verily, all power should be first of all—service. Power is sacrifice. And when the leaders of the future shall be filled with the spirit of true service, then a new degree of evolutionary structure of life will approach. The leaders will then rule in complete accord with the Cosmic Magnet, which is the bond and communion with the Higher World in the order of Be-ness.

Thus, you may well emphasize that the character of the future order of life will be based on the realization by the people of Great Service for the General Good. Not I but *we*—here is the key to future achievement!

And now, several remarks. Usually there are two kinds of the elect—from two worlds. The Elect of the Higher World will affirm, whereas the offspring of the masses will deny, for the engenderment of the masses is not effectual. Try to put together all the hopes and strivings of the masses, and they will amount to a pile of motley rags. The masses are still unable to coordinate their wishes. In connection with this, reread paragraphs 445, 446, and 447 in *Fiery World III*.

The Ruling Principle of the Universe is one of Harmony and Love—God is Love. Therefore, if we wish to embody the most ancient axiom, "as above, so below," we should become unified precisely upon this principle of Love and should be subordinate to it, regarding it as our only boundless Ruler. But if, nevertheless, we make the attempt to apply human concepts to the structure of the Universe, it will be closer to "Eidocracy" (in the Platonic sense as an "example" or ideal and moral "prototype") or ideal democracy, than to a limited monarchy. Certainly, since no organism, no structure can exist without the Hierarchic principle, the heavenly Eidocracy must also have its own Hierarchy, but this Hierarchy is lost in Infinity.

Esoteric Science states that the world is governed by Cosmic Mind, which is an *aggregate* of the Minds of the Highest Hierarchies. The term *personal* is *absolutely* unsuitable to this principle, and so is the concept of power.

In the Heavenly Hierarchy nobody is appointed, everything is achieved. Indeed, in Cosmos there is an immutable subordination of the lower to the Higher; in this lies the basis of evolution. Reread attentively the book *Infinity*.

* * *

There is no need to see the emanations of people. That ought to be done by means of physical photography. Indeed, it is very difficult on the earthly plane to see the human aura at will, for everything requires special conditions. It is impossible to transfer all the conditions of the Subtle World to the earthly plane. It would be unbearable to suddenly see the auras of everything that surrounds us!

* * *

"Some people dream that the rulers of the future will be able to read the thoughts of people who come in contact with them, and, through clairaudience, not only hear the opinions of people close to them but also of those who are far away. ... A perfect knowledge of the universal laws must be the essential quality of future rulers."

It is possible that when our planet enters the Seventh Round and the Seventh Race, we shall have such rulers, but in the near future we shall have to be satisfied with much more modest demands. Even Buddha (according to the Pali Suttas) never claimed the omniscience which was attributed to him by his disciples and followers: "Those who told thee, ... that the Teacher Gotama knows all, sees all, and asserts His possession of limitless powers of foresight and knowledge and says, 'In motion or immobility, in vigilance or sleep, always and in all omniscience dwells in me,' those people do not say what I said, they accuse me despite all truth."

Even a perfect Arhat, when in an earthly environment, is able to use *all* his spiritual attainments only while in a certain state. That explains why the Great Teachers require seclusion.

Thus, let us be modest in our expectations of the leaders, rulers, and judges of the future. It will be excellent if they possess well developed straight-knowledge, which will help them to correctly assess the true essence of each work and event, and if they will always be guided by the voice of the heart balanced by the intellect. We affirm that the pearl of strength of the future leader will be in his communion with the Hierarchy by means of psychic energy. Thus, psychic energy is the key to all achievements and to the solutions of all problems, for the psychic sphere concerns all the planes of Being.

However, some concrete advice could be given by pointing out that justice signifies a high standard of nobility in government. Judges should undergo tests regarding the perception of the human heart. One could also indicate the necessity for adaptability of laws and accelerating the processes of the Courts of Law. Nothing is more dreadful than dead laws, for in the Cosmos each law is, primarily, goal-fitting. There are as many laws as there are degrees of consciousness.

Attention should be called briefly to the possibilities that will open before humanity when the laws of psychic energy are discovered, and also to what an extent the discovery of the conditions of help through psychic energy will renovate all of life, will facilitate the construction of life, and will provide solutions for the most complicated problems.

16

16 April 1936

I looked through your questions, and it seems to me that my answers this time will satisfy you even less, but I beg you once more to take into consideration that many things *cannot be* trusted to paper. The sacred Teaching ceases to be such the moment it is written in a popular style or language.

And now for your questions:

1. Not only are the keys to many of the mysteries of the zodiac lost but, properly speaking, also to almost all the mysteries of Existence. It is said in *The Secret Doctrine* that in this work the key was given one turn, but for complete knowledge it needs to be turned seven times. Yet judging by the questions that some people ask after they have read *The Secret Doctrine*, we may say that they have not accomplished even the first turn of the key. The knowledge of all the seven keys is the knowledge of the Arhat. But even the second turn of the key already pertains to esoteric knowledge and must be discovered by the disciple himself. Everything should be achieved independently, and if the intuition of a disciple helps him to find the truth, the Teacher must confirm it. Such is the rule.

2. Do I agree with the article "How to Utilize the Solar Energy"? The article itself is interesting and contains much correct information. It is quite true that modern man has even forgotten how to breathe correctly, therefore, some exercises in rhythmical breathing, provided the air is pure, will bring nothing but benefit. However, the danger of public instruction in such exercises is that ignorant people may begin to exaggerate them; this may cause an influx of blood to some particular

center, which may often be situated in a diseased organ and thus could cause radical worsening of its condition. In all mechanical exercises there must be a careful regulation of the blood pressure, for much trouble develops, owing to unbalanced tension. As a matter of fact, in order to avoid the danger of blood pressure, which inevitably follows the opening of the centers, the yogis withdraw from crowded localities and retreat to the mountains, where they stay on great heights. Thus, the process of the opening of the centers is accompanied by great dangers and cannot take place without a lengthy preparation of the organism. Indeed, sometimes it is even necessary to draw off an excess of blood, but, of course, this is possible only if the disciple is under the special observation of a Great Teacher who knows the course of the inner processes of the disciple.

Therefore, knowing all these dangers, I am against broad, enticing advertising that promises how to become a superman through mechanical exercises! Indeed, ignorant people are attracted by these methods, and, as a result, often awaken their dormant mediumistic potentialities, or lower psychism (spirituality is never achieved through any mechanical methods), and thus they become the victims of various obsessors of different caliber. At present, both the Eastern and Western worlds are flooded with cheap books proclaiming how to develop one's hidden powers. But not one of those most harmful publications even points out at the same time the dangers connected with the methods broadcasted. Therefore, it is a pity that the author of the excellent article you have sent does not mention the necessity for caution.

3. If synarchy is understood as co-rule by the best minds possessing spiritual synthesis, who can be against it? The Universal Synarchic Union is realized in the higher worlds.

4. What is *Tactica Adversa*? The Great Minds, before carrying out a certain plan, foresee and take into consideration all the worst possible circumstances and conditions with which they may have to deal. Thus, when both the active ill will and the wavering free will of the fireflies, or the "lukewarm ones", have been taken into account, there can be no failure. The plan is then fulfilled regardless of any circumstance. The evil ones and the dark ones, while thinking that they construct a prison, actually build a temple. Verily the Jinn build temples. Thus, we can say—praise to the enemies.

5. Of course you realize that there must be special reasons why, in some paragraphs of the Teaching, only the first initials of certain names are used. But in order not to disappoint you entirely, I can tell you that S. G. are the initials of the Comte St. Germain, and L. of Louis XVI. The other I cannot disclose.

6. The International Government is the Invisible Government, the Hierarchy of Light—Jacob's Ladder.

7. The Wings of Alaya? Alaya—the Universal Soul—in its mystic sense is identical with *Akasa* and in its essence with *Mulaprakriti*, for it is the root of all things. Each individual soul conforms with the Universal Soul.

It seems that I have answered your questions, as much as one can trust to the mail. If it would not make it too difficult, I would like to have some idea about your work, for this will give me the key to a better understanding of your consciousness, and in the future I can better coordinate my answers with your questions.

Consciousness is growing, and the quests of the spirit and heart are expanding. In spite of the aggressiveness of the old and outworn consciousnesses, a new comprehension is setting its path. All the dams can only temporarily hold back this current; and it will be all the more powerful when it breaks through. Everything in the Cosmos lives and changes. The foundation and essence of Consciousness is an eternal movement. Following this principle of motion, the New World strives in concordance with the Cosmic Magnet, which indicates the way through the Dictates of Be-ness.

17

17 April 1936

Although I am touched by your vigilance, I must tell you that the defense of the Teaching should be expressed, not by criticism or condemnation of others, but, first of all, by applying the covenants in one's personal life. As usual, the best defense and the strongest conviction are brought to bear by concrete example. Therefore, the criticism of the article "The Solar Path" is baseless. You say that " The Solar Path" is presented by the author as "a path of negation," but indeed I did not get this impression from the article. In accordance with the general sense of the article negation is given a positive aspect. All statements cited correspond to the Eastern concept, which sees true reality only in Brahman, and considers the whole manifested world from a negative aspect as Maya, as something transitory and therefore having no real being. Likewise, in the second paragraph on page 10, the author only paraphrases the Eastern thought, namely, that the whole world is nothing but the play of the Divine Mother or, as the Buddhists call it, the Great Stream.

You are indignant at the statement, "The Solar path negates time, space, etc." Yet with a broadened consciousness time and space acquire an entirely different significance and dimension. Ordinary earthly dimensions are not applicable where the union of the worlds has taken place. Besides, what is said above fully corresponds with the words of the Teaching that "neither time nor space exist between united consciousnesses and hearts." Who of the truly spiritual people has not experienced and is not aware of this transcendental truth!

Likewise, the Hierarchy is not denied by the author. Does he not say on page 9, "Therefore, whoever follows it [the Solar path], with equal love and reverence embraces all, past, present, and future, known and unknown, cosmic solar Co-workers and Creators of the General Good—he will always stand before Them all, realizing that sometime he also will enter Their ranks."

In truth, it is so; he who loves and reveres and embraces them all—the Creators of the General Good—also accepts the Hierarchy of Light.

It is also right that the one who in his heart bears love and reverence does not need a school (as it now exists), for truly the Great Brothers disclose to the approaching brother the meaning of the manifestations of life and teach him to read the book of Great Mother Nature. The bee gathering honey is the most ancient symbol of discipleship.

And again, further on, "The Solar path knows no leadership save the inner guide of its divine spirit." But all the Eastern Teachings, as well as that of the Living Ethics, instruct us to develop our straight-knowledge by all means, otherwise there can be no progress. Indeed, Higher Leadership lies not in constant commands, but in hints, in solicitous leading of the consciousness toward the given milestones so that nothing violates the independent achievement, which alone has value. Also, when the disciple is receptive, the invisible touches of the spirit kindle the fires in him. All is based on mutual help and collaboration. Thus, the author of this article adds, "The principle of mutual help enriches those who follow it, and therefore each one is assured of visible and invisible active help from all."

Can the principle of Higher Leadership be expressed more clearly than this?

"The Solar path knows no organizations and societies." The meaning of this is that the path of truth, the higher path, exists above all organizations and societies, since it includes all seekers of the General Good, all those who have chosen the Higher Service, thus it excludes limitations and fanaticism.

And again: "The Solar path invisibly unites in one Brotherhood all those who follow it." This is a very precise definition—truly *invisibly*, in the spirit. It is likewise true that "only an individual consciousness can guage it."

Those who do not understand this article, also do not understand the foundations of the Eastern Teachings, whence the entire Western occultism has come. True, a peculiarity of these occult or esoteric teachings is that in order to understand them one has either to have rich experience from the past or to seriously study and acquire the history of human thought.

And now regarding the article by Vivekananda. When you criticize Vivekananda for his seeming approval of acquiring wealth, you forget that he referred on these very same pages to the duty of the householder, the builder of life, but not to that of the hermit, or spiritual teacher. Each position in life brings its own obligation, or duty and responsibility; and it is hardly possible to apply the measure of a spiritual teacher to a builder of life. Commensurability and goal-fitness are cosmic laws, and if violated, chaos results. Moreover, Vivekananda suggests, first of all, the acquisition of knowledge, and only then, of wealth. The whole sense is in this word *then*. With knowledge, in the way a Hindu understands it, wealth would also become a blessing, for it would serve not just personal aims but the General Good. Learn to read with a consciousness enlightened by the heart. The dead letter deadens the mind!

I shall quote here a parable from the life of Buddha. " ... Anathapindika, a man of incalculable wealth, called 'the supporter of the orphans and the friend of the poor.'... Hearing that Buddha was stopping in the bamboo grove near Rajagriha, ... set out in that very night to meet the Blessed One. And the Blessed

One perceived at once the pure heart of Anathapindika and greeted him with words of comfort.

"Anathapindika said, 'I see that Thou art Buddha, the Blessed One, and I wish to open to Thee my whole mind. Having listened to my words advise me what I shall do. My life is full of work and, having acquired great wealth, I am surrounded with cares. Yet do I enjoy my work and I apply myself to it with all diligence. Many people are in my employ and depend upon the success of my enterprises. Now I have heard your disciples praise the bliss of the hermit and denounce the unrest of the world. "The Holy One," they say, "has given up His kingdom and His inheritance and has found the path of righteousness, thus setting an example to all the world of how to attain Nirvana." My heart yearns to do what is right and to be a blessing to my fellow beings. Let me then ask you, must I give up my wealth, my home and my business enterprises, and like Thee, choose homelessness in order to attain the bliss of the righteous life?'

"And the Buddha replied, 'The bliss of the righteous life is attainable by everyone who walks in the noble eightfold paths. He who is attached to wealth had better cast it away than allow his heart to be poisoned by it; but he who does not cleave to wealth, and who, possessing riches, uses them rightly, will be a blessing to his fellow-beings. I say to thee, remain in thy station of life and apply thyself with diligence to thy enterprises. It is not life and wealth and power that enslave men, but their attachment to life and wealth and power. The bhikshu who retires from the world to lead a life of leisure derives not profit. For a life of indolence is an abomination, and want of energy is to be despised. The Dharma of the Tathagata does not require that a man choose homelessness or resign the world, unless he feels called upon to do so; but the Dharma of the Tathagata requires each man to free himself from the illusion of self, to cleanse his heart, to give up his thirst for pleasure, and to lead a life of righteousness.

" 'And whatever men do, whether they remain in the world as artisans, merchants, and officers of the King, or retire from the world and devote themselves to a life of religious meditation, let them put their whole heart into their task, let them be diligent and energetic. And if they are as the lotus, which, growing in water, yet remains untouched by water, if they struggle in life without cherishing envy or hatred, if they live in the world a life, not of self, but a life of truth, then surely joy, peace, and bliss will dwell in their minds.'"

Similarly, the article by Vivekananda is also full of the spirit of goal-fitness in everything.

* * *

One should not worry overmuch about beginners. They will stumble, for this stumbling is inevitable, upon the next steps also. One thing, however, should be reiterated—in everything avoid the dead letter and one-sided judgment.

* * *

Be careful regarding certain pains, and do not necessarily think them to be sacred pains. You are still young, and many sacred pains would be premature. Moreover, the atmosphere of the city is not favorable for such manifestations. Therefore, I ask you to take good care of your health. At present, the warriors of Light must fight day and night, because Armageddon is frightful. Therefore, be careful, and do not allow any excesses, for they will lead nowhere but to the ruin of your health. Spirituality can be achieved only by the purification of thoughts and by labor. Strive upon this highest and shortest path.

* * *

Events are piling up, and everything accelerates accordingly. Judases, Cassiuses, and Brutuses in modern images are inevitable on the Path of Light. No Teaching ever entered life without being attacked by the hosts of darkness, and the same thing takes place today. Verily, the dark ones assist the manifestation of each work of Light; hence, we know the value of all obstacles and even of slander. Long ago, N. K. wrote an article, "Praise to the Enemies." Each betrayal gives an opportunity to all faithful co-workers and friends to be united even more closely. There will be all sorts of actions, even up to and including betrayal, but on the earthly plane such manifestations are necessary. The victory of Light over darkness must be revealed

I recall a well-aimed remark by one of the contemporaries of H. P. Blavatsky, "In spite of all that was written about H. P. B., she was never embarrassed by any slander, for she knew the value of the drumhead." *Thus, let the drums beat.* And in the Teaching, there are already enough definitions of slander. Let us not fear!

But I must tell you frankly—I am amazed at the hostility of certain people mentioned by you. Surely, nothing can be built on malice. Wherever there is malice and hatred, there is deadly deterioration. One feels like telling them, "Why blind yourselves by a bloody fog of malice?" Thus they may overlook many useful possibilities. But may God help them! As for ourselves, let us radiantly and joyously continue our work, for while the slander grows, the ranks of friends are generously swelled by new, valuable co-workers. Never before have we received so many and such fiery letters from our friends, and often from quite unknown people. All takes place in Inscrutable Ways. The year that was predicted long ago began in thunder and lightning. But after a thunderstorm, the atmosphere is purified.

I shall end this letter with a quotation from the Buddhist *Anguttara Nikaya*: "Warriors, warriors, for indeed such we are. We are fighting for noble courage, for high strivings, for the highest wisdom. Therefore, we call ourselves warriors."

18

2 April 1936

The thoughts you expressed about a symbol are very beautiful and quite true—the Chalice of Amrita, the Chalice of Beauty and Attainment, the Chalice—the Holy Grail! The legend about the Chalice—the Grail—also came from the East as one of the versions of a great spiritual achievement and the very same mysterious Shambhala. Incidentally, some investigators of the symbolism connected with the Grail perceive in this Chalice the Stone, which is at present in the world, accompanying historic events; later it is supposed to return to the "Heart" of Asia. This interpretation is also close to the truth. But the Chalice itself does exist, and before the beginning of a new era, it is sent to where the Teaching of Kalachakra shall be affirmed. Many legends exist about this Chalice. One of these says that the Chalice always comes unexpectedly and through the air. Thus, at the proper time, it was brought to the Lord Buddha. The origin of this Chalice is Egyptian, and its antiquity goes back to some twelve thousand years B.C. After the death of Buddha, this Chalice was for some time in a temple in Karashahr, from which it disappeared, and since then has been guarded in

Shambhala. According to all the legends, this Chalice will again appear before the New Epoch of Maitreya.

And now—the serpent that is entwined around the Chalice also signifies a belt, and, as you know, in ancient days the belt was regarded as a sign of dignity, power, and the greatest trust, even more than the ring. Thus, in these symbols we can see cosmic significance as well as practical application: The Covenant of the Times, the Great Advent, the Epoch of Fire and Regeneration of the Spirit, Wisdom and Synthesis, the Chalice of Achievement and Immortality, the signs of the Highest Trust, and the Call, which is clothed in purple, the color of valor.

Likewise, excellent are your thoughts regarding the Universal Symphony. Verily, each spirit resounds to its own tone, and nothing can be compared with the beauty of these sounds. The one who has heard the music of the spheres has the right to say in the words of the Teaching, "The former song will become the noise of the wheel."

Of course it is true that the primary aspect of Manifestation is the Divine Tremor in the Bosom of the Great Mother. Tremor, or vibration is, at the same time, Light, for Light is the movement of Matter, and it creates forms. "In the beginning was the Word, and the Word was with God. ... In him was life; and the life was the light of men." In this statement is the whole profundity of the sacred knowledge.

You ask whether it is possible to understand the indication regarding the appearance of Christ in lesser images and in reality. Certainly. Medievalism made an inaccessible idol of Christ and deprived him of any humanity, therefore also of divinity. Thus, all the Teachings of the East proclaim that there is no god (or gods) who was not at one time a man. Such a forced separation of Christ from human essence threatened and still threatens a complete break in the communion of humanity with the Higher World. One can trace how in the Middle Ages there appeared every now and then great saints who tried to re-establish this almost lost communion, and all of them insisted precisely on the *human* essence of Christ. Especially strong affirmations of this can be found in the pages of the autobiography of St. Theresa, the Spanish saint of the sixteenth century, and still earlier, in the visions and writings of St. Catherine of Siena and St. Gertrude. Thus, the form and the quality of the visions and communications received through such communion always *correspond* with the level of the consciousness of those who see and receive them, and also with the needs of the time. As it was said, "It is precisely by following the character of the visions that the best history of the intellect may be written."

I strongly recommend that all read the autobiography of St. Theresa. In spite of the fact that this work went through the "spiritual" censorship of the Church, some amazing pages have been preserved. By propagating the dogma of Jesus Christ as the *only begotten* Son of God, the Church contradicts the very sense of the prayer given to us by Jesus Christ himself, "Our Father which art in heaven." And also the words of the Scriptures, "So God created man in his own image." (Genesis 1:27)

Thus, by claiming the exclusiveness of *sonship* and divine *origin* for Jesus Christ, the Church, by that very claim, forever divorced him from mankind. From this came a whole train of grave events; the exclusion of Jesus Christ from the life of humanity, the obliteration of his human Sacrifice and the awful suggestion implying that the death of Christ on the Cross saved humanity from "original" sin (?!) and from all subsequent sins. Thus: "As a phantasm he roams the earth while his body is imprisoned in the Church in conventionalized figures. We must find his body in the world, and that which is imprisoned in the Church we must set free."*

You also ask whether there is a trace of psychism in the tears that sometimes come from inner exaltation during the reading of the Teaching. Certainly the exaltation experienced by the heart during the reading of the Teaching cannot be considered as a manifestation of psychism in its lower aspect.

Yet one must watch oneself, for one can become so absorbed in the sweet savor of such feeling that imperceptibly one might lose control over one's senses and thus be deprived of the ability to work. There have been such cases, and therefore all the Teachings indicate the necessity for balance and a complete discipline of one's emotions. There was a time when I also wanted to dwell on the exaltations of the spirit and to cognize the mysteries of cosmogony. And then I was reminded of the present grave times: "Again thou hast forgotten the Heavenly combat. None go to school during the assault of the enemies, etc." Thus I was

---

* Dmitri Merezhkovsli, *Jesus the Unknown* (New York: Charles Schribner's Sons, 1934) p. 47.

turned back to Earth and earthly activities from my exaltations. And I was trained to find joy in the most tiresome routine work, to verily bring each task to the altar of the service of love. All the warriors of Light will feel particularly close to the "Book of Sacrifice." Thus, beautiful are the exaltations of the spirit, but we must be on guard in order that they shall not weaken our energy, but strengthen it. The time will come when a certain isolation will be permissible for the exaltation of the spirit, but at present the time is threatening, and all who are in the Great Service are called upon to make use of their weapons—the battle is unprecedented!

"The time of action is but begun. Comprehend devotion, faith and courage. I shall safeguard thee with a helmet of faith, an armor of devotion, and a shield of victory. And on the banner shall be inscribed: Love, the Conqueror,"

At present, all those yogis who attempt to attain Samadhi are regarded as deserters by the Great Teachers.

* * *

You ask how to understand the words from the book *Leaves of Morya's Garden I*, "But the daughter of the world ... will join the pieces of this Raiment." Indeed, it could also be understood in the way you interpret it, for it is true that in the coming Sixth Race the tissues of the physical body will become more refined and rarefied and will approach what is called figuratively the densified astral body. It is interesting to note that this process of rarefaction, or dematerialization, of the physical body is also pointed out in the most ancient Chinese Medicine. So-called asceticism played a great part in it, but like everything forced, it did not bring the desired results.

19

24 April 1936

First I shall answer your last letter, for you have touched upon a certain question which should be cleared up so that it will not become an obstacle on your path.

If my explanations are not sufficient, write me, and I shall try to explain in more detail, as far as the present conditions of the mail will allow. But now I appeal to your heart and ask you,

Could you bear to inflict upon fine young souls, and even your dear ones, a great danger?

You know that the task of the books of Living Ethics is to broaden the consciousness by every means, and therefore in the first book—*The Call*, the foundation for this task is already given. In short formulas, everything is told and set forth in that book. I suggest that you reread it attentively, at least, pages 72 and 73

The New World is coming, and it can be assimilated only by a new consciousness. Destructions and sacrilegious denial of great concepts are disgusting, for they are engendered by chaos and ignorance. But as there are no effects without causes, let us look back, and honestly, without prejudice, call to mind and investigate the historical records. Even if they were compiled by earthly minds, maybe an enlightened consciousness will be able to clarify them.

You are rightfully indignant at the Jesuitic formula, "The end justifies the means," this formula is particularly frightful, since those who accept it do not hesitate to use the most revolting means for the achievement of purely *personal* and *covetous* aims. But all the Teachings, even Christianity, justified a sacred concealment when it was used for safeguarding holy things, for saving a fellow man, or for the General Good. Whence came the esotericism of all the Teachings? Each new disclosure of the truth, each new discovery of science always has to be concealed from ignorant minds. Let us think of all the terrors of the Inquisition, all the wars caused by new Revelations! Whence came all those most complex symbols in the works of the prophets and great workers in science, at whom ignoramuses will sneer, but who nevertheless evoke profound amazement and admiration from those who even partially discern their deep meaning. Unfortunately for humanity, the key to many of these is lost, and only the rarest of minds find this key and are able to turn it at least once or twice. I think that at the present time, there is no one on Earth able to turn this key the entire seven times. The whole Mystery is preserved in the Stronghold of Knowledge.

If, in the Middle Ages, the *Akasa* of the alchemists was personified by the image of the Heavenly Virgin, and Jehovah and other sacred names and definitions hid the secrets of the structure of the human brain and organism, *modern times* require *different* images and veiling. Life is complicated, and only the one who comprehends *all its complexity* is able to receive the knowledge.

Thus, each evolutionary thought that indicates the direction of a coming epoch was always met, and now meets with frightful *resistance* from people whose consciousnesses are obscure and immobile; hence come all the terrors of disgusting excesses.

Therefore, when something is given which directs toward the *General Good*, one must manifest all the broadness of an enlightened consciousness. Thinkers have always been persecuted, but each such thinker is a focus, in which the thoughts that fill space are gathered and reflected in a contemporary garb. Thinkers are the seers of the future. From the books of Living Ethics you know how dreadful is a static consciousness; verily it causes deterioration, and, as it is said, the most terrible cataclysms and earthquakes cannot be compared with the catastrophe of a deteriorated consciousness.

Thus, think of *all the causes* that have brought on the effects that now set the whole world atremor. Try to investigate each manifestation from all angels, and especially beware of *one-sided, prejudiced* judgment, both of persons and of any and all events of life.

* * *

The Silver Lotus is to be found in the heart, and one sometimes is able to see it within oneself. Bear in mind that we see within ourselves all the fires and rings of the centers in the place where this or that center is aflame. Sometimes fiery rings, hoops or wheels, or suns are seen and at times, a flame, but all this is mostly *within oneself.*

The Silver Lotus can be even larger in size than a flower, and the tongues of flame form petals, as it were.

* * *

Let the heart speak, and may it not dare to blaspheme against the most pure and the Inaccessibly High! The true disciple trusts the Leading Hand, and no hen's evidence is able to confuse him, for he knows.

20

29 May 1936

I am sending you my entire faith that you will accept the spiritual heritage of F. D. [Lukin] and will personify his symbol, that of the Leader of the Heart. Let all those who seek Light and who are overburdened by grief find response in your heart; and let all those who have gathered under your guidance feel that heartfelt sympathy which warms one even in spite of stern criticism. Indeed, the most difficult art is to create the right relations between people. No single art requires so much patience, tolerance, and refined sensitiveness. One should learn to penetrate into the consciousnesses, the hearts, and moods of all those who surround and come to us; it is necessary to feel the fundamental undertone upon which one can be united with them and unite them with others.

However, if the great magnet of love lies in the heart, everything will be made easier, since the sincerity of this feeling can conquer the most hardened hearts. To the heart that has touched Beauty this language of the heart must be close; therefore, I have faith in you—a Leader of the Heart.

Please give my most hearty gratitude to the nearest co-workers, who have expressed their readiness to fully collaborate with and help you in all the tasks of the society. Let every member of the society feel that his true home and his spiritual abode is within the walls of the society. Let each one be not only a welcome co-worker but also a member of one spiritual family; and let each one personally learn to give the very best in him for the benefit of all. Thus, let Love, the Unifier, be the motto for the new cycle of the society.

21

14 May 1936

You are quite right in saying that personal burdens are easier to bear when we face some great task and are responsible for others; nevertheless, I am deeply touched by your courage.

We are most happy to hear about the development of the activity of the society. In view of the dreadful disorganization now taking place all over the world, each united, constructive effort based on the furtherance of the foundations of Living Ethics is, verily, a light in the desert. It is horrible to observe all attempts of darkness directed toward the corruption and disruption of consciousness.

I approve of your excellent decision to establish a philosophical section. Truly, for the battle with the dark forces, it is necessary to be fully armed, and certainly, augmented knowledge is indeed a most powerful shield and weapon. In this connection I am answering your question as to whether the versatility of Leonardo Da Vinci might be taken as a worthy example for emulation. Indeed, yes, providing there is real study and not a superficial diffusion. It is a fact that an advanced disciple possesses certain abilities. Even in the Buddhist scriptures it is said that each Bodhisattva should possess the mastery of three arts, or fields of knowledge, and be perfected in one of them. The more we know, the better we are able to perceive all the depth and dimensions of the great plan of evolution and all the complexity of life's structure. Moreover, each systematic study brings to us that discipline of mind which is essential for independent thinking. And only he who is able to think independently can become an active servant and co-worker of the Forces of Light. That is why a versatile education is so important.

It is certainly not possible to become a specialist in all spheres of knowledge and art, but it is essential to have at least some understanding of them. Also, in our desire to embrace as much as possible we must learn to co-measure our forces, and chiefly to be able to continue what has already been started; for only in this way can the most essential qualities of discipleship, such as constancy and patience, be developed.

You mention that a member of the society asks whether the events in the world at present will lead to the Common Good. I must say that I firmly believe that whatever happens leads to good in the long run. Lessons must be learned in order that consciousnesses may advance further. Everything is created by people themselves, and cruel national disasters are the results of many centuries of causes and effects. All over the world, a great sifting is taking place, and a new balance of the world *is being established*. Thus we may say, all is for the best. You ask how the following statement from *Leaves of Morya's Garden* can be understood, "Karma will overtake one, but its quality may be altered by a voluntary sacrifice to unknown people." Imagine that someone caused suffering to his dear one and repented of his conduct when that dear one had already passed into the other world. Not being able to expiate his guilt or atone to the wronged one, he can nevertheless actually improve his karma by a voluntary sacrifice to other people, and, as it has been said, "to unknown people." True, karma will sometime overtake him and bring him face to face with his victim, but the redemption will be of a higher quality, because his whole being will have been elevated by the voluntary sacrifice.

And now, with regard to mint. All kinds of mint can be used both externally and internally. In India, where there are so many intestinal diseases, essence of mint is widely used. Combined with magnesia, it is one of the best remedies. It also helps during inflammation of the centers. During the summer months, I am never without menthol and rub it thickly over the whole of my face and the back of the head, since I cannot endure heat, even in the mountains. Mint tea is definitely a good disinfectant, and in certain kinds of asthma it is also very helpful to inhale the steam from mint. The entities of the lower strata of the Subtle World do not like the smell of mint, therefore it is useful to keep it as a plant in the house.

"The Lord of Compassion" is a title of the coming Maitreya, but it could be equally applied to all the great Sons of Light. Everyone is free to choose and follow the Image that is closer to him. The concept of the unity of all that exists is the knowledge of an Arhat. But people who are blinded by the illusion of selfhood and isolation are unable to embrace the whole beauty of this Truth, and thus all the Higher Concepts are reflected in their consciousness as in turbulent muddy waters and lose all clearness, transparency and beauty.

Gupta Vidya means the Secret Knowledge. Gupta—secret, vidya—knowledge.

The Alberichs are the servants of darkness. In "The Ring of the Nibelungs" the dark force is personified in Alberich, the adversary of the resplendent Gods of Valhalla; he seized the Gold of the Rhine and was an accomplice in the slaying of Siegfried.

A further question you ask is how the following sentence should be understood, "I shall assert the might of My Teachings upon those of limited mind." By "limited" is meant those who are deniers and are ignorant, for limitation is the result of ignorance. The power of Light will conquer darkness, and the power of the Teaching will pierce through ignorance.

Intuition, straight-knowledge, and the accumulations in the Chalice are certainly one and the same concept. There are cases, however, when Hiero-inspiration is taken for intuition.

But this, too, will not be an error, for without the accumulations of the Chalice, it is impossible to receive the ray of Hiero-inspiration.

You ask, "Where do all the betrayers come from?" This is but a sign of the significant period through which our planet is now passing. However, we know of the victory of Light.

"Victory will become evident within a certain time, but all the phases of the Battle should be accepted. Let us not forget that all the best Forces are gathered on Our side. Thus it will be possible to approach the next step. The servants of darkness will themselves help to bring success. It is necessary to understand how near are the dates, in order not to postpone new possibilities. There can be no resistance to the Forces of Light. If the forces of darkness take upon themselves the foul work—let them perform it. The greatest names and concepts are already involved. Everything can proceed only through expansion. ... Certainly the Battle is terrifying. ... Certainly with each day the New Forces, the Invisible Ones, are evoked. From such approaches to the earthly spheres the most unexpected tensions can take place. Let us accept the Battle with the united force of all Our participants. Unity will be the unconquerable Banner. Satan will be defeated, and his warriors will, as usual, abandon the field of battle. Who will understand the tension of the Forces of Light? Who will fail to take into consideration the extent of the battlefield? The united ashrams, the strongholds of spirit, are now needed more than ever before. ... The Teaching never entered the world without a struggle. Thus, let it enter as usual, otherwise people will forget it. But imagine the dimensions of the Battle, in which all the planets are involved. ... Thus, with all the strength of the spirit, and with all solemnity let us participate in the Battle of Light against darkness."

For the ascent of a new step it is essential to accept the battle and to surmount all obstacles. The drinking of the chalice of poison is inevitable on the last steps, and betrayal, like a shadow, must accompany the Light on the earthly path. Thus, let us accept this initiation also. But let us understand that the traitors act not only against us but against the whole Great Plan of Light.

Let us gather all our forces, and in unity enter upon a new step.

22

24 May 1936

You say you have only one wish—"to reach the Teacher, and if that is not possible, then to reach his disciple." I must say that I have not yet met anybody who, after learning something about the great White Brotherhood, has not attempted the search for it. But rarely, almost never, does one question himself as to whether he is ready spiritually and physically to endure that tension. Can his physical shell stand the awful tension of the atmosphere that surrounds this Stronghold? Only he can approach it who, here on Earth amidst the struggles and surmounting all possible difficulties, has outlived all habits and attachments and in self-sacrificing achievement has fierily transmuted his energies. Without going through the earthly purgatory it is impossible to enter Paradise. *The Fires of the Higher Energies would burn the overloaded aura.* Therefore, only one or, at the most, two people in a century ever reach this Stronghold. You also know that the Great Teachers never invade the karma of man, and therefore they make *no* exceptions. Karma can bring a man into Their Community, and if such karma is present, no one and nothing, except the man himself, can impede its fulfillment. Therefore, as best you can, apply in life all your aspirations and all the Covenants of the Teaching, and leave the rest to karma and to the great knowledge of the Lords.

We must likewise learn only in life, in the midst of the hardships of everyday living. The Community of the Brotherhood is too far removed from early conditions, and therefore it cannot provide the necessary touchstone for the spirit. The Teaching is given to us; each aspect of it is analyzed from all angles, and therefore we cannot say that we have no Teaching. Besides, there are the senior disciples who are always ready to explain what is not clear. The application of all the Covenants in life will actually prove to be the work of which you dream and which will quicken your path toward the Community of Light.

But do you really think that if you could get into the Ashram of the White Brotherhood, you would acquire the power to convince people? All historical examples prove the opposite. The complete assimilation of the Teaching is possible only for the spirit that has prepared itself for it during many centuries. This explains why the great Teachers of humanity have so very few disciples. For this same reason, the Teaching of Living Ethics advises *not* to entice anyone and *not* to force anything upon him. The Ocean of Wisdom is given to humanity, and the Teaching, like the sun, sends its rays everywhere—to the wise and to the foolish, to the good and to the bad. Each one can absorb and understand what is accessible to him, and to the limits of his growth; of course, the difference in the state of consciousnesses and understanding gives birth to those contradictions which immature spirits claim to see in all Teachings. However, this is unavoidable.

Now for your questions. Certainly, all achievements are stored potentially within us. In all Teachings it was and is sufficiently emphasized that man is the microcosm of all the Macrocosm, and undoubtedly the most powerful means for achievement is love for the Divine Principle and the Hierarchy of Light.

As for pranayama, you overestimate its significance. Correct breathing is always beneficial, but those exercises which are advocated by irresponsible self-styled yogis are extremely dangerous. I thought I had already written sufficiently about this, but apparently it is necessary to return to this question again. Therefore I shall once more remind you that only he who has completely purified his heart and his mental body from all earthly dross is able to enter the Holy of Holies of Yoga. *Without this purification, no pranayama, will help one to reach even the first gates of true knowledge.* Pranayama can develop mediumship, which would close the Gates. Long exercises in pranayama or in Hatha Yoga make the study of Raja Yoga *impossible.* All the psychic faculties that are developed by means of pranayama, means of the artificial stimulation of the physical and astral bodies, are limited to a *psychic plane*, and not by far a high one; this is proved by the quality of the visions of psychics and mediums. It is important to realize that psychism is *not spirituality.* Precisely, as is said in the Teaching, "Psychism is the antithesis of spirituality," and it only hinders the possibility of approaching the Great Teachers. That is why the Teaching begins and ends with the realm of spirit and so severely condemns all exercises for the development of lower psychism. No doubt, the path of spirituality, the royal path, is much more difficult and slow, but it is the *only* one that deposits all achievements in the Chalice. Those who follow this path have their psychic powers awakened *naturally* and they are developed on all the seven planes, *from the highest* to the lowest; and by fusing them into one this path upholds the great synthesis. No true Teacher will help a disciple to enter the astral spheres by way of mechanical exercises. One should have *no illusions* about this, for otherwise it might be easily possible to contact an entity from these spheres impersonating a Teacher. So many warnings about this were written by H. P. Blavatsky! This very fact created many enemies for her among mediums and psychics, but she fulfilled her ordained mission and pointed out the harm of spiritualism, due mainly to the ignorant approach to it of all classes of society. From my personal experience I know with what hostility all such indications and warnings are accepted.

* * *

Certainly, the ability to concentrate and to think creatively, provided the thought is pure, is not only very useful but is also necessary. Without the ability to think, it is impossible to progress in knowledge. Likewise, the development of will power, beginning with small daily matters and ending with high self-sacrificing action, is the foundation of every discipline and achievement.

Pure thinking, with the will directed toward the Good and self-purification, will certainly result in excellent emanations.

Having love and will you already possess striving and are therefore able to bring a prayer into action.

You are quite right in thinking that in cities exercises in pranayama may be dangerous. But since pranayama, as such, cannot give us spirituality, we should not concern ourselves with it. The most important thing is to train ourselves in purity of motive, thought, and deed, and we do this only amidst people and obstacles. Thus, even the city at times has its uses.

* * *

You appear to be worried about the attacks on the books of Living Ethics, but this also is inevitable. Not a single Teaching entered life without counterattacks. Similarly, the New Teaching must enter, accompanied by shouts and attacks from dying consciousnesses. Such is the earthly law. Humanity heeds and remembers only that which undergoes ostracism or martyrdom. I have often mentioned in my letters the statement by Vivekananda, and I shall repeat it again, that the reason humanity so well remembers Buddha and Christ is because they both were fortunate in having powerful enemies.

Thus, let the New Teaching come into the world and also be affirmed in the usual way, by persecution. Again and again, one must be reminded that the Teaching spreads by Inscrutable Ways. This is why I have always advised you *not to recruit followers*. I have also suggested that you organize cultural-educational gatherings, and only after getting to know people, to put into their consciousnesses a few new seeds. It is always advisable to enlarge our own treasury with knowledge. A well-disciplined, enlightened mind will more easily assimilate the Teaching of Light in all its manifold scope. Truly, a lack of knowledge is an obstacle on the path of evolution. "*Hell is ignorance*"—so said one of the great spirits of the early era of Christianity.

Verily, there is nothing more sacrilegious for human consciousness than to limit the Ineffable Grandeur of the Divine Principle that is poured out over the entire Universe. Assuredly, from this monstrous, ignorant belittling issue all the *unworthy concepts of God*. Man, in his conceit, tries to bring everything down to his own level and likeness. Enough is said about this in the books of the Teaching. Indeed, the books of the Teaching are full of concepts of the Divine Principle, or God, and of Spirit and spirituality. The line you have quoted, "The Spirit of Christ breathes across the desert of life," expresses that very same august pantheism, to which human thought cannot rise.

The God in us is the sole reality; all else, as beautifully and poetically expressed by the East, is but the "Play of the Great Mother of the World."

Yes, you are quite right in saying that not in a single book of the Living Ethics has the great Foundation of Being been abrogated; likewise, there is no disparagement of the concept of Christ (Chrestos), or of Jesus, who brought, and suffered for, that which had long since been known to the world, but which had been forgotten by people again and again. So it was, and is; but let us hope that it will not always be so.

And as far as the labels which the ignorant stick on everything that is above their understanding, who among serious-minded people pays attention to them? The same can be said about the attacks against us; we are used to them, and know their value. And, in truth, all these attacks have been beneficial. It is said in the Teaching, "without slander grateful humanity would have interred the most vital manifestations." Moreover, I beg you again and again not to be sorry for those who have fallen away—

these are immature souls. Leave them to follow their own path. One cannot serve two masters. Let them honestly choose, and avoid betrayal, for "the fate of even a small traitor is horrible!"

It is excellent that you are working on self-perfectment. How else can one become an apostle of Living Ethics, unless one proves by personal example the benefit and beneficence of the Teaching? Who can be attracted to the Teaching if the followers do not apply it in life?

Also, do not be troubled by slander. Slander is painful only if it comes from people whom we respect. Praise from unworthy people can only humiliate and offend.

You have a number of questions, I shall answer them in your order, but will not repeat them, since I presume you have kept a copy.

1. The Subtle World corresponds to the astral world, from the lowest to the highest strata.

2. The Fiery World is the world of the Spirit. The highest degree of the Fiery World is often called the Highest World.

3. All the psychic centers correspond to physical centers. Each organ has its own nerve center; some double organs, such as the kidneys, lungs, etc., also have double branches.

4. It is theoretically correct, but life reveals many variations. Many women are almost men, and men, almost women, spiritually as well as physically. Often, women have masculine magnetism and vice versa.

5. The mystery of the "Book of Lives" of the Highest spirits is sacredly preserved.

Indeed. in the true cosmogony there are no angels or archangels who were not, once upon a time, humans. This is fully confirmed by the entire East. "There is no God, or Gods, who was not at some time a man." If you have read *The Secret Doctrine*, you will remember that the Great Spirits, who in the East are known variously as the Sons of Light, the Sons of Reason, the Sons of Fire, the Kumaras, etc., correspond to our Christian archangels. Of course, these angels are not adorned with wings, which have been conferred upon them by the imperfect vision or poetic imagination of certain clairvoyants, who were anxious to inculcate this symbol of a Messenger. This symbol is not bad, and it is true that the rays that emanate from the centers of the shoulders might give the impression of shimmering wings, as it were. But if even we, the Earth-dwellers, can move through space in subtle bodies without these birdlike attributes, are the Highest Spirits in need of them? Alas, one more disappointment—the angels have no wings! Truly, the rays are much more beautiful than these ornithological appendages!

And so, the Guardian Angels, or the Great Brotherhood, these rulers of our planet, were High Spirits on other planets and Men-Gods on our Earth. Belonging to the higher evolution, They came to our Earth in order to accelerate the evolution of its humanity. Indeed, They are, in the full sense of the word, the Protectors, the Guardians, and the Saviors of our planet.

* * *

I rejoice with all my heart at your devotion to the Teaching of Living Ethics, for only through this can we achieve the opening of the Gates. I am also happy to hear what you say about your other co-workers. Let them temper their spirit through the achievements of every day. Let each labor, even the most monotonous and tiresome, be improved in its quality. The path of discipleship is full of thorns and hardships, mainly because of our old habits and attachments. Therefore, only the firm and fearless ones, those who have burned their selfhood in the fire of self-denial, will reach the destined Gates.

* * *

The year is passing; a most difficult year, which was indicated long ago as the year of the beginning of the battle between the Archangel Michael and the Dragon. The threatening Armageddon takes place on both planes—visible and invisible. The forces of darkness are fiercely attacking all the undertakings of Light, but we solemnly accept this battle, because we know for whom and for what we are fighting. And many illnesses are connected with the unheard of tension on both planes.

* * *

What you write about people is an old truth: In need we are remembered, in prosperity, we are forgotten. Also, what you say about obsession is most characteristic of our time, but please be careful, for there are certain degrees of obsession that are most contagious. All cases of obsession can be cured by the power of psychic energy in contact with the Higher Power. Certainly, auxiliary means, such as lofty music, wonderful aromas, purity of atmosphere, and the color of the room—all of which should harmonize with the tastes of the patient—can be very helpful. It is good to keep by the bedside during the night a vessel of hot water containing a few drops of eucalyptus oil, this is also useful during the day. Yet a severe case of obsession cannot be cured by any auxiliary means, only by the action of a pure and powerful psychic energy.

You are right about *The Call*. It does contain in concentrated formulas the ideas that are analyzed in more detail and from different angles in the later books of the Teaching. But it is in vain and incorrect to condemn and reject *The Mahatma Letters*. A. P. Sinnet wrote his *Esoteric Buddhism* based on these Letters. Their contents but more extensively treated, were also used in *The Secret Doctrine*. This volume of *Letters* is one of the greatest books, and it is fully appreciated in the West. To repudiate it is to deny the entire Teaching given through H. P. Blavatsky and all the books of Living Ethics as well. Unfortunately, only a few letters, or rather incomplete extracts from them, were used in the volume you mention. But alas, even in this form, as you can see, they are digested with difficulty by certain consciousnesses.

You are right in saying that Jesus Christ was an exceptional manifestation in history, but it can be equally said that not less exceptional were all the Kumaras, or Men-Gods. And only a conceited ignoramus will try to measure the respected statures of these Highest Spirits. An excellent formula is given us in the Teaching: "People will ask, 'Who is greater, Christ or Buddha?' Answer, 'It is impossible to measure the far-off worlds. We can only be enraptured by their radiance.'"

You write about the sadness of all the disputes and polemics about lofty concepts. This is perfectly true, but especially sad are the *ignorant polemics* that bring nothing but irritation. It is impossible to explain to others what is not clear to ourselves, nothing but harmful confusion will result. The exchange of thoughts between highly educated people is most creative, because from an exchange of ideas and contrasting opinions sparks of Truth are struck. Precisely, an *exchange of thoughts* is needed, not ignorant argument.

It is also true that incomplete statements in books often create an impression of contradiction to the superficial reader. Even the Great Teachers have been accused of such contradictions. But the accusers forget the most important factor, namely, their *own ignorance*. He who sees everywhere a call to atheism and Satanism is, verily, far from enlightenment, and none of your arguments will convince him. Those who were disconcerted by the book *The Foundations of a New World Contemplation* are to be pitied and left alone. And as for the clergy, they have even forgotten that in 1906, during the reign of Nicholas II, freedom of religious creed and *freedom of speech* were granted. Many of them would probably be glad to return to the times of religious intolerance and even to the *Domostroy*.* There are symptoms of this in some quarters. Thus, the author of the pamphlet, *The Orthodox World and Freemasonry*, was rewarded by an approving decree from the Synod—apparently for defaming the best sons of his country. Nevertheless, Light conquers darkness.

The new book, *Aum*, is now being published. Undoubtedly, those in the opposing camp will again raise a hue and cry, "Why this pagan term? How dare they compare divine Bliss with the heathen *Aum*?" etc. To this we may answer, "Leave ignorance to yourself," and we shall quote the lines from the Teaching: "If scholars were told of magnetized water, they accept such an expression; but if you speak about enchanted or bewitched water, you will be classed with the ignorant. Whereas, the distinction is only in name, for in essence the same energy is applied. It is time for science to broaden its horizon, unhampered by casual designations. *All the dramas of life arise precisely from denominations* One should accustom oneself from childhood to ascertain the essential nature of things."

"In the study of the history of faiths it is possible to observe how humanity has repeatedly grasped subtle conceptions only to forget and later cast aside that which had been cognized. One may see how in ancient times people grasped the law of reincarnation only to reject it again in a spasm of rage. The reason for this ecclesiastic denial is understandable—a caste was protecting its prerogatives, for the law of Existence threatened to equalize the rights of people. so it has happened in different ages, yet the waves of cognition and of ignorance are everywhere identical.

"They create an agitation of the waters so needed for the advance of consciousness. Therefore, each one striving for knowledge achieves tranquillity of spirit amid storm and stress.

---

* A book of the sixteenth century on the organization of family life and household.

Let us not remain in ignorance when knowledge is knocking at all gates."

I want to give you an extract from an article about "Original Sin" in an English magazine. A spiritual instructor was asked by a schoolboy, "Why is it claimed that sin and evil came into the world with Adam and Eve if in Paradise there was a tree bearing the fruits of Good and Evil? Whence could come the fruits of Evil in Paradise? How could the Devil be in Paradise?" Indeed, some contemporary school children are more clever and *introspective* than those of the past generation., It is quite impossible to push back consciousness. Great sin is committed by those who forcibly retard enlightenment and the development of thought in people. Any kind of compulsion is against the laws of the Universe and inevitably must cause explosions and destruction. When we look back, we can see the profound causes that prepared the fall of the old world. Indeed, the suffocation of thought and spirit bred all the subsequent madness. The long-controlled dam broke, and everything in the way of the torrent was swept away. Thus, nothing and no one can stop thought, this fiery energy and the Crown of the Universe. Great shifting has taken place in the consciousness of the masses of all countries, but some people still refuse to accept this fact. The reason for all the calamities that are now taking place lies in ignorance and monstrous irresponsibility, which was, and still is reigning and is to be observed among the so-called "vested with power." People need care, and this care should be manifested first of all in the UPBRINGING of people and in their true education. Man does not live by bread alone.

And so, do not look for followers, but work on yourself, on your own self-perfectment.

23

25 May 1936

You are quite right when you say that, owing to the poverty of definitions in our Western languages, we meet with almost insurmountable difficulties in attempting to express or explain not only the Higher Concepts but even an unaccustomed approach to an already known idea. Western thought is comparatively crude and heavy, and in consequence has not yet evolved all the subtlest nuances in definitions in which the East is so rich. The main reason for the lack of understanding is that the people of the West are not used to, or rather, not trained in refinement of thinking. How many are able to read with true assimilation? Most people read with their eyes, not with the spirit and the heart; therefore, the inner meaning remains inaccessible.

Certainly in the word *religion* is contained a concept of the greatest significance, but this significance is now lost by humanity. Actually, it signifies the bond of man with the Higher World or Higher Principle. Yet everyone tries to usurp this great and sole link as his exclusive possession; therefore, every nation has kept it apart, limited and stamped it with the stigma of fanaticism, while condemning all and any unaccustomed expressions of this concept by those close to it. Thus, from one all-unifying religion, we have made many pseudo-religions which exclude each other. But if you try to say that the main cause of all adversities is not religion but pseudo-religion, each one will point to his neighbor, and in his conceit will never admit that this bitter truth applies equally to himself. A new obscurity and a new temptation will result. The meaning of words in all languages can be absorbed or correctly understood only by the heart and straight-knowledge.

Likewise, do not be afraid of any attacks or slander. All this is but slime from stagnant swamps. I have already written that not a single Teaching has entered life without cruel opposition,. The same will happen with the books of Living Ethics. As Jesus said (St. Luke 6:26). "Woe unto you, when all men shall speak well of you! for so did their fathers to the false prophets." It is impossible to say it more clearly. And who of the workers for Truth would like to assume the badge of a pseudo-prophet? Those who cannot accept *The Chalice of the East** should be told that the world is wide and the light is great, and that in many homes *The Chalice of the East* has lighted a new candle and a new spiritual joy. It would be inexcusable to pin down the consciousness to a single locality or to just a casual group of people. The Teaching spreads by Inscrutable Ways. Nobody and nothing can arrest the Cosmic Magnet in its evolutionary movement; all dams will lead only to destruction. Whole continents and races that have perished bear witness to this. Mankind of our race, in

---

* Extracts from *The Mahatma Letters to A. P. Sinnett.*

its mad disunity, accelerates the cycle of its own displacement. Our ship is rushing toward wreck, and the dark instigators spitefully rejoice, for they hope to escape upon the wreckage.

I would not call the opponents of *The Chalice of the East* even "reasonably intelligent," for precisely, it is most difficult to find in such opponents the evidence of any intelligence. Their intelligence is like a reflection in a crooked mirror. Such casuistry causes degeneration of the higher centers and cognition becomes impossible. Someone has said that if one were to accept literally and flatly the statement about the evil of religions, one would also have to accept the logical conclusion of the fatal formula that religion is the opium of the people. Literalness and insipidity are attributes of limitation, and undoubtedly limitation would eventually arrive at such a formula. But, then, nobody turns to limitation in order to contain the new understanding! Only a prejudiced mind will not agree that every insular, limited, and decadent religion is actually opium, the most evil poison of disunity and deterioration. The same can be said of ignorance in science, and, in general, about any and all ignorance. The new consciousness struggles to establish the one link with the Higher World and the one Source of all teachings, philosophies, and knowledge.

Likewise, those wiseacres whom you have in mind should have known that a certain degree of knowledge corresponds to each epoch, and what was essential or goal-fitting for one century cannot be fully so for succeeding ones. If it were not so, what would happen to evolution? Humanity, in each phase of its development, is given only that portion of Truth which can be assimilated by the *minority*. In each epoch, in each religion and nation, besides the Great Teachers who brought a new understanding of the forgotten ancient Revelation, after a certain time there appeared High Spirits to purify the newly received Covenant. These Spirits stand out as resplendent beacons against the background of the ignorant representatives of religions. Usually, these Torch-bearers became martyrs, and often their works and they themselves perished at the hands of various zealots. No one would think of linking Them with any one religion, and They stand isolated from any church dogma, which is not surprising, for They were almost always denouncers of unworthy church servants.

Similarly, St. Sergius adhered to the spirit, not to the external church dogmatism, and he who understands otherwise is blind and deaf. We may meet people who insist that St. Sergius was an orthodox ecclesiastic, because he built churches and monasteries and established austere Rules, rituals, etc. But the significance of the entire work of St. Sergius was not in external dogmatism, but in his highly moral and ethical influence on his contemporaries. In establishing austere Rules, in bringing discipline to the savage temper of those times, he helped to mold the character of the people, thus building up the might of the nation. We know from history in what a chaotic condition was the spirit of the nation during the grave period of the Mongol yoke, and because of the licentious morals of the ruling princes who warred among themselves. Severe schooling and curbs were necessary, and they had to be based on concepts that were near and understandable to the people. Symbols and ceremonies were essential to consciousnesses that were just emerging from an infantile state. And even now, as we see, some cannot yet give up these symbols; one has to be lenient with weak consciousnesses. However, Christ said, "But the hour cometh, and now is, when the true worshippers shall worship the Father in spirit and in truth; for the Father seeketh such to worship him. God is a Spirit: and they that worship him must worship him in spirit and in truth." (St. John 4:23, 24)

The Troitsky-Sergievsky Monastery may disappear, for even during his life it was almost destroyed; but the memory of Sergius himself will never die, for great was the magnet of the spirit which he planted in the soul of the Russian people. The history of the development of spirituality in the Russian soul and the beginning of the assembling and building of Russia are indissolubly linked with the name of this Great Spiritual Toiler. Precisely this explains why all the forces of darkness took up arms against this great name. What relics are left of all the Great Bearers of Light, of Buddha and Christ (a handful of ashes in one case and a conventional tomb in the other), but their memory lives and will be even stronger in the centuries to come when it shall be purified of the accumulations of ignorance.

If one wishes to replace the inner meaning by "any algebraic signs" or terms, one may *just be left with them.*

Likewise, he who sees in *The Chalice of the East* the limitations of atheism displays his complete ignorance. Someone grieves because the Elder Mahatma did not give fifty-six years ago that apotheosis which he now gives in the *Fiery World*. But how can anyone know what was given and what was not given by the Elder Mahatma? To the mind familiar with Eastern teachings and Eastern thought, this apotheosis is the fundamental principle. Likewise, all the quotations that you give from *The Call* speak of the same august pantheism which saturates the volumes of *The Secret Doctrine* and *The Mahatma Letters*. Furthermore, the creativeness of the Mahatmas is so great and manifold that it is impossible to expect them to address, in all cases and at all times, various nationalities and consciousnesses always in the same formulas. Even a average artist or poet, when interpreting various epochs and localities, changes his style and idiom accordingly. Set thought, set formulas are discordant with Cosmos, the life of which is perpetual motion, perpetual change of forms. Diversity is life; monotony, death.

I have no desire to rummage in the husks of the casuistries of the dialectical wiseacres; this would be an inexcusable waste of time.

I send you courage and fearlessness. Above all, do not disturb your consciousness with the whisperings of those clever ones, who in our opinion are complete ignoramuses.

24

26 May 1936

Please regard calmly the attacks on the books of Living Ethics. Indeed, everything new that leads the consciousness away from habitual stagnation is always accompanied by malicious outcries and opposition. There are numerous examples of this in the history of religion and likewise in the domain of science. For those who call themselves Christians the most vivid example should be that of Christ himself, but precisely him they are apt to forget. Who persecuted and crucified Christ if not the dogmatists and scribes, and did not the Pharisees say of him, "He casteth out devils through the prince of the devils"? (St. Matthew 9:34) And also, "But some of them said, 'He casteth out devils through Beelzebub the chief of the devils.' And others, tempting him, sought of him a sign from heaven. But he, knowing their thoughts, said unto them, 'Every kingdom divided against itself is brought to desolation; and a house divided against a house falleth. If Satan also be divided against himself, how shall his kingdom stand?'" (St. Luke 11:15-18)

It is strange that the ones who howl the most and attack the books of the Teaching, not only know nothing about it, but also know nothing of their Scriptures. If by chance someone has read something, he garbles and explains it in the way most advantageous to him. We always emphasize and advise not to entice and force immature consciousnesses—it is to no purpose and even harmful. All must take place through a natural process. A ready spirit knows exactly where the truth is, and nothing can confuse or frighten him. But, of course, such are in the minority. Yet they are more numerous in this era than before, for no repressions can arrest evolution. Remember how few followers and disciples Christ had, and even among those few one was Nicodemus and another, Judas! However, do not worry about the work of enlightenment, for it proceeds by special ways. The number of searching souls increases over the entire span of Earth.

The first task of the Living Ethics is to broaden the consciousness, therefore, let us not pin ourselves down by thought to one accidental, small place and one group of people. Broad is the Universe, and the Light is not weak. While in one place slander is expressed, in another the new thought is assimilated a thousandfold. Somewhere betrayals take place, and elsewhere, examples of a remarkable fire of the spirit and self-sacrifice. One must learn to find equilibrium of the spirit and to calmly face the inevitable manifestations of darkness. You already know that we are living in a grave time, long since foretold by all the scriptures of the world, the time of the battle of the Forces of Light with darkness; thus, let us not be surprised by all the craftiness and attacks of evil. Indeed, after this battle, which will last several years, and after the victory of Light over darkness, the power of the Prince of Darkness will not be in ascendance any more, and his power will be on the decline. But since one cannot serve two masters, let everyone finally decide in his heart whom he will serve, in order not to become a traitor to one of whom it is said in the Revelation of St. John, 3:16, "So then because thou art lukewarm, and neither cold nor hot, I will spue thee out of my mouth."

Therefore, if one is not strong enough to overcome fear and

doubt, it is better not to test oneself; if someone follows dogmatic Christianity, let him extract the very best from it. Precisely, the New Epoch will shine with a new realization of the Teaching of Christ. Enlightened spiritual teachers (and there are such already) will return to the true covenants of Christ, to the covenants of the first Fathers of the Church, and to the works of the great beacon light of Christianity, Origen, who laid the foundation for the whole philosophy of Christianity.

In conclusion, I again repeat that no aggressions can ever frighten us, for we serve the Great Light. Moreover, where lies true achievement? In general recognition? Never did the enthusiastic shouts of the crowd follow the awakeners of the new consciousness and the bearers of new discoveries. As it is said in the Gospel of St. Luke, 6:26, "Woe unto you, when all men shall speak well of you! for so did their fathers to the false prophets." It would be useful to reread such schoolbooks as *The Martyrs of Science*. All this is seemingly old, but nevertheless, eternally new. Therefore, we say, "Let us be without fear!"

Live by the heart, develop tolerance and magnanimity, and the new consciousness will be strengthened in you.

25

8 June 1936

Let the new Cycle bring a new understanding. Let us not fear any assaults or battles, for the Hierarchy of Light requires victory, and is a victory possible without a battle? Is it not a victory to have published so many most essential books in this most difficult year? Indeed, such an accomplishment is a most serious defeat for the enemy.

And now for your questions. I have written much about karma. Truly, around this concept have grown many monstrous distortions, and one of the worst misconceptions is the refusal to help one's neighbor for fear of complicating one's own personal karma.

Would this not be a manifestation of the greatest selfishness? If in rendering benevolent help to our fellowman we take on a particle of his karma, then it cannot encumber our spiritual development, which alone determines our karma.

On the contrary, the refusal of help may immeasurably burden our own karma, for who can tell to whom or when we are repaying an old debt? Only the Arhat knows where help must be withheld, yet we must stretch out a helping hand when it is needed. As St. Sergius used to say, "And he who forbears to aid his brother shall not draw the thorn from his own foot." Indeed, everywhere and always one must practice commensurability and goal-fitness. There are people who will give away everything, and later become dependent on others. But to such people we shall give a reminder from the Teaching, "Who hath said that one must renounce madly? Madness doth so remain." Moreover, people often forget about spiritual help, which is the highest. But one fact is neglected much too often, and that is that karma is created, eased, and weighed down mainly by our own thoughts. Precisely thought and motive weave our aura, this magnetic field which either attracts or repels all possibilities. And this decisive factor is very often forgotten during discussions of karma. But were it otherwise, it would be impossible to break out of the magic circle of karma.

Thus, if people thought less of karma and more of purifying and perfecting their feelings and thoughts, they would succeed immeasurably. One should not fear new karma, but only strive to *improve* its quality. By fearing to engender new karma, one may enter such a chicken coop that there would by only one way left—involution. One should remember that commensurability rules in Cosmos; therefore, insignificant karma will bring insignificant results. Although the karma of great responsibility is burdensome, it alone brings great achievements. Therefore, people should avoid neither actions nor responsibilities.

And we should remember that difficult karma does not mean a low karma; in fact, it is quite the reverse. Easy karma is the karma of insignificance. Often easy karma is in itself a serious test, for very seldom does a man raise himself to the next degree of spiritual perfectment amidst material well-being. That is why among the wise an easy life is considered a curse. If Joan of Arc had been rewarded by her king with an estate and had ended her life in luxury and well-being, she would not have been the Joan of Arc she was. However, it was not her personal karma that required death at the stake. We must remember about the missions voluntarily undertaken by great spirits. And the attitude toward them of those to whom they are directed determines the karma of their nation for many centuries. Thus, these great spirits serve as touchstones for the consciousness of peoples.

Likewise, if an action or offering, performed with lofty motives, is accepted in the same spirit of understanding, and is applied to an equally high goal, this thrice-created energy will, in return, bring results that will be intensified as hundredfold. It is possible that the results may not come in this incarnation but in the next, since the larger the circle encompassed by the action, the more the time required for its turning; yet so much the more powerful will be the results and possibilities gathered by it. That is why in all the Eastern scriptures it is indicated that the help (not in the narrow sense of the word) that is given to a great Spiritual Toiler exceeds all others in its results. But precisely this great truth served as a basis for the most terrible misuse by the priestly caste. Offerings of sacrifices, the financing of the building of temples, adornment of the ikons with precious stones and golden vestments, the forty-pound candles, etc., all have as their basis the very same distorted truth. With the passing of centuries all the spiritual values were replaced by material ones. People forgot that gold and material treasures have no application whatever in the supermundane spheres. The richest man here is a beggar in the supermundane world. Therefore, the improvement of karma should not be sought in refraining from actions, but in an intensive development, and accumulation of spiritual treasures.

And now regarding paragraph 230 in *Fiery World III*, balance and harmony are one and the same concept. Therefore one may say that Cosmos is held by the action and harmony of atoms. Man is the reflection of the Macrocosm, therefore, he must aspire to the harmonization of all the atoms which enter into his microcosm. Karma is action, and each action creates a consequence. As it is said, "Equilibrium [is] affirmed in correspondence with the development of the will." Therefore, action directed by a disciplined will that is in accord with the cosmic laws affirms harmony and creates equilibrium. The base will, colored by selfish cravings, breeds the terrors of destruction, for collisions between disharmonious forces cause explosions in the Cosmos and open the way for chaos. In fact, an ignorant and vicious man causes poisonous explosions and chaotic disturbances in his own chemical laboratory, and thus extensively pollutes the atmosphere.

And it is also said, "The scales of man's karma affirm their measurement of free will." That is to say that the quality of karma reveals either a high or low degree of a person's will. The will is the main factor and creator for all that exists. Thus, man is punished or rewarded, not by the High Forces, or Divinity, but is drawn to this or that environment or sphere only because of the affinity of the atoms that enter the whirl of his aura with the atoms of the corresponding spheres. It is said that karma cannot overburden a harmonious body; therefore, let us strive to perfect our energies. Perfectment will lead to balance, or harmony.

And now, about the sacrifice of Christ. Of course, it is absolutely unthinkable to understand the significance of the sacrifice, or crucifixion of Christ in the way it is understood by some consciousnesses. Its meaning is that Christ, wishing to emphasize the power of spirit over physical matter, accepted the chalice of sacrifice, and sealed by his blood the Covenant which he brought, "Greater love hath no man than this, that a man lay down his life for his friends." And in the book *Agni Yoga*, paragraph 8, it is said, "One can point out why the Teachers of Knowledge experienced such suffering on departing the earth. Of course, this suffering was *conscious* and *voluntary* . As the host fills to the brim the cup, so does the Teacher desire to impress this last sign of His Covenant."

Therefore, if the great examples and sacrifice of Christ kindles the fires within our hearts, and if we apply his Covenant, it can be said that he did not suffer in vain, and that precisely the Cup that he accepted, sealed his Covenant. But if we imagine that, regardless of what we do and what crimes we commit, the blood that was shed by Christ will save us forever from the power of the devil, then we ourselves become these very devils! No one can save another. Only by personal efforts can the spirit ascend into the preordained beautiful worlds. "Faith without works is dead."

All the Great Teachers are called Saviors of the World, because again and again they point out to us the Path of Light. However, They are able to help and safeguard us only so far as we ourselves accept Their protection. The whole of Cosmos is based on the law of reciprocity or mutuality, and where there is no response, there is no result. This explains why Christ could not perform miracles where there was no faith in him, and where there was no striving of the spirit toward his healing ray.

* * *

The Sacrament of the Great Sacrifice has its origin in the most ancient Mysteries. At the last initiation, the neophyte was offered a cup filled with the juice of pomegranates (symbolizing blood); accepting it, he had to spill the contents in four directions as a sign of his readiness to give his soul and body for the service of the world, that is, to suffer for Truth. Thus, Christ also wished to affirm this symbol among his disciples, in order to infix the memory of his sacrifice and Covenant for future generations. But no mechanical communion is able to save our souls, for "faith without works is dead."

I remember my conversation with a woman missionary about Christ's sacrifice. She was beating her breast and shouting hysterically that she knew that Christ had suffered for her, and so had saved her from eternal damnation. To which I answered, "You are mistaken. Christ suffered not for you, but *because of you*." Of course, we never met her again, were proclaimed pagans and spies, and were rewarded by other corresponding titles.

Nothing seems more sacrilegious to me than the concept of an All-Merciful Father-God, who sacrificed his only begotten and consubstantial Son for the sins of the people, the people whom, according to the Scriptures, he himself created! It reminds one of a certain Akkadian ruler who sacrificed his son in an attempt to avoid the consequences of his own sins. Ancient history recorded and condemned such a barbarous concept of fatherhood. Is it possible for later generations to accept such an example of parental love and to elevate it to the stature of Divinity? Every truly loving earthly father or mother would gladly sacrifice their lives for the salivation of their son. Can a Divine Father be morally inferior to the people whom he himself created!

It is by voluntary sacrifice or self-renunciation that the world is held together. In the higher worlds the chalice of self-sacrifice is radiant with all the fires of unutterable joy, and only on our plane, the plane of tests and sorrow, is this chalice full of bitterness and poison. The Spirit that has realized the joy of self-sacrifice is itself the highest Beauty. Beauty and self-sacrifice lie in the foundation of Being.

You ask how to understand the appalling example of betrayal by Judas. We know the occult law that Light attracts darkness; therefore, the stronger the light, the denser the darkness. Thus, on all paths, the encounter with the servants of darkness and with betrayers of varying degrees is inevitable. They follow the Source of Light like shadows. Indeed, the very hatred of the dark ones binds them to the object of their hatred. The potentialities of such betrayal definitely were hidden in Judas himself. That is why the dark forces used him, as well as the priests' and Pharisees' hatred, as a tool for accomplishing their criminal purpose. Therefore, Judas can be regarded as the representative of a collective betrayal.

People are not fully cognizant of the extent to which the visible and invisible worlds participate in their deeds and in events, and of how often they become the semiconscious and subconscious instruments of the servants of darkness. Indeed, one can assert that two-thirds of all the actions of people are performed under the influence of visible and invisible counselors. And, alas, because of the mental side of mankind those counselors are for the most part denizens of the lower spheres adjacent to Earth. The influence of the lower spheres is more easily assimilated by the denizens of the earthly plane, whereas the pure, higher influences can be received only by a pure vessel.

It is said that the ray of the Higher World is not "wet muslin," and if the ray is not assimilated by the heart, the head could come off as a result of such an unaccustomed influence. Let us remember that for the acceptance of Hiero-inspiration the great Spiritual Toilers used to prepare their bodies for years by means of various purifications and abstinence. Let us also remember the shocks experienced by even very lofty Spirits, while in the physical body, when visited by the Dwellers of the Fiery World. Let us recall the shock experienced by St. Sergius and how his hair turned white, in spite of the fact that his spirit belonged to the Higher World.

Now it must be clear to you that those who describe being visited by the Highest Spirits and who do not mention the sacred tremor which throws the heart into an indescribable state approaching heart failure either speak an untruth or are deceived by impersonators from the Subtle World.

* * *

Your definition of God is correct. Verily, one has to show that the true concept of God is all-embracing. "In him we ... move, and have our being." If the concept of Infinity exists, then, indeed, God is that Infinity. Therefore, all discussions about Him must inevitably limit Him. All we can do is to bow before this Unutterable Power and Beauty with profound reverence and the highest joy of the heart and strive with jubilant spirit to this *Mystery of Mysteries* of the *Great Infinity*. Indeed, the path of the approach to God is infinite.

* * *

It is right to collect as many indications as possible about the great significance of the heart. The heart is the Abode of God. The nearness of God can be felt only through the heart. Truly, the heart makes Him very near or very distant.

Yes, space is full of heart-rending cries, but earthly ears seldom hear them. These are not from sadness or grief, but precisely—wails of *terror*.

* * *

Undoubtedly the sounds caught by us but inaudible to others indicate a refinement of the center of the ear. And the pains in the solar plexus may also be connected with the refining of the sensitivity of centers. I strongly recommend taking bicarbonate of soda the moment you feel such pains. If the pain is not relieved you can repeat the dose. Soda is irreplaceable in many cases of inflammation. Remember that soda is called "sacred ashes." It prevents excessive inflammation. In general, soda is useful in almost all diseases and is a preventative of many illnesses, therefore, do not be afraid of taking it, as well as valerian.

* * *

The dark forces certainly attack, first of all, pure undertakings and those who are under the direct ray of the Forces of Light. The traitors are admitted, for according to the law the force of a return blow is proportionate to the force of resistance. Armageddon is necessary; the collision of the opposing Forces is necessary. Conflagrations are necessary in order that the human spirit shall *cry out* and *realize* at last that it has to struggle, not with its neighbors, *but with its own self and with the forces of chaos and the elements*, which offer a vast field for creative testing.

I wanted to conclude this letter, but one more sheet is left so I will write some more, about the redemption of sins. In the esoteric Teaching it is declared that the redemption of personal sins can only be performed through Christ—Christ crucified, suffering during the entire Maha-Yuga (the great cosmic Cycle) upon the cross inscribed in space by the intersection of the line of matter by that of spirit.

The redemption of personal sins is performed by the soul, the bearer of Christ, almost without cessation during the earthly lives of the individual Ego. When the strivings of the souls directed toward obedience to the Divine Law overcome the desires of the body to impede the Divine Law for the sake of self-indulgence, a complete change, or transmutation, takes place in the lower nature. The process of vanquishing and transmutation culminates in the fusing of the individual souls with the Higher Soul.

"The Christ on the cross, of every human being, must descend into Hades at some point of its evolution, in order to bring back to normal conditions the soul that has been plunged therein as an effect of the evil deeds of its lower self. In other words, Divine Love must reach down into the heart of man, conquer and regenerate the man, before he can appreciate the enormity of his offenses against Divine Law and forgive himself for the sins committed against himself, and forgiveness must be obtained to complete at-one-ment." [Loc. cit., p.10]

Thus, only the transmutation of energies—of feelings, and qualities of thoughts—can take us out of the magic circle of karma. Therefore, blessed are all the higher emotions, which lift us out of usualness and heighten our vibrations, refining and opening our nerve centers.

I am sending you thoughts of valor and joy. Do not be disturbed by the feeling of depression, for at the moment all such feelings are inevitable. The whole world is in a dreadful, unheard-of tension, and, of course, sensitive organisms react to it more strongly. The rhythm of the waves of tension will change, and after the depression a wave of exaltation and joy of the spirit will come.

26

15 June 1936

Hearty thanks for all the beautiful feelings expressed by you. I was especially glad to learn about your unprejudiced attitude toward *The Mahatma Letters to A. P. Sinnett*. You are quite right in your judgment of certain circles. Even sufferings teach a certain class of people little or nothing at all. Inert consciousnesses probably know that the series of books of Living Ethics is considered dangerous by some Theosophists, and an order not to read them was issued. We can only say once again, "They do not recognize their own!" Nevertheless, the groups gathering around the Teachings of Living Ethics are increasing and spreading, though there are some among them who, while accepting all the books of Living Ethics, cannot accept *The Mahatma Letters* given during the life of H., P. Blavatsky and through her cooperation, regarding them as atheistic! You have the right to ask, "But can we really believe that they truly understand the books of Living Ethics?" It makes me very happy therefore to meet a consciousness which is devoid of prejudice and predisposition. The ability to discern independently the merit of these or other teachings is, in itself, not a small achievement.

You write that someone regrets that the books of Living Ethics are published in the new Russian orthography, for "various Ahrimans are taking advantage of this for their own propaganda." To that I must say that we should ignore such insinuations, for in this case the "Ahrimans" display their inherent ignorance. We can remind them that the change of orthography was introduced by the Imperial Academy of Sciences long before the Revolution, but war interfered with this innovation. In connection with this, I recall a rather distressing incident. In 1917, during our stay in Finland, we were visited by Professor R. In a conversation with him, I mentioned that I had recently received a book published in the new orthography, and that I could not read such incompetent illiteracy. In addition, I strongly expressed my disapproval of those people who only think of ease of assimilation, probably measuring other intellects by their own. You can well imagine my embarrassment when the esteemed professor told me that this measure had already been introduced before the war by a special committee of the Academy of Sciences, and that he himself was one of its members!

27

18 June 1936

I want to believe that unprejudiced minds, analyzing the happenings in the world in the light of the Teaching of Living Ethics, will be able to assimilate evolution, understanding that the old world is gone and that regenerated and broadened consciousnesses are needed to accept the new forms of construction prompted by life itself. I have already written time and time again that all events, all that takes place, clearly indicate the trend of evolution. An epoch is being created of general collaboration, work in common, and collective solidarity of all workers, irrespective of class distinction. The most essential problem that now faces humanity is precisely to synthesize the spiritual with the material. New achievements in science, new investigations and discoveries of the laws of psychic energy, will demand new penetration and understanding of the subjective, or spiritual, world. Undoubtedly, the discovery of the laws of psychic energy will help to establish a new order of life. The bond between the dense world (the physical) and the Subtle (the world of energies) will become evident, and the Higher Wisdom will become affirmed by the Force that directs and links all existence.

The world of the future, a higher world, will be heralded armed with the rays of the laboratories. Precisely the laboratories make manifest the advantages of the higher energy; and the supremacy of the psychic energy of man over all hitherto known energies not only will be proved but the obvious difference in its quality will be manifested. Thus, the significance of spirituality will be wholly established.

Perception of the higher laws will subjugate technology to the spirit; hence, the recognition of higher aims will be affirmed, which will lead to a regeneration of the whole material nature. This regeneration of nature and the regenerated spirit of the people will prompt new, better forms of the structure of life. Therefore, I advise you to watch most attentively all the signs that come from the New Country.

* * *

And now regarding your question about the Sixth Race. Yes, in many Theosophical books, even in *The Secret Doctrine*, we find the indication that the Sixth Race is gathering in America. But precisely in *The Secret Doctrine* I encountered a contradiction. In one place it is mentioned that it is in America that the sixth sub-race of the Fifth Race is commencing to be formed, while in another part it is given as the Sixth Race. Certainly, there is a vast difference between the concept of a sub-race and that of a root race. One should also take into consideration the possibility of a misprint. At the birth of America the majority of migrants belonged to the sixth and even the seventh sub-race of the *Fifth* Race. It is rather remarkable that no one pays any attention to the strange fact that almost nowhere in Theosophical literature is our country mentioned, as if a sixth part of the world had no place in the cosmic plan and in evolution. Almost no one asks, "Why is this and what is the reason for it?" I will answer, That which is secret is *carefully guarded*, and if it were announced prematurely that this country has a great future, it would be torn to pieces. Moreover, the Teaching of the Secret Doctrine *would not have been accepted*. As for the Sixth Race, those single individuals who belong to it are indeed born in all countries, and at the proper time the majority of them will be assembled in the principal and safe place. Just as the seeds of the Fifth Race were saved, so, also, the seeds of the Sixth will be safeguarded.

* * *

Yes, each spirit, or monad, is born under the rays of a definite luminary, and therefore the seed of that spirit contains in its potentiality the same energies inherent in that luminary, which remains its guiding star throughout the whole Manvantara.

Thus, the whole of humanity, in the seed of the spirit, belongs to various planets even while on Earth, one of its temporary stations. True, there are hosts of spirits belonging to a luminary or to the ray of the Dhyani-Buddha, that engendered them, but only the one nearest to this ray becomes the head of the planet. Consequently, each great Teacher gathers around him those nearest to his ray, or to the potential of his energies; that is why all waverings, and departures from the Teacher, once he is chosen, are so destructive. In the madness of wavering, we may leave our cosmic Father, who alone can kindle our centers in their entire perfectment. Now you will realize how sacred is the bond between a Guru and disciple! For who could know, if it were not revealed to him, that the Guru chosen by him is not his cosmic Father and also his Guru? And amidst the ones who approach the Teaching there are those who run from one Teacher to another, hoping to accelerate their progress. But only the ignorant can think thus; they do not realize the significance of the occult bond, nor do they know with what difficulty and patience it is woven, and how anger, irritability, and doubt—to say nothing of betrayal and apostasy—can instantaneously destroy a work even of many years.

It is said in *The Secret Doctrine*: "The [human monads] 'triads' born under the same. ... Planet, or rather the *radiations* of one and the same Planetary Spirit (Dhyani-Buddha) are, in all their after lives and rebirths, sister, or '*twin-souls*,' on this Earth." "The star under which a human Entity [monad] is born, says the Occult teaching, will remain forever its star, throughout the whole cycle of its incarnations in one Manvantara. But *this is not his astrological star*. The latter is concerned and connected with the *personality*, the former with the INDIVIDUALITY. The 'Angel' [or the Ruler] of that Star, or the Dhyani-Buddha will be either the guiding or simply the presiding 'Angel,' so to say, in every new rebirth of the monad, *which is part of his own essence*, though his vehicle, man may remain for ever ignorant of this fact. The adepts have each their Dhyani-Buddha, their elder 'twin soul,' and they know it, calling it 'Father-Soul,' and Father—Fire. It is only at the last and supreme initiation, however, that they learn it when placed face to face with the bright 'Image.'" [Op. cit.]

Thus, our true Angel Guardian is the Dhyani-Buddha of that planet under whose, or which rays our human entity was conceived.

* * *

In all epochs there can be found empty tombs, or tombs containing substitute bodies. Thus, there exists the grave of Comte Saint-Germain, but, in fact, a substitute body is buried there. Still, one must treat occult novels with great discrimination. At times, no doubt, their authors catch certain things from the spatial records, but often a great deal that is refracted is exceedingly distorted.

* * *

Yes, you may consider one more historical cycle ended. A river does not flow backward. The new coming cycle will certainly be more beautiful, for all the celestial signs in their combinations affirm a great Renewal and Beneficence. Let the heart tell you whence comes this Beneficence. Watch attentively all signs, and you will see how many events are now taking place, and the heart can rejoice at the swiftness of events. There is no power that can stop the Wheel of Karma. All the calamities which have overtaken this or that country were not accidental; therefore, there is no place of either malice or self-pity. But let us watch with cognizance and apply all our efforts for the broadening of consciousness and understanding of events. Watch events keenly and you will see how all the inflated values shall crumble in obedience to karma.

* * *

It is quite true that it rests with us whether we extract either filth or goodness from anything. The Golden Mean, or Path of Great Equilibrium, has been decreed by all the Great Teachers. If someone is not attracted to the often mediocre cinemas or dead rituals, let him not force himself. To do so is simply a pernicious waste of time, which could be better used for interesting labor for the Common Good. I do not think that it is possible to convert the narrow consciousnesses, congealed in old prejudices and concepts, just by being in their midst and conversing with them. However, if they themselves knock at your door, that is something quite different; but to go to them in an attempt to open their eyes is useless.

28

22 June 1936

Thank you for the books from Shanghai, but as we already have them would it not be better to return them to you? Concerning the book written by Bajenov, I have not had time to read it attentively, but I looked through it and noted that there are some correct dates and explanations, based on astrological and cabalistic data. So you already know about the significance of the year 1936 and the importance of the month of September of the same year with its good portents for our country. It is also correct that Israel has come to mean "the chosen;" therefore, Israel can be encountered in all peoples. In general, the book is not bad, and even if it has a certain amount of errors, what book has not, whatever the subject? Therefore, Bajenov's book could be recommended to help people to think.

True, the author of the English book that was the source of information for Bajenov is not free from the common human weakness which attributes all the best to his own country and nationality, and that, of course, should be taken into account;

however, it seems to me that Bajenov himself noticed this. In connection with these books I recall an article written by H. P. Blavatsky about interpretations of Biblical prophecies. In this article, "Hosea's Prophecy about Rotten Rails," she says that according to the cabalistic reading by the method of the Notaricon it is possible to obtain from each prophecy and each sentence of the Bible any sort of meaning. As an example, she gives a case of a cabalistic calculation and interpretation of the 14th verse, chapter 13 of the Book of the Prophet Hosea. The verse, if read according to this method, prophesied the catastrophe of the imperial train at Borki and the miraculous escape from it of the imperial family on the 17th of October, 1888, or, according to the Hebrew calendar, the year 5649. Of course, this verse has this meaning only if read in Russian, but, she adds, if it were read by an English cabalist, it might indicate that Hosea foretold the appearance of the infamous murderer, Jack the Ripper, in White-chapel (the Jewish quarter of London), etc.

I myself once heard intelligent people trying to prove that the Bolsheviks were predicted in the Apocalypse, and that even the number of the days of their power was mentioned, and that the Michael mentioned there was none other than the Grand Duke Mikhail Alexandrovich! I certainly do not mention this to discredit Bajenov's book, but simply to warn those who are greatly attracted by research into Biblical prophecies. Mistakes often arise, not from incorrect data, but just from incorrect interpretation. For instance, the new earthly Jerusalem is not in Palestine, however, its true whereabouts cannot yet be disclosed. Incidentally, do you know the prophecy made by L. Tolstoy not long before his death? We have recently received a little book, written in Russian; I could hardly finish reading it. Artificial language with "three-storied" scientific terminology kills any kind of thought. Clarity of consciousness manifests itself first of all in its simplicity of expression.

I advise you to strive toward psychic energy, toward thought, and to all concepts that could regenerate life. While speaking of the Brotherhood, one must exercise the greatest care in order not to profane this sacred concept with sacrilegious remarks. Give this advice to everybody.

* * *

And now, about Atlantis. The article about the discoveries of

Schliemann is interesting, except at the end where manuscripts are mentioned as having been found in Mexico and Peru, containing quotations from the chronicles of old Buddhist temples in Lhasa. The latter should be *most earnestly investigated.* Lhasa itself, as far as the city of that name is concerned, is no older than the seventh century A. D. Furthermore, the first Buddhist temples were built there in the very same century. Finally, knowing all the secludedness of this nation and that locality, one may ask, How could these chronicles get into Central America? Even supposing that some cuneiform characters were brought from Central Asia to Central America during the time of Atlantis, certainly Lhasa could not have been referred to as such at that time, or have Buddhist temples, because they did not then exist. Did you receive this article from S.? It bears the stamp of the very same hand. W. Scott-Elliot's book which you mention, I cannot recall. However, in *The Secret Doctrine* Atlantis is well covered, and the excavations of Schliemann are also mentioned, as well as quotations from Plato. Likewise, in the second volume of "Lucifer,": page 465 in the English edition, there is a *remarkably interesting article called "Atlantis."* It is based on Plato's works Timaeus and Critias. I suggest that you translate these extracts from *The Secret Doctrine* and write an interesting article of your own based on them and on the article in "Lucifer" and Scott-Elliot's book.

* * *

Do not think that we are seeking recognition. Nothing is further from our intention. The Teaching that is now being given must, and will, be appreciated for its own inner merit. If someone, sitting in his own coop, is unable to grasp the cosmic scope of this Teaching, we can only suggest that he abandon his limited position as soon as possible. Therefore, we never entice anybody. Only those who themselves knock find our doors open, and we have quite a number of friends among the Theosophists as well. In 1925 it was indicated that N. K. should do a painting called "The Messenger" and donate it toward founding a museum named for H. P. Blavatsky. By this gift, and by establishing the museum, the Great Teacher M. wished to perpetuate the memory of her, which, till quite recently, certain of her successors attempted to expunge.

* * *

If we do not receive an immediate answer or affirmation, it means that there are *special* reasons for this. You know what an unheard of Battle is now taking place on all planes! The Forces of Evil are directing the subterranean fire in order to cleave the crust of the Earth at a most dangerous point. And only by the tireless watchfulness of all the forces of Light is our planet held back from the final explosion. Their tension in this cosmic Battle is stupendous. The often mentioned drops of bloody sweat are not an exaggeration, but a grave reality. Apart from this, the Forces of Light smother the flashes of fury and hold back the warlike spirit of many nations, in order to safeguard that which must be *protected*. Thus, amidst the chaos of the cosmic, supermundane, and earthly battles They fulfill the Plan of Light and protect those elements that are qualified for evolution by directing them into the right channels. Whole spheres of the lower strata of the Subtle World are not crumbling! And are there many consciousnesses able to realize the significance and consequences of such destruction?

Therefore, knowing of the gigantic scale of this unprecedented Battle, how can we burden the Forces of Light by our pleas and questions? Co-measurement should always be observed. We know that everything urgent, everything essential will be communicated in due time; therefore, we wait patiently, and often the answer comes without delay.

Thus, all the warriors of Light must now deeply realize the significance of all that happens during Armageddon. Courage, firmness, and unremitting vigilance are necessary.

* * *

I received the book *Photographing the Invisible* by James Coates. It would be useful to publish an article on this subject, and also on transmission of thought at a distance. All this relates to the realm of psychic energy. There are also many interesting statements in the book by Professor Rhine of Duke University.

29

25 June 1936

It is good that you have realized that the main condition for progress is honesty with oneself, and I might add—always and in everything. Precisely, "for the inner work, let them sell the shield of lie."

1. The concept of a concordant soul in animals does not exclude the concept of the existence of the individual seed of the spirit in each animal. The concept of consonance in itself excludes indivisibility. To me this is so clear that it does not actually require any special explanations. When individuality awakens, then, of course, certain corresponding gradual changes and the withdrawal from the basic group take place. I strongly advise you to thoroughly analyze this question and not to apply the formula, "I am I," while talking of animal "individualization." Consciousness of self belongs only to human development.

2. "To outdistance karma" or "to change the quality of karma"—any of these expressions is understood by him who has completely adopted this law.

3. And now, regarding locusts being mentioned in the books of Living Ethics which has so greatly puzzled some people, it refers to the fact that space, polluted by the chaotic vibrations of base energies or thoughts and emotions, actually attracts the most unwelcome guests in the form of all kinds of microbes, which cause various epidemics; and the disharmonious currents call forth various calamities, etc. Therefore, negative manifestations such as clouds of locusts can also be attracted by corresponding vibrations. All low entities *cannot* endure *high* vibrations. Thus, in India, people firmly believe that, by his presence, a Sadhu will protect a village near which he settles down from epidemics, earthquakes, floods, and other calamities.

And so it is. If such a Sadhu is really a hermit of saintly life, he raises the surrounding vibrations by the power of his aura and brings them into harmony, preventing the intrusion of chaos. As you see, the beginners, just like all ignoramuses, laugh readily, without suspecting that they are actually laughing at themselves. The fact is that precisely ignorant people or those having little education are very fond of the most complex, three-storied words, which they themselves hardly understand, but they use them in order to appear learned; whereas everything clear and simple seems unscientific to them, and therefore subject to ridicule. But it is in the East that simplicity of expression is considered the highest achievement, because simplicity vouches for clarity of understanding. The highest Truth is revealed only in the grandeur of simplicity. Certainly, such simplicity is of a special kind, just as the highest joy is a special wisdom.

The one principle, the one fiery element is manifested under different aspects or qualities in the human microcosm, and is also contained in his auric space. The subtle body is sometimes divided into the higher and lower (or etheric). This etheric body, or double, is very easily projected, and in the case of mediums this happens without their will. Most of the phenomena in spiritualistic seances are performed by this double, which creates a means of communication, as it were, between the soul and the physical body of man, similar to the state of the etheric waves that are brought into motion between wireless telegraph stations. The subtle body has many degrees, but the highest state of the mental body corresponds to the Fiery World.

I appreciate very much your determination in striving—this is the "open sesame" to achievement. Remember all that is said in the books of the Teaching about striving. "Striving is the boat of the Arhat."

* * *

I can judge the condition of your bodies, and therefore I advise you to bring them into equilibrium. Try to achieve psychic calmness, and do not overburden your brain. Read more slowly and ponder more. Write down the thoughts which come into your mind, and reread this after a while so that you can observe your progress in clarity of understanding and expression.

And now I would like to warn your group. Often, the beginners and those who have just approached the Sacred Teaching remind one of first-year medical students; when commencing to study different ailments, they feel in themselves the symptoms of all existing diseases. Similarly, some novices in the Teaching begin to ascribe to themselves sacred pains and the most lofty achievements, about which they read in the books of the Teaching. They must be warned against such tendencies, for these indicate the presence of undesirable qualities of the spirit such as conceit and lack of discrimination. Unless these qualities are overcome, no progress on the spiritual plane is possible. Moreover, it must be remembered that until the age of thirty is reached, the opening of the centers is impossible without harm to the organism.

Of course, I am referring only to *normal, healthy* organisms.

So-called mediums may have various manifestations at an earlier age.

* * *

Cold showers may be harmful for very nervous people. Do not force your brain in the late evening hours. It is better to rise earlier and dedicate an early morning hour to reading.

* * *

No one thinks of such a thing as profit from the books of the Teaching. All the money from the sale of books is used for further publications. I may personally add that many a time we were convinced that people do not appreciate what is given to them freely and easily. The book *Agni Yoga* in Russian is actually not attainable, and we know some sincerely striving people who sit and copy the whole book for themselves on a typewriter. These are the valued readers, whereas the majority of those who easily pay for it will just as easily place it upon a shelf, maybe without even reading it in the end. A truly aspiring disciple will find a way to obtain the book.

I am enclosing some paragraphs from *Aum*:

"227. The particle of higher energy which exists in each human organism correspondingly exists in the other kingdoms of nature. The animal kingdom and the vegetable kingdom know how to preserve the particle of energy also in the Subtle World. Especially certain animals that lived around man preserve a certain bond with the organism of the Subtle World dweller. When I advise kindness toward animals, I have in mind that it is better to encounter small friends than enemies. Indeed, one should preserve co-measurement in everything, otherwise one may receive harmful emanations from animals. Likewise, when I indicate a vegetable diet, I am guarding against nourishing the subtle body with blood. The essence of blood thoroughly permeates the body and even the subtle body. Blood is so undesirable in the diet that only in extreme cases do we permit the use of meat which has been dried in the sun. It is also possible to use those parts of the animal where the blood substance has been thoroughly transmuted. Thus, vegetable food has a significance also for life in the Subtle World.

"278. It is often asked, 'Do animals retain their appearance in the Subtle World?' Rarely, because the absence of consciousness renders them formless; sometimes there are foggy outlines, like impulses of energy, but most often they are imperceptible. In fact, the manifestation of animals pertains to the lower strata of the Subtle World. Such obscurities can terrify one by their confused appearance. I consider that the subtle body of man should not remain in these strata, but in their consciousness people frequently resemble animals.

"279. The Subtle World is filled with prototypes of animals, but only a strong consciousness perceives them. Indeed, the aspects of such animal representatives are innumerable, from the most complicated to those which are decomposing as dross. It should not be thought that the dwellers of the Subtle World all possess identical vision. Good clear sight is due to clarity of consciousness, therefore from beginning to end We advise showing care in the matter of clear consciousness. Long ago it was said that good does not dwell in a muddy well."

30

23 July 1936

It is amusing to hear the assertion that the Great Teachers live in the town of Shigatse. One should know Tibet in order to understand what an absurdity such a statement is! Probably the author you have mentioned obtained this information from *The Mahatma Letters to A. P. Sinnett* in which in one letter the Mahatma K. H. mentions the betrayal of H. P. Blavatsky by the Coulomb couple and the dimensions it began to assume. The Mahatma wrote to Sinnett that the Mahatmas had not only not stopped this affair but it had been even, or rather inflated from Shigatse! The Mahatmas often allow hostile elements to bring their evil deeds to a point of absurdity in order that the defeat of evil may be more effective. You remember *Tactica Adversa*, do you not? "From" by no means implies that the Mahatmas dwell in Shigatse. The Stronghold of Light is many, many miles away from there. The entrances to this Stronghold are very well guarded. Many ways lead to it; often one must walk on subterranean paths, going under rivers also, in order to reach the Sacred Summits. But for those who are called there are signposts.

Be cautious with "well-informed" people. Do not try to contradict them, for they are often hopeless. It is better if they busy themselves in trying to help humanity according to their own understanding, rather than thinking of its destruction, poisoning it with gasses, etc. Therefore, look for the young and those whose hearts are open and who are still unprejudiced.

And now, regarding the article that we received. The thoughts are not bad, but the expression "closed communities" is not a good one; for any shutting out implies isolation, and this does not conform to the broad plan of cooperation. Yes, there were, and still will be many more or less successful attempts to organize societies and communities. Of course it is difficult, very difficult indeed, if the members of such a community differ widely in their consciousnesses.

The most essential is not to accomplish a tightly knit communal life, but to learn to manifest in general a spirit of collaboration and magnanimity in everyday life and in all conditions; for new problems in all spheres of life now confront humanity and require the participation of many forces and specialists in order to attain a synthesized solution and practical decision. In fact, even scientific problems cannot now be solved without the cooperation of specialists in the most diverse fields of knowledge. Everything has grown so complicated and has assumed such gigantic planetary dimensions that no single mind is able to grasp all the details necessary for a decisive synthesis. Thus, life itself will work out a new type of cooperation. Therefore, each attempt at friendly cooperation should be welcomed, for all these efforts will become steps on the great ladder of achievement.

And now something else. The astronomer you mentioned is mistaken in thinking that every planet eventually becomes a sun. According to the Sacred Teaching, it is just the opposite. Actually, our planet, before becoming an abode for humanity was a sun, and still earlier, a comet, etc. Thus, the moon after imparting its vital principles to Earth did not become a sun, but is a decomposing body.

* * *

You are right in thinking that all the terrors engendered by the errors of the Prince of the World are nullified by that Light which was brought and is now poured over humanity by the very same Seven Kumaras, or Angels, who came to Earth together with Lucifer. Moreover, Lucifer himself, before his fall, was also a light-giver, for he, too, participated in the awakening of the higher abilities in man. The gift of awakening the higher thinking powers cannot be compared with anything, for only by the path of opening the higher centers can true immortality be attained. Verily, each man is responsible not only for himself but also for others, for man is a creator of the whole world in the full meaning of this concept. All possibilities are contained within him. Of all creatures, only man has the gift of *conscious free will*. The sole expression of this freedom is the freedom of choice, and this choice can make him either a god or a devil.

We also know that each power grows through resistance. Therefore, all the difficulties which arose upon the path of humanity because of the apostasy of the Host of Earth, at the same time give to people the possibility of especially straining and refining their abilities and thus accelerating their progress. Long ago, it was said, "Blessed are the obstacles, by them we grow." Thus, also in the most ancient Hindu scriptures it is said that the Kali Yuga is particularly useful for spiritual perfectment, and that which in the Satya Yuga could only be achieved through hundreds of thousands of incarnations can be attained in Kali Yuga in a few lives. Hence, we may conclude that the Forces of Light will, in the final analysis, turn to good even the apostasy of Lucifer. But, of course, here as ever, only strong spirits who love to overcome difficulties are particularly successful, whereas lukewarm ones, who choose the easiest and irresponsible path, are destined to hard toil, which will finally lead them to a most difficult path. Therefore, profoundly just and scientific are the words from the Apocalypse, "So then because thou art lukewarm, and neither cold nor hot, I will spue thee out of my mouth."

Likewise, your remark about Christ reproaching his disciples is very appropriate. Yes, during all ages the Great Teachers have often been compelled to emphasize the fact of the inertness, division among, and lukewarmness of so-called good people, and the fury, solidarity, and resourcefulness of the dark ones. In fact, at present, the fury and solidarity have become even stronger, for they sense that the decisive Battle will bring defeat to them. Indeed, the signs of the Great Victory are already visible; given more time, much will be instituted. The signs of Benevolence are guarding the New Country.

We should not grieve too much about Abyssinia; in time, the victory will reach there, too, but one should not understand this crudely. The time of brutal conquests is over. Each nation has the right to live its own life and to learn cooperation.

I return, with appreciation, the projects you sent to me, and once more will say—let each one build in his own way; the more versatility in such experiments, the more beautiful will be the crown of achievement. I shall quote from *Aum*:

"441. A cooperative is not a closed community. Cooperation based on the law of nature contains within itself the element of infinity. The exchange of work and mutual assistance must not impose conventional limitations. On the contrary, the cooperative opens the doors to all possibilities. Besides, cooperatives are interconnected, and thus a working network will cover the whole world. No one can predetermine what forms of cooperation may be developed. Institutions founded by cooperatives may be highly diverse and cover the problems of education, of industry, and of rural economy. It is impossible to imagine a single field which could not be vastly improved by the cooperative. One should not prohibit people from gathering together for cooperation in completely new combinations. The cooperative is a bulwark of the state and a nursery for public life. Whence will come public opinion? Whence will be formed the longed for progress? Whence will solitary workers receive help? Surely, cooperation will also teach unity."

You are also right when you say that the dark ones are now working cunningly and very skillfully in an attempt to distort every beautiful thought that has found expression. Verily, the devil is the inventor of a crooked mirror!

Therefore, practice unity. Preserve striving, and fulfill as well as possible the task of friendly cooperation.

Here are a few more useful paragraphs:

"Who, then, are they who do not esteem and love unity? They have never experienced the feeling of steadfastness which is always connected with unity. They do not know valor, which is indissoluble from unity. They have renounced advance, which is strong in unity. They have not absorbed the joy existing in unity. They have scorned the stronghold of unity. What, when, is left for them? Either to crumble under the hurricane, or to wither under the sun, or to rot in the moldiness of prejudices. Who, then, are those who disdain UNITY?

"The most obvious illustration of Maya and of reality is found in the heavenly bodies. Though such a body may have been destroyed thousands of years ago, its light is still seen on Earth. Who, then, can attempt to define the boundary between the existing and the visionary? We find similar examples also among earthly manifestations.

"Earthly victors, where is your being, and where is your phantom? Who will define—is it victory or the reflection of distant events? Where is the boundary of reality? Though all figures be amassed, the ciphers of solutions will not be found. Only the subtlest energy can distinguish between life and catalepsy. But people prefer to live amidst phantoms." [*Ibid.*, 443-5]

31

3 August 1936

The Great Teachers decidedly do not contemplate uniting all the existing groups into one or several "closed" communities—this would be tantamount to death. Life and beauty exist only in diversity, therefore, let the cells of Light flourish freely, like beautiful flowers on the meadow of life. Unification does not necessarily mean that one has to have communal headquarters or identical methods of application and achievement, etc. Unity, as a true motive power, must first of all be born in spirit and must manifest in magnanimity and cooperation in all circumstances of everyday life. Cooperation, collaboration, and community imply the broadest admission. There is no room for forcing where there is unity of consciousness.

Another concept, the renunciation of property, is often wrongly understood. To renounce property does not mean to give everything away and refuse to possess anything. Things are the result of human creativeness, and they should be appreciated. The improvement of their quality is a step toward the perfectment of the spirit. The Teaching tells us that the true significance of objects should be understood, while not being enslaved by them. One has to learn to love everything, and, at the same time, be ready to leave everything for new achievements. Love for beautiful things without a sense of possessiveness is one of the purest and most uplifting of feelings. Without love, nothing can be created and improved. Thus, let people learn to love without the sense of possessiveness. Let them admire beautiful creations without the conventional concept of ownership.

It was interesting to read in the newspaper clippings which you sent us about the rash of reincarnations appearing in a number of cities. Your remark, that the dark forces are attempting to prevent people from accepting the law of reincarnation and are therefore trying to bring it to the point of absurdity by instilling in their agents or unconscious collaborators the idea of these same reincarnations, is not far from the truth. Moreover, they are helped in this by some undisciplined psychics, who see mostly what they want to see. Also, let us not forget that honesty in everything and at all times is the rarest quality. Indeed, according to the mediums there are many Napoleons, Tamerlanes, Ramseses, Cleopatras, Semiramises, etc., all of whom are simultaneously visiting our Earth. And it could be asked, Which of these are genuine?

That is why proofs of reincarnation such as occurred with the little Hindu girl Shanti, a case which could be checked by so many still surviving witnesses of her previous life, are so important. Probably you read about it, for I sent the newspaper clippings.

Here is the explanation in paragraph 491 from *Aum*: "Frequently you hear absurd tales of how there occur simultaneous incarnations of one and the same person—a conclusion both ignorant and harmful. Deniers of incarnation make use of such fictions to dispute the possibility of reincarnation. Besides, they forget the reason—which somewhat lessens the guilt—namely imaginative invention. Certain people remember the details of a definite epoch; when they dream of being a well-known person, their remembrance of the dream molds the imagining of an incarnation. The resulting error is in the person, but not in the epoch. A child imagines himself a field marshal, and such a representation already sinks into his Chalice.

"Many remember their past lives, but through obscuration of consciousness they call forth their own past imaginings. One needs to be careful also not to censure too greatly the mistakes of others. Aside from conceit and ignorance, there may be only partial errors without base motive. Indeed, there may also be different forms of obsession and whispering with evil intention, but enough has already been said about obsession."

Yes, the dark forces are trying their best to distort and destroy all that leads to the knowledge of other spheres and worlds, and to the continuation of life in them. They realize that the awakening of such knowledge will inflict upon them a mortal blow and considerably reduce the ranks of their followers. Indeed, the nature of the dark ones will become obvious, and few will want to join their legions after being convinced of the terror that as a final consequence awaits those who live in evil. Since they can subsist only on the fluids of destruction and decomposition the absence of this substance causes them unbelievable misery.

You are also right in observing unusual signs in all the manifestations of life. Definitely, the approach of the fiery energies affects the whole of nature. Indeed, at the present time, the reduction of crops by leaving the fields fallow in order to maintain price levels cannot be thought of. Some countries have already felt the harm of such measures. Verily, "Man proposes and God disposes." If people had studied psychic energy earlier, it could have helped them to avoid many calamities.

* * *

A few more paragraphs from *Aum* will fully answer your questions:

"450. Remember the advice that the book of the Teaching should lie at the crossroads. Be not tormented as to whence will come the wayfarers, whence will come the friends who have a presentiment of cognition. Be not distressed by those passing by; they may attract someone without knowing it. They may be indignant, and their cries will attract many. But let us not enumerate the inscrutable paths. They cannot be revealed, yet the heart knows them."

"452. It is necessary to help everywhere and in everything. If obstacles to assistance be encountered through political, national, or social lines, or in religious belief, such obstacles are unworthy of humanity. Help in all its aspects should be extended to the needy. One must not scrutinize the color of hair when danger threatens. One should not interrogate as to religious belief when it is necessary to save from conflagration. All covenants point to the necessity of unconditional assistance. Such help may be considered true inspiration. It has been emphasized already, but numerous conventionalities compel one to again affirm the freedom of assistance.

"453. Anxiety of heart is inevitable if you know of misfortune in the home of a neighbor. And the open centers can indicate many disturbances near and far—the heart quivers from them.

But people often fail to pay attention to heart signs; they are inclined to attribute them to illness. Yet it will be just to remember that the heart beats in unison with all that exists. Cosmic events and national conflagrations are like hammer blows. People talk about the development of heart ailments. Indeed, the symptoms are increasing, but it is superficial to think only about the nervous tension of the age. Where, them, lies the reason for these disturbances? The condensation of currents provokes psychic energy to new manifestations. But people fail to give the energy paramount significance, and from this result so many perturbations and all sorts of conflicts. Someone has said, 'Do not drive energies to the point of madness.' Such a warning is not far from the truth. One can picture to oneself the frenzy of energies, wrongly overstrained, broken and abused. In such chaos is it possible for the heart not to be atremble?

"454. Gratitude is a great motive force. No one solicits gratitude, but great is the quality of this power. Gratitude acts as a purifier, and whatever has been purified is already more easily moved. Thus, gratitude is a means of hastening the path. Some believe that by a transport of gratitude they lower themselves. What ignorance! Gratitude only exalts, purifies; it attracts new energies. Even a machine works better without dust."

* * *

Dark forces creep out of all holes, but, at the same time, the hearths of Light are kindled everywhere. Be valiant, be courageous, the times are very grave, but the dawn is already aglow. The Higher Help is prepared; let us learn to accept it with a courageous heart, in readiness, gratitude, and full trust.

32

14 August 1936

The thoughts expounded in your project are excellent, but their execution requires other conditions than those which now exist and are forming under the pressure of approaching events. Of course, the most urgent problem is the birth of the true man; that is why it is so essential to spread more extensively the seeds of the new, broadened consciousness and understanding of cooperation on the widest scale.

Before building communities, co-workers with a prepared consciousness are needed. Otherwise, the result will be nothing but a terrible burden and an ugly caricature of a community. For this purpose, it is first necessary to create new schools where from very childhood will be laid the foundations of the understanding of the destination of man, his place and role in the world, and his cosmic dependency. With such concepts, he will realize his social role, and, mainly, his personal responsibility, which will be given a fitting significance. But such schools need appropriate teachers. That is why it is so useful to have groups that gather around the Teaching of Life, for from such groups can come forth bearers of the new consciousness.

Verily, the Teaching of Living Ethics regards the whole world as one World Community. We are told to cultivate cooperation, unity, and magnanimity, but nowhere is anything said about jostling one another! The exchange of labor and mutual help should not impose any conventional limitations. Any exaggerated attachment to a particular place is condemned, because it is limiting. The Great Buddha, the fountainhead of world community, taught his disciples not to stay too long together in one place, but to leave frequently to visit new countries and have contacts with different people.

Communities dedicated to scientific research are excellent, they facilitate the work of the scientists who are occupied with a common problem. Excellent are the sanatoriums and experimental laboratories that unite various specialists for the work of the Common Good. I can well imagine whole educational settlements and cities of knowledge, and also cooperatives dealing with all spheres of life; however, knowing human nature, I can hardly visualize a successful narrow *closed* community of entirely different people. In a narrow, closed community, given the present average state of consciousness, the tendency to leveling would be unavoidable, and such leveling inevitably transforms talent into mediocrity, causing a loss of culture and lowering of the level of civilization, that is, to primitiveness, and, alas, to the next stage—coarseness.

Therefore, community and cooperation should be understood broadly and practically. Precisely, the new scientific discoveries and life itself will prompt new forms of collaboration. The international postal system and means of communication have already shown what mutual benefit and excellent cooperation can be achieved between different countries. And so, I believe in the broadest development of cooperatives in the most diverse combinations. Cooperatives organized broadly will prove what kind of national benefit can come from such collaboration. As there is now evidence of an awakened desire in many people to establish working communities, a desire which is undoubtedly in response to the trend of evolution, I consider it appropriate to quote some paragraphs from the new book of the Teaching, which indicate the need to prepare the consciousness of people for the beneficial results of any undertaking.

"Picture to yourself how an ignoramus approaches a complicated machine. He does not think about the meaning of the apparatus but clutches at the first lever, not realizing the consequences. Exactly comparable is the case of a man who has remembered only one detail of the entire Teaching and is amazed that he does not see the whole effect. Just as careless handling of the machine threatens the ignoramus with ruin, so does a man who disregards the essence of the Teaching find himself in danger.

"One person is concerned only about the quality of food; another tries to avoid foul language; another attempts to avoid irritation; a fourth avoids fear; but such useful details are nevertheless separate levers—none by itself will lift the entire weight. One needs to delve by degrees into the synthesis of the Teaching; only the rainbow of the synthesis can bestow advancement. If someone notices that one aspect has taken possession of him, let him diligently repeat also the other parts of the given indications. We give much in a veiled form and gradually bring realization nearer to people. Let man not be afraid, but draw near until he assimilates the rhythm of the entire mosaic. Thus, an approach to the synthesis teaches one to make use of all the details." [Aum]

Therefore, primarily, we should think of education and the broadening of the consciousness. This realization will bring the most beneficial results. "Disharmony of details can break up all construction." Therefore, let us learn magnanimity and cooperation in our groups where the Living Ethics are studied; this is good schooling for the closer type of community. Let us be solicitous abut one another, exercising the maximum of sensitiveness and response to each other's characteristics.

* * *

It is quite true that in all countries the Societies for Psychic Research are, at the moment, on the first steps, but the entire, infinite field of knowledge lies ahead of them. You are right in saying that they are, in a way, at a dead end, the reason being that most of them are pursuing their researches with the aid of inferior mediums. Investigations in the realm of psychic and parapsychic manifestations with the aid of mentally and spiritually developed individuals are interesting, for only they can provide the new steps of understanding of the higher energy and of the conditions of the Subtle World in its higher spheres. As for the harm that comes from dealing with the lower spheres that are adjacent to the earthly plane, you already know about this from the books of the Teaching. I can here add another paragraph:

"Ectoplasm is the storehouse of psychic energy. Actually, the substance of ectoplasm is midway between the earthly and the subtle being. Psychic energy, which is inherent in all the worlds, has, first of all, a relation to the substance close to the Subtle World. From this it may be seen that ectoplasm should be preserved in purity, the same as psychic energy. It should be remembered that by giving out ectoplasm for casual comers the medium is subject to great danger. It is inadmissible to place such a valuable substance at the disposal of uninvited visitors. More precious are the higher communions; they do not drain our strength, or rather, they bestow a new current of force. It must be understood that psychic investigations should be carried on prudently. It is inadmissible to drain another's essence." [*Ibid.*]

I presume you know that all the phenomena that take place in spiritualistic seances are performed by means of ectoplasm, which is exuded by the medium and all those who are present. And you can well imagine the polluted condition of the ectoplasm when it returns to its owner after it has been used by the visitors from the lower and middle spheres! That is why it is so essential in psychic research for all people that are present to be both in good health and of a high moral level. Eventually, when people know more, this, too, will become evident. Thus, in the new book *Aum* much has been said about this energy, and it is emphasized that those who undertake research into this energy must be self-denying and have keen discrimination and purity of heart. Research into and the study of psychic energy is the science of the near future.

The followers of Christian Science, whom you mention, are quite numerous in America, and occasionally they perform remarkable healings. But it also happens that some of their ignorant followers ruin themselves as well as those near to them, for often these healers are impure and weak. Moreover, not all diseases can be healed directly by psychic energy. When a surgical operation is inevitable, psychic energy alone, without the use of the needed instruments, will not be of help.

* * *

When I spoke of leaving the Teacher, I meant departure from the CONSCIOUSLY chosen Teacher, and not just the matter of leaving the particular church into which one was accidentally born. Only a conscious choosing of a Teacher is significant, and not, because of one's birth, the acceptance of a conventional creed which automatically binds us to one or another Founder of a particular religion. Truly, conscious choosing is the call of the spirit. The Great Brotherhood represents one Single Ego; therefore, the Teaching that issues from them is one in its essence. But each of Them, though belonging to a particular luminary, is linked in His essence with all those who have been conceived under this same luminary. Hence, it is especially beautiful when spirits having the same essence gather together under the guidance of their own Lord. Each Teacher also has his own individual method. I cannot imagine a departure from the consciously chosen Teacher in the future, for the higher we ascend, the closer becomes our bond with the Teacher.

* * *

Certainly, smoking carries away our vital force. It is quite true that H. P. Blavatsky smoked, but, then, her condition was so exceptional that one should attempt no comparison with her. Her life, spent among strangers to her, was incredibly hard; she was never understood properly by them and was often even betrayed, both consciously and unconsciously. All these reasons, as well as her smoking prevented her from finishing her work and the writing of the last volume of *The Secret Doctrine*. There are also many people who mistake the Takur, Gulab-Singh, the hero of her book *The Caves and Jungles of Hindustan*, for the Mahatma

K. H. However, in this remarkable book, written for a wider public and therefore greatly embellished by the rich fantasy of H. P. B., the Image of another Mahatma is actually portrayed. It is true that the Teacher K. H. in his letters to Sinnet sometimes signed them: "Lal Singh," but the Mahatmas use many names, and in some cases they sign with a single, general one. In fact, none of the Mahatmas smoke, and the legend about the pipe used by one of them was actually based on a story told in a light vein by H. P. Blavatsky, in which she mentioned the Hindu pipe smoked by Master M., but omitted to explain with what the pipe was filled. The reason was that M. M., coming down from the heights, of course felt the entire burden and pressure of the atmosphere of the valleys; thus for relief He smoked, or inhaled a special preparation of ozone. Hence, the legend about the pipe and smoking.

* * *

True, there are no large and small matters in Cosmos, but the daily life of human beings has so greatly departed from cosmic concepts that it is filled with the most trivial and abominable matters. And yet cosmic goal-fitness and co-measurement sweep away our present-day sand piles to make room, let us hope, for better creations.

* * *

Guard your health, the currents are extremely heavy. Events are piling up. The place of the future great construction is indicated, but not yet pronounced, and the thoughts of men are far from it. Thus, all that is sacred is guarded for the time to come. Someone reads Nostradamus and attempts to apply the great signs to himself, but he may be far astray. The Great Initiates knew how to protect the most sacred when they left their writings. Without the key no one is able to understand Their indications. But when the predestined shall come to pass, the key will be found.

Thus, let us remember the Leading Hand and be without fear.

33

24 August 1936

You ask how you should react to the "Call of the Mother of the World" issued by the T. Society. I would suggest that you accept it in a friendly and sympathetic way. In the Epoch of the Mother of the World we must welcome every mention of her. And why be surprised that A. Besant could write it? In the East, the cult of the Mother of the World, of the goddess Kali, or Durga, is widespread, and one may say that it is predominant in Hinduism. But even among other sects, one finds more worshipers of the Great Mother than of any other aspect of Divinity. In Mongolia and Tibet Dukkar, or the White Tara, and other Taras—Sisters—are greatly worshiped. In all the most ancient religions, the feminine deities were considered the most sacred. At the head of all, or rather, behind the veil is the "Eternal and Everlasting Breath of all Be-ness." But on the plane of the manifested reigns the eternal Feminine Principle, or the Great Mother of the World.

And here are several dates:

In 1924 the rays of the luminary of the Mother of the World reached Earth, and in pouring upon it they awakened a new consciousness; the hearths of many women were kindled with aspiration toward new life.

In 1924 N. K. painted several variations of his painting "The Mother of the World." They were exhibited in the museum in New York and made a tremendous impression. The reproduction of one of these paintings, which was based partly on my vision, received very wide distribution.

In 1924 N. K. wrote an article entitled "The Star of the Mother of the World," which was published in *The Theosophist* at Adyar.

Since 1917, being already outside of his motherland, N. K. continued his campaign for culture and unity through art. His motto expressing the significance of art was used on the shield of the Institutions in New York and has appeared in many books and magazines. Thus, let us recall paragraph 375 in *Agni Yoga*: "What comprised the success of a Yogi? It is not in the attraction of crowds, not in the conversion of multitudes. But near the works of the Yogi one may begin to remark imitation, conscious and unconscious, voluntary and involuntary. People begin to do the same thing. Even enemies, while cursing, follow by the same way. It is as if a special atmosphere had gathered about the actions of the Yogi. This is veritable success; when not money, nor multitudes, but the invisible fire kindles human hearts. But, desiring to imitate, they enter the same atmosphere and bear away with them drops of the identical creative dew. The success does not come alone from without. It is created by the correlation of human hands with the thought of space. But the Yogi becomes the primary channel, the primary receiver of the energies of space. Therefore the Yogi is luminous as an evocative fire. He builds that which should be built. He lays together the predestined stones. And even enemies, atremble, reiterate the words he brings. The Yogi is not a preacher. He seldom appears; but the works entrusted grow with a special color. Others do not even acknowledge the flourishing of these works. For their destiny is not to absorb, but to kindle.

"Where will flow the spark of fire? Could one see all the lighted fires and all the travelers warmed by the fire of an Agni Yogi? The fire lights up successfully because it burns not for itself."

And so, let us welcome everything that does not contradict but confirms the indicated direction.

Recently, I received an excellent appeal to women written by Mrs. K. I fully agree with her statement that a theory must be linked with practice, however, I do not quite accept her conclusion that "the first step on the path is to establish a community house to give an opportunity of living together to those people who have decided to follow the path of the new great epoch of regeneration and spiritualization of life." Personally, I would be interested least of all in such communal hothouses and in the leveling of minds. Security and ease of achievement are the greatest obstacles on the path of spiritual growth. Youth exists for the very purpose of testing all obstacles and tempering the spirit upon them. In connection with all such proposed communal houses and the thoughts of giving complete security through clothes, food, and shelter, I recall the numerous camping communities organized in America in recent years with the view of helping unemployed youth. All of them, as I was informed, ended unsuccessfully. The young people, being provided with everything, became incapable of that labor to which they had dedicated themselves. The majority of them preferred to continue with the easy, minimal physical labor in such a community camp, which guaranteed to them a replete and calm life.

It is not the comfort of youth that we should be concerned with, but with equipping them better for the life struggle which is an immutable cosmic law. That is why, in the structure of the New Epoch, the main factor of the national welfare will be the education and upbringing of people. It is urgently necessary to pay attention to the betterment and broadening of school programs, especially those of the elementary and high schools. Woman must raise her voice and insist on one program for the education of both sexes. From very childhood, *respect for knowledge* should be taught. In schools, this true and only propeller of evolution should be pointed out through concrete historical examples. It is necessary to reach a state where the aspiration to and respect for science enter our flesh and blood and become an inalienable part of our daily life. Only then will it be possible to say that the nations have entered the path of culture. Only then will the bearers of knowledge be considered as true treasures, not only of any one particular country but of the whole world. Then it will be possible to speak about the acceleration of evolution and bringing into life the dreams of communication with the far-off worlds. Thus, we may repeat the words of a thinker and leader who said, "First, all should learn; second, all should learn; third, all should learn; and then see that knowledge does not become a dead letter, but is applied in life."

Thus, let us leave communal houses and legitimate forms of all kinds of relief to those who need the rest because of *old age* or illness. Mrs. K. begins with the kindergarten, and it is excellent. Why should she not continue to look for helpers in her own country in the task of introducing *a new type of school* into life? Talented youth loves everything unusual, and life in communal houses may seem flat to them. Only the most mediocre ones will be reconciled to an all-leveling environment. Moreover, only that which is achieved with difficulty, and even with a certain amount of danger, is especially liked and appreciated. Therefore, the persecuted and semi-proscribed societies were often far more successful in attracting truly valuable workers than the recognized and well-publicized organizations. Easements never achieved their purpose.

And now, regarding paragraph 80 of *Fiery World III*. We must first of all fully realize what is meant and what is expressed by "fortified by a fiery esteem for Hierarchy." The Hierarchic Chain has been manifested, and it is impossible to omit a single link of it. But in order to remain in the powerful Chain in its onrushing motion, one should not lose hold of the nearest link. Breaking from the Chain is terrifying, for it throws us into space and casts us into chaotic rambling. How many centuries must pass before the spirit that broke away can again grasp a new link! For it is impossible to overtake the previous link, since it is too far ahead. That is why it is so dreadful to break away from, or to leave the manifested Hierarchic Chain.

Certainly, every union is already a great power, but like everything else in the manifested world it has two sides, and if such union is not strengthened by fiery reverence for the Chain of Hierarchy, it may find itself on the side of darkness instead of that of Light. That is why the fiery reverence and devotion to Hierarchy are so persistently and repeatedly indicated.

Please tell Mrs. K. that I received her heartfelt and kind letter, and I was especially pleased with her words that *she does not like to look back*. This is already a great achievement. Looking back is like putting heavy weights on one's feet. Creative striving comes only from the contemplation of the future. Of course, now is the time of spiritual regeneration and accumulation; and yet, at the same time, all knowledge should be used for the benefit of all. Each broad thought, each display of magnanimity and dedication to peace is a good deed in everyday life.

With all our heart let us strive to where the great task is being fulfilled, and let us harken to all tidings that come from there. Events of tremendous significance are taking place before our eyes. And in spite of many tragedies, the country is growing and moving forward, and is undoubtedly creating its own future. Thousands and thousands have awakened to the cultural life. The virgin soil is in need of a sweeping approach. Striving toward knowledge indicates the right path.

Let us rejoice.

34

31 August 1936

Unquestionably, weakness of character indicates a comparative immaturity of spirit. Old spirits know exactly what they want and are usually very persistent in their decisions and achievements. You should advise that one's thinking should not be based on visions. There is nothing more deceptive than these illusions from the Subtle World, which are perceived through the lower manas. It is essential to have discipline, a firm control of all emotions, and years of the most refined observations before it is possible to correctly discriminate between visions of the Subtle World. One must investigate all such visions most objectively, honestly, and with keen observation, otherwise we will become playthings of the denizens of the lower strata of the Subtle World. That is why disciples are advised to write down their visions, so that eventually they can ascertain their correctness and significance. But there is a great difference between writing down and observing them, and unconditional acceptance of and guidance by them. The visions that are most deceptive are those which concern our personality and our immediate surroundings. In the normal development of spiritual perception, visions embrace seven circles, or planes, as indicated in he second volume of *Leaves of Morya's Garden*. Visions that concern the personal life become rare. It is true that the lower entities attack poorly protected auras; in addition, the lower manas of those attacked readily prompts the suggested image.

Now, regarding the questions connected with the Teaching. When reading *The Mahatma Letters*, you should bear in mind that the explanations in them were given to people having a definite way of thinking, which had to be considered in order to be understood by them. Moreover, you should thoroughly correlate the questions and answers. But you ask quite correctly how to understand the words, "or—be annihilated as an individuality." Certainly, a High Individuality cannot be annihilated upon completion of the earthly evolution, for such an individuality has had to assimilate the eternal life-power of the seventh principle and to fuse the fourth, fifth and seventh principles into the sixth. By the way, the example of Lucifer is sufficient proof that individuality is not annihilated. In your quotations from *The Mahatma Letters* that eternal, infallible forward motion, which impels all that lives to follow this fundamental impulse, it is emphasized and therefore each stoppage inevitably throws it back. Thus, even a highly evolved person will cease to progress, and if he does not realize suddenly that in his rushing descent he may reach such a low level that all his higher centers will become silent, his higher individuality will lose contact with the vehicles that are necessary for its nourishment and those elements which enter the whirl of its auric surroundings, and finally, it become separated from its lower principles. Deprived of their cohesive power, the lower principles of such a soulless entity will decompose and will be reworked as cosmic dross. The detached higher individuality itself, after many cycles of time, may receive a new possibility for incarnation on another planet, but it will have to build its vehicles, or sheaths, for incarnation, beginning with the lowest kingdoms of nature, until finally the human form shall be built in which it can again manifest.

We should remember that in the first days of the Theosophical teaching it was necessary to devise certain definitions for concepts that were entirely new to the Western mind; hence there is some lack of clarity. In that era no distinction was made between the personality, which comprised by one earthly incarnation, and the individuality, which is the eternal witness and accumulator of the achievements of a multitude of such incarnations. Even now, in the consciousness of the majority of people, personality and individuality are one and the same. A High Individuality cannot be annihilated, but its separate manifestations in the form of personalities can. Thus, at the end of a Manvantara, looking back through the book of lives of each individuality, in some such books there will be missing pages (earthly incarnations). In those pages the individuality failed to gather, through its personality, the harvest of higher energies which nurture it.

Now, regarding the same Letter, Reply No. 7, in which it is said that "During earthly life ... the whole individuality is centered in the three middle or 3rd, 4th, and 5th principles," pay attention to the following lines: "Mr. Hume has perfectly defined the difference between personality and individuality. The former [personality, or 3rd, 4th and 5th principles] hardly survives—the latter [individuality, the incarnating Ego], to run successfully... [let us say, more simply, in its further ascent] has to assimilate ... the seventh [principle] and then blend the three (fourth, fifth and seventh) into one—the sixth." (*The Mahatma Letters*, pp. 77-78, Letter XIII.) Thus if immortality, or to be more precise, continuous consciousness on all planes of being can be achieved only through a lengthy process of nurturing the seed of the spirit by the higher energies, it becomes clear that if this nurture of the seed ceases, the thread of consciousness is interrupted, and one may say that this is the annihilation of the personality, and a relative annihilation of the individuality. Furthermore, we must bear in mind that people tend to think that something is annihilated in each transformation.

The seventh and the sixth principles without the fifth have no consciousness on the plane of the manifested Cosmos. Yet we know that in the Cosmos everything strives toward conscious life, therefore, thought (Manas) spiritualized by the primary energy creates the Crown of the Cosmos, which, with the completion of each new cycle or Round, or Manvantara, becomes more and more beautiful, and so unto Infinity.

The primary energy, or psychic energy, brings immortality. If something is not clear to you, I shall always be glad to explain further.

And now, from paragraph 3 *Infinity I*, "Humanity does not even realize what extinguishing means. But you know that each extinction of a flash of fires ignites supermundane torches." Here is meant any kindling of fire, any extraction of fire from space. When, let us say, we light a candle, by this very act we summon to earthly manifestation the fire that is concealed in space. The extinguishing of such fire returns it again into space, but already in a transformed condition. And this condition will be saturated with the fluids that accompanied its lighting and the process of burning. This implies that the fire that is called forth from space with a benevolent intention and for a benevolent purpose will bear in itself benevolent fluids, and after its extinguishing will kindle supermundane torches of entirely different significance than the fires caused by malicious arson and destruction. That is why, when calling forth fire from space, it is advisable to accompany these actions by the most benevolent sendings and benediction.

Likewise, the extinguishing (death) of the earthly fires, or vital fires of the human body, kindles so much the brighter the fires of the subtle body.

35

5 October 1936

You ask how one should explain the karma of drowning in the case you have described. By refusing to save a drowning person in the past, because the memory of it deprived the man of the power of self-preservation.

* * *

Upasika means a female lay disciple. So, the Great Teachers called H. P. Blavatsky.

* * *

You are surprised that the proximity of certain auras is so oppressive for you, but there are many reasons for this. It could be lack of correspondence in tension, difference in color, disharmony of currents, or that weaker or sick aura are drawing strength from one's reservoir. Especially heavy are the auras of people whose consciousness is extinguished, they should be avoided. Moreover, during the cosmic battle, when the spatial currents are so terrible, an acute sensitiveness toward everything and toward all atmospheric conditions, is most natural. The spatial battle can interfere even with a correct reading of a horoscope. Incidentally, not many people understand that astrology, as a science, is a double-edged sword; a little knowledge of it can be dangerous. I particularly advise you against reading your own horoscope, especially upon the first steps. Only very strong spirits are able to read certain signs intelligently and calmly. Do not forget that a strong will and pure striving toward the Hierarchy of Light can change many things. The reading of horoscopes has become more complicated at present, because of the new combinations of luminaries, which bring about entirely new currents. Indeed, our astrology is to be regarded as quite relative, and the astrology of the Higher Knowledge differs greatly from ours. Thus, the most sacred signs and decisions are beyond the usual astrology. Were it not so, there would have been a world cataclysm long ago. Here is a quotation from *Brotherhood*: "We have spoken about the mixture of strata. In cosmic storms the current of chemism is constantly being unsettled and the rays refracted. It is not easy to assimilate such perturbations unless we remember about the inviolability of the laws. Astrology, remaining a science, can still undergo many fluctuations due to earthly lack of information. In addition, many signs have been concealed. We say this, not by way of disillusionment, but on the contrary, in order to remind observers about the complexity of conditions." Therefore, let those who perceive difficult signs in their horoscopes be not too dismayed, but remember that pure striving toward the Teacher can turn everything to the best. Moreover, one must be aware that an easy horoscope is not a blessing, but the reverse. We grow by obstacles. All great spirits have difficult horoscopes.

36
23 October 1936

The attitude of Vsevolod Soloviev toward H. P. Blavatsky is imparted in his book *A Modern Priestess of Isis*, which was written after her death. To any reader with even a little discrimination this book is a severe condemnation of the author himself. Soloviev did not realize what a harsh verdict he rendered upon himself, with this book! All the dull conceit of mediocrity, all the meanness, betrayal, falsehood, and pettiness of his nature show through on every page.

The meeting of H. P. Blavatsky with Soloviev is described in *Letters of H. P. Blavatsky to A. P. Sinnett*. These letters are remarkable. I shall never tire of repeating how important it is to get acquainted with *The Mahatma Letters* and *Letters of H. P. Blavatsky to A. P. Sinnett*. In these volumes is the whole history of the Theosophical Society, as well as that of its chief participants. The biography of and the articles on H. P. Blavatsky are greatly needed, but it is also very important to acquaint Russian society with all her basic works. When we know the works of a person, his biography acquires an entirely different meaning and significance.

I know that the Mahatma M. was displeased with all the biographies written about Blavatsky. Indeed, at that time there was not to be found one sensitive and thoughtful co-worker who could have evaluated this titanic nature. Of course, Mead did not write badly, but probably A. Besant wrote best of all about Blavatsky, because she herself was a big spirit; yet she did not give a full biography of this self-sacrificing life.*

* * *

On the path of discipleship it is most difficult to maintain co-measurement and balance in everything. Precisely, one must fulfill the indications as they are given—not more and not less. But often, in his striving, the disciple is inclined to overdo,

---

* In 1937 an excellent treatise about our great compatriot H. P. Blavatsky was published by Helena Pisareva.

forgetting that all superfluousness is just as harmful as incompleteness, and perhaps even more so.

* * *

I return to you herewith the dreadful letters. Rarely does one come across such black human documents. Verily—"bombastic passions"! Of course, complete ignorance stands out above all. To such a type it is absolutely useless, and even harmful, to write or communicate anything at all. The aura of the letters is frightful, it reveals signs of the gravest obsession. Such a degree almost no longer admits of any action.

Leave this obvious servitor of darkness alone, particularly since he is so convinced of the humaneness of the dark forces! Severity that issues from Higher Justice, is, of course, beyond the understanding of such unmitigated ignoramuses. What can this blasphemer know about Buddhism? Each thought of his, each word, contradicts the very foundations of this great Teaching.

Incidentally, this blasphemer referred to the concept of the natural path. I shall quote some paragraphs for you from a book not yet assembled: "What is the natural path? *The most unrestricted way of learning, with tolerance and patience, without any sectarianism.* Unrestricted cognition is not easily adopted. Everything connected with human labors is limited. Every occupation cuts short, as it were, many ways of communion. Even excellent minds have been driven into a narrow channel. The disease of self-limitation bears no resemblance to self-sacrifice. Man limits himself for *his own comfort.* Indeed, bold actions for the sake of unrestricted knowledge will be the exception. Malice and hatred carry out their actions in straitness of mind. For unconfined action it is necessary for one to be filled with magnanimity and to discover causes and effects with a benevolent eye. Austerity of labor has nothing in common with a censorious attitude. Only limited people condemn. Not out of condemnation is perfectment born. Is it possible to dream about unlimited knowledge when in confusion? One may learn everywhere and always. Possibilities themselves are attracted toward irrepressible striving. *Only in motion lies the natural path!*

"Verily, one has to seek! One has to keep in mind that a small spark produces a great explosion. A single thought may both attract and repel. Those who rule human minds are often themselves being led. And what empty sounds can stifle the will of a man and forever impede the path already molded! Good does not hinder, but evil does. Thus, let us remember that small sparks produce great explosions.

"Are such preparations needed for Brotherhood? Definitely, not only preparation but also illumination. Will not he who decides to devote himself to the Great Service regret it? From faint-heartedness there will arise many thoughts about comfort and convenience. There may be even smiles of regret. How, then, to overcome such assaults without illumination?" [Brotherhood]

By the way, have you heard of the phenomenal ten-year-old boy in Athens, who, as they say, comes out every night at eleven o'clock on the balcony of the house where he lives and addresses the crowd with a speech. He talks on political and social topics and reveals extraordinary knowledge. He can answer the most complex questions, but only at that hour. The rest of the day he is an entirely normal child. It is supposed that through this boy speaks the spirit of Venizelos. Also of interest is another case, in America. A boy sees through impenetrable surfaces, but also only at certain times when some impersonator acts through him. There is a photograph of this boy in the newspaper, in which he is shown with tightly bound eyes fencing with an expert in this art. According to the expert, the boy (or the impersonator who acts through him) displays an unusual skill. All this comes from the newspapers, therefore it needs verification. However, in principle it is quite possible.

* * *

Do not be disturbed by anybody or anything. As it is said, "Danger becomes salvation for many things." Perhaps, in connection with some events it can even be said that the more dangerous, the better. Danger can help to outlive a great deal of ugliness.

Let us remember the Helmsman of the World Ship, and let us not fear.

37

25 October 1936

I was happy to learn that the formula for independent achievements appeals to you, for this will help you to evaluate all the beauty of the Teaching, which, though it indicates the direction and generously gives hints, sometimes very transparent ones, never forces the consciousness and leaves freedom for individual decision.

It is true that the time is ripe, but it ripened first of all in the realization of the threatening time and of the cataclysms that await our planet if the human spirit does not cry out and fails to strive toward a shift of thought and the purification of the heart. The poisoned atmosphere around Earth must be dispersed, for it prevents the penetration of the beneficial rays of the luminaries. However, this can be achieved only by an increase in vibrations, that is, by the awakening of spirituality in mankind.

All apparatuses for collecting psychic energy or for measuring the fiery tension of space, which are of such interest to you, in the hands of the covetous and chaotically thinking representatives of humanity, would become premature detonators. The accumulated psychic energy would not be used by them for construction, but for destruction. There are many identical examples in other domains.

The greatest benefit that we can contribute consists in the broadening of consciousness, and the improvement and enrichment of our thinking, together with the purification of the heart, in order to strengthen our emanations; and by thus raising our vibrations, we restore the health of all that surrounds us.

True, it is impossible to increase our store of psychic energy without the help of the Teacher; however if our hearts are open and purified, and if our organism permits it, the Teacher will not tarry in manifesting himself.

The books of Living Ethics have in mind the Image of the Teacher that every disciple carries in his heart. Of course, these images differ greatly. Judging by many hints, each disciple creates the Image that is closest to him. However, there is no Image which completely accords with the reality. We have one of the closest Images in our Ashram, but even it does not express the beautiful reality.

Yes, there are many interpreters of the Sacred Teaching, and they all claim to be members of the White Brotherhood. Who can forbid this? Besides, if they are working sincerely to contribute to the Light and help to bring order into the chaotic consciousness of the majority of humanity, they may call themselves members of the White Brotherhood. For has not the whole of humanity now divided itself into the followers of the Black or

White Brotherhoods? And, actually, the vast majority are with the dark ones, and there are as many degrees of these members as there are consciousnesses.

I have heard about D., and I have read his good and useful booklets, but his followers make some sort of a sect out of his teaching. There are even rumors that those who leave are threatened with punishment. However, realizing that often the leader differs greatly from his followers and treating rumors and gossip with great caution, I would not believe it were it not that in this case I have come across a certain fact myself. D. forbade one of his disciples to translate into the local language and publish the books of Living Ethics. Truly, one has the right to expect more broadmindedness and tolerance from a teacher whom his disciples regard as "a teacher from the White Brotherhood" and even "belonging to the Solar Hierarchy"! The Teaching of Life or Living Ethics does not entice anyone; it is given broadly and freely; it does not threaten or persecute anyone who for some reason desires to leave it.

What interpretation of the Teaching in the magazine *Occultism and Yoga* have you in mind? Each one has the right to take from the Teaching that aspect which is closest to him. I greatly love these words from the *Bhagavad Gita*, "By whatever path ye come to Me, by that path will I bless ye, for all paths are Mine." This beautiful statement clearly indicates that the form has no significance, it is the idea that is essential. How far removed are some spiritual teachers from such tolerance and breadth of containment! First of all, they lack GENEROSITY OF HEART.

* * *

And now for your question about the details regarding the isolation of the substance of electricity. Much information and exact formulas cannot be entrusted safely to the post.

Here are the paragraphs from the Teaching which should interest you:

"Is it possible to acquire psycho-technics without a Teacher? It is impossible. This technic is accompanied by dangerous processes. Do you send your children into a physical laboratory without a guide? How to find the Teacher? Let us not forget that the laws of the will possess the property of attracting the attention of whomsoever the call concerns. One's Teacher is not necessarily discovered in a neighbor's house; it is possible to guide at a distance. But moments occur when an experienced forewarning is unavoidable.

"A series of psychic manifestations is closely connected with atmospheric and astrochemical events. There exist invisible but perceptibly deadly magnetic storms; the physical guide will give useful advice on how to avoid the danger contained in each metal. There are psychic storms in which the hand of the Teacher becomes indispensable. You know that physical manifestations react on large groups of people. This cannot be called insanity, but is a particular manifestation of collective unity. One may visualize the reaction of subterranean gases and the dust of atmospheric bodies. Some paralyze psychic actions, but on the other hand there are such exciters that the Pilot must take urgent measures. Speaking about the possibilities of psycho-technics, We have no intention of destroying anyone's apparatuses. We, as Members of the Community, pursue the task of true economy, and each psychic apparatus must be safeguarded. Carefulness is the more needed because often the potentiality of psychic energy does not coincide with intellect, and it is necessary to determine the quality of psychic possibility. Forcing psychic energy into a direction foreign to it will be a most dangerous aspect of compulsion.

"Precipitations of luminous matter and astrochemical rays communicate to psychic energy an unusual sensitivity and saturate it periodically with rays. Indeed, the quality of the consciousness will provide the determining factor, therefore let us treat psychic energy with solicitude."

* * *

"The concept of the magnet transcends the physical sphere. Apply the magnet to the psychic domain and you obtain a most valuable observation. The association of ideas has a certain basis in the magnetic wave. If one will investigate the passage of magnetic waves, it will be possible to establish the advance of ideas in the same direction. The quality of the ideas may be different but the technique of their spreading will be similar. A certain experiment on the connection of the magnet with thinking gives an adequate example of the influence of a physical invisible energy upon the psychic process. The qualities of magnets are diverse; they can be tuned like [musical] instruments. The ... [length] of magnetic waves is inconceivable. Their reaction on people is not according to age but to psychic aspiration. For distant radiations, magnetic waves serve as an exceptional conductor. Thus, we began with distant horizons and end with that future task of humanity. Observe, the system of exposition is followed not in monotony but in the spiral of diverse conditions of one aspiration. Think about magnetic waves and about psychic striving."

"The manifestation of atomic energy is connected with the investigation of psychic energy and with the study of the theory of magnets. Without these factors it is possible to appropriate only certain manifestations of primary energy." [New Era Community]

Yes, *Materia Lucida*, so called, will enter as an ingredient into the formula for a new energy promised to humanity. Indeed, rays and light waves bring the solution for the coming evolution.

Finally, I should like to say that at the moment humanity is so much enslaved by mechanization that the majority have become, consciously or unconsciously, robots. It is necessary to liberate them from this calamity, which threatens to destroy many subtle abilities of man by benumbing his spirituality. Honest and great scientists openly declare that many of their discoveries cannot be revealed at present. They are so much in advance of average humanity that the application of these discoveries in life might bring more harm than benefit.

Therefore, the Teaching of Living Ethics insists primarily upon the development of spirituality, for without this fundamental factor all manipulations with the subtlest energies will not only be destructive but impossible. All the apparatus of the future for collecting and condensing the subtle energies will need the presence of psychic energy of the highest quality, or spirituality in the operator. Many of the most subtle combinations are possible only in the presence of an aura of a definite tension and composition. Thus, the preparation of the fabled philosophers' stone also requires the specific aura of the two Principles (masculine and feminine) completely and spiritually harmonized.

I will quote here from a book written by a pupil of Professor Yourevitch. "After a decade of detailed experiment, Professor Yourevitch brought the results of his investigations before the International Psychological Congress at Copenhagen.

"The difference between the human emanations and those of Radium and the Roentgen Rays is that human emanations are far subtler and can penetrate dense walls, whereas the Roentgen Rays and Radium depend upon a definite density of the bodies which they penetrate. The emanations, for instance, transform gaseous streams, otherwise non-conductors, into remarkable conductors of magnetic force. Their far-reaching conductivity is the chief basic quality of the Y-rays. Without respect for distance and intensity, these gaseous streams become conductive under the influence of human emanations. Their far-reaching and penetrative power is conditioned by the cosmic contact of human emanations and therefore they are conceded to have a stronger effect than all other rays.

"Beyond their capacity for far-reaching conductivity and power of penetration, the Y-rays have the power, when piercing thick obstructions, to exercise mechanical functions as well. When piercing thick metal plates, the Y-rays cause molecular sediments as soon as the rays pass through in a consciously concentrated way. During certain experiments they induce refraction of light-waves. They may also be photographed. The Y-rays of the aura are at the basis of levitation and telekinetic phenomena. The work of Professor Yourevitch ... is called 'Y-rays as Conductors of Biophysical Energy'." [*The Magnetic Aura of the Cosmic Man* (Trier: Fr. P. Reiss).]

Thus, science, *nolens volens*, is compelled to direct its research toward spirituality. The dawn of the new era of cognition of the spirit is verily approaching.

38

9 December 1936

I have the little book you mentioned, but I have to postpone reading it until I have more time. The quotations you sent from this book amaze me by their ignorance and, I might even say, by their intentional slander. Apparently, the author could not be bothered to read *The Secret Doctrine* and speaks of it from hearsay of an obviously most hostile kind. However, if he insists that he knows this work, it is still worse, for this would reveal that he did not understand it at all. In saying that "For Blavatsky responsibility does not exist, and she has no understanding of the problems of freedom," he has indeed shown that he himself has no comprehension of the essence of Eastern philosophy, and that such concepts as karma and dharma are for him an empty sound. Certainly it is not Blavatsky who thought that "man is a marionette," but such unscrupulous critics who are themselves marionettes of their own irresponsible statements and prejudices. You are right in being amazed at such judgments.

And now regarding your question. The rabbis whom we used to know unanimously agreed that the word *Israel* has come to mean precisely "the chosen." Therefore, every unprejudiced and pure mind that reveres the Revelation of ancient times, or the sole Source of all religions and philosophies, is called "the chosen" or "Israel"

It is always advisable to mention the gravity and unusualness of the time we are now experiencing, and the necessity for a new approach to the Foundations of Life and a return to the primary Sources of all Teachings, particularly to all the great Spiritual Toilers, who indirectly or closely followed the real Founder of one or another Teaching.

Did you succeed in finding the *Dobrotolubye*? In spite of numerous corrections, one can still find there many remarkable parts. The words of the great St. Antonius are difficult to oppose.

Yes, "Compulsion upon thought is a grave offense. It cannot be justified. It serves only to provoke new violations, and where then will there be an end to outrage? It is a mistake to presume that something created in the name of hatred can remain firm. Only construction, not subversion, can gather power for free thought. Thought must be safeguarded. The very process of thinking must be loved."

No, we are not grieving. On the contrary, we watch with tremor in our hearts how the salutary feeling of love of the motherland is awakened under the signs of war. One may recall the ancient saying: "And I saw a new heaven and a new earth; for the first heaven and the first earth were passed away." Thus, the whole world is now undergoing a purgation, and darkness will devour darkness. *Podvig* is ordained for all. Let us arm ourselves with patience, for the time is approaching when all those who can bring a grain of the true Knowledge will be sought. Where everything was taken away, where all creativity was suffocated, where human dignity was forgotten, there especially powerfully will be awakened, and is already awakening, the thirst for knowledge and for true freedom. In due time, the Abode, unheard of before, will come into its full glory. Therefore, now, during the threatening time, we are bidden to preserve solemnity. We have entered the thick of the Battle of Armageddon.

* * *

Certainly, the concept of heaven understood broadly is that of space, whereas, taken in a religious sense, it signifies the higher spheres surrounding our planet—the Fiery World and the Higher World.

Actually, the term in itself has no significance; only that concept which is linked with this term is important.

One outstanding American scientist when asked how he pictured heaven gave a fine answer, "It is what scientists call the true world, and our earthly world is but its reflection." (One could have added—a dreadfully distorted reflection.) This is a truly Eastern explanation. Who knows, perhaps this scientist, alone in his bedroom with closed door, read *The Secret Doctrine* and similar works of the great Carriers of Light, who, even now, are so cruelly persecuted by ignorant representatives of our biped kingdom. Verily, the extinguishers of Light do not deserve to be called men; they are on an even lower level than the animals.

A wild beast attacks only when hungry, but man in his hatred is ready to destroy all and everything at any time, exercising the most exquisite cruelty. Indeed, hell is here on Earth! But in order to better appreciate paradise, one must also know hell. The Gates of Paradise are ajar; it depends on us to enter them.

Preserve wise joy!

39

10 December 1936

Once again I attentively read your letter and my advice is to put away the so-called occult books and concentrate with all your soul and body on studying the lives of the great saints.

You write that "there seem to be the right conditions for entering the Path," but prior to this you enumerate your hesitations and doubts. Yet the fundamental condition for entering the Path is a firm decision to follow the chosen road without deviations. Although there are a multitude of ways that lead to the one Truth, as has been beautifully expressed in the *Bagavad Gita*, nevertheless, if we run from one path to another, we shall only waste our forces and arrive nowhere. Therefore, if the very beautiful Image of St. Francis is so close to you, do choose him as your Teacher. Why should you turn to another's Guru—have your own. I myself deeply revere St. Francis, and I love St. Theresa of Spain no less. Why not try to follow the great example of St. Francis? Who knows, perhaps someday, if your heart becomes really aflame, you will be inspired to write a book, *The Imitation of St. Francis.* In our present age, with its almost universal worship of the golden calf, a revival of the teaching of poverty would be a most salutary counterpoise.

And so, put aside the books on occultism, and do not burden yourself by criticizing them. In order to be able to criticize soundly, one has to know much. You write that certain people, or even some organizations, consider the book of the author you mentioned to be a Masonic work, moreover, "Jewish-Masonic." There is nothing new in this; it is the same old favorite formula of dull-witted and malicious ignorance. In the Middle Ages, all that brought Light was labeled with the seal of Satan, and now this stamp has only changed its name, that is all. Similar accusations, as well as the titles of "charlatan" and "spy" were, and still are bestowed upon many of the best minds and great workers for the General Good. Great is the assembly of the bearers of knowledge who have perished at the hands of ignorance! At one time, these honorable titles were bestowed upon the great Paracelsus and Comte Saint-Germain, and also on our compatriot, H. P. Blavatsky. Nowadays there are people who have labeled as "betrayers of their motherland" such great patriots as Subvorov, Golenishchev-Kutusov, Prince of Smolensk, Novikov, Lopukin, Prince Repnin, Karamzin, Prince Kurakin, Speranski, Pushkin, Griboyedov, and others, only because these people joined the highly cultural and progressive movement known at that time as Masonry. Take these minds from Russian culture, and what will be left? Let us not forget that even now a certain section of Russian society particularly traduces Tolstoy. Thus, in Harbin, it was forbidden to celebrate the centenary of his birth! Judge for yourself—can we, without deep shame before educated foreigners, face such a manifestation of medievalism? Not that I want to defend Masonry, since now, this movement has degenerated for the most part into mere trappings, clubs, etc. But it is only fair to admit that the original founders of Masonry in both the West and East were people of great intellect and high morality, and above all they were truly great patriots.

By the way, do you know that there are some people who ignorantly believe the Order of the Knights of Malta to be also Masonic? Whereas it is a purely Catholic organization and only Catholics are accepted as members.

As for the enemies of our country, they are numerous, and one may find them in many countries and among various nationalities. During recent years, a number of most valuable documents have been published, revealing the sinister reality in its full power. It is painful to read these documents. At this time, human hatred has reached its climax and threatens the whole world with destruction. Thus the karma of our planet unfolds, woven, above all, by ignorance, for the cause of all misery lies in ignorance. "Hell is ignorance" said one of the great Spiritual Toilers of the first centuries of Christianity.

You would like to be convinced of the law of reincarnation. But this depends upon you, for every conviction or knowledge comes from within. If our former accumulations are meager, it is difficult to expect a speedy enlightenment. And much must be gone through and suffered before the consciousness will be prepared for the new receptivity, yet if there is only a temporary obstruction, one may hope that the eyes of the spirit will open. My counsel is—observe more and ponder upon the cosmic laws, and perhaps you will realize the entire absurdity and monstrous injustice of only one life for man on Earth, and at that in the most unequal conditions of birth.

There is infinite perfectment in Cosmos, based on the law of goal-fitness and the leading Principle of the Hierarchy of Light, or Jacob's Ladder! Were it otherwise, chaos would have devoured the Universe long ago. Indeed, everything positive is in the leading Principle. There is no such thing as eternal damnation, nor is there eternal bliss as it is understood by the majority. There are only periods of this or that duration in full conformity with the accumulations of the spirit. In Cosmos there exist only perpetual movement and diversity. Beautiful is the path of limitless perfectment!

And so, follow the Image you love. I do not doubt that, with the striving of your heart, you will find what you seek. My knowledge of certain details from the life of St. Francis would not satisfy you, for it is based on a different source. I shall quote for you a most edifying story from this beautiful life, which I have recently read in an Indian magazine. It is very probable that you know this story, but I like it so much that I shall repeat it with pleasure.

"Once, Saint Francis of Assisi said to a young monk, 'Brother, let us go and preach in the city.' And so they left the monastery, and, talking of lofty subjects, they passed through the whole city and returned to the monastery. The young monk asked in amazement, 'Father, and when shall we preach?' And Saint Francis replied, 'Brother, did you not notice that we were preaching all the time? We walked with dignity, we discussed most lofty subjects, the passers-by looked at us and received peace and comfort. Indeed, preaching does not consist of words alone, but also of behavior itself.'"

So, imbue yourself with such spirit, and bliss will come to you.

40

17 December 1936

I certainly would not publish fragmentary details about the remarkable personality of Comte Saint-Germain; better to translate completely the book by Cooper-Oakley. I consider this work the best among those I have read about Saint Germain. In this particular volume are included pages of a quite extensive bibliography, which are most valuable.

There is no doubt that Saint-Germain played a role in Russian history also. In international literature one comes across brief references to the prophecies he made while he was in the capital of Russia. The time has not yet come for making these public, but times change, and at the destined date we shall hear about these prophecies.

* * *

Yes, in a certain epoch, in some countries there appears one or another envoy, who brings the message and benevolent help from the Stronghold of Knowledge, which are usually rejected. The East, once upon a time, understood how to accept these messages—of course, not always—but the Western nations were very stubborn in their rejection. Only once were the advices and help accepted by the so-called New World, precisely in the time of Washington, at the Declaration of Independence of the United States of America. The result of this acceptance was the powerful development of the United States. Who knows, even at present, somewhere such help was offered, but in our age of deterioration and the reign of human madness, it was certainly rejected.

And so, let us be witnesses to the karma of rejection of the great help. If, in former ages, many decades sometimes were needed to reveal the consequences of such refection, nowadays dates are much shorter. Under the unprecedented acceleration of the cosmic influence of new combinations of the rays, all events acquire an entirely different tempo. So much has already happened, even in the course of the past year! Therefore, let the wise ponder upon events and look for causes in the past, and sometimes, in the very recent past. During a grave time one must think about new sowings of causes. Let us hope that enlightened minds will be found, who will arrest a total destruction by laying timely benevolent foundations.

* * *

In all ages the Elder Brothers rendered help to people, but the profound ignorance and intolerance that reigned in the ruling circles rejected the salvation of whole countries. Human egoism hates most of all those who are able to foresee, who know more than the self-satisfied ignoramuses. What a minute number of people really wish to learn; everyone is interested only in teaching others! But during all his life the wise one collects the honey of knowledge like a bee, gathering it through observing seemingly most insignificant circumstances.

Of course, one should not interpret the advice about urgency in a narrow sense. This advice primarily concerns fulfillment of the tasks already assigned, and it deals particularly with the inner growth and broadening of the consciousness in order that one may meet and understand the meaning of current events. The brown gas envelops our planet, and the mixing of currents grievously affects sensitive organisms.

* * *

I would greatly like to get acquainted with your new work. I believe that such a book should not be written in a hurry. It is necessary to collect more material. You will find much of value in the Epistles of the Apostle Paul. I found the quotations from *The Life of H. P. Blavatsky* by Sinnett that you mentioned, but I do not know from where H. P. B. picked up this information. Probably they should be referred to the existing Apocrypha, which, in most cases, are more reliable than the so-called historical data. In the *Encyclopedia Britannica*, in the brief description of the Nicaean Council, a curious detail in connection with the choice of the canonical Gospel is absent. I doubt if such details are to be found in the *Encyclopedia of Religion and Ethics* (English edition by Hastings), for they would hardly be allowed to pass by the censorship of the Church of our times. Thus, it remains to look for them in the Apocrypha. However, the decision of the Council of Constantinople in 553 rejecting the doctrine of reincarnation is mentioned in the *Encyclopedia Britannica*. One must give credit to the author who furnished this information about the Councils for the *Encyclopedia Britannica*, he certainly did not feel any compunction in speaking critically about the authorities who headed those Councils. So, my advice is not to hurry with this responsible and greatly needed work. Patiently collect your materials.

* * *

Your answer to the inquirer was very good. Precisely, conscience and heart must prompt the best way to fulfill one's duty. I, personally, approve of all and any defense of one's motherland. And so, let us courageously meet all the accelerated events. As you see, the year 1936 was filled with the most significant events, but do many understand their profound meaning?

In a book recently published in America, *The Story of Prophecy*, [Henry James Forman (New York, Farrar & Rinehart, Inc. 1936)] the author mentions historical events predicted during many centuries, up to the present day. He also mentions the words and prophecies of N. K., which were told to the author of this book in 1934. Not only the year, but the day and the month of a certain predicted event were indicated. This prophecy was fulfilled on the day and the hour—the dot, as they say. Therefore, let us not grieve, but let us bear in mind the destined new world.

Thus, do not be disconcerted by anything, preserve calmness, and watch your health. Accustom yourself to a solemn mood, for precisely solemnity is indicated to us above all else in these days of the Apocalypse. Remember about the wisdom of joy!

Part III

1937

1

1937

To some of your questions I feel like saying, Trust more the voice of your heart. Those greatest Egos, or Individualities, who came to our Earth from higher worlds at the end of the Third Race, continue to guide the movement and growth of human consciousness. The Greatest among Them, the Avatar of Vishnu, as He is known in the East, was manifested, is manifested, and will be manifested in various aspects throughout the whole Cycle of the existence of our planet. This Individuality laid the foundations for every shifting of our humanity's consciousness. Verily, this Highest Spirit stands at the head of the Hierarchy of Light, and He has taken upon Himself a ceaseless vigil.

It is impossible to give the truth to people, for they are incapable of assimilating it. One can even say, The nearer to Truth, the farther it seems to be from us. It is too simple in its grandeur. Try to sell people a golden coin at a reduced price, and no one will buy it from you. So it is with great truths. People require all the trappings, all the age-old masquerade that has accumulated around great concepts.

Christ came, and only fishermen accepted him. But when the centuries laid upon Him all the weight of the church dogma and golden vestments, making out of Him an inaccessible idol, multitudes believed in Him.

I also advise you to put less trust in all sorts of rumors. During the days of Armageddon the entire Hierarchy of Light is gathered in the One Stronghold. For thousands of years the Great Spirits have been preparing for this time. Awesome is the battle, only madmen do not see the terrors of destruction. How can one, after all the sayings and affirmations of which you write, believe in some sort of esoteric knowledge possessed by a few impostors? As for the denial of the existence of the black lodge, one could answer them with the words of a European philosopher, "The victory of the Devil is that he has succeeded in convincing people that he does not exist." The black Lodge does exist and is very powerful, because it acts through the masses, and its best servants are recruited from the feeble-minded, the lukewarm, and the wavering. The dark ones try to imitate the White Lodge in everything, and under the disguise of Light they try with all their might to penetrate to the spiritual hearths, so that they can disturb and corrupt them. That is why it is so important to acquire the qualities of discrimination and self-restraint.

In *The Mahatma Letters* there are many affirmations by the Great Teachers regarding the existence of the Brothers of Darkness. Thus, Armageddon is a decisive battle between the forces of Light and darkness.

I shall end my letter with a paragraph from *Brotherhood*. "The primary energy [psychic] seeks admittance into all the nerves of humanity. It is, it does exist. It has been tensed by cosmic conditions. It is unfitting to ask whether one should develop it. It is impossible to develop the primary energy; one can only safeguard it against the waves of chaos. One should manifest great solicitude toward the treasure of evolution. Much was said in antiquity about the time when the primary energy would begin to be intensively manifested. People must not deny that which so imperatively claims its goal. Who is filled with such arrogance as to fall into denying the tidings of the epoch? Only the ignorant and those vaunting a false wisdom will begin fighting against the evidence. But let us not take to heart the attempts of the ignorant. They only make a wreath to each advice about helping humanity."

With many passers-by apply the wise proverb "Speech is silvern, silence is golden."

2

7 January 1937

We were glad to receive the information regarding the development of the cultural activity of the society and also the report of its president. The latter is written excellently and with hearty aspiration. The Congress that is now being planned may become quite useful in many respects. Therefore, let us bring our best thoughts for its materialization and for deliberation pertaining to the program. We are very touched to know that friends do not relinquish the idea of the Pact. They understand the urgent need to impress upon the consciousness of the masses, starting from early childhood, the value of true treasures, without which humanity would return to savagery. However, there are those limited minds that consider the Pact and Banner only as a problematic defense during military operations, entirely losing sight of its fundamentally profound educational significance.

* * *

Since our friends have taken to their hearts the advancement of the Pact and Banner of Peace, I am enclosing a Discourse from *Brotherhood*. These words should inspire all the friends of the Pact and Banner even more.

"You remember how undeviatingly We try to preserve the creations of Beauty. Already foreseeing the approach of Armageddon we began to disseminate advices as to how best to protect the treasures of the world. We know that the forces of darkness will apply all their efforts to oppose this urgent indication. The forces of darkness understand very well the power of the emanations emitted by objects of art. Amidst the assaults of darkness these emanations can serve as the best weapon. The forces of darkness try either to destroy objects of art or, at least to drive humanity's attention away from them. It should be remembered that a creation rejected and deprived of attention cannot emit its beneficent energy. There will be no living bond between a cold spectator or listener and the locked-up creation. The meaning of the transmutation of thought into creation is very deep; in other words, it becomes an attracting magnet and a collector of energy. Thus, each creation lives and contributes to the exchange and accumulation of energy. Amidst Armageddon it may be proven how extensive is the influence of works of art. The key to the whole epoch is comprised in this concern about precious creations of art. We have saved not a few creations of art. We saw how the dark ones were exercising their craftiness in impeding such salutary conditions, and from the very highest spheres We see when humanity needs help. In the Subtle World this preliminary plan was known long since. We do not conceal the urgency of the measures, because Armageddon, now in action, is aimed at the task of corrupting all human energies. Thus hope the dark ones, but We know how to counteract them. Therefore, observe where Our solicitude is being directed."

* * *

And so, someone accuses us of using Theosophical ideas without mentioning Theosophy anywhere! But quite logically we can point out to these accusers that all of contemporary

Theosophy is borrowed completely from Eastern philosophy. H. P. Blavatsky did not conceal the Sources from which she derived her knowledge. Even the Introduction to *The Secret Doctrine* is ended by H. P. B. with the words of Montagne, "Gentlemen, I have here made only a nosegay of culled flowers, and have brought nothing of my own but the string that ties them."

Any pretense of monopolizing the Universal Teaching, or Truth, or Communion with the Great Teachers sounds utterly wild!

I am quoting a paragraph from the new book *Brotherhood*, which completely puts a stop to such usurpations.

"The Sacred Teaching cannot become congealed at one level. Truth is one, but each century, and even each decade, contacts it in its own way. New scrolls are unrolled and the human consciousness observes in a new way the manifestations of the Universe. Even in its wanderings, science discovers new combinations. Upon such discoveries are the previously proclaimed fundamentals affirmed. Each transmission of the Great Wisdom is indisputable, but it will have its own followers. Those who honor Hierarchy reverence also its Messengers. The world lives by motion, and the issuance of the Sacred Teaching is evoked by advancing. The mediocre call such advancing a violation of foundations, but the thinkers know that life is in motion.

"Even knowledge of languages increases the flow of new discoveries. How much more, then, will unfettered thought bring! Each decade reveals a new approach to the Sacred Teaching. The readers of a half-century ago read it completely differently. In comparison with those who are reading it at present, they emphasized entirely different thoughts. One should not speak about new Teachings, since Truth is one! New data, and new perception of them, will be only the continuance of cognition. Each one who impedes this cognition performs a transgression against humanity. The followers of the Sacred Teaching will not impede the path of learning. Sectarianism and fanaticism are out of place on the paths of knowledge. Whoever can impede cognition is no follower of Truth. The age of shiftings of peoples must especially safeguard each path of science. The age of the approach of great energies must openly encounter these luminous paths. The age of striving into the higher worlds must be worthy of such a task. Quarrel and strife is the lot of litterers."

Now I must tell you that N. K. prefers the original sources, and he is well acquainted with Eastern thought and with those books from which H. P. B. obtained her information. Likewise, I can say about myself that my first earthly teachers were the books of Ramakrishna, Vivekananda, the *Bhagavad Gita*, books on Buddhism, the *Lamrin Chembo* of Tsong-kha-pa, etc.

I only became acquainted with the Theosophical literature in America, and I can say that after the Eastern pearls and the works of H. P. B. this literature was not particularly interesting to me, and some of the works actually repelled me. It would be appropriate to ask the Theosophists why they do not publish in Russian *The Mahatma Letters to A. P. Sinnett*. If it is too difficult for their leaders to translate the whole volume, I am convinced that some members would readily volunteer to share this work among themselves. Likewise, why were the small books of the early letters of the Mahatmas and the volume of *The Letters of H. P. Blavatsky* not translated? Why should the Russian Theosophists walk in blinders and know nothing about the real history of the Theosophical movement and its leaders? While casually referring to Alice Bailey, why are they silent about the far older and more significant center in California which is led by the Great Teacher H.? Why do they never mention the remarkable book *Teachings of the Temple*, which was published by that center?

And as to accusing the Teaching of Agni Yoga of encouraging the growth of psychism, this shows clearly how far those accusers are from the understanding of the great psychic energy! And all the works of H. P. B. did not enlighten their consciousnesses. To deny psychic energy and to veto its development is equivalent to an attempt upon human life. These "wise ones" do not realize that psychic energy is the primary energy and each suffocation of it threatens explosion or death.

Here is one more paragraph from the Teaching: "One should receive guests graciously, but it is inadmissible to haul them in forcibly—every householder knows this. It is exactly the same in the application of psychic energy—one should not force it, but its manifestation should be received worthily. Let the ignorant prattle about the undesirability of applying psychic energy. When the energy is already at work it is impossible to deny it, and it remains to find its natural application. Let the learned tell what takes place if spatial electricity be limitlessly intensified. Let them tell how such excessive tension will end. It cannot be denied that at present spatial currents have been especially intensified. This is no time to deny them; it is needful to make haste with their application. Many times already has the danger of lower psychism been pointed out. *Consequently, it is necessary to reflect about the higher energy, which is understood as spirituality."*

Besides, as you have rightly pointed out, the slanderers did not even bother to get acquainted with all the books of the Teaching. It is equally ignorant to claim that the methods of development of the psychic and spiritual powers indicated in Agni Yoga can be applied only in Mongolia and Tibet and are not suitable for the Aryan race. Nowadays, who does not know that all the Yogis come to Tibet and Mongolia from Aryan India and not vice versa?

What, precisely, are the physical methods for the development of the psychic and spiritual powers mentioned in Agni Yoga which would not be suitable for the Aryan race? And are not all the books of the Teaching filled first of all with the foundations of ethics? Indeed, how many warnings against the harm of the lower forms of psychism are in those books! But, as it is said—no one is as blind and deaf as those who do not want to see and hear.

* * *

Regarding St. Sergius of Radonega, you can answer that N. K. depicted in paintings the events from the life of this great Spirit and Toiler for humanity when nobody was even writing about him. Do these accusers have access to our inner life and to our sacred records? Also, let them cite those private letters in which N. K. speaks *against* the Theosophists. It was I who wrote in my private correspondence about the Theosophists, because I was asked for many explanations of certain Theosophical statements. And again and again I am ready to repeat that some Theosophical luminaries are not authorities for me. Likewise, we are not looking for followers among the Theosophists, and *our rule is never to entice anybody.* But if it happens that people who are interested in the books of the Teaching sincerely address us, we do answer them, leaving them complete freedom to enter into and to form this or that group. Thus, one such group recently sent us a message from New Zealand, and earlier another message came from Canada; and, as usual, among them there are also Theosophists. Just now we received a message that a group of Russian youths is ready to walk around the world, carrying the Banner of Peace.

I also hear for the first time that the messengers of the White Brotherhood were reluctant to affirm themselves as such whenever it was deemed necessary. *Did H. P. B. ever conceal the fact that she was sent by the White Brotherhood, and did she not affirm her mission?* Of course, the envoys, or messengers, *do not* broadcast in the market place their approach and mission. Whatever is given through them speaks for itself and is assimilated by sensitive hearts, but *they must declare it* whenever it is necessary and is indicated to them. However, the difference is that the real messengers would not call themselves World Teachers or future Dhyan Chohans, or even apostles. Nor would they ascribe to themselves alien incarnations, and, particularly, they would not write false and tasteless books or claim monopoly of communion with the Great Teachers.

As regards the accusation pertaining to valerian and musk—these remedies are used in Ayur-vedic medicine. And it is a revelation to me that Ayur-vedic medicine pertains to the Fourth Race! Once again, one may say-Learn more!

It is ridiculous to read about the highest degrees of initiation that can be attained in contemporary occult schools. The highest degrees are attained only through inner perfectment, which no contemporary esoteric school can give. Initiations take place face to face, between a Great Teacher and the disciple; the next degree of perception of the higher energies, or rays, is the result. Therefore, such Initiations always take place unexpectedly and often simply in the bedroom or workroom of the disciple. And this Festival of the Spirit remains unforgettable in the consciousness and heart of the disciple. These Festivals of the Spirit have nothing in common with the trappings of the initiations described in some occult books.

Let our accusers not worry, H. P. Blavatsky is revered by us, perhaps even more than by those who are silent about her. Thus, in 1925, N. K. painted "The Messenger," dedicated to H. P. B., and he personally brought it to Adyar, laying the foundation for the museum of H. P. B. Indeed, it is our dream to worthily honor the memory of our great compatriot when the time shall come.

Neither should any of those protesting ones worry, we certainly shall not expound or interpret their teachings, for we have the whole Ocean of Teaching, the works and foundations of H. P. B., and all the treasures of the Wisdom of the East as well.

Never try to dissuade skeptics. The Teaching cannot be lowered by their non-acceptance or elevated by their acceptance. Truth speaks for itself. And on that we shall finish.

3

14 January 1937

The letter I have received ends with a rather ill-chosen expression, "The priceless cargo of the Teaching sinks with the vessel of *The Chalice of the East*." But the author of this letter did not realize that Truth, being life itself, does not burn in fire and does not sink in water. Therefore, the Teaching-this Source of Life-cannot be trampled upon by the passing crowds of darkness. Moreover, *The Chalice of the East*, in this instance, is not really a vessel, but is the cargo itself. Indeed, an inexhaustible Chalice of the East is preserved in the Invisible Stronghold, and not one drop will ever be spilled from it. The Eternal Guardians know when and how many drops must be poured from it in order to cleanse the consciousness of humanity. *The Mahatma Letters to A. P. Sinnett* became the foundation of *The Secret Doctrine*, which was published, as you know, almost fifty years ago. At that time there were already minds in the West that were able to assimilate this knowledge and spread it among the less advanced consciousnesses. That is why it is so absurd and wild, after fifty years, to listen to apprehensions because of the publication of *The Mahatma Letters* expressed by people who have drawn near to the Teaching and who should have understood the exceptional time which we are now experiencing—a time when the Vessel of Humanity is perishing; when only the most exceptional measures can awaken the wailing of the spirit; when the masses understand all the inability, all the ignorance of their "spiritual" leaders, even Academy graduates (your enclosed report bears testimony of this); when these masses, which were not led in due time toward the new Path, have like a long-restrained dam overthrown the extinguishers of fires, and then themselves perished in blasphemies and crimes. Criminal delay in pointing out the way was practiced precisely by the "spiritual" and voluntary guardians, who were interested in their own welfare first of all.

Yes, the path of bringing Light always was and is the path of achievement, and that makes it so beautiful. There is no selfhood or fear in it, only the high joy of serving the Great.

At the approach of a cosmic date for a new awakening of consciousness, more or less high Carriers of Light are sent to those who build the new steps of human consciousness; material is given and it is indicated exactly what should be put into the foundation and what should be laid aside for the exceptional minds. One must take into consideration that every period brings its own form of expression which corresponds to contemporary times, and it also brings broader information about the fundamentals of the Teaching, for in accordance with the law of evolution everything grows, everything expands. This latter circumstance also unavoidably attracts those consciousnesses which are unable to embrace all the vastness and depth of the Teaching, and which stumble, even upon the first steps, which were openly laid for the West *fifty years ago*. Truly, the frail vessel of such people is unable to carry the priceless Cargo. In past centuries their consciousness was not concerned with building a strong ark, which would have saved them from the deluge of ignorance and set them upon the Mount of Light!

Yes, many, or rather, the majority take gold for copper, but, then, what of it? Truth remains intact. Slowly but surely humanity moves forward on the ladder of ascent. Therefore, we should not grieve that somewhere somebody does not accept the foundations of the Teaching. Verily, the Teaching of Life is not just for one country or nation, it is for the whole world. Therefore let us rejoice with our spirit that the current of the Teaching of Life does not cease. Writings are being revealed and new, new hearths are being kindled in the most unexpected places. Precisely the year 1936 brought much joy for those who are able to see.

Let me remind you of the words from the Teaching of Life: "The waves of cognition and of ignorance have passed through all ages. They create an agitation of the waters so needed for the advance of consciousness. Therefore, each one striving for knowledge achieves tranquility of spirit amid storm and stress. Let us not remain in ignorance when knowledge is knocking at all gates."

Perhaps you remember the story in the Gospel about the angel who came down to stir the waters in a font so that healings could take place.

Throughout the whole history of humanity we see that precisely the Jinn build temples. Very edifying is the legend about the building of Solomon's temple by the Jinn. This is an inevitable law of life on that level of evolution. Enemies and unknown people help to uplift the things that so-called appeasers take for granted and often conceal. There are very few true friends in the present state of human consciousness. But we consider ourselves lucky, having a number of true friends who surround us. We value them, and we protect them with our heart. Let Light be with them!

In all respects our time is exceptional. Never was the borderline between Light and darkness so strongly marked. And now we observe a remarkable process when one darkness devours another darkness.

The great Guardians of the Chalice of Wisdom and Truth, the Protectors of humanity are bringing about the Divine Plan, knowing when and what should be given to humanity. Those who have placed themselves upon the Path of Service to humanity are not groping *in darkness, but are proceeding in complete knowledge of all events.* They also know the persons who approach them, but, due to the complicated laws of karma, much has to be tolerated. Each Carrier of Light takes upon himself the entire complex of karma of the people attracted to him. This explains the inevitability of betrayal. But for him betrayals are transformed into a crown—so it always was, so it is, and so it shall be.

You write, "I know that in this incarnation I must undergo the most tiresome and boring work in the world—cleaning the dirty cellars of my soul."

To this I shall answer that there is no work that is more exciting and worthy than the cleansing of the soul, and self-perfectment. Therefore, it is unseemly and blasphemous to call it "the most boring work in the world." Where, then, is the understanding of the Teaching? In addition, sincerity and honesty are the most essential qualities on the Path; without them there is no progress.

4

27 January 1937

My heart is full of profound gratitude to the Teacher for his unwearying care of all those who are devoted to the service for

General Good. Guard your health—this is most important. So much has still to be done, and you know how sparse are the ranks of conscious fighters for Light and for the foundations of Be-ness, and how numerous are the adherents of darkness. True, cosmic justice and goal-fitness are coming to the rescue, and we are now witnessing the unrolling of the scroll of the Karma of nations. More than at any other time, protection should be given to him who is able to become a leader in numerous branches of knowledge, or else we shall plunge for a long time into darkness that will be worse than the epoch of the invasion of the so-called barbarians. (It is rightly said by the eminent contemporary English philosopher, Bertrand Russell, in his recent work *The Scientific Outlook* that if, in the 17th century, a certain hundred people had been killed in their childhood, the modern world would not exist.) The time approaches when nations must realize that people who possess the power of synthesis, the power of psychic energy, are invaluable treasures of their countries. Indeed, all the welfare of nations depends on these pillars and keepers of the balance of the world! One may say that the realization of the significance of psychic energy will be the conquest of a new, powerful step in world evolution.

* * *

It is indeed extremely timely to send unified benignant thoughts in order to render somewhat less harmful the surrounding poisonous atmosphere. I whole-heartedly approve such an undertaking, and in order to confirm its correctness I shall quote a paragraph from the new book: "It is useful to advise friends to send out mutually good thoughts at a definite time. In such an action there will be not only a strengthening of benignity but also a disinfection of space, and the latter is extremely necessary. Poisonous emanations not only infect man but are precipitated upon surrounding objects. Such sediments are eradicated with great difficulty. They can even accompany objects for long distances. In time people will distinguish the aura of such infected objects. Meanwhile sensitive individuals can feel the reaction of such stratifications upon themselves. Good thoughts will be the best purifier of one's surroundings. Affirmations of the sendings of good are still stronger than purifying incenses. But one should accustom oneself to such sendings. They need not be made up of definite words but only of a directed good feeling.

Thus, in the midst of daily life it is possible to create much good. Each such sending is like a cleansing bolt of lightning."

From these lines you can judge how important it is that the participants in these sendings be harmoniously attuned and really full of good will. For thought can be beautiful, but if it is not spiritualized by the fire of the heart, it will remain dead. It is good to listen to music before sending such messages.

5

19 February 1937

Please extend my hearty gratitude to your co-workers for their thoughts and good wishes, I am sending my best thoughts to them. I shall answer your questions briefly, for I am literally overloaded with urgent work. But first of all I must tell you—you are blessed in realizing so intensely the value of time. Indeed, the loss of this value is irreparable.

And now your questions. In order to answer some of them to your satisfaction we must come close to the most sacred aspects of the foundations of Existence. However, letters often go through many hands before they reach the addressee, therefore I hesitate to put certain things on paper.

Of course, in principle Spirit has no sex, and differentiation takes place only on the plane of manifestation. As the manifestations of the monad become more conscious and pronounced and the individuality is enriched, the sex in it becomes more emphasized, which means that incarnations belonging to one definite Origin begin to predominate. Undoubtedly, there are certain exceptions when sex is chosen in conformity with an accepted mission; and there is also one other condition, which has its origin in the law of Equilibrium, and which belongs to a cosmic right. However, I shall not elaborate upon this law in a letter, for the reason mentioned above.

* * *

Yes, according to the ancient Hebrew scriptures, there were spirits of both Elements among the Elohim, for each creation, on any plane, is based on two Origins. This fact should be well understood. Likewise, we must understand that each creation requires the participation of the energies of man, since man is the bearer of the highest principles of Cosmos. It is said in the Sacred Teaching, "The worlds not populated by men could not develop, and therefore they perished." Thus, the dependence of the worlds or of the planet upon man and his spiritual and moral level becomes clear.

* * *

1. Regarding the Mother of the World, it seems to me that in my previous letters I have discussed this theme rather fully. In Cosmos, in its visibility and invisibility, spirit and matter are indivisible; one is naught without the other. Unification of the energies of the Elements gives birth to all existence; precisely, there are Logoi of both Elements. This highest Mystery of Being degenerated into a crude phallic cult. It is said, "As above, so below." But the light of great truths is reflected on our earthly plane as the light of the sun in a puddle.

To understand the greatest mystery of spiritual Be-ness is impossible for those people who are attached to its earthly manifestation in all its animal-like imperfection. One must often recall the saying of Jesus Christ, "Give not that which is holy unto the dogs, neither cast ye your pearls before swine, lest they trample them under their feet, and turn again and rend you." (St. Matthew 7:6)

2. You should not think that in your previous lives you were far from the Teaching of Light. You could hardly be so kindled by the Teaching were it not for a previous bond. The bond is forged by many thousands of years, not just in one hour or in one life. A centuries-old and exceptional bond with the Great Teachers is, of course, extremely rare; yet there are many degrees of approach, and only man himself determines his present and future nearness. Cosmic right in this, too, has a tremendous significance, but the will of man can neglect even this right and so postpone the approach for endless millenniums.

Even so, if one comes to the Teaching at a mature age, it does not mean that one is far from the Teaching. There are various destinations.

Also, it is only after the age of thirty that all the centers are able to act. Moreover, it is essential that the personality or the character of the aspirant be fully formed. We know many cases when people who have approached the Teaching of Life in their youth became easily tired and gave it up at the first obstacle that came across their path. But a man who has gone through a life full of difficulties, who has experienced doubts and struggles of the spirit, such a man may prove to be a reliable co-worker upon entering the Path of Light. Of course, considering the shocks and upheavals that have taken place in the consciousness of many nations during the past decades, evolution has been accelerated, and it is already possible to bring the forces of youth nearer to a conscious and active collaboration.

* * *

3. You are applying your psychic energy excellently. Work dedicated to carrying out the counsels of the Teaching of Life in your daily routine, in discourses, and in your writings, which are awakening the mind and bringing the joy of the new consciousness and of strengthening of the spirit, is this not the best application of psychic energy? Do you not possess this energy already? Yet the complete mastery of it comes when we unceasingly strive toward Light, toward Hierarchy. Indeed, psychic energy is primarily the striving of the heart. Remember, it was said that, "Striving is the key to all achievements. Striving is the boat of the Arhat." And so, do sail in that boat.

The mechanical methods so broadly recommended for the development of psychic energy cannot give the higher quality of this energy; they only develop the black fire, which leads to disastrous results. But a realization of this energy within oneself and all observations of its manifestations certainly assist its natural awakening. You probably have noticed that when you were profoundly interested, when all your attention was concentrated on some particular thought or problem, not only were new thoughts born in your mind—and sometimes even came as if from the outside—but in life itself, in daily routine, the necessary helpful elements and conditions came to you. Psychic energy, first of all, possesses the property of a magnet.

* * *

Certainly, if healing is possible through psychic energy, then transmission of this energy is also possible. We have witnessed such transmission and even participated in it. But an absolute spiritual unity was necessary for this. Tell your friends that the paramount and first discipline for mastery of psychic energy is the betterment of quality in everything, in all life. Let them be imbued with this discipline.

* * *

The Elder Brothers of humanity stand on vigil, and wherever possible they strengthen and intensify the divine energy. Therefore, let the friends be patient, and let them read attentively the books of the Teaching, which are full of advices and indications pertaining to the necessary discipline for the mastery of this power.

"No doubt you have been asked many times how to develop psychic energy and how to realize its usefulness. But it has been said enough that the heart that aspires to higher quality of all life will be the conductor of psychic energy. No forcible, conventionally accelerated movement toward a display of the heart's action will be useful. The heart is a most independent organ; it may be set free toward good, and it will hasten to be filled with energy. Likewise, only in a friendly communion is it possible to secure the fruits of unified energy. However, for this it is indispensable to understand what harmonious agreement is." [Brotherhood]

All mechanical apparatus, if used while consciousness is not yet completely freed from the least presence of selfishness, can result in serious misfortunes. The Fishermen of the Gospel undoubtedly had a store of psychic energy, and its main lever was their unbreakable faith in Jesus Christ. For the right action of psychic energy it is necessary to have a completely unobscured bond with Hierarchy.

4. Cosmic Right, like all the laws of Being, has several aspects. Truly, man, primarily, is the carrier of this Right. One of the aspects of Cosmic Right is affirmed from the moment of birth of the human monad under the influence of this or that luminary. It seems to me that I already wrote you about the cosmic fatherhood and sonship, or about each monad belonging to a definite planet for the duration of an entire Manvantara. Thus, each Logos will be the father of all the monads that were born under the rays of his luminary. Also, we must not forget another aspect, namely, that the seed of the spirit belongs to one of the elements, which gives a pre-eminent mastery over a certain element. Of course, all the achievements of man are recorded upon the electro-magnetic space which he occupies, or

his aura, and this, too, comprises his inalienable cosmic right to a definite step or place in the scale of the evolution of Cosmos. Similarly, a verdict of karma may also be called a cosmic right. The actions of the Cosmic Magnet are always conditioned by Cosmic Right.

But the most sacred, the most beautiful concept connected with Brotherhood Cosmic Right is transmitted by the Teacher to a disciple, orally and face to face.

5. The pages sent by you beautifully explain the questions which were put to you. As can be seen from the letter of your friend, he came independently to the correct solution. Precisely, "not for the life of our body must we take the Body and Blood of Christ, but for the life of our spirit. Therefore, the partaking of the Body and Blood of Christ must be understood spiritually." Not a single church today is able to give an answer to the fundamental problems of Existence. In their exclusiveness and immobility churches have reached a dead end. How far are many spiritual leaders from the understanding the simple words of Christ, "God is a Spirit: and they that worship him must worship him in spirit and in truth."

Work on your book, but *do not* hurry, collect the essential materials. This work should become very significant. I advise you to look through the writings of Origen and through *Dobrotolubye*, and to quote many remarkable passages from them. By the way, did you read an excellent book *Open-hearted Stories Told by a Pilgrim to His Spiritual Father*?

Your book brings a great deal of joy. Quite recently I heard from a Russian physician who enthusiastically admired it and said that this book answered all his questions.

* * *

How is your health? Your bees? I hope you did not give them up. In many countries there is now an interest in apiculture. Many more useful properties of bees are being discovered. The venom secreted by bees cures certain diseases. It is said that one or two stings by a bee cure the most chronic rheumatism. Here are some paragraphs regarding honey and milk:

"People are vainly seeking new remedies and medicaments without making use of the old ones. Even milk and honey are not sufficiently in use. Whereas what can be more beneficial than vegetable products reworked through a succeeding evolution? Milk and honey are to be had in infinite variety, and they constitute the best prophylaxis when employed rationally and scientifically. The point is not simply to drink milk and eat honey; first of all, one must consider what kind of milk and what kind of honey. It is right to assume that the best honey will be from places that are replete with curative herbs. It may be understood that bees bring together not mere chance combinations of their extractions. Nature lore about bees has importance in the way of directing attention to the particular quality of the honey.

"Moreover, many vegetable products require investigation. People regard things so primitively that they are content with the expressions 'good and bad,' 'fresh and spoiled'; besides, they are elated by the large size of a product, forgetting that artificial enlargement diminishes the qualitative value. Even such primitive considerations are lost sight of. In the development of vitality, its essence ought to be derived from all the kingdoms of nature." *Brotherhood,* 148

"The best curative products are often neglected. Milk and honey are considered nutritious products, yet they have been entirely forgotten as regulators of the nervous system. When used in their pure form, they contain the precious primary energy. Precisely this quality in them must be preserved. Whereas the sterilization of milk and the special processing of honey deprive them of their most valuable property, there remains the nutritive importance, but their basic value disappears.

"Indeed, it is indispensable that the products be used in their pure state. Thus, the animals and bees must be kept under healthful conditions, but all artificial purifications destroy their direct usefulness.

"The ancient knowledge protected cows as sacred animals, and it wove an attractive legend about bees. But in time people lost the conscious regard for the remedies as first given to them. In the old manuals of healing, each remedy was looked upon from the standpoints of both usefulness and harmfulness. But such valuable substances as milk, honey, and musk carry no injury when they are pure. It is possible to point out many useful remedies in the plant world also, but the majority of them are best in the pure state when the basic energy inherent in them, over and above so-called vitamins, has not been lost. The juice of carrots or radishes, or of strawberries, is best in the raw, pure state. Hence it may be understood why the ancient Rishis subsisted on these wholesome products." (*Ibid.*, 201)

6
9 March 1937

Protection of the sacred names of the Great Teachers and to be able to reply to all attacks with dignity is our direct duty. That is why such watchfulness and care are required with the treasure entrusted to us. In connection with this I shall quote a paragraph from the new book: "Standing on guard is a sign of broadened consciousness. Many do not understand at all what it means to guard that which is most precious. It is impossible to rely upon those who do not know about value. But one may rejoice at each wakeful sentinel. Brotherhood teaches such a vigil."

To avert the danger that you have described is certainly a gigantic task. Indeed, the Great Forces of Light have fought against this danger for centuries. One could even say that the meaning of Armageddon consists in this. But the cosmic forces themselves come to the rescue, and after stern fiery purification the human spirit will cry out and will strive to comprehend the spiritual foundations in all manifestations of Being.

True, human consciousness, with the rarest exceptions, always has stultified whatever it contacted, and the form gained victory over the contents. And now, more than ever, we see this enslavement and engulfment by form. Though church dogma decayed, they were replaced by others, which are forced into the consciousness of the masses in a like manner. It is distressing to see that humanity, while dreaming of freedom and seeking after it, is nevertheless busy with the invention of new and still tighter fetters. Freedom, this bird of paradise, sings only in pure hearts liberated from their only jailer, whose name is Selfishness.

7
1 April 1937

Precious to us is each unity in the work for General Good and for preparing the consciousness to accept the New World, which is coming, but by different ways than many of us can now imagine. The luxury of destruction in all its aspects must depart into the past. Realization of responsibility, search for synthesis, and creativeness with broad cooperation will bring about a salutary balance on the planet.

* * *

With sadness I have read your letter in which you describe the condition of the sick man. How can I help when his condition is almost hopeless? Healing is possible at the beginning of disease, but it is very difficult to produce a beneficial influence when there has been neglect. One cannot resurrect that which is on the way to disintegration. I shall quote for you a paragraph from the new book: "There are many examples of people having remained deaf to the most urgent Indications. At the moment when misfortune is taking place they recall in a flash how help was offered them, but it is already too late. People usually think that equal help can be extended in all the stages of circumstances. But can a cure be expected when the organism is already disintegrating? It is impossible to grow a non-existent hand, it is impossible to reanimate an already dying brain. Many examples can be cited when people beseeched resuscitation of the dying. Such an attitude merely shows complete lack of understanding of how to deal with energies."

Yes, psychic energy when sent from outside can help when there is evidence of it in an ill person, cooperation is necessary in everything. Indeed, all the so-called "miraculous healings" are performed only through a powerful surge of psychic, or nervous, power in the ill person himself, which is called forth by contact with a more powerful energy. But if the store of this energy has become depleted in him, then how or through what will the sent energy be received? Verily, miracles do not exist. For each action of energy special conditions are necessary, and if the essential condition is absent, how can one expect a positive result? That is why spiritual and physical prophylaxis are so persistently advocated.

8

6 May 1937

We welcome the publication of separate issues dedicated to a definite theme, and we shall be waiting particularly for serious articles which deal with the significance and power of thought, the transmission of thought at a distance, and psychic energy. At present one must pay attention primarily to everything that directs thought ahead toward new discoveries in the realm of the subtlest energies. The time has come for these energies, and various manifestations are flashing out all over Earth. By gathering newspaper and magazine articles alone one can acquire a collection of most remarkable manifestations and discoveries.

And now I shall answer your questions.

1. Live flowers, preferably uncut, are always and in all cases useful because of their aroma and beauty. Vitalizing aroma drives away the low entities which seek to fasten themselves to any source of decomposition. Perhaps it is more practical to spend money on charity instead of on a wreath for the grave, but if one were to insist upon it, people, in their human way, might easily renounce the beautiful custom of bringing the best gifts of Earth to the memory of the departed one and would limit themselves to putting a quarter into the charity box.

You might be interested to know that precisely in Atlantis there existed the following custom: The deceased was not touched, but was thickly sprinkled with oil of eucalyptus and was immediately covered with the sacred shroud and showered with flowers. For three days and three nights fire was kept burning around the body in a closed circle, and immediately following the departure of the astral body, the physical body was burnt. This is a very wisely conceived ritual. When the will is lazy, the astral body emerges lazily. Some can do everything on time, whereas others are late in everything; yet this is no reason for scorching someone's heels! In India the discarded shell is often burnt too soon, and that may cause considerable injury to the subtle body. This information is taken from my notes about Atlantis. This ritual and the sacred shroud were called "Purificatory of Peace."

2. Unnaturally large ears on the images of Buddhas were a later innovation, and they symbolize omniscience. "They signify the power of Him who *knows and hears all*, and whose benevolent love and attention for all living creatures nothing can escape." The idea was borrowed from an esoteric allegory. One can observe a similarity with such elongated ears only among the Burmese and Siamese people, who artificially distort their ears. This is confirmed in the second volume of *The Secret Doctrine*

in the section on symbolism where the statues at Bamian are discussed.

3. Since all phenomena are performed by concentration of the will it is of no importance what object is chosen for concentration. That is what H. P. Blavatsky meant when she spoke of concentration upon the little finger.

4. All outer impulses are located in the head, therefore it would be more correct to call them the impulses of *chakras*, rather than *chakras*. Moreover, they influence but do not direct the nerve centers. The essence of all the *chakras* lies in the heart.

5. How is it possible to approach the New World with an outworn consciousness? New consciousnesses cannot be put into old vessels. The approach to the Teaching of Life, which will be laid in the foundation of the New World, requires a clear and incisive consciousness. One cannot suppress achievements; the thirst for true freedom, which dwells in freedom of thought and conscience, has awakened in the midst of the masses. No incense and holy water will drive people into the former chains. Only KNOWLEDGE enlightened by the full power of the discoveries of new energies will find its way into a spiritually revived country. Everything beautiful must be preserved, but all the unnecessary accumulations and all the frippery of the centuries must fall away. Verily, the new understanding of the Testaments of the Great Teachers must enter the transformed life.

Here are some paragraphs from the new book: "Wherein, then, is progress? Some assume that it is in constant recognition of the new. Will not such aspiration be one-sided, and must there not be added to it regulation of the old? More than once it has been shown that people abstractly strive toward something new, and yet continue to dwell in an old pigsty. Someone gives lectures about cleanliness, yet is himself extremely filthy. Will such instruction be convincing? Or a lazy man summons to labor, but who will give heed to him? Let us not be afraid to repeat such primitive examples, for life is full of them. Whoever thinks about harmony knows that a house is not new where old rubbish has settled. And yet one can see how beautiful attainments wither because they cannot grow in filth. Not only is such a fate of useful attainments deplorable to see but it is sad that their dissolution litters the already discovered paths for so long a time. This is why I speak about equilibrium.

"Do not permit any quest to be traduced if it is sincere and has a good basis. Solicitude and care are necessary. As a gardener grows new fruit and fertilizes the soil, so let us be ready to assist the new and regulate the old."

Thus, let us rejoice and preserve solemnity.

9

14 May 1937

Today we observe the ever growing interest in the study of hidden powers inherent in man. Besides the existence of many partly scientific and semi-amateurish societies for psychic research, in some countries (England, America, Sweden) special courses have been established in universities for the study of psychic and parapsychic phenomena. Unfortunately, the majority of these societies have dealt, and still deal, almost exclusively with the so-called kinetic phenomena, apports, and materializations, completely ignoring manifestations of that same basic energy, but of a higher order—for example, the action of thought at a distance and the increase or decrease of this action owing to various degrees of psychic tension or the qualities of thoughts of the participants in such experiments.

And yet one can cite a series of earnest attempts to study the transmission of thought. Thus, Professor Rhine of Duke University successfully experiments along these lines, and he has succeeded in attracting the attention of the scientific world by using a new scientific name for his experiments—"extrasensory perception." As you know, mesmerism was also cruelly ridiculed and rejected at one time, but as soon as it was labeled with a new name, *hypnotism*, it was accepted by science. As H. P. Blavatsky wrote, "Mesmerism is a new nose on a very old face." Indeed, one could write a scientific treatise on the significance of terminology and of its psychological effect upon certain types of consciousnesses. Nevertheless, the most ancient *Fohat* or the Egyptian Tum are destined to be acknowledged in the coming epoch. Thus, psychic, or primary, energy will at last attain citizenship, regardless of what name or appearance it was manifested under before. Such recognition will mark the entrance of humanity into the new era of greatest discoveries, which will bring about the so much needed reappraisal of values.

Therefore, owing to the beginning of the New Epoch, which

brings an unusual influx of psychic energy, it is necessary to awaken and to educate within ourselves the right attitude toward this two-edged power. In the books of Living Ethics (the Agni Yoga series) a manifold explanation of this energy is given for the first time, and methods of rational approach to its study are presented.

A High Spirit, when in a physical body and in complete possession of the quality of divisibility of the spirit, can consciously act simultaneously on Earth and in interplanetary space, even visiting the nearest planets. At the same time, this divisibility of the spirit is in no way reflected in a lowering of the quality of His manifestation or activity in the earthly body, because the high energies released by Him do not as yet have application on our Earth.

* * *

In order to participate in the cosmic creativeness it is necessary to comprehend precisely the laws of cosmic forces and to act in complete accord with them, otherwise destruction is inevitable. Verily, when acting in harmony with cosmic laws, man becomes a creator. He is the creator of his own destiny, and collectively he creates the destiny of the planet. All forces and energies of the Cosmos are revealed to man only if he possesses a powerful accumulation of higher energies and has reached the state of illimitable ascent. Ponder upon the immensity of power of the cosmic forces which surround us.

* * *

It is wrong to say, "By the quality of their spirit ... people are alike." It is precisely that quality of the spirit which is different in each case. Therefore it is better to say, "By the fundamental principle of spirit all people are alike." Certainly, psychic energy is the quality of the spirit. But one may picture infinite varieties of this energy, which depend on the very early conditions of the inception of the seed of the spirit.

* * *

We must emphasize the significance of action or labor for awakening and developing psychic energy, since psychic energy, first of all, needs to be exercised. It must not be limited by accidental impulses; only constant, systematic, and rhythmic labor can attune its current. The correct exchange of psychic energy is based on rhythm. Do emphasize the harmful effect of laziness, which stops the action of psychic energy in us and thus ruins our entire evolution, finally leading to complete destruction. Indeed, it now becomes obvious that the busiest people live the longest, provided there is rhythm in their work and no excessive poisoning of their organisms. It must be pointed out that each labor should be performed with complete consciousness. Also, striving toward the betterment of the quality of each labor and each action is the best method for growth and for intensification of the psychic energy.

But it is also necessary to state that an excessive outflow of psychic energy is dangerous. Co-measurement should be applied in everything. A person who immeasurably expends his psychic energy disturbs the balance of his organism, thus opening himself to the possibility of infection and also to the attacks of evil forces, consequently damaging his health and energy. When it is said that the more the spirit gives, the more it receives, this does not mean giving it out excessively at one time, but constant rhythmical use of it. Certainly the mastery of divisibility of spirit can be achieved only when psychic energy is considerably developed.

Here is a paragraph from *Brotherhood:* "Self-sacrifice is one of the true paths to Brotherhood. But why then is it enjoined, 'Guard your strength'? There is no contradiction in this. The Golden Path, the combining path, affirms both qualities—achievement and caution. Otherwise all would be driven to suicide. Achievement is created in full consciousness and responsibility. Again someone may suspect a contradiction; but a higher devotion, an all-conquering love, can teach the combining of higher qualities. Madness does not bring achievement. Faintheartedness cannot answer for true cautiousness. The conscious realization of duty prompts the right use of energy. Let people reflect about the concordance of qualities. Madness and faint-heartedness are not suitable for the Path." But how few people realize what the concordance of qualities means!

We are constantly warned about the careful expenditure of energy, especially now when the spatial currents are incredibly tensed.

Likewise, during the division of one's psychic energy, at those times when a decrease of forces is felt, we should not force ourselves to work. Time must be allowed for renewal of energy. Of course, one should be particularly honest in all such occurrences, for there are many who like to take things easy, and each lazy spell might be attributed by them to an excessive outflow of psychic energy.

Where there is no correct exchange of psychic energy, there is also no divisibility of spirit. When the fire is inactive or is about to leave an unsuitable receptacle, then, of course, divisibility of spirit is unattainable. Likewise, you must bear in mind that psychic energy is a two-edged force, and many fierce dark forces possess a great supply of this energy, but in its lower manifestations and properties; therefore, the actions of such energy are limited to the lower spheres and are of small scope in comparison with the energy of higher quality. It is necessary to stress as strongly as possible the significance of thought and a disciplined mind for the development of a high quality of psychic energy.

Hypnotism is also a manifestation of psychic energy, therefore the influence of this property of the energy should be studied and understood as broadly as possible. Do not forget to mention the transmission of thought at a distance, for it takes place with the help of the very same psychic, or primary, energy.

* * *

Many of the best people, and even those who possess a comparatively broad consciousness, would not accept the true Images of the Great Teachers. Pay attention to the unhealthy reaction of the majority of people to everything that does not meet with their fancy; the atavism of ages is strong!

Yes, counterposing one false image against another, no less fantastic, is a most dreadful and corrupting manifestation. People who do this are actually unable to become reconciled to either, and as a result there occurs a dreadful dual personality, something like crossed eyes; and finally they end with a completely "crossed mind."

According to esoteric Eastern Teachings, during the entire Manvantara, or great Round, of our planet, we are given one Manu (The Teacher of Teachers) who stands at the head of his High Brothers. Thus, One Individuality takes upon himself responsibility for the planet for the duration of the entire Manvantara.

* * *

It is proper to write only the best about a friend, and particularly about a departed friend. For who would dare to judge all the motives, all the secret feelings that caused one or another deed of the friend? Each disparagement, even an unconscious one, nevertheless brings its bad karma. The first advice given to us was "to increase ten-fold all that is good and to decrease twice all the bad," only then is it possible to give a more or less correct evaluation.

Not knowing the motives and inner reasons and actions of a person, people often allow themselves to judge by appearances; thus they perform a grave misdeed against justice and immeasurably burden their own karma. That is why the custom of writing and speaking only in good terms about the departed one is so beautiful and practical. In such a way people at least compensate somewhat for their injustice.

* * *

Many things are ripening in the country you mention. Perhaps this country, too, when it reached a turning point in its history, was given a warning and was offered help by the Forces of Light. But, as usual, among those in power there was not a sufficiently enlightened and, mainly, a spiritually strong personality to utilize the salutary counsels. And from all the history of mankind we know that wherever the Messenger was rejected, and even persecuted, the whole country is held to account for it. The Messenger comes at a difficult hour, therefore to reject him means to accept the full brunt of karma. All the calamities which strike the country, are they not a grave omen? Did not the country choose the hardest path? But how hard is the karma of those who have rejected the help of the Forces of Light, and who therefore have taken upon themselves the whole responsibility for the future! There were some rarest exceptions in history when the great leaders of a nation understood how to accept the Help, hence the amazing development of certain countries. But in our time of total negation and the supreme rule of gold a small coin covers up even the sun.

* * *

I have looked through the collected material on Armageddon. A very impressive record indeed, but great caution is required in dealing with this topic; all the grave warnings when they are scattered on separate and few pages are one thing, but when they are put together, they may frighten small consciousnesses and even cause undesirable actions. People prefer to be lulled by rosy hopes, and they very much dislike those who attempt to open their eyes in time to the coming danger. Each salutary warning is taken by them as a personal threat. Therefore, my advice is to keep this very useful compilation for inner familiarization and reading.

10

17 May 1937

I very much approve of your idea of writing an essay on the problem of women's rights. Indeed, this very problem will be the cornerstone of the New Epoch, and without the correct solution of it there will be no order and equilibrium in the world. When you write, harken to the voice of the heart. So-called intuition, or the voice of the heart, is very accurately defined in the books of Living Ethics as "straight-knowledge." I can attest from my personal experience that all enlightenment is based precisely upon "straight-knowledge," which brings true knowledge.

You are rightly indignant about some of the lines that you quote from the writings of the apostles. One might ask where are the originals of all these Epistles? Who has seen them, and when? And then, who can guarantee that the hands of zealots did not insert corrections in the originals (if they were preserved) wherever something did not conform with conventional customs and rules. Was not this the case with all the works of the great Spiritual Toilers? As it was said, "Not one document of antiquity has reached us without distortion." And how many inaccuracies were permitted by the translators of those Epistles! It is sufficient to look through the Bible in three translations, English, Russian and French; in fact, in translating certain works, I constantly had to deal with this, and where contradictions were too evident, I had to quote two or three translations.

Besides, why should the apostles be regarded as infallible? It is not only in the Gospel that they are revealed to be far from the high moral level that is to be expected of the closest disciples of Christ, but reading their own writings, one sadly realizes how many discords and all sorts of sinful abominations went on in those first Christian communities out of which came the Fathers of the Church. And even among the apostles themselves there was plenty of disunity. Let us, for instance, recall the perpetual contention between Peter and Paul, which has survived as a symbol of all dissension among so-called Christian zealots, who have split the one Teaching of Christ into sects and churches warring among themselves. I advise you to read Merezhkovski's book *Paul and Augustine*. You will find interesting material in it. As usual, this writer offers a complete treasury of most valuable information.

Thus, let us remember that only an enlightened heart or a mind illumined by the light of the heart can become a reliable guide in reading all the Sacred Scriptures. Religions which allowed, or rather affirmed the humiliation and subordination of woman are destined to extinction. By humiliating woman, the later religions were indeed serving Satan; knowing the power of woman, the Prince of this World, for the fulfillment of his plan, first of all schemed to demean her—the bearer of the higher energy.

But when woman (who, by a strange paradox, is the main supporter of the church) awoke and understood where her age-long oppressors were hiding, the downfall of the church took place. Religion, or rather quests of the spirit will never leave the people, but the awakened consciousnesses will demand new forms and new ways from spiritual teachers and leaders.

The most ancient Teachings always highly regarded the Feminine Principle, and even female divinities were considered by them to be the most sacred. We can now find traces of these most ancient cults among the American Indians, whose priesthood is headed by women; women also head the clan, and the whole line of inheritance is considered as coming from the woman's side. Likewise, there is no distinction between the two Origins in the Teaching of Buddha, and woman, as well as man, can reach the state of Arhatship. And even now in India, in spite of the fact that the later Brahmins humiliated woman because of greed and self-interest, the cult of the Goddess Kali is nevertheless spread most widely. The last of the known sages of India, Ramakrishna and Vivekananda, were worshippers of the Divine Origin in its aspect of the Mother of the World. Indeed, it is the ignorant and avaricious distortion of the cosmic law that has placed woman in a subjugated position.

Certainly it would be wrong to blame the Masculine Principle alone for the situation created; woman, too, is at fault. Many women welcomed being constantly in custody as wards, and precisely this weakened their strength and dulled their abilities. Therefore, nowadays a reverse order is necessary. Woman must accept the struggle against life's obstacles in order to temper her strength and manifest her true nature. True, the struggle for her lost rights will be a hard one, but with the refinement of thought and acceptance of the higher, psychic energy much will be eased. Indeed, not a single high experiment with the subtlest energies can be performed without the presence of the Feminine Element. The famous philosophers' stone cannot be discovered or created without the participation of woman. Thus, Cosmos itself, Nature herself, affirms the equilibrium of the Origins in their higher functions. And one may say, "To confirm rights does not mean to possess them."

The first task which faces women is to insist in all countries upon full rights and equal education with men; to try with all their might to develop their thinking faculties, and, above all, to learn to stand on their own feet without leaning altogether upon men. In the West there are many fields which are now available to women, and one must admit that they are quite successful in all of them.

It is necessary to awaken in woman herself a great respect for her own Origin; she should realize her great destiny as a bearer of the higher energy. Indeed, it is woman's intuition which should again, as in the better periods of history, lead humanity on the path of progress. And meanwhile, one can only profoundly grieve and, at times, watch with inexpressible shame how woman humiliates herself in her desire to win the admiration of the stronger sex. The combinations of the luminaries are favorable for the awakening of women, and I believe that the new influx of psychic energy will be utilized by women for lofty tasks and in search of new achievements for the good of humanity. Let the fire of achievement in the name of great service be truly kindled in woman. The quality of self-sacrifice is fundamental in woman, but she should learn not to limit her self-sacrifice to the narrow concept of home life, which is often nothing more than encouragement of the family's egotism—she should apply it on a world scale. I believe that woman should be even more educated and cultured than man, for indeed it is she who instills in her family the first concepts of knowledge, culture, and understanding of statesmanship. When you finish your essay, I shall be glad to read it, and I do not doubt that your heart will prompt fiery words to you.

Thank you for your beautiful words about your pupils. The warmth of the heart is that magnet which holds the whole structure. Ability to encourage is the fundamental quality of teaching. Therefore I rejoice at your words concerning the work of your pupils. The first encouragement is particularly important, for it may mark the whole future path. By being too severe in evaluating the first work we sometimes hinder and even stop the growth of outstanding abilities. It happens so often that the first successful attempts of a pupil do not necessarily indicate talent, and, on the other hand, it often happens that the first weak and even crude attempts later develop into something very serious and important. After all, the dormant abilities awake in us the different times.

"The happiness of the Teacher is in encouraging the disciples to dare toward Beauty. Long lists of tedious, torpid incidents do not promote this achievement. The Teacher himself must be aglow so that his approach alone may be passed on fierily. Such an everyday task is difficult, yet people are tested precisely in everyday life, which is the sister of Infinity." Therefore, I am happy to see your heartfelt understanding and your attitude toward your pupils.

11

17 May 1937

1. You ask, "Does every man have a permanent Teacher?" But it should be made clear what kind of a Teacher you have in mind. Regardless of whether he realizes it or not, one could say that almost everyone has a more or less permanent guide from the supermundane spheres; these guides are of diverse qualities and levels. Moreover, in the present state of humanity such guidance often brings more misery than benefit. It is difficult even to imagine the number of dwellers of the spheres above Earth who are trying to interfere in earthly affairs. Still, if a man has kind-

led within himself a flame of pure striving toward Light, and if devotion is inrooted in him, then his call to the Elder Brothers of humanity will be heard, and it will depend upon him alone to strengthen the sacred bond with the chosen Image. Owing to an immutable law, the disciple will have to undergo a test, the duration of which will also be completely in his own hands.

2. "You must reach Us on Earth" certainly means that actually in the earthly life, through broadening of consciousness and through earthly attainments, one may approach the Great Teachers.

3. Indeed the spirit is free to choose either sex for incarnation. But when a spirit belongs to the Great Service, he takes on the incarnation that is indicated to him by the Great Teacher. Besides, it is sometimes necessary to change the sex for a certain incarnation, due to the law of Great Equilibrium, which is linked with the mystery of Existence. But this mystery is revealed by the Teacher only when the disciple can satisfactorily pass the ordained tests.

4. You ask, "Supposing I do not want to return to Earth anymore, what can make me do so?" The answer is, "The Cosmic Law." As hunger leads the hungry one to food, so the law of incarnation impels the spirit ready for the time of the next incarnation. A spirit that has reached a great transmutation of its energies during earthly life is able to considerably prolong its stay in the supermundane worlds, up to a certain point; and then the moment will come when it will feel acutely the magnetic attraction toward an earthly incarnation, for only Earth is that furnace in which our energies can be transmuted, obtaining renewal and accumulation of new energies.

We can be liberated from earthly incarnation only when all our energies are sublimated to such an extent that further stay on Earth can give us nothing. Precisely, one cycle of karma terminates for man when all the elements, or energies, that enter into the essence of his being are united into one striving and in this tension have reached the state of perfection ordained for this cycle.

One should not fear reincarnations, on the contrary, a true disciple accepts with joy a new experience and new possibilities of achieving most valuable accumulations. Indeed, the disciples of the White Brotherhood walk the shortest path, and with the help of the Elder Brothers they accelerate their incarnations in order to outlive their karma and help their retarded brothers.

5. "What should one do in order not ever to forsake the Teaching and not to become a traitor?" The answer is given in all the books of the Teaching—strengthen in your heart the foundations of love and devotion and apply the Teaching in daily life.

6. There are as many consciousnesses as there are expressions. Therefore, each one has a right to express his feelings completely individually.

7. You have understood correctly that it is inappropriate to turn for help to the Highest, where we ourselves should apply our own understanding; aside from an appalling lack of co-measurement, we not only lose all possibilities but also dull our abilities through such expectation of help, and thus weaken ourselves. Without incessant effort in tensing our abilities and resourcefulness in overcoming obstacles, there can be no progress on the spiritual plane. Not reliance is needed, but precisely full trust in the Teacher and realization with all one's being that when we have reached the limits of tension, help will come, giving us a possibility to direct our efforts toward new and higher achievements. Without such independent overcoming of obstacles, the transmutation of our energies is not possible. Only when the limit of highest tension is reached can the blessed sublimation take place. The laws are alike in everything.

8. "What is a unit, and is it not a constant magnitude?" From the metaphysical standpoint a unit is a symbol of unity and includes everything in itself, consequently it is the Absolute, or in other words it is a constant magnitude.

9. "What is a number?" A number is a symbol of divisibility, consequently it is movement and rhythm, and a manifested consciousness.

10. All and any debts must be paid, for a debt is an obligation of the spirit.

11. Karma is woven by thoughts. Thought can either weaken or intensify any karmic effect. Purified thinking liberates from bad karma, for it does not generate evil causes. Thought and will are the rulers of karma.

12. Only the heart can prompt the choice of the earthly teacher.

13. "Is it possible to reach the Brotherhood on Earth, while

still in this life?" It all depends on the man, on his past accumulations, and in some cases, also on the mission accepted by him before incarnating.

14. Always and in all actions the only criterion is straight-knowledge. But if direct straight-knowledge is perceptible with difficulty and is weak in its knocking, then each action should be weighed on the scales of the heart. Straight-knowledge is nearest to the heart.

15. The path is indicated in the books of the Teaching; without application of the foundations of the Teaching in life, there is no access to the Brotherhood.

16. "Where is the point of no return?" When the fires of the centers are kindled, and the crystal of psychic energy is formed.

17. "How can one work consciously on other planes of being and remember about it in the physical body?" By following the Teaching and by training oneself to consciously remember such work. But, being in the physical body, it is not always possible to remember the activity of one's subtle body, because the dimensions of the Subtle World do not correspond to ours, and the physical brain is often unable to record such subtlest vibrations without suffering damage. Only mediums, because of their peculiarities, are more often able to remember such actions, but one should not envy them.

18. Precisely, let this striving of yours become constant and ever-growing. But you should test yourself in such constancy. Patience is one of the major qualities which one must acquire on the Path of Service.

19. "How can one help the Great Brothers?" By application of the Teaching in everyday life, thus giving an example to others. Personal example is the most convincing action.

20. "From what else should one be liberated?" The most harmful worm and the most imperceptible to oneself is egoism. Therefore, do check yourself often, for this worm likes to cover itself with the most exquisite justification. In some circumstances egoism may not be so evident, but the moment circumstances are changed, this worm makes itself felt.

21. "How should one act in order to deserve the confidence of the Great Teacher?" One should apply the Teaching in life, and one should be ready to courageously accept all life's obstacles, constantly proving this in action.

22. If the Teaching is applied, if patience is indomitable, if

courage, fearlessness and devotion burn in your heart with an inextinguishable flame, you will attain your aim, and the Great Teacher will not delay in manifesting himself in some way.

23. When sensing an invisible presence, you should display complete calmness, for senseless fear may weaken the protective net of the aura. If the entity whose presence you feel is approaching you with evil intentions, the fear that you manifest may aid in inflicting harm on you. That is why all the Teachings put such stress upon fearlessness of spirit. If one has complete self-control, no astral entity can inflict harm. In such cases I advise concentrating on the Great Image and pronouncing the Name seven times, surrounding yourself mentally with an impenetrable armor of light, as it were.

And now, questions from your second letter.

1. Undoubtedly, the publication of the books of the Teaching is a great help in building the New World. What are the books given for if not for wide dissemination?

2. Of course, those who are striving and seeking sincerely, yet are unable to pay for a book, should receive it free of charge. But are there many such? Through long experience we know that nothing given free is appreciated. The majority will not even bother to open a book that was given free to them. But when they know that something is difficult to obtain, they will seek it, and there were cases when people did not sleep nights in order to copy the books of the Teaching. Great benefit is derived from each small obstacle. It is better to utilize the money which is received for the books for further publication, rather than to scatter the books freely, without any benefit, thus losing the possibility of publishing the next edition for those who are longing for it.

3. Spirit overcomes physical illness. Often, precisely physical defects enable the spirit to soar.

I shall rejoice with all my heart if you feel the desire to perfect the quality of your work, in this already lies a guarantee of every and all success. Whoever looks for quality understands that perfectment is a guiding principle and that he is already on the Path.

Indeed, all can be achieved through the striving of the heart, but do not forget the most essential quality—patience. "The great man is he who is strongest in the exercise of patience."

If you realize that each obstacle is a benefit for the growth of the spirit, you are already on the Path. It is said in the Teaching: "Let us refer, with regret, to the generally accepted idea of comfort and security. In it is contained torpor and vacuity. We learn to welcome all inception of thought, and We always esteem the pressure of a forward striving. A multitude of examples may be cited from physics and mechanics showing pressure as a motive force. For many, it is not easy to agree that pressure is but the gateway to progress. But if humanity will recognize this truth, in so doing it will also understand the meaning of progress. From the point of such cognition it is not far to Brotherhood."

I appreciate that you understand how overloaded I am by work. Indeed, if I do not answer, it is only because of the complete inability to do so, otherwise I am always glad to answer questions. I do not like meaningless letters. When there are questions, it means one is thinking, which is especially valuable, for the development of mind and incisive thinking brings us closer to the Higher Consciousness, and great Collaboration becomes possible.

4. "What is meant by a responsible mission which, if refused, would especially burden karma?"

There are many kinds of such refusals. The most common case is when a person who has approached the Teaching turns to the Great Teachers begging them to be admitted into the building of the New World, and then in a short while for some reason becomes disappointed and drops out. But there are other particularly grievous cases when the spirit of a very advanced student, who for many years has prepared for the fulfillment of a definite action or mission, suddenly regrets the acceptance of the obligation and also the wasted years. That is called a refusal of a mission, since one who evidences regret is unable to fulfill successfully what is entrusted to him. Regrets extinguish the fire that lies at the foundation of each success. Such regret already borders on betrayal and greatly encumbers the karma.

My young friend, from all your questions it is clear that you wish to enter the Path of Great Service, therefore, seriously test your strength to the fullest.. Service requires great self-renunciation and tension of all forces. Earthly happiness is replaced by realization of the wisdom of higher happiness, which comes to the student only in rare glimpses. Persecution, slander, obstacles grow in proportion with progress, because the servant of Light lights up the gloomy hiding places of the servitors of darkness. There is no higher attainment than Service for the good of humanity, nor is there a more difficult one. If your spirit is strong, you are blessed.

Of course, even a partial approach to the Teaching of Living Ethics broadens the consciousnesses, and if the foundations of the Teaching are intelligently applied in life, the earthly path is eased up. But remember that dedication of oneself to the Service of humanity demands complete self-renunciation—indeed, a true achievement. Are there many who are able to lift the Burden of the World? Therefore test yourself in all conditions of life.

If your intentions are profound, the trials will not delay, and you will face many psychological problems which you yourself will have to solve. As it is said, "As water develops the heat in caustic lime, so does the teaching bring into fierce action every unsuspected potentiality latent in him [the disciple]." Precisely, each embryo of good and evil in him will be revealed. Thus, if your intention is firm, be prepared for tests.

12

28 May 1937

I have no doubt that your new book will be as successful as your first one. But before starting such work it would be advisable to observe certain care and to have in mind the covenant of the Teaching of New Life: "On the path to Brotherhood one must lose the habit of belittlement. ...Let no injury take place, even through ignorance." Historical facts put together will speak eloquently for themselves.

Only upliftment and affirmation should issue from the followers of the Teaching of New Life. Your point of view, which is not in the least a belittling one, will reveal itself through further exposition. Speaking of the aspects of the Trinity in a philosophical sense, since Macrocosm and microcosm are one, each human being represents in himself not only the first, the second, or the third aspect of the Trinity, but contains within himself the whole Trinity, for how otherwise can one understand the triad of Atma, Buddhi, and Manas in him? Therefore, is it possible to limit the Son of Eternity to one Image of the Trinity? Indeed, much thoughtlessness is in such division of the Indivisible.

In your new work you should set forth broadly the discord and ignorance that have prevailed among the majority of self-appointed authorities and leaders of human consciousness. And then, based upon all the ancient Teachings and the newest achievements in the realm of thought and science, prove the unity of all religions, all philosophies, or teachings, and also the greatness of their Heralds and Founders.

* * *

Certainly, the Divine Element permeates everything that exists, and its power can create and also destroy whole worlds. Therefore human consciousness must raise its spiritual perception to such a level that good causes can be created in full harmony with this Power. Each violation of good laws evokes grievous consequences. Yes, everything has meaning, but the value is not in outward manifestation or application, but only in its being assimilated by the consciousness.

I agree that the words of Christ, "If any man come to me, and hate not his father, and mother, and wife, and children," etc. sound cruel (should we not ascribe this phraseology to those who wrote it down, or perhaps translated it), but nevertheless the inner sense is clear. If man serves his family more than he serves the spirit of the Teaching of Good, what good will come of it? In the spirit of the Teaching of Living Ethics blood relationship and spiritual relationship are indicated. When and where is the one who brings light into any sphere recognized by his family or contemporaries? Name him. In daily life is it not those closest to us who most often misunderstand and belittle us? Because of their physical and blood ties, they impose upon us some of their own laws. People refuse to understand that above all earthly relationships there is a spiritual bond, and it is a blessing when both these relationship, spiritual and blood, are combined on Earth, but this rarely occurs. Often in the same family spirits with entirely different past accumulations are gathered.

* * *

Just as the words of Christ "Heaven and earth shall pass away: but my words shall not pass away" indicate the truth of his Teaching (because Truth and Eternity are synonymous) so also his other saying "Whatsoever thou shalt bind on earth shall be bound in heaven: and whatsoever thou shalt loose on earth shall be loosed in heaven" indicates the law of karma. How can it be put more clearly that if on Earth we shall not settle or reconcile our contentions with our near ones, we shall not solve them in the Subtle World, or heaven, either. What we sow here has to be reaped by us there. True, this saying has been interpreted differently, namely, that Christ authorized the apostles to use the power of binding and releasing, or, in other words, of punishing and forgiving almost forever and ever. Upon this saying, as we know, the Church has asserted its power. However, when we read this passage as a whole a great deal will become clearer, for it is impossible to interpret it otherwise than as an explanation of the law of cause and effect, or karma.

* * *

Regarding redemption, it is only in an earthly sense that we can make a redeeming sacrifice, that is to say, take upon ourselves the effects engendered by another person. But in a spiritual sense it would be impossible, for the causes that we have generated are reflected primarily upon our inner, or spiritual nature. Therefore, only spiritual regeneration can change, or rather weaken the reaction of the effects which we have generated. A High Spirit can help a man in his spiritual regeneration only if that man's spirit is propelled by a firm decision to redeem everything that he has done. But no mother's prayers will help unless his spirit feels a high impulse toward purification.

Regarding forgiveness and redemption of sins I write more than once, therefore I may as well quote to you this extract: "Just as one chemical ingredient is able to change the whole character of a substance composed of several others, so is the action of a high impulse or quality able to neutralize and overcome the results of the action arising from the base qualities of human nature, and thus to change the entire character of the man, transforming his nature." And, as you know, the transmutation of an inner substance lies in the change of emanations, which, when purified, will react differently upon the effects of the formerly created causes. Only man himself is the creator and also the living record of each motive, each thought, and each deed; therefore, who can change anything in his nature without his personal and direct participation?

* * *

Regarding incarnation. In each new incarnation we receive

an organism limited by the general level of human development and the hereditary influence of ancestors, in addition to the conditions dependent upon our own karma. We are attracted to that environment which is accessible to us, precisely, through our karma. Therefore, the seed of our spirit, in spite of its numerous accumulations can be only partially manifested in each new earthly sheath. It can be observed how a former musical virtuoso will maintain in his new body the understanding of and more or less inclination to his art, but not having the necessary coordination of the centers for particular musical abilities, he could not be a virtuoso.

The quotation from the Gospel of St. Matthew is beautiful. You should emphasize the tolerance and containment in the Teaching of Christ. There are other quotations, similar in meaning which could be found.

When one reads about the concepts and arguments of the Fathers of the Church in the "History of the Councils," one cannot always clearly understand their point of view. For this one has to be able to transport one's spirit into that epoch and feel the whole complexity of the transitory period which created it. Based on a few fragments it is difficult to have a clear picture of what they tried to express. The language and symbolism of concepts change greatly even during a few decades, therefore, one should be careful with interpretations.

The quotations from Athanasius the Great, first of all, are full of beauty, and where there is beauty there is truth. Thus his statement "God became man so that man could become God" confirms the occult truth, for the spirit of Jesus Christ in its purified, fiery, Divine Essence is indeed, for us, a personification of the Divine Principle. Accepting the earthly body during a grave epoch of degeneration and corruption of spiritual values in order to give a new impulse to the human spirit and thus unite man with his divine essence, He verily deified him. We commingle with the Divine Essence within us in proportion to our acceptance of it into our consciousness. Indeed, "through sacrament of the spirit we become participants in the Divine Essence," thus reaching the divine state. Using modern language, is it not said in the Teaching that only by accepting the high energies into the consciousness can we reach and master them?

* * *

It is likewise correct that by rejecting the spirit we open ourselves to the dark forces, obsession, etc. "The one who is baptized puts off the old man, he who is born from above is regenerated by the bliss of the Spirit." We must not forget that during the first centuries of Christianity such rituals as baptism and communion had great inner and spiritual significance, and only later did they degenerate into state ordinances, which were to be observed under threat of forfeiture of rights, etc. Originally baptism and communion were the symbols of adherence to spiritual life. After all, the Mysteries of antiquity were in themselves rituals full of profound inner significance, and the majority of our Christian rituals were actually borrowed from the rituals and symbols of the pagan world. But everything has significance only in spirit, and of course no mechanical manipulations can bring to us a spiritual rebirth or make us adhere to anything, without the participation of our spirit. However, those rituals helped to create certain conditions and moods that enabled our spirit to perceive and to rise more easily. Even nowadays one should not deprive man of the church with all its ceremonial. What actually is needed is a new purification and *spiritual* understanding of rituals and, mainly, not to make them compulsory. Let the spirit choose its own way. We must not forget that the ritual of baptism in the early centuries of Christianity was performed in most cases upon grown-up people, who, through this symbol, wanted to emphasize their break with the old and adherence to a new understanding. But, of course, when afterwards this ritual became compulsory and was performed upon unconscious infants, it *lost all sense*. Particularly appalling was the casting of the bodies of unbaptized dead infants behind the fence of the cemetery. In general, cemeteries should be destroyed, being nurseries of all kinds of epidemics.

Few, very few people can experience and not lose the memory of an exaltation of the spirit unless something visible and touchable reminds them of it. Therefore, the nearest task is not the destruction of a temple but a purification and new explanation of the rituals, as well as of the foundations of the great Teachings. It is indeed essential for people to realize that without a spiritual transport within us no ritual has any meaning. It is necessary to remind constantly that the Divine Bliss can be received only consciously and voluntarily.

* * *

According to the ancient Teachings all the highest Cosmos Concepts acquire their form, or personify themselves in God's likeness in man. Thus, the Highest spirits are personifications of the Highest Concepts. The Seven Kumaras, Seven Logoi, Seven Fires or Flames, Seven Sons of Reason, Seven Sons of Brahma, or Sons of God—all are such Highest Spirits, who (like the Avatars) took on human bodies for the upliftment of man's consciousness and to bring about his adherence to his Divine Essence.

It is not quite correct to state that formerly, people—in this case the Jews—did not know about their sonship or about the law of reincarnation and that Christ was the One who revealed to the Jews the meaning of that which is said in the Bible. Truly, much was known to the ancient Teachers of the Jewish people, and perhaps a great deal more than is known now. But at that time many concepts were already obscured by the zealous interpreters, who were greedy for gain. The Pharisees were actually familiar with the ideas of resurrection, angels, and spirit—this is obvious from the Acts of the Apostles (23:6,7,8).

* * *

Someone says, "It is possible to create only out of something, but not out of one's own self. God is everywhere, and there is nothing aside from him, therefore to create out of oneself is not quite right." I wonder why? In the first place, if God is omnipresent and nothing exists outside of him, that is to say, he is both creator and substance, it seems to me that it is utterly non-essential whether we say that he produces, creates, or generates, because all these concepts are but his manifestations. But even every earthly creator creates or produces precisely through his spirit, from out of himself. Man can be surrounded by the most exquisite materials, but if his creative fire is weak, he will create nothing. Verily, thought and thought-energy create. Remember the Eastern Teaching about the creative power of thought.

* * *

The time has come to indicate that the greatest God of all peoples is the One Living God in Nature, the Only Universal Divinity—the God of Unfailing Law, the God of Just Recompense, but indeed not of Arbitrary Mercy. Verily, this hope for undeserved Higher Mercy probably serves as the strongest stimulus for repeated crimes.

* * *

The answer of Christ to his disciples: "Destroy this temple, and in three days I will raise it up" should be understood correctly as his Resurrection in the subtle body in which he appeared before his disciples. In almost all ancient Teachings the human body is likened to the Temple of God. And Christ hardly meant a miraculous raising of a temple made of stone as a proof of his power. This would contradict the whole spirit of His Teaching.

* * *

There is enlightenment, and enlightenment! *The scope of our consciousness determines the dimensions of the truth of our visions and feelings.* We can receive illumination only through such symbols and feelings as are akin to us, and no more. Pay attention to the visions of saints, how exactly they corresponded to the character and demands of the epoch. Likewise, visions characterize best of all the moral and mental aspects of man. Yet we should not forget that people often do not possess an essential quality—honesty; and they invent much on the basis of what they have heard or read. Visions of cosmic character are sent or revealed to the eye of a clairvoyant only if there is honesty within him. And the characteristic feature of such visions will be Beauty and Grandeur in Simplicity.

You may say that the moral and mental level of Pascal, to whom you refer, was high. Nevertheless, he might not have had spiritual synthesis, and this could have been a stumbling block. Are there many who have attained this quality? Great intellects have often lacked it. One may be an intellectual giant, and yet not possess synthesis.

* * *

Why do you consider the verse from I Corinthians (11:10) so characteristic of the spirit of the teaching of Paul? If, based upon numerous testimonies, we must admit that there have been frequent distortions of the texts of the Scriptures, we may as well admit the possibility of like distortion, or even a later insertion in this Epistle. Indeed, subordination of woman and slavery became so deeply rooted in the course of the decadent centuries, and especially during that epoch of the approach of intellectual darkness, that it was more than difficult to give up those prerogatives. True, the Apostle Paul was a very high spirit, and in his sacred messages he could hardly have allowed such barbarism. But you know that it becomes necessary to make concessions to the conditions of the epoch. The whole truth cannot be revealed to people, because it would not be accepted and might bring more harm than benefit. It is undesirable to rouse too much resentment in the ignorant masses, who, in their fury, may destroy the most precious.

It seems to me that it would have been advisable to cite the decrees of the Ecumenical Councils collected according to sequence. They reveal amazing contradictions and thoughtlessness, which gradually become more and more obvious. The decrees were promulgated, not by individual lucid minds, but by the representatives of the ignorant majority, and this circumstance should be particularly emphasized for precisely these decrees eventually became the dogma of our present Church. Indeed, all the enlightened minds among the theologians revered at present, such as Basil the Great, Athanasius the Great, and John the Divine, were persecuted by their own clergy because they did not agree with those decrees.

Likewise, it is most essential to include the decrees of the Second Council of Constantinople which rejected the teaching of reincarnation and of the pre-existence of the soul. Also of interest is the movement of iconoclasm and all the arguments regarding genuflection and other ceremonials. Why not include those passages from the Gospel which clearly indicate reincarnation?

Your interpretation of the Beatitude "Blessed are the poor in spirit" appeals to me very much. This Beatitude is one of the deepest in meaning. Indeed, in this precept is indicated the need for humility in self-sacrifice, or the absence of any conceit and vanity, as well as the renunciation in consciousness and spirit of all greed, possessiveness, and attachment to transitory objects. Precisely, this *renunciation in one's consciousness* was emphatically insisted upon by all the great Teachers of antiquity. Do you remember the example of the two disciples mentioned in the books of Living Ethics? One had no possessions, yet the Teacher reproached him all the time for his attachment to things; the other was surrounded by things but did not receive the reproval of the Teacher.

* * *

Perhaps some curious person will say, "Explain to us the Image of Christ." To this, answer in the words of the Teaching. "It is impossible to measure the far-off worlds. We can only be enraptured by their radiance." The mysteries of the Spirit are so beautiful that we can only advise not to speak about the Unutterable. The heart alone can tremble with exaltation when coming into spiritual contact with the Supreme Beauty.

* * *

You are completely right that timid elements should not be attracted, for they can cause much harm. Not in vain did all the ancient disciplines require first of all the conquest of any and all fear. Only through fearlessness can be approach the Light and assimilate the ordained Truth. Each Manvantara, or Cycle of Life reveals a new facet of the Diamond of Cosmic Beauty.

And so, with all solicitude and wisdom continue your useful activity. Do not be confused by the isolated cries of darkness.

13

4 June 1937

You are right, people have been asking me about *Chalice of the East*. However, there were not many who thought that this book violated their established ideas and made them feel indignant about it.

I beg you to be calm and patient, for it is not so easy to answer your letter. First of all, for clear mutual understanding, as I have already written, it is necessary to have at least a certain degree of unification of consciousnesses, but this does not exist as yet. Secondly, you do not put direct questions, but simply criticize separate sentences taken out of context, and, in addition, you support your perplexities by examples taken from daily occurrences that are not always applicable to the topics with which these letters deal.

I should also remind you that *Chalice of the East* is unfortunately only a small portion of the large volume of *The Mahatma Letters to A. P. Sinnett*. Often only a few quotations are extracted from a whole letter, and this inevitably makes it difficult for an unprepared reader to understand the many themes which are touched upon. Moreover, these letters are actually answers to the questions of individuals who were already somewhat acquainted with Eastern philosophy. This, too, has to be taken into consideration.

Replying to your criticism, I shall follow the order of your statements, and for better clarity in answering I shall have to quote the sentences that are causing you perplexity. I shall also check the translation with the English edition of this work which is in my possession.

1. "And now it is your province to decide which you will have: the highest philosophy or simple exhibitions of occult powers." The reader (in this case—yourself) answers, "I want both, for the manifestation of the occult forces would once and forever prove their existence." I sympathize with your wishes, nevertheless, I have to say that it is to no purpose to think that people can be convinced of any kind of phenomena from the occult realm if they face these for the first time and have no idea of the occult, or as yet, hidden, laws. I have not met such people. The very suddenness of the manifestation of these phenomena and the conditions in which they take place contradict the preconceived ideas and concepts of the observers and evoke their suspicions and doubts. And the supposition that hypnotic power is being used is not the least of these. It would benefit you to read the book by Sinnett, *The Occult World*, in which he describes the numerous and remarkable occult manifestations that took place with the participation of H. P. Blavatsky. But as a result, all these manifestations did not convince anyone; on the contrary, because of these manifestations H. P. Blavatsky was accused of various frauds, deceits, and similar base stratagems.

Your question, "Is not the greatest philosophy also a manifestation of the occult forces?" is not devoid of justice. The only difference is that in philosophy these powers are manifested on a mental plane corresponding to them, whereas manifestations which are meant to impress the skeptics must be performed on the physical plane; furthermore, they must be adjusted to conditions that are accessible to and fixed by skeptics and ignoramuses who demand them, contrary to the laws to which such manifestations of subtle energies are subject.

Consciousnesses that do not understand the actions of the hidden subtlest forces or energies do not wish to accept the fact that the subtlest energies demand the very same subtle and strictly scientific approach to them. Unfortunately, the majority of people approach these manifestations precisely with an axe and with their own mechanical calculations. Yet in the realm of subtlest energies any primitive physical coarseness is inapplicable. Moreover, you should realize that not only each plane of existence has its own definite laws but each realm of science also has them and needs corresponding conditions for the desired results.

Someone may ask, "Water transformed into wine—is this not a suggestion?" Or, "How can the blind see?" But such things took place, are taking place, and shall take place; the least educated person understands that such phenomena are performed. Therefore, who will deny the miracles of Christ? And do we not know from the very same Gospels that "He did not many mighty works there because of their unbelief"? Thus, even Christ himself needed particular conditions for the performance of miracles. But for us the miracles of Christ are not so much in these manifestations as in the new shifting of consciousness and the new affirmation of achievement.

And now tell me—are there many among those who would like to be convinced of the existence of the hidden forces not yet manifested on our physical plane who possess the necessary qualities of their radiations (aura) suitable for creating the essential conditions? Does it not seem to you that in most cases the emanations of people cut off any possibilities, or at best distort and lower the quality, of phenomena? In the fragments from the first letters used in *Chalice of the East* it is explained very clearly that occult manifestations for the purpose of convincing people are useless.

Often those who approach the subtle manifestations with an axe forget that even a touch of the subtlest energy can reduce them to ashes.

However, in our time there exist in many countries societies for psychic research, where through the aid of mediums the so-called spiritualistic and parapsychic phenomena are studied. Likewise, in some countries in the universities courses have been established for the study of psychic phenomena, transmission of thought at a distance, etc.

But in spite of all this the vast majority continues to doubt the existence of these phenomena.

There is also a large literature on spiritualism; of course, it exists only in those countries where the freedom of conscience and thought is less suffocated by all sorts of zealots of the old as well as the new order.

But since you have "sent Martha to manifest in the kitchen," I in turn will tell you a parable from the wisdom of the East. "To Him of the great Illumination there came a pupil seeking a miracle: 'After the miracle I shall have faith.' The Teacher sadly smiled and revealed to him a great miracle. 'Now,' exclaimed the pupil, 'I am ready to pass through the steps of the Teaching under your guidance.' But the Teacher, pointing to the door, said; 'Go, I no longer need you!'"

2. "Of the theologian we would enquire what was there to prevent his God, since he is the alleged creator of all—to endow matter with the faculty of thought; and when answered that evidently it has not pleased Him to do so, etc." You remark that "such would be an answer of an author who is a narrow theologian, because a cultured and educated theologian not only would not prevent 'his' God from doing this, but would even encourage Him to do so." And you cite the example of St. Sergius of Radonega, who could converse with a bear, and St. Francis of Assisi, who talked with the birds, ending with an example of the responsive vibrations in stone. You conclude, "Then all the further structure of the Author would crumble away." But, precisely this crumbling away I do not see, because neither Sergius of Radonega nor Francis of Assisi were theologians. Besides, in their letters the Mahatmas did not have in mind the exceptional spirits of the individual enlightened minds among the theologians who are anathematized even to this day, but they meant the majority of theologians, who now have the power to forgive and to punish. Indeed these are the heirs of that majority who participated in enacting the edicts of the Councils, which became the dogmas of the present-day church. And the most amazing of these dogmas is the one that separates God from the Universe, or segregates him from Matter. The Eastern pantheism is especially hated by our ecclesiastics. I was glad to hear from you that there are some among them who are able to accept into their consciousness the majestic pantheism which lies at the basis of Eastern philosophy. But if those enlightened ecclesiastics whom you know accept God as the Divine Origin, which is present in all existence, I wonder how, then, do they deal with the only begotten Son and the second aspect of the

Trinity and the Immaculate Conception, etc.? I am in correspondence with some archbishops, and it would be of interest to me to learn also about the point of view of your enlightened theologians.

3. "*Our ideas on Evil.* Evil has no existence *per se* and is but the absence of good." And later on you quote some examples expressing your perplexity. I have to remind you that you expressed the desire to remain at the feet of the Teacher for the sake of the *greatest Philosophy*, but you have failed to acquire the necessary knowledge for this purpose. Without fundamental preparatory training one is unable to approach higher mathematics; similarly, high philosophy is not applicable to everyday discussions. In order to understand the assertion about evil quoted about, one should fully assimilate the Eastern Thought and accept its basic principles, namely, the existence of One (Absolute) Transcendental Reality, its dual aspect in the manifested Universe, and the illusoriness or RELATIVITY of all that is *manifested*.

After you ponder over these concepts you will understand why there can be no evil as such in the higher aspect of perfect Be-ness. Imperfection or RELATIVITY is perceived only in the perpetual motion of forces in the light of the existing concept of One ETERNAL REALITY. You will realize that it is only in our consciousness that all manifestations acquire one or another coloring and one or another quality. There are as many degrees of knowledge and qualities of manifestations as there are consciousnesses.

But let us come down to the planes which are nearest to us. Undoubtedly in the world of man evil does exist, and it was born with the first glimpse of consciousness. Imperfection of consciousness combined with freedom of will gave birth to all types of evil. And the concept of sacrifice is synchronous with the first manifestation of evil. Likewise, it is correct that there are conscious sacrifices and also unconscious ones. But I do not agree with the example given by you. Certainly in the usual interpretation it could be understood that here is a victim of malice and ignorance, but the man who knows the action of immutable cosmic laws will realize that one can be a victim of one's own past misdeeds. Verily, each manifestation has several aspects, and therefore it inevitably becomes relative.

4. "In other words, we believe in MATTER alone" and also

"Only thus, and not otherwise, does it, strengthening and refining those mysterious links of sympathy between intelligent men—the temporarily isolated fragments of the universal Soul and the cosmic Soul itself—bring them into full rapport [unity[. Once this established [or assimilated], then only will these awakened sympathies serve, indeed, to connect MAN with—what for want of a European scientific word more competent to express the idea, I am again compelled to describe as that energetic [dynamic] chain which binds together the material and Immaterial Kosmos" "Immaterial Kosmos—what nonsense? This is verily hailing matter and ending with a prayer for the repose of the soul." Such is your hasty conclusion.

You are indignant because it seems to you a contradiction; but is it really so difficult to assimilate the point of view of the East that Spirit and Matter are one? That everything issued from the One Element—Spirit-Matter? That Matter is only a differentiation of Spirit, and that Spirit devoid of Matter has no manifestation, or in other words, does not exist? Indeed, whether in actions or in thought we cannot become detached from matter; we approach the highest or the grossest aspects of the very same matter. Matter, or the subtlest substance—Spirit-Matter—is infinite in its differentiations and in its visible and invisible manifestations, but one cannot act with pure spirit alone. Ignorance disunites and dissolves everything, whereas the great knowledge of the East unifies and synthesizes all. For millenniums the Western consciousness has been accustomed to divide everything into material and immaterial or physical and spiritual to such an extent that it is difficult in discussions with Westerners to fully exclude this terminology. The Author whose letter you are criticizing had to deal, precisely, with the Western mentality of the past century, which not only had difficulty in assimilating new concepts but even in accepting the more suitable terminology for the old concepts. As for the quotation which you cite, instead of "Immaterial Kosmos,:" we, using the modern language, would say: "The Cosmos of subtle Substances or Energies." In the modern energetics of the Universe matter has lost its "density." In the science of thought, in the realm of philosophy, the East was, is, and shall be our teacher.

You are puzzled by the words of the Author, "Once this established. ..." But really, all the previous statements in this letter explain "this.:" Precisely, on the very same page of the letter it is stated that a pupil should learn the elementary rules of arithmetic before he attempts to solve the highest problems of Euclid. And only his progress in the assimilation of the elementary foundations of the Sacred Knowledge will bring him understanding of the great Thought of the East. And only in such a manner, constantly strengthening and refining the links of sympathy, or, in other words, by unifying the consciousnesses of intelligent or learned people is it possible to achieve mutual understanding and accord.

Only then can the cosmic laws, which unite the physical world with the subtle one (or the "hereafter"), be revealed to them. Harmony is the law of the Higher World. Man has three natures within him, and he must perfect all three in order to fulfill and accomplish his earthly evolution. And that will come when he learns to consciously act through these natures on the three corresponding planes of existence.

5. "Nature is destitute of goodness or malice; she follows only immutable laws when she either gives life and joy, or sends suffering [and] death." Here you conclude that "if the Author wishes to say that life and death are relative states, that there is no death, then in our conception there should be no life." Again the same thing; therefore, we must return again to what has already been said—in order that we may understand relativity we must know that the *World of Reality is the Eternal IS, and that the whole relativity is born only through differentiation and through the endless transmutations or changes in the perpetual motion of the manifested Be-ness.* Could you call death the change of one sheath for another, the awakening to a more refined, more broad activity? (The latter, of course, only in the case of a developed and spiritualized consciousness.) And the concepts that you have enumerated such as Devachan, Kama-Loka, and others are but different states of our consciousness.

6. "Nature has an antidote for every poison . ... The butterfly devoured by a bird becomes that bird. ... I can see that you do not approve of the cosmic laws. I agree with you that there are many imperfections and even cruelties in manifested nature from our human point of view. But in the majority of cases of cruelty and imbalance in nature, alas—it is primarily man, the so-called "crown of nature's creation," who is guilty. Man is summoned to perfection, to collaboration, to constant giving. But, instead, we see that man applies all his forces for disunity, disruption, and

destruction. Man has violated his collaboration with nature and thus has transgressed against great Equilibrium. Perhaps you will try to explain the cosmic laws, which seem so cruel to you, from your own point of view; or from the point of view of the All-merciful and All-powerful. Heavenly Father We know only one law: the law of causes and effects.

7. "And today the followers of Christ and those of Mohammed are cutting each other's throats in the names of and for the greater glory of their respective myths [faiths]." Well, do you not agree that the degenerating religions are a great evil? Do you not agree that religions caused the greatest bloodshed, and that the majority of the servitors of religions have hindered every discovery of science and extinguished each bold thought revealing the infinitude of Knowledge? But it is fortunate that historical chronicles are still preserved!

Also, one has to understand that the Author of this letter has in view only the *distorted, declining* religions and not the foundations of the Teachings of the Great Bearers of Light. I think you will agree that some established dogmas and actions of the representatives of the Church very often did not, and do not to this day meet the spirit of the "teachings of their Founders. Surely we should not go back to the history of the Councils of Churches; to the persecution of such great fathers of Christianity as Origen, Clement of Alexandria, John the Golden-Mouth, Gregory, Athanasius the Great, and others by their ignorant colleagues! Should we resurrect in our memories the papal chronicles with all the terrors of the Inquisition and St. Bartholomew's Night? Likewise, let us not dwell upon the destruction of Buddhist temples and communities and the murder of Buddhists by Brahmins, Mohammedans, and Chinese, or the perpetual enmity between Hindus and Moslems, which yearly carries away many lives because of a slaughtered cow, or a pig thrown into a temple! All this continues and will continue until the best minds among the spiritual fathers realize where and how cruelly they have sinned against the covenants of the Great Teachers and Founders. The consciousness of humanity cannot be helped with impunity in a vise of ignorance. Sooner or later, the human spirit will awaken and will cry out and throw off all fetters. Looking back we can find profound reasons which caused the fall of the old world. The stifling of mind and spirit which took place in certain countries has engendered the subsequent madnesses. Thought is the crown of creation, and its murder is the greatest crime. Persecuted, the best spiritual fathers realized this long ago and declared that "hell is ignorance."

8. You feel indignant that "in *Chalice of the East* there is no disclosure of the Highest Mystery." But, just think—is it possible in the face of Infinity to attain the Highest Mystery? And where is that synthesis and pure consciousness which can comprehend the beauty of the Highest Be-ness? The subtlest concepts and feelings are inaccessible to an impure and coarse consciousness, it would be blinded by the very approach to them. Mysteries, and not even the highest ones, are revealed only through flights of the spirit. Therefore, grow your wings!

9. "If, for generations we have 'shut out the world from the Knowledge of our Knowledge,' it is on account of its absolute unfitness." To this you ask, "Who should have prepared the world?" I will say: the common efforts of the human spirit toward the cognition of the great reality. The Greatest Minds have reincarnated on Earth in order to advance the consciousness of humanity toward an understanding of the cosmic laws which require complete cooperation between all the temporarily disunited particles of the One Universal Soul. But the free will of man pushed him onto the path of a limited, isolated selfhood toward complete disunity, and wreck.

Further, you quote: "and if, notwithstanding proofs given, it [humanity] still refuses yielding to evidence..." and you immediately put a question, "proofs of what, which, where, and when?" To this I may tell you: acquaint yourself with the history of the development of human consciousness and thought from the writing of the greatest minds, who often were rewarded with "Honorary" titles of heretics and charlatans. And then at the end of the sentence: "... then will we at the End of this cycle retire" you sense a threat there, and, as you declare, an undeserved one. But to begin with, there is no threat that the Great Teachers will accept the voluntary rejection by humanity of the higher knowledge, in which case they would apply their knowledge and energies for the benefit of other humanities on other planets. It seems to me that it is sufficient to fathom even slightly the present events in the world in order to be able to realize to what end all is hastening. And as there are no effects without a cause, we can well imagine what were those causes and where we can look for them.

Therefore, only a prejudiced consciousness can perceive some sort of threat in the words quoted by you. In that case, every sign at a railroad crossing, "beware of the train," etc., could pass for a threat. A free consciousness will understand and gratefully accept every warning.

Thus, you write in conclusion: "First of all, the impression from this book is as if it were written by people of various degrees of spiritual development; but if the book has been written by one person he is entirely devoid of any knowledge of his subject, and has with great aplomb strung upon one thread the picked-up crumbs of knowledge as if they were beads of various sizes, colors, and values." By using your own manner of expression I may as well say that in this particular case you blame those who are well for your own ailment. It is impermissible to attribute to the Great Teachers of humanity one's own ignorance and lack of understanding.

The book in question is written by the Greatest Minds, but the unprepared consciousness had better not touch it, for it would result in nothing but blasphemy. One may know and may not understand a great deal, this is no crime, but to blaspheme is unpardonable. The one who sees contradictions everywhere but in his own consciousness reveals not only his own ignorance but conceit as well.

Thus, the great Buddha, when selecting disciples, used to test them on their ability to contain, as it were, pairs of opposites. If a disciple could not master this, Buddha would not advance him to further knowledge, since this not only would be useless but harmful as well. *The awareness of reality is achieved only by way of perpetual change and confrontation of pairs of opposites.*

You will probably feel indignant after reading my letter, but I am well used to the fact that those people who tell fine stories, thus heaping all kinds of blasphemies upon the most High, most sacred, and dear, become enemies when justly reprimanded. It is not in my nature to utter hypocritical sweet words to avoid personal defamation. Likewise, I dislike cheap sentimentality, which encourages any kind of lie and becomes a hotbed of injustice.

14

11 June 1937

Every affirmation of unity is a great action, and it is difficult to evaluate its effects by earthly measures. Therefore, from the bottom of our hearts we express our gratitude to all who are spiritually attuned to us and who brought their best sentiments for the day dedicated to the Festival of Unity. Let there be light and joy for all, let self-denial in unity adorn the life of every true servant of Good. We are happy that your group is so mobile and active. The most important is to stir the waters. Then only are possibilities born. However, we have to bear in mind that often we expect quite a definite result from our actions and feel disappointed when we do not see the immediate and presupposed outcome; with all this, we fail to notice that our actions may have brought or sown seeds of new possibilities in another no less important direction. Therefore, let us be vigilant, let us seize the possibilities that are brought to us through our actions, our meetings with people, etc. Life is action, stagnation is dissolution. Therefore, blessed are those who are striving toward action.

And now I come to your questions. You want to know more about psychic energy.

You know that psychic energy is called PRIMARY energy, therefore it includes all other energies, which are only its differentiations.

Thus, Parafohat is the fundamental, or primary psychic energy in its highest cosmic aspect, and Fohat is its next aspect in the manifested Universe, the same psychic energy manifested as life force is diffused everywhere as PRANA. The time has come to bring into oneness the meaning of Primary Energy.

Here is a paragraph from the Teaching: "No doubt you have been asked many times how to develop psychic energy and how to realize its usefulness. But it has been said enough that the heart that aspires to higher quality of all life will be the conductor of psychic energy. No forcible, conventionally accelerated movement toward a display of the heart's action will be useful. The heart is a most independent organ; it may be set free toward good, and it will hasten to be filled with energy. Likewise, only in friendly communions it possible to secure the fruits of unified energy. However, for this it is indispensable to understand what harmonious agreement is."

Psychic energy is the Holy Ghost; psychic energy is love and striving; psychic energy is the synthesis of all radiations of the nerves; psychic energy is the great Aum. Therefore, the development of constant, invincible striving toward perfection, to Light in all its manifestations, will be exactly the unfolding of this life-giving energy. Do you remember paragraph 55 from *New Era Community*? "Striving is the boat of the Arhat. ... Striving is the key to all caves. ... Striving is the multitude of stars." I am so fond of this paragraph! One can say that wherever there is absence of striving there is also absence of the lofty psychic energy.

You are right—psychic energy can be assimilated only if the nerve centers are ready to accept it. But no one can give it forcibly. It is possible to transmit a certain amount of one's own store to another person, but only if he is able to assimilate it. This explains many miraculous healings. Likewise, psychic energy acquires power from space, but only if it has acquired the *quality of a magnet*. All phenomena, such as telepathy, transmission of audience, psychometry, etc. are connected with the manifestations of various qualities of psychic energy. It must always be remembered that the qualities of psychic energy are infinite in their diversity.

Kundalini is the very same life force, or psychic energy, that acts through the center at the base of the spine. But it manifests through the heart in highly evolved spirits. In past centuries attention was directed mainly to the center of Kundalini for attainment of the visible result of the action of psychic energy. But in the coming epoch, with the worlds coming closer to each other, the *center of the heart will be especially intensified*. Action through the center of Kundalini is convincing and real chiefly in the earthly condition, whereas for attaining the higher worlds and for the sojourn in them it is essential to refine the energy of the heart. This is the reason why the Teaching speaks so much about the heart, this "sun of suns."

Psychic energy is infinite in the variety of its qualities and manifestations. It is dual in its aspects, as is everything else in the manifested Universe, i.e., it can serve both good and evil. Therefore, just as its most diverse qualities were manifested in the times of Atlantis, so, too, in the coming epoch, one may expect its most varied manifestations. But upon the awakening of greater spirituality in mankind through the influence of the new spatial rays that are now reaching our planet, let us hope that the higher manifestations, or qualities of psychic energy will predominate. All depends upon the spiritual development of man, on the quality of his heart.

Now, your next question. "How to understand the words in the Gospel of St. John, 'Whosoever sins ye remit, they are remitted unto them; and whose soever sins ye retain, they are retained'?" Obviously, these words were not transmitted exactly. Indeed it is impossible to expect that the Gospels, the first of which was written almost a hundred years after the departure of Christ and after they had gone through the censorship of so many zealous hands, could preserve the thought of Christ explicitly. However, I interpret it this way: if we forgive the sinner, by so doing so we do not make his karma more burdensome. Whereas, if we hide malice and implacability within ourselves, we complicate his karma still more, and at the same time, we will not help ourselves, but vice versa.

Let us recall what is said in *Brotherhood*, paragraph 445: "Around the concept of forgiveness there is a great lack of understanding. One who has forgiven someone assumes that he has accomplished something out of the ordinary, whereas he has merely preserved his own karma from complications. The forgiven one thinks that all has been ended, but, of course, karma remains ahead of him. True, the forgiving one did not intervene in the karma of the forgiven one and thus has not made it more burdensome, but the very law of karma remains with both participants. The Lords of Karma can alter this to a certain extent if the fire of purification flashes out brightly, but such a flame cannot easily be set alight. Great sacrifices have been performed for the kindling of the fire. One must revere the memory of such self-sacrificing deeds. Beauty lives on in such calls. Neither time nor human confusion can stifle the calls to self-sacrifice. The Teachings of Brotherhood also tell about the same thing. It is beautiful that even now the concept that has existed throughout the ages is not forgotten. Let us not reject even a little understanding of the supermundane path."

Let us return to the words in the Gospel of John, which usually are quoted parallel with the saying from the Gospel of Matthew (18:18): "Verily I say unto you, Whatever ye shall bind on earth shall be bound in heaven: and whatsoever ye shall loose on earth shall be loosed in heaven." Actually these are the words upon which the Church, claiming to be a successor to the apostles, bases its power to forgive and to punish, including excommunication. I have already written about this, therefore I shall now quote for you these lines: "In order that one may correctly understand the words of Christ mentioned above one should carefully read the preceding verses in the same chapter (St Matthew 18:15). Indeed, the 18th verse is, so to say, a summary which issues from the above parable, and it fully explains the action of the law of Karma.

"Verily, if we do not resolve our arguments with our near ones here on Earth, they will not be settled in the Subtle World either. For we reap in the Subtle World what we sow here. That is why we should always try to neutralize karma as much as possible or, in other words, to settle our relationships with others while we are on Earth. Why should the word 'you' in the 18th verse apply only to the apostles and not to people in general? Certainly, it is not difficult to understand why these words were interpreted as being the right given by Christ to the apostles to 'bind and loose,' or in other words, to punish and forgive. ...

"Indeed, strictly speaking, even the Greatest Spirit is unable to forgive sins that have been committed, as it would contradict the law of Karma. He could ease Karma to a certain extent, but that is all. If man is the only creator and recorder of each of his motives, thoughts and deeds, who then can alter anything at all in his being, and therefore in his destiny, without his direct will? The High Spirit can do no more than help us in our efforts to reform our inner beings. Precisely, cooperation is necessary in everything."

In concluding my letter I would like to ask you to remind from time to time all those who have approached the Teaching that tests, as you know, are inevitable. Verily, the disciples must find the strength of spirit to vanquish the enemies, who of course, dwell first of all in ourselves in the form of all sorts of passions and habits not outlived. Often, under the pressure of outer circumstances and conditions, these rise in our heart and poison our consciousness. Point out to your friends the following paragraphs from *Brotherhood*.

"483. In ancient communities each one undergoing testing was hailed. He was dealt with solicitously since it was known that it was inadmissible to forcibly interrupt the process of his experience. It was considered that each testing is a threshold to progress. No one could twist the path of effects, but brotherly encouragement enabled him not to slacken his pace, even before the most frightful images. Of course, chaos in its terrible ugliness inevitably tries to impede the path of each one being tested. But let these images be dreadful; the manifestation of the most horrible one will be in itself the forerunner of the end of the test."

"529. Habit is second nature—a wise proverb indicating to what an extent habit dominates man. Precisely, habits render a man immobile and unreceptive. One can suppress habits, but it is not easy to eradicate them. People are continually encountered who boast of their victory over habits. But observe the daily routine of such victors, and you will find them slaves of habit. They have become so imbued with habits that they do not even feel the weight of such a yoke. It is especially tragic when a man is convinced that he is free, whereas he is really shackled in the fetters of his habits. It is most difficult to cure a sick man who denies his illness. Each one can name such incurable ones among people known to him. Yet in order to assimilate the concept of Brotherhood, mastery of existing habits is indispensable. Under habits We have in mind not the service for good, but the petty habits of selfhood.

"It is Our custom to test those who are approaching the Brotherhood on liberation from habits. Such testings must be expected. It is best to begin with small habits. Man is often concerned with defending them more than anything else. They are considered to be natural qualities, like birthmarks. Yet the newly born have no habits. Atavism, the family, and school foster the growth of habits. In any case, a routine habit is an enemy of evolution."

15

19 June 1937

I was glad to hear that you intend to pay attention to psychic energy and the power of thought. At present this is the most essential question. It is necessary to awaken men's consciousnesses to a correct evaluation of the significance of thought.

The coming evolution will be based on cooperation and on the significance of thought. Therefore, try to gather as much material as you can regarding practical achievements in the realm of thought transmission.

What remarkable tests in discrimination of people are being sent to you! But I am sure you will pass these tests victoriously.

So let us acquire wisdom by comparing different personalities. Let us remember which personalities have already been disclosed within a short period of time. Let us practice goal-fitness. It is said in the Teaching that a man who does not realize what is co-measurement cannot be considered spiritual. Co-measurement is the Golden Mean.

Referring to Lord Buddha, Vivekananda said that the heart of the Great Spirits is as soft as butter, but they know how to discipline it. In other words They know what is co-measurement. Verily, They are guided by co-measurement. Co-measurement borders upon goal-fitness, which reigns throughout Cosmos.

I looked through the enclosed letter and feel like helping the author to clarify his thoughts regarding the complexities of the human being. But first I must emphasize that the *Buddhists do not declare that man is "That"* or God, perfect and eternal. This declaration belongs to the followers of Vedanta. Further, one should not think that the presence within us, or our adherence to the perfect Divine Principle, makes any evolution senseless. On the contrary, only the presence of this eternal Principle within us makes evolution possible, because all the Universe, all Be-ness exists only because of this life-giving Principle. Verily, the perfection and eternalness of this Divine Principle in its potential is the guarantee that man, its carrier, can perfect himself eternally. While acknowledging the changelessness and perfection of the Divine Element, the Vedantists recognize also the whole complexity of the human being as the reflection of the Universe—this complex of complexes. The Macrocosm is in a perpetual process of unfoldment, or becoming; so, also, man, the microcosm, tirelessly uncovers and accumulates new possibilities, precisely owing to the presence within him of the perfect eternal Divine Potentiality.

Buddhists deny the existence of a *changeless* soul in man and in all Existence, because in man, as well as in the whole manifested Universe, they see impermanency and transitoriness, or, using modern terminology, the evolution of all that exists.

However, not a single educated Buddhist, whose ontological concepts are nearer to contemporary thought based on energetics, would deny the existence in man of Divine Energy, which is fundamentally eternal and changeless. Therefore, it is of no consequence whether we call this energy God, Spirit, or Eternal Witness, or even Divine Fire, its majestic transcendental meaning would not change.

It is useful to recollect here what is said in *Agni Yoga*, paragraph 275: "Vedanta correctly states that the spirit remains inviolate. The fiery seed of the spirit remains in its primary consistency because the essence of the elements is immutable.

"But the emanation of the seed changes, depending on the growth of consciousness. Thus one may understand that the seed of the spirit is a fragment of the elementary fire. And the energy accumulated around it is consciousness. This means that Vedanta was concerned with the seed and Buddhism spoke of perfectment of the bodies. Thus the movable and immovable are completely correlated.

"It is quite understandable that Buddha, who directed humanity toward evolution, pointed out the nature of mobility, whereas the Vedanta expounded the foundation. You may add any chemical ingredient to a flame and thereby change its color and size, but the primary nature of fire will remain unchanged. I do not see any basic contradiction between Vedanta and Buddhism."

Thus, Vedantists like to compare the evolution of a human being with a necklace, each bead of which is one of the physical manifestations strung on the thread of the Spirit. But from the point of view of the Buddhists it is more correct to imagine this evolution as a complicated mixture, into which a new ingredient is added with each new manifestation upon the earthly plane, and, of course, this changes the entire mixture.

Someone protests against the division of man into spirit and matter. Certainly, in their ultimate state, spirit and matter are one (matter is crystallized spirit); but on the plane of manifestation, or differentiation, everything changes, and the nearer to the dense strata, the sharper the differentiation, or division becomes. Thus, if, in the Fiery World, differentiation between spirit and matter is almost intangible because matter acquires the appearance of light, then, alas, on our earthly plane it acquires a monstrous coarseness. Therefore, bearing in mind the complexity of man's organism, it becomes necessary in many cases to resort to a division into *spirit* and *matter* in order to be understood.

During the span of his earthly life, a mentally developed human being lives and acts upon two, and even three planes; each plane has its own corresponding sheath; therefore it is natural that the sheath in which man acts on a higher plane receives corresponding impressions. But because of the subtleties of these vibrations, they can be impressed upon the coarse physical brain only in rare cases, since otherwise the brain would not be able to stand the strain. Therefore, because of the poverty of our terminology for such concepts, it is customary to speak of man as "a spirit" when he manifests himself in his subtlest sheath, whereas, his physical envelope is termed *matter*.

Besides, do we not know about the Chalice of accumulations, which is only partially manifested in each incarnation? And would not these accumulations of the Chalice be indeed knowledge, or precipitation of energies around the fiery seed of the spirit? Therefore, there are no contradictions, whether we say that man is an imperfect spiritual being, or if, when analyzing certain aspects of the human complex, we resort to division into the higher and lower manifestations of this complex.

We know that spirit without matter has no existence. Wherever there is Existence there is matter, even if it be entirely invisible to us. And man is just a complex of infinite gradations in the differentiation of one Element-SPIRIT-MATTER.

One should always bear in mind the two fundamental contentions of Secret Knowledge, namely: 1. The Non-separateness and Inalienability of Good, or the Divine Element, from the Universe; and 2. The unity of the basic Element—Spirit-Matter. From non-realization and non-acceptance of these fundamental occult theses come all misunderstandings and delusions.

With the new understanding of matter by scientists and with the interest shown in the power of thought, the Teaching of Buddha will occupy a fitting place in the coming epoch. Actually, Buddhism makes no difference between the physical and the psychic world. Reality ascribed to the actions of thought is of the same order as the reality of objects that we perceive through our senses.

Stand as a warrior on watch, and do remember the inevitable tests.

16

2 July 1937

The entire Universe is permeated with One Divine Element whose visible and invisible Existence is manifested in the eternal never-ceasing Motion (Breath), engendering ever new differentiations and combinations in ceaseless change and in the process of unfoldment of this immense, ineffable, eternally unknown Mystery of Mysteries.

At the basis of all Creation lies a great impulse, or striving toward manifestation. This is the very same impulse, or thirst for existence that induces man to incarnate. In its higher aspect it is divine Love and also sublimated human love. In ancient times, precisely Kama, the God of Love, was revered as the greatest God. God is Love, and in love and through love is each of his manifestations conceived. The whole Cosmos is held by the Cosmic Magnet, or Divine Love, within the order of Be-ness. Thus, tell your friends that Divine Love generates all worlds.

In the Divine Consciousness there is neither beginning nor end, only the eternal IS. Just as it is impossible to imagine Infinity having a beginning, so it is inappropriate to talk about the beginning of Creation. Could the human mind imagine the beginning of even one of the Great Manvantaras, the number of which is lost in Infinity? From the Sacred Teaching we can formulate a certain idea about the germination of our planetary chain, and by analogy, with the help of some existing hints, we can attempt to catch a few glimpses regarding the engendering of the cycle of the solar system.

You also know that, during partial Pralayas, or renovations of the planet or solar system, the Highest Beings (Jacob's Ladder), who collectively represent Cosmic Reason and the Creative Element, stand on guard and plan the future cycle of life of the solar system or planet. Later They themselves become the chief executors of these plans. How else could all the legends about the pantheon of Gods, or Avatars and Man-Gods be explained? Indeed, the Hierarchic Principle is the cosmic law, the leading principle. Therefore, there is a Highest Spiritual Being, or Hierarch who takes upon himself responsibility for the whole cycle or a certain Manvantara. In human conception such a Greatest Spirit is merged with the Image of a personal God or even Universal God.

* * *

Regarding psychic energy I shall quote these words from *Brotherhood:* "No doubt you have been asked many times how to develop psychic energy and how to realize its usefulness. But it has been said enough that the heart that aspires to higher quality of all life will be the conductor of psychic energy. No forcible, conventionally accelerated movement toward a display of the heart's action will be useful. The heart is a most independent organ; it may be set free toward good, and it will hasten to be filled with energy. Likewise, only in friendly communion is it possible to secure the fruits of unified energy. However, for this it is indispensable to understand what harmonious agreement is."

Thus, advise your pupils to strive toward the betterment of quality in everything, in all life. This will result in the best accumulation of psychic energy.

Straight-knowledge was formerly called intuition. Straight-knowledge is built out of accumulations from past lives and is preserved in the Chalice. Indeed, it is not just knowledge, but straight-knowledge, because all knowledge gained by us is based primarily on feeling. It is especially strongly expressed in all transcendental experiences. Straight-knowledge is awakened together with the intensification of the action of psychic energy. As you see, everything is interwoven in a mutual collaboration, and everything is interdependent.

17

6 July 1937

Now—your questions. Suicides usually stay in the strata that are closest to Earth, because the magnetic attraction of their energies to Earth has not yet been outlived. Their etheric, or lower astral body especially attaches them to earthly sensations. Only in the case of exceptionally high Spirits is this lower sheath dissolved while still in the earthly life. Clarity of consciousness assists such transfiguration. Indeed, the sphere that is closest to Earth is very dense, but if, even at times, during his earthly life the spirit was striving toward Light, he will be able (if he can collect and direct his will) to find here also the influence of the Higher Forces, and with their help he can improve his condition. But most of the time precisely suicides are the ones who never thought about the supermundane realms, and therefore they are unable to comprehend what has happened to them. If during life, their consciousness was clouded, then this haziness will be still more intensified after the separation from the physical body. Consciousness, in its highest aspect, psychic energy, must be very clear and active during the earthly life, so that the impressions, or precipitations of the energies can be impressed upon the centers of the subtle body; otherwise, after the change of envelopes the human essence remains in the Subtle World in a semi-somnolent state.

Psychic energy is absolutely necessary during the crossing, or the changing of one condition into another. Our psychic energy carries us into the sphere that is conformable with our accumulations, and the stronger the striving of one's spirit before death, the higher will it be able to rise. And if the fundamental store and the quality of his psychic energy do not allow the spirit to remain in the higher sphere where the last powerful surge bore him, nevertheless, while dwelling in the sphere that corresponds to his spiritual achievements, he will forever preserve the memory of that exaltation of the spirit. That is the reason why, in antiquity, one was so concerned with the last moments on Earth, trying to make them joyous and filled with aspiration toward the most Beautiful. Conversely, the unfortunate suicides precisely cut off every current of psychic energy within themselves. The despair that drives them to commit this act of madness causes the complete ebbing of the psychic energy and thus they are left in the power of earthly attraction. Their anguish and sufferings will last until the very day of their natural death. In exceptional cases when consciousness has been obscured only temporarily by the grievous concatenation of circumstances, these unfortunate ones may remember about Light and thus find within themselves sufficient will power to turn toward the Higher Help and to strive for redemption. Therefore, a sincere prayer of the heart to the forces of Light, asking for help for these unfortunate ones, is not left without an answer, provided of course, that these unfortunate ones shall themselves strive to rise in spirit.

Certainly, the low entities among suicides can practice all sorts of excesses. Vampirism is not a rare occurrence; their not yet outlived, not yet transmuted energies drag them with special power toward earthly sensations.

Everything told in *Chalice of the East* is true. Separation of the monad causes loss of the memory of personality, but not of the individuality. However, the final separation of a monad from the other principles of man is indeed a terrible occurrence, the worst that can happen, since this arrests the evolution of the individuality for many, many millenniums. Such a monad would have to build up a new vehicle, or conductor for itself, going through all the low forms.

You wish to know about death, or rather about the change of condition. But there are so many indications about it in the books of the Living Ethics—which one is not clear to you? I shall repeat once more—one must firmly remember that the quality and the dimensions of our earthly condition provide the clarity of our consciousness in the Subtle World. Whatever is not realized here will not be realized there. Somnolent consciousnesses remain so in the Subtle World. We acquire new energies, for their transmutation into knowledge, only here on Earth. Therefore, every striving for knowledge, every accumulation is most important.

Thus, if here on Earth there was not built into our Ego an irresistible longing for knowledge, whence will it appear in the Subtle World? There thought-creativeness and spirit-creativeness reign. But is such thought-creativeness easy? One must first learn to think here on Earth. Thus, it is impossible to acquire in the Subtle World those qualities that we have disregarded in our earthly lives. After all that is said above, you probably will be able to more clearly understand the *fundamental* and determining role of refined psychic energy during all changes of the bodies.

18

19 July 1937

"Cautiously touch the tarred knots of destiny" and let us cover the flow of karma with the ice of understanding.

You do not understand the meaning of these words, but they seem so clear to me. The better part of our being can help us to recognize an old debtor or creditor during karmic encounters, and then, precisely our straight-knowledge can prompt us to cautiousness and actions that accord with the situation. But, indeed, in most cases thoughtless touching upon his many-hued past entraps man and he again and again gives in to any and every feeling, thus making his old karma more burdensome, so that it will drag behind him in numerous existences.

"The flow of karma can be covered by the ice of understanding" or, in other words, its action can be slowed down or even stopped altogether. This can be achieved through the *transmutation* of our inner essence and through the approach to the Hierarchy of Light. Truly, the Hierarchy of Light helps a disciple to discriminate in life's encounters, so that he may learn not to allow karmic recollections to take possession of his feelings.

"But beware of destroying this covering by foolishness or by cruelty, which is forbidden under Our Shield." If the Highest Hierarch has explained to us the meaning of our encounters, and if we, not being able to overcome our feelings, give way to them in either direction, that is, either by senseless giving and self-sacrifice or by cruelty, we shall bind ourselves by a new and still worse karma, thus depriving ourselves, perhaps for many ages, of the privilege of approaching the Great Teachers. A man who is overburdened with karma cannot be brought close. He may receive some support, but an approach is something entirely different.

Likewise, one should not assume that the Higher Forces *send* tests to us. Life itself is replete with them. And definitely, the most dangerous tests are those that have their roots in past lives. The tests performed by the Great Teachers are, rather, their *observations* of the conduct and resourcefulness of the tested disciple in all life's manifestations, often insignificant in their outer appearances but what is small and what is great is only so in our limited earthly conception.

"Since the worlds are on trial, each particle of them is being tested. One may foresee that someone will be terrified at such a supposition. But only injudicious thought can stand in the way of welcoming the law of evolution. Through expansion of consciousness one grows to love this incessant motion; would it be better to remain in the unchanging prison of errors and delusions? On the contrary, it is much more joyous to sense the constant testing, which engenders the feeling of responsibility. In each cooperation on the path to Brotherhood responsibility will the be basis of growth." [Brotherhood]

But are there many who comprehend the meaning of responsibility? People often interpret the most sacred responsibility as the greatest violation of their freedom.

I welcome your mettlesome spirit! A storm cloud which passed, happily without harm, helped you to look into the depth of your being, and now you will be better equipped for new encounters; they will not come upon your unawares, and your heart will be on guard. Do you remember my writing you that discrimination of people is one of the major qualities required on the path? It is very difficult and brings many bitter moments, but we must steel our courage and will and discipline our emotions.

One must learn to meet every person as the x in the problem, yet at the same time one must not admit an iniquitous contempt and indifference. In our entire life, upon each step, we meet with counterpositions, and we must be able to make them compatible. The science of making opposites compatible and of finding equilibrium is that great Discipline which everyone must undergo on the path to Brotherhood.

Austere is the path of approach to Brotherhood. Earthly joys leave us. But much higher and deeper joys come to take their place, however one must learn to grow up to them, to the joy of the nearness of the White Brotherhood, the joy of the possibility of cooperation with Them, the joy of constant broadening and deepening of the understanding of life and active cosmic laws. Likewise there is no small joy from contacts with the harmonious hearts of the closest friends and co-workers.

"If people would only realize the visible and invisible cooperation in which they could participate. If people would realize to what an extent they could multiply their strength in cooperation with the Brotherhood. If they would at least think about cooperation, which could be revealed each instant. But people not only do not approach the Brotherhood in thought, they even consider thoughts about Brotherhood ludicrous.

"Each moment each one can apply his strength; one has but to think that there is incessant labor being performed on the heights to help mankind. Such thought alone creates and influx of energy. It will propel the consciousness toward the service of humanity. It will whisper that love for humanity is possible. Because of earthly conditions it is often difficult to imagine the possibility of such love. But let the thought about the existence of Brotherhood help to open the heart. Then cooperation will appear not as a duty, but as JOY. And the drops of sweat and the sacred pains will become the crown of knowledge.

"Let us not take these words as an abstraction, because such negation will close the best receptacle—the heart. Each drop of labor's sweat, each ache about humanity lives in the heart. Hail to the containing heart!"

Thus I shall end my letter of JOY for lofty collaboration. Be full of light and joy. Walk the path of great service to humanity, and in everything and to everything apply the measure of the highest path; precisely, do not lose sight of great COMMENSURABILITY.

19

31 July 1937

We received your long letters with the enclosed photographs, and we send you thanks for both. Your description of the situations among the various groups and certain strata of society coincides largely with what we have heard from other sources. Likewise, our own premonition told us long ago about all the discord that you have been observing, I shall tell you frankly—I grieve that the group you have mentioned is occupied with reading and discussing the books of Living Ethics. If this group consists of people whose consciousnesses are still on that level which excludes one another, then really one should not have introduced the books of the Teaching to them. How is it possible to study the "foundations of ethics" in an atmosphere of mistrust, irritability, and even open hostility? Indeed, one should safeguard the Teaching and the great concepts from blasphemy. Therefore I earnestly beg you to keep the Teaching for yourself if it resounds in your heart and to exchange the thoughts pertaining to what you have read only with devoted friends. The Teaching is spread by Inscrutable Ways. From all corners of the world we and our friends receive letters from harmonious and flaming hearts. Therefore, why should we burden ourselves with unreceptive consciousnesses? Is it not more useful to give time and strength to those who really need a word of enlightenment? We do not attempt to convert anyone, and we accept only those who come to us voluntarily. Let everyone follow the path that is closest to him.

To your question, "Why do the Great Teachers not point out the many mistakes which were and are committed?" I shall answer with paragraph 14 from *Fiery World III*: "It is asked why We do not put a stop to the false sources. Why do We not expose those who distort the Sending? [Answer:] If one were to stop by force the current in whose wake humanity is proceeding, fanaticism would turn into brutality. Thus, the evil free will flows like lava, engulfing also those who rise against the Good, as history reveals. Surely, violent manifestations of force cannot carve a righteous path for humanity. Hence, all the subtle energies can be accepted only by a fiery consciousness. Thus, tolerance is truly the lot of the fiery consciousness. Of course, one should purify wherever there are accumulations of filth, and the lot of the fiery consciousness is to purify the records of space. Among the accumulated pages of human writings there will have to be noted those pernicious records which have clouded the brains of even well-meaning people. Thus, on the path to the Fiery World one should understand the great significance of receptivity of higher energies and of subtle sendings." Also reread paragraph 11, 12, and 15 from the same book.

You ask why the Great Teachers do not point out the significance of the new Teaching? But They do point this out to those who are able to accept it. This requires an open consciousness. Penetrate more deeply into the Teaching and a great deal will become clear. Light is thrown on each question from many sides.

Yes, the Teaching of Living Ethics is based upon reverence of the Hierarchy of Light and recognition of the high authority of the Teachers. And the greater the spirit, the broader and higher is his understanding of the great law of Hierarchy. I shall not tire of repeating that the principle of Hierarchy is the cosmic law. The whole Universe is filled with, exists, and is held only by this principle. Each form in the Universe has in its foundation a kernel, and each center of striving exists upon the principle of Hierarchy. Precisely, in the cosmos the lowest is subordinated to the highest. Evolution is based on this. In the books of the Teaching it is said, "Of all [leading] principles ... Hierarchy is the most powerful. Each manifested shifting is created upon the principle of Hierarchy. Whither can the spirit direct itself without the Guiding Hand? Whither can the eye and the heart turn without Hierarchy ... the seed of the spirit is imbued by the Cosmic Ray of the Hierarch." Verily, the sign of belonging to the Sixth Race will be the acceptance of the law of the Highest Leadership, the acceptance of Hierarchy in all its magnitude.

Leave people to their own unlimited leadership and a dreadful involution will immediately assert itself. Today in the West people revel particularly against any and every authority and are afraid to lose their individuality, which, in the majority of cases, they do not even possess, for they are chained by prejudices, atavism and ignorance. The spiritual knowledge of many is minimal, and they go through life led by the voice of the lowest egoism, which they mistake for higher intuition. Are we not witnessing the consequences of such madness?

I have already expressed my views regarding the visions and scenes of initiations that are described in some books, and I certainly shall not take back my words. Furthermore, there is nothing more blasphemous than the assertion that the at the power of rites is so strong that the ethical level of the priests performing them is of no importance as long as the formula and the order of succession in initiation are fully observed. "Verily, the subtlest can be accepted only by the subtlest; during the action of the subtlest energies, full harmony, or concordance, is needed. One cannot make the pure from the polluted." Truly, "An impure servitor cannot perform a pure action. The most affirmed ritual will not free the servitor from impure thinking. Thus, many are mistaken in thinking that the outward ritual will cover the inner abomination. ... No sacraments, without the purification of consciousness and corresponding good deeds, will help anyone or anything. One should remember that all exists only in consciousness." Broadened and purified consciousness is a panacea for everything as well as an "open sesame" to everything. As to the stories about the various festivals and initiations attended by certain people—let this be their personal responsibility.

You are, of course, right, it is not so easy for people to discriminate among the abundance of present-day self styled adepts, and this is the reason why the foundations of the Teaching of the White Brotherhood were given through H. P. Blavatsky—but who cared to study them? People preferred the simplified and convenient interpretations, instead of focusing their attention on the fundamental Covenants. I affirm the H. P. B. was the only messenger of the White Brotherhood, and she alone KNEW.

After her a remarkable Teaching was given by the Teacher H. through Francia La Due. But did many know about it? Why is it being hushed up by certain groups of Theosophists? Why is this manifestation never mentioned by those who pretend to be the messengers of the White Brotherhood and teachers who claim to belong to the Solar Hierarchy (!)?

The Ocean of the Teaching of Living Ethics is being given at present; having studied it man will be equipped for a further journey, because his consciousness will be broadened, and discrimination will accompany him upon his path of life. Yet many are already up in arms against this Teaching!

Since every Teaching should enter life accompanied by the shouts of enemies so that humanity shall pay attention to it and not forget it, let us observe the action of this law, which testifies to the low degree of the development of our earthly humanity. The Jinn will still build temples for a long time, and they will endow men with new Gods. The crucifixion of Jesus Christ gave the world a new God and a new religion.

You ask, How can a lofty spirit deceive people by claiming the title of the Teacher of the White Brotherhood? Assuredly, not a single High Spirit would stoop to deceive, but first of all we must set up a criterion for defining a Teacher of the White Brotherhood. The earthly criterion is entirely different from a supermundane or higher one. Affected devotion and insipid, frequently hypocritical, kindness are not the signs of greatness of spirit. It is best to judge the greatness of the spirit by its tolerance, containment, and magnanimity and also by its active resistance to evil.

Amazing is human consciousness! It is ready to trust any self-opinionated, earthly authority, not substantiated by proof, which claims to receive and transmit a message from the Highest Source, as it were. But when this message proves to be a sterile flower, not one of the followers care to accuse the impostor, but will hasten first of all to blame the Highest Source! Once again I would like to ask, Why search for mistakes in the indications which come purportedly from the Great Teachers, instead of looking for them in the pocket of their transmitters?

Yes, we can point out how people regarded the Great Brothers of humanity as dark forces. We can enumerate cases when the greatest calamities were attributed to Them, and how They were accused of violence and threats! Especially persistent in their accusations were those who did not care to listen to Their Word. People reach such extremes of falsehood and blasphemy that they even say that the Great Brothers denied Christ! Can one believe such blasphemy? Nevertheless, many servants of darkness are ready to spread such slander just to sow disunity; but everyone who knows the structure and the composition of the Brotherhood will be aghast at such slander. As a rule, slander is based on ignorance, but even grown-up people are not averse to repeating obvious lies. One feels like saying, "Shame on you, ignoramuses! Shame on you, bearers of disunity!"

Ask yourself, "Am I not mistaken? But the ignorant ones do not think that they can ever be mistaken, for they dwell in their mistakes, and therefore cannot fall into them."

Actually, mistakes, too, were attributed to the Great Brothers according to people's judgment. Thus, examine such accusers and negators and you will see that their negation is rooted in ignorance. Usually, those who do not perceive the new do not have any cognizance of the old. An observant, vigilant mind will perceive something new in an everyday event, but this privilege belongs to an open mind, not a negative one. Each epoch brings forth concepts that are necessary for the next stage of evolution; and these particular concepts are emphasized in the books of Living Ethics—Collaboration, or Cooperation, the Woman's Movement, the Significance of Thought, and the Study of Psychic Energy. The best and the more receptive minds already respond to these vibrations, and we are happy to note it.

Fire and psychic energy are inseparable, for the latter is the quality of fire. Psychic energy is the primary energy.

It is also true that for the correct assimilation of the Teaching inner realization is necessary. Indeed, when consciousness is open and free from prejudices and all atavism, perception becomes considerably easier. But in a majority of cases precisely people enslaved by prejudices talk the most about the necessity of open perception, without noticing that they are bound by fear to accept someone's authority. Indeed, limitation and enslavement are present in such fear. A free mind is not afraid of enslavement, for it is always open for new accumulations.

Certainly, all the existing teachings, religions, and philosophical systems, as well as the Teaching of Living Ethics, came from the East or were echoes of Eastern thought. Can anyone name an independent Western philosophy or religion! After all, Christianity also came from the East, and Christ was an Asiatic!

Those who refuse to accept the existence of the White Brotherhood deprive themselves of the greatest idea and the highest beauty to which human thought ever ascended. The White Brotherhood is a dream of humanity, it is a stronghold of knowledge, and a treasury of life-giving energy. Verily, the whole world and its humanity are held together only by these Guardians!

The one who asks about the connection of the Great Teacher K. H. with the Teaching of Living Ethics obviously does not realize what the White Brotherhood is. Could it be possible that one Brother would renounce the Teaching given by another Brother? Verily, people are unable to comprehend even the concept of "Brotherhood"! We shall salute those who consider only Christ as their Teacher, in the same manner that we shall salute the followers of Lao Tze, Confucius, Buddha, Krishna, Zoroaster, and Maitreya. But we shall ask them to truly study the Teaching of Jesus Christ and practice it in life. Then there will be no place for discord, for, verily, all great Covenants come from One Source. Remember what was said in the Teaching, "People will ask, 'Who is greater, Christ or Buddha?' Answer, 'It is impossible to measure the far-off worlds. We can only be enraptured by their radiance.'"

I recall a characteristic case which happened in our area. A Moslem asked for the Gospel so that he could get acquainted with the Christian Teaching. After having read it he remarked with astonishment, "I read the Gospels attentively, but I could not find in them anything that would correspond with modern Christianity." This should be taken into consideration by all those who want to follow the true Teaching of Jesus Christ.

Likewise, ask those people who feel offended because the coming epoch is being called the epoch of Maitreya and not the epoch of Christ whether they really understand the significance of these Names. If they knew more, they would not feel offended. The coming epoch will be under the Rays of Three Lords—Maitreya, Buddha, and Christ. Once again one has to regret that all those whose feelings are easily offended are so little acquainted with the foundations given through H. P. Blavatsky. However, it is possible that many of them would not be able to properly digest all this and would even scoff so much the more.

Atavism is unusually strong in some people. Their minds simply cannot enter upon a new path; they are in a habitual rut which prevents any further progress, but they do not even notice it. Besides, age-old blinkers, put on as a precaution in the form of all sorts of dogmas and prohibitions, deprive them of a broad horizon. This explains why the process of evolution is so slow; the cosmic equilibrium has been violated, and humanity is compelled to pay for its inertia by experiencing dreadful calamities and revolutions.

To all those who gather together, not for the honest study of the given high concepts, but only for criticism, one may say with the words of the Teaching when, it is advised to preserve unity, "Such an indication will not be merely a moral lesson. Disunity can be likened to a most abhorrent dissonance. Nothing strikes space as sharply as a dissonance; and when people are imbued with malicious disunity, the immediate results are destructive devastations in space. Thus, such people not only harm themselves but also create a spatial karma, involving in it many who are like them. It is frightful to battle with this newborn chaos. People who bring in disunity are called creators of chaos. Grievous are the consequences brought about by these evil calumniators ... such a battle with them is more arduous than the encounters with certain spatial currents. Wherever one has to meet the free will of man, a special expenditure of energy takes place. The power of free will is vast. It is equal to the most powerful energies. In malice people can attain the destruction of the astral strata. What vast efforts by experienced weavers will be needed to heal these spatial wounds! We must battle against disunity. Not psalm-singing with harps, but labor and battle."

And now, regarding the capitalization of certain pronouns in the books of the Teaching, the fault is mine, if this could be called a fault; I do it from deepest reverence and love for the Great Images and Highest Concepts. I assure you that in the personal letters of the Great Teachers there is no such capitalization. But what a pearl of nonsense is the statement of a certain "envoy" who said that "even Christ would not allow his Name to be capitalized in a pronoun!" What is it? Barbarous and coarse ignorance or simply a brazen evaluation of his audience? It would be appropriate to explain to this ignoramus that wisdom and love are synonymous in the understanding of every cultured man. But love without wisdom is simply a candidacy for the lunatic asylum. Can people be found who can calmly listen to the stupidities of this "envoy"?

Now something else. Certainly the defense of one's country is the direct duty of every man. Blessed is the soldier of that country which is not the aggressor. Defense of one's own country requires various means and defensive measures, no one can deny this. But one should avoid by all means applying methods of complete extermination, such as, for instance, poison gases which lessen the vitality of the whole planet. The criminal madness of invaders has no justification whatsoever. Those who push the whole world toward the invention of means for only abominable destructions and crimes, indeed, do not deserve to be called men.

But until humanity realizes its place and destination in the Cosmos, until the law of reincarnation and the law of karma are accepted, until the interdependence of all that exists and the correspondingly great responsibility of man is realized, until the supermundane worlds and the Hierarchy of Light are cognized and perceived, until thought is acknowledged as the main moving force and spiritual synthesis is given priority in the life of the state—until then the peace, freedom, and happiness of man, and the great Service for the General Good will remain in the realm of the abstract. But the spirit of man will not cry out and turn to the Highest Guidance until he has passed through all the terrors of the calamities and cataclysms caused by his own madness. Verily, in this madness of frightful disunity and intolerance, in this refusal to accept the new higher energies that are directing the whole world to the next steps of evolution one should seek the cosmic cause and meaning of all the upheavals which periodically affect our unfortunate planet.

Let us hope that the coming epoch, with its particular combinations of the cosmic rays, will bring a new awakening of consciousness and that the new generation will realize all the criminality of the instigators of self-destruction—self-destruction not only by means of cannons and gases but mainly through disunity and impermissible evil and destructive mental sending. Indeed, more murders occur from malicious thought-transmissions than from cannons. But even this truth is not yet accessible to humanity.

It seems to me that I have covered most of your questions. Your answers and objections are correct. When you become more familiar with the Teaching, you will find answers to all your questions, especially since the arguments of most of the deniers are rather stereotyped.

In conclusion, I shall add—do not proselyte, do not entice, but heartily meet those who are sincerely seeking. Each and every importunity can only bring the greatest harm.

I quite understand that the book *The Foundations of a New World Contemplation* is not to the taste of some people. It is not pleasant when someone treads upon your sore toes.

I shall end my long letter with a wish that you may go vigorously and courageously through life, making it easier by applying in daily routine the principles of the Teaching.

20

9 August 1937

I have read with great interest your essay about "The Question of Woman in the New Epoch." I approve of your idea of tracing historically the attitude of the great Founders of religions and philosophical schools toward this question and also pointing out how eventually, with the downfall of culture, these traditions were more and more distorted. Certainly, this idea is very fine, and several pages should be dedicated to this historical review, but I would not advise you to base your opinions on the works of Schure. This author has many touching pages, even glimpses into great Truth, but his fantasy carries him far beyond the bounds of historical authenticity. Therefore, one should, with much regret, rank his works with similar rhapsodies of St. Yves d'Alveidre. Fabre d'Olivier, who is often quoted by Schure, also suffered from excessive imagination at the expense of historical truth.

You ask about the Druids. The Druids were the Masons of very ancient times. The authenticity of information about this lofty teaching, which we find in the Greek classics, becomes more and more evident as we delve more deeply into the most ancient epochs; in other words, the more ancient the testimony, the nearer it is to truth. At the head of the Druids was a woman, who bore the title of Mother of the Druids.

The information given by Schure about Rama, the hero of the Hindu epic poem, the *Ramayana*, is most inconsistent. Rama was the purest native of ancient Aryavarta; he was the king of Ayodhya and never left India. Long before Rama, the Indo-Aryans come from the steppes of Central Asia, and descended into the valleys of India by way of Afghanistan. Thus, Rama was not a Druid and had not the slightest relationship with the Celts.

Likewise erroneous is the statement that Krishna affirmed Brahmanism. All the Great Teachers belonged to the Kshatriya caste, which, in ancient days, was considered the highest. There are many legends which relate that it was actually the Brahmins who learned from the Kshatriyas, and not vice versa. Only with the downfall of the high and heroic spirit of the peoples who inhabited ancient Aryavarta did the Brahmins take the power into their hands. This usurpation of priority was, and is grievous for India.

Furthermore, Krishna was of royal birth, was himself a king, and all of his Teaching is permeated by a noble, courageous spirit, it even culminates in the form of a most beautiful poem dedicated to the great battle on the field of Kurukshetra. All the legends about Krishna, the cowherd, who passed his time in dancing and playing the flute in the company of cowherds and milkmaids, are a later development of folk-fantasy which originated amidst the tribes of Dravidian origin. The Dravidians belong to the Fourth Race, and there are hints in the Sacred Teaching that the Basques are the descendants of tribes of the Dravidians who migrated to Europe. Likewise, the gypsies can consider India their birthplace, from which they were banished.

Rama, the Aryan, fought with the descendants of the Atlanteans from the island of Lanka, and his allies were the warlike Dravidian tribes, among whom was developed a strong reverence of monkeys. This reverence was a relic of the ancient knowledge about the descent of the anthropomorphous monkey from man. Thus, in folklore this knowledge was interwoven with fantasy, the Hanuman, the leader of the Dravidians, took on a monkey image.

I advise great caution in drawing information from the works of Schure. His books can stimulate many consciousnesses, but one should use discrimination and cast aside the embellishments by human fantasy, which yield in beauty before great reality. As for Moses, he was not an Egyptian, but a Jew; he could not have been hostile toward woman, for he was an initiate. Keep in your work what you have quoted about Pythagoras.

But I do not agree with your affirmation regarding the greater knowledge of life coming through the Masculine Principle. The tragedy of life touches woman more than man, and we know that suffering is a great teacher. Also, let us not belittle the abilities or talents of woman. Give to woman a proper education and a chance to participate directly in the building of life, and she will not be inferior in common sense to the stronger sex. According to the definition of a certain thinker, genius consists of one-third ability and two-thirds hard and systematic work. The miracles of a genius are always the miracles of work, but what in the eyes of ordinary people constitutes hard work is always a joy for a genius. Therefore, wherever the conditions were favorable for such labor, woman has not yielded any ground to the stronger sex in her achievements. And now several outstanding scientists have definitely stated that there is no basis whatsoever for regarding woman's intellectual faculties as below those of man. Logically speaking, this should be so, because the spirit has no sex, the latter belongs to the realm of forms. Therefore any belittling is ignorant. To all such mockers let us quote the answer of Buddha to a woman-disciple. She asked how could she, with the limited mind of a woman, attain the knowledge and state of Nirvana which is so difficult for even the wise to achieve. He said, "When the heart is at rest, when the consciousness is unfolded, then truth is perceived. But if one will think I am a woman, or I am a man, or I am this or that, let Mara be his concern." "The gates of immortality are open to all beings. Who has ears, let him approach, let him hearken to the Teaching and have faith."

The organism of a woman in itself manifests a synthesis, and thus woman possess all cosmic energies and creative energy in a greater measure. Therefore it is erroneous to think that woman is deprived of independent creative power; however, for the development of any kind of ability constant practice is needed and also suitable conditions. By the way, flights to the far-off worlds are the prerogative of woman. Perhaps this is the reason why so many woman are at present turning their interest to aviation.

In all domains of science, art, social work, and government, woman has proved to be capable of reaching the greatest heights when circumstances were favorable. Among the names of women that you have mentioned should also be included that of the mathematical genius, Sophie Kovalevsky, whose image is extremely close to me. The Paris Academy honored her with the Prix Bordin in a contest in which all the eminent mathematicians took part. The problem that was set at the contest was, "To perfect in one important point the theory of the movement of a solid body round an immovable point."

This very same problem was set by the Berlin Academy for a period of six years, but with no results. The solution of the problem by Mme. Kovalevsky was so remarkable that the prize was doubled in order to emphasize this extraordinary service to science. Kovalevsky died at the age of 41 in 1891, when she had reached great fame and was even recognized in her own country, Russia. She was elected to membership in the St. Petersburg Academy of Sciences. With all this, let us not forget the difficulties which she had to overcome. At that time women were not allowed to enter universities, which made is necessary for her to go to Heidelberg and Berlin to study privately under the local mathematical celebrities. In 1874 the University of Gottingen granted her a doctorate *in absentia* for three dissertations sent by her. One of them dealt with the theory of partial differential equations, and is considered one of her most remarkable works. In addition to her outstanding mathematical abilities, she was also a writer. Her novels, *Vera Vorontzoff, The Nihilist, The Sisters Rajevski*, and also her autobiography (unfortunately unfinished) prove her great literary talent. Let us also not forget another genius—H. P. Blavatsky, who has not yet been fully recognized. Also Marie Sklodowska Curie, whose daughter continues with her mother's research and has achieved remarkable results. And the many other talented women—actresses, painters, poets, among all nationalities. So many wise leaders, warriors, and great saints among women! The image of St. Theresa, the Spaniard, is not less than that of St Francis of Assisi. Let us also recall the ancient times when, in spite of the fact that masculine egoism always attempted to suppress the achievements of women, there were always some illumined minds that did not submit to this shameful weakness. It would be well to also remember the slandered image of Aspasia. Socrates used to call her his teacher, and the great Plato mentioned her reverently in his writings. Also, through her many useful reforms the reign of the woman-Pharaoh, Hatsepsut, far surpassed that of many

Pharaohs. And was she not the one who, by her wise rule, paved the way for the latter victories of Tethmosis III?

According to the Sacred Teaching, the fall of humanity began from the time of the abasement of the Feminine Principle. Therefore, with the beginning of the Epoch of the Mother of the World woman should realize that she herself contains all forces, and the moment she shakes of the age-old hypnosis of her seemingly lawful subjugation and mental inferiority and occupies herself with a manifold education, she will create in collaboration with man a new and better world. Indeed, it is essential that woman herself refute the unworthy and profoundly ignorant assertion about her passive receptivity and therefore her inability to create independently. But in the entire Cosmos there is no passive element. In the chain of creation each manifestation in its turn becomes relatively passive or active, giving or receiving. Cosmos affirms the greatness of woman's creative principle. Woman is a personification of nature, and it is nature that teaches man, not man nature. Therefore, may all women realize the grandeur of their origin, and may they strive for knowledge. Where there is knowledge, there is power. Ancient legends actually attribute to woman the role of the guardian of sacred-knowledge. Therefore, may she now also remember her defamed ancestress, Eve, and again harken to the voice of her intuition in not only eating of but also planting as many tree, bearing the fruits of the knowledge of good and evil as possible. And as before, when she deprived Adam of his dull, senseless bliss, so let her now lead him on to a still broader vista and into the majestic battle with the chaos of ignorance for her divine rights.

In conclusion I want to add that women must without delay begin to perfect themselves in all fields, and this is not done at a moment's notice. First of all, we women have so much to outlive. Let us develop primarily a sense of our own dignity and learn to lean courageously on our own strength and knowledge, in order to join in, as well as accept, responsibility for the great structure of General Good.

21

16 August 1937

So often when we turn back to our past, we feel ashamed and sad that we allowed ourselves to be grieved or troubled by the daily cares of life. Our hearts should be so firmly set upon the chosen Path that no fluctuations in our surroundings can disturb our balance. This does not mean to get used to indifference, but rather to simply transfer the focus of our attention. All the feelings of the one who has accepted the great fellowship of service with his heart must be subordinated to the main aspiration. Verily, the path of the heart is light, and through the silver thread the current of courage and joy passes incessantly. Only in the heart, in this "sun of suns" are all our achievements and all our happiness. Happiness experienced through kindling the fires of the heart surpasses the illumination that follows the rise of the Kundalini. But, as all the authorities on Yoga agree, the most difficult achievement is the kindling of the fires of the heart, because for this the heart must first be cleansed of all burdening thoughts. Advise everyone to watch the life of their hearts. Let them not allow bad thoughts. One bad thought can sweep away the labors of many years.

At the moment we send many thoughts to the proposed Congress. Let there be laid the first foundation stone of unity for the future joint, broad cultural projects. The very highest and most worthy are fitting where the foundations of the Teaching of Life, Culture, and Beauty are laid.

The greater the man, the more quickly he reacts to all enlightenment. Small consciousnesses have no horizon, and it is almost impossible to compel them to leave their chicken coops. It is lamentable when people with small consciousnesses occupy important posts. These small consciousnesses may be divided into two kinds. The first are always afraid that they may lower their dignity, and therefore they always deny and reject whatever is above their understanding; the second, not being able to rise in consciousness above petty evidence, imagine everything in correspondingly diminished measures. Both are almost equally harmful in their results. We have long ago agreed, always and in everything, to draw the longest line and to follow the highest measure. The benefit of such action can be seen from very simple examples. In order that one may cross the river and moor at a certain place, every experienced helmsman will advise, "Set the helm higher upstream, for you will be carried down regardless." Thus, also, in the Teaching, striving as high as possible is constantly indicated. The spiral of striving will inevitably subside, but the higher it was aimed, the higher will be its next starting point. A small consciousness starts everything from below, the broadened consciousness, from above. I shall quote a paragraph from *Brotherhood*.

"The thought about cognizing the manifestations from below or from above is correct. Usually cognition is acquired along with the growth of consciousness. Man raises himself with difficulty, as if climbing toward a mountain top. That which he observes hanging above his consciousness oppresses him. Many concepts appear to be difficult, and he begins to avoid them. But there may be another means of cognition—man heroically uplifts his consciousness and then observes manifestations from above. Thus, the most complex manifestation will appear to be below his consciousness and will be easily apprehended. The second means of perception is the path of Brotherhood. By austere and inspired measures it awakens the consciousness and leads it upward, in order the more easily to perceive the most complex manifestations. This means of uplifting the consciousness is especially needed in time of pressure and cumulations. It can be applied in each sagacious school of thought, but it should be known as the path of Brotherhood."

One more paragraph which is quite useful for the knowledge of the disciples. "'The stronger the light, the denser the darkness'—and this saying is also not understood, whereas one must accept it simply. It should not be thought that darkness increases from the light. Light reveals the darkness and then disperses it. The bearer of light also sees the dark shadows, which vanish at the approach of light. The timid assume that darkness will fall upon them; thus thinks timorousness, and the light trembles in its hands, and because of this tremor of fear the shadows come to life and play antics. In everything fear is a poor counselor.

"The neophytes of the Brotherhood are tested upon fear. A most hopeless situation is shown to them, and one waits to see what solution will be chosen by the tested one. Very few will think, What is there to be afraid of since the Brotherhood stands behind us? Precisely such a premise liberates one from fear and brings to light a free, beneficial decision. But most often, before thinking about the Brotherhood, a man will promptly get distressed, irritated, and filled with imperil. A plea from one filled with poison will not be useful. The Light of Truth is the light of courage, the light of devotion—with these words the Statutes of the Brotherhood begin."

"Some will say to you, 'We are prepared to understand the Fundamentals of Brotherhood. We are ready to build up cooperation, but we are surrounded by such intolerable conditions that it is impossible to manifest greater readiness.' In truth, there may be conditions that do not permit putting into practice that for which the heart is ready. Let us not expose innocent workers to danger; they can apply their abilities under other conditions. For a time let them construct Brotherhood in their thoughts. With such construction they can purify the surrounding space, and such thoughts will be salutary. But let them not fall into conceit, believing that it is sufficient to build mentally. No, the wayfarer will affirm the manifestation of achievement by human feet and human hands. Likewise, although we will show solicitude for the overburdened ones, let us warn them not to give way to unwarranted fear. There can be no cognition about Brotherhood when the mind is contracted with fear. The best approach to Brotherhood may be darkened by fear. Let us not forget that people are accustomed to being afraid of everything at all times."

* * *

Now—your questions. It seems to me that in my previous letter I spoke about psychic energy being a primary energy, hence, all other energies are only its differentiations.

1. Prana is the very same psychic energy in its quality of vital force, which is diffused everywhere and is absorbed by man chiefly through breathing.

2. Kundalini is the same energy, which acting through definite centers, separates man from Earth, giving him a feeling of unearthly bliss.

3. Fohat, or cosmic electricity, is the foundation of all the electrophorous manifestations, and among them thought will be the highest quality of this energy.

4. *Tushita* is the same as Deva-loka, or the heavenly abode of the Gods (Highest Spirits) within the boundaries of the Fiery World.

5. Levitation can be explained by the disturbance of equilibrium in the polarity of magnetism, when the negative pole acts with the greatest strength.

6. And "the spirit ... is able to cognize up to the fourteenth gradation of hearing" signifies the most refined scale in the

quality of the gradation of tones, at present almost inaccessible to our earthly hearing, however, there may be even twenty-four such gradations. Thus, the ears of Hindus are receptive to a far broader scale of tones than the ears of Europeans.

7."The Lunar Life must be outlived..." refers to the semi-conscious life led by the majority of human beings. Aside from the rarest exceptions, humanity came to our planet from the moon; and it is about time for mankind to accelerate its evolution, but unfortunately precisely the majority have not departed far from their lunar state.

8. "A smile to My enemy will be turned into a grimace," There is no doubt that whoever smiles at the enemy of the Great Teacher out of fear or thought of gain, by this very fact condemns himself, and such a smile will eventually turn into a grimace of terror.

9. Dgul Nor is just a Mongol-Tibetan name.

10. There are various degrees of alcoholism and one who possesses a considerable degree of hypnotic power is undoubtedly able to cure certain stages of it. All depends upon the condition of the organism of the sick man, or the obsessed one. The hypnotic treatments should extend over a long period of time.

I will add more about psychic energy. Psychic energy is EVERYTHING. Psychic energy, being the primary energy, lies at the foundation of the manifested world. Psychic energy impresses images upon the plastic substance. Psychic energy is fohat, it is the Holy Ghost, it is love and striving. Psychic energy is the synthesis of all radiations of the nerves. Psychic energy is the great AUM. The development within oneself of a constant uninterrupted striving toward Light in all its manifestations will indeed result in the growth and development of this energy. Striving toward the perfectment of quality is at all times and in everything the shortest path for the development and refinement of psychic energy.

22

19 August 1937

Yes, it is sad to observe how people waste the most precious, namely, time, by treading on one spot or carrying water in a sieve. I love the saying of Peter the Great, "Waste of time is like unto death." Indeed, absence of independent action is the stumbling block of very, very many. It is a strange paradox that though they wait for instructions in everything, they nevertheless will often rebel against the Hierarchic Principle. The difficulty also lies in the fact that all forcing is useless, because only that is strong and valuable which is born of consciousness and heart. One has to cautiously direct people toward the realization that is beneficial for them. But sometimes this requires such an amount of time and patience that one should use commensurateness and decide whether that particular person is worth such an expenditure of precious strength.

* * *

Certainly it is useful to have some understanding of astrology; however, when studying horoscopes one should always bear in mind that the free will of man is the most powerful factor in everything and can change many signs. Furthermore, the most difficult signs may turn out to be the most conducive to success. One person will be able to create a great structure out of small signs, another will create only a chicken coop from the best possibilities. Usually, all great spirits have a difficult horoscope. The science of astrology is very complex. The one who studies it, and particularly the one who interprets its signs, must have an accumulation of psychic energy. The most important key to astrology is lost to the West. Moreover, in ancient times the learned astrologer was, in addition, a chiromancer and could sometimes read people's auras. Only such combined knowledge can give an accurate definition of the character and its destiny. But above all this stands the secret knowledge of astrology that is inaccessible to ordinary mortals; this knowledge is possessed by the Great Teachers of humanity.

I am not surprised at your horoscope, for otherwise whence would come such refinement of feelings? Earthly life is difficult for people with refined feelings, but on the other hand they can attain flights and exaltations of spirit that are not even dreamt of by most Earth-dwellers. I love a comparison that is often quoted in Buddhist writings. "A fluff of wool settling on the hand is imperceptible, but entering the eye, it causes severe pain. The palm is like an ignorant man, the eye is like a sage."

* * *

It might have been a useful task to write down from the

books of the Teaching all that is said concerning doubt—that dreadful viper—and to read these indications often in the group meetings. Indeed, there is hardly anybody who would not want to drive away with all his might this terrible visitor.

All great people were great precisely because they did not doubt. Absence of doubt is the "open sesame" to all achievements. Pay special attention to all who doubt. They should not allow this destroyer and poisoner of the whole surrounding atmosphere to become enrooted in them. You have probably noticed what a healthy feeling one has, how easy it is to breathe, what joyous creativity there is, in spite of life's many difficulties, when one is in the presence of those who are full of great faith, or rather, knowledge of the existence of the Stronghold of Knowledge and Love and that continuous care, which the Great Teachers pour out upon all the co-workers of Good. This help and care are filled with wisdom and goal-fitness and therefore do not always correspond with our rather near-sighted expectations and hopes. But the heart that is in touch with this Stronghold will carry through all dangers the unutterable joy of this straight-knowledge, which cannot be forgotten for ages and ages.

And now I shall answer your questions.

1. In *Hierarchy*, paragraph 247 the Manvantara of the Sixth is meant. Its selection has already begun.

2. From the very sense of the word *Manu* it is clear that the Great Individuality who bears this name is closely related to the concept of the World Teacher, or the Teacher of Teachers. Who, if not Manu, strikes the basic note, or establishes his own vibration, which must resound during a specific Round? Who brings the first Proclamation? Verily, the Manu, who manifests at the end and at the beginning of each Race.

A planetary Round comprises the birth and the end of all the seven Races. It is under the leadership of one and the very same Individuality throughout its whole duration. That is why in *The Secret Doctrine* it was stated that the Lord Maitreya will appear in the Sixth and the Seventh Races.

3. Certainly there are aeons of various lengths. Possessing the esoteric key, one can find even in the distorted translation of the bible much similarity to all the ancient Teachings.

4. Thus, the narrative about the Community on Mount Zion can refer to the Abode of the Great Brotherhood in the Subtle

World. In the second part of *Brotherhood* it is said, "We have complete Strongholds in the Subtle World. You already know their names, you have already heard about the amazing tree and the structures created by thought. One should realize these circumstances with complete clarity in order to wend one's way to Dokyood. Thought unhampered by doubt will lead to Our supermundane Abodes. The Ashram in the Himalayas is in constant communion with the Abodes in the Subtle World, and the earthly battle resounds and thunders equally in the Subtle World. People do not want to understand this correlation, therefore they regard Armageddon as only an earthly conflict of nations. The most important region of Armageddon remains unaccepted. Yet how can one participate in something if one is aware of only a small part of what is happening? We affirm that a much mightier battle takes place in the Subtle World than on Earth. Verily, a great deal of the spatial Battle will re-echo on Earth. Earth often attempts to warn people of the grave danger, but in vain."

5. *Tushita* is also a stronghold of the Brotherhood within the boundaries of the Fiery World. It is correct to find correlations in all religions.

I am not against the books of Kryjanovsky, St. Yves d'Alveidre, and Schure, or against books of this type in general. Many minds need enticing, fantastic subjects for inspiration. One should not disparage such consciousnesses. They cannot be satisfied with grey everydayness, and they instinctively feel that somewhere there exists another, beautiful reality. That is why they are attracted to everything unusual. And they are right, because there is that reality which surpasses all human imagination. But this reality is so far removed from our limited earthly concepts that no fantasy can fully contain it. However, in searching for the unusual and the fantastic we should not depart from the point of equilibrium between mind and heart. First we must affirm ourselves upon the stable foundation of true beauty. But the trouble is that the majority still associates beauty with the pomp and tinsel of luxury and with a frightening vulgarity and poverty of thought.

Dear to me is all you say about flexible consciousnesses that bring joy to the heart. But I am also aware that there are many others who have to be treated like glass vessels or sometimes like dynamite, as it were. Examples of this were met by us in our life-journey. It was sad to observe how excellent abilities could not receive proper development, due to a dynamic stubbornness, touchiness, or jealousy, which was inevitably followed by suspiciousness. Such a heart is locked within itself in total loneliness, and not receiving any nurture, it withers.

23

2 September 1937

I am always against the broadcasting of personal experiences. Mainly because in this manner a ready program, or canvas, as it were is offered for embroidering certain designs. After reading such descriptions many impressionable psychics at once begin to see and sense similar manifestations. The value lies precisely in that each one must independently observe his own fiery experiences, for these manifestations should not be prompted; moreover, they *should be different* in every individual. That is why it is so important for serious investigators to write down their observations and later to compare them.

* * *

The question, "How can an imperfect human being approach the Teaching?" should be answered also by a question, "And where are these perfect ones?" Besides, the criterion of the Great Teachers differs considerably from the earthly criterion. Often, the outer man is far better than the inner one, and the Teacher considers precisely the inner man. Furthermore, our task is not to create angels—let the church occupy itself with this task! By the way, the thousands of years of the existence of the church and its world-wide expansion and dominion prove its obvious failure in this—the results speak for themselves. Our task is far more modest. We simply wish to help those who come to us at least broaden their consciousness somewhat and receive an answer to many of the problems of life, answers which the church could not give. The books of the Teaching of Life, in their cosmic span of thought actually give answers to all questions. Therefore, let us not look for angels, but let us occupy ourselves with people.

* * *

The greatest mysteries cannot be explained in human words.

The grandeur and beauty of Infinity cannot be stowed into our limited concepts or into our terminology. They must remain within the bounds of the Unutterable. I remember, while still in Russia, we asked the poet Blok why he did not visit the religious-philosophical meetings any more. He answered, "Because there they speak about the Unutterable!" Thus, let your sensitivity prompt you as to where lies the boundary of human interpretations and where the Unutterable begins.

In the eternal whirlpool of life, in the course of the process of evolution, man's great destiny as a co-worker of Cosmos in the support of the equilibrium of Cosmic Life will become more and more evident. The worlds are begotten and dissolved, whereas man, after having transmuted all his feelings in the fire of the spirit, is transfigured into a superman and takes a place amidst the Highest Spirits, thus living in Eternity. The Highest Spirits are the co-workers of the Great Architect and of Mother Nature—they are the builders of worlds and the leaders of nations.

* * *

In the East much is known about the centers, but actually only a small portion of this knowledge is accessible to Europeans. Partly because the language is hard to acquire, but mainly because of the *sacredness of this knowledge.*

* * *

Actually, the subtle body is somewhat larger than the physical one, nevertheless, it is *erroneous* to suppose that it *cannot be lodged* in the physical body. It becomes larger only when it emerges. In fact, all the bodies are contained within the physical envelope. All the designs of a man with the lotus over his head are only figurative, just like the names of the centers, which are called lotuses. The number of petals corresponds to the branches of a nerve center.

All indications regarding the size, color, and number of the petals of the lotuses are relative; *one should not forget the individuality of all manifestations.*

Regarding the protuberance on the top of the head during the time of the opening of the brain center, this too, should be understood as a symbol. The opening of a center is always accompanied by the enlargement of the blood vessels, which causes some swelling, but not the protrusion of the bone. On many images of Buddhas and Bodhisattvas one can see this symbolical protrusion of the crown of the head. It is termed *Ushnisha* and is known as the symbol of the opening of the brain center. Likewise, when the Tibetans wish to symbolize the opening of the third eye, they put upon sacred images a wart between the two eyebrows. Clairaudience is usually symbolized on the sacred images by enormous ears.

* * *

The touch of the Mother of the World should be understood as the manifestation of the Primary Energy. The *Kundalini* energy is called in India the power of the Mother.

The development of the heart is the main task in our era. The *Kundalini* cannot act with full force unless the heart is developed. Verily, the fires of the heart give the sensation of inexpressible bliss. In this epoch of the *rapprochement* of the worlds the center of the heart is particularly intensified. However, it is even more difficult to kindle the fires of the heart than it is to accomplish the rise of the *Kundalini*.

* * *

The center of the Chalice is located near the heart amidst the knots of nerves. The Chalice is the focal point of all emanations. This is the focus in which and through which all emanations of the seed of the spirit are refracted and spread. The Chalice forms a triangle between the center of the heart and the solar plexus. It is located above the solar plexus at the level of the heart. The Chalice belongs to those nerve-knots that are not investigated as yet. In the very ancient scriptures the center of the Chalice was sometimes called the "Celestial Axis."

Indeed, "Very rarely is the Chalice filled to overflowing. As a synthesized center, the Chalice preserves the most essential, indescribable accumulations. ...

"The Chalice is the repository of everything loved and precious. Sometimes, much that has been gathered into the Chalice remains concealed for entire lives, but if the concept of Brotherhood has been impressed upon the Chalice, it will resound in both joy and yearning in all lives." [Brotherhood]

I will quote here a discourse about the centers. "Many questions must be understood outside of earthly limitations. People often observe but one detail and elevate it into an immutable law. The centers of man are understood rather relatively. Their very names have changed in different languages over thousands of years. Some may call the Chalice, 'Celestial Axis,' but its function does not change because of this! Others speak of the influence of the Mother of the World [the *Kundalini* energy is called by the Hindus the power, or *Shakti*, of the Mother of the World], but *Shakti*, in its essence, already contains the great significance of the Primary Energy. Moreover, we are forgetting about the collective action of the centers, which is always individual. In fact equally individual is the transmutation of the centers in the subtle and fiery bodies. They retain their essence in all bodies, *but their development depends upon their passing through earthly existence.* It would seem that the muscles have been sufficiently studied, but their functions depend upon a man's character. Each member of the body acts individually. The gait depends on the psychic condition, and thus the muscles will work in a unique combination. The relativity of judgment is quite clearly expressed in the judgment about subtle energies.

"It is not possible to establish a certain number for the petals of the Lotuses. Besides, each petal will differ from another. Let us not limit the multiformity of the structure of the world. The most unexpected growth of the tissue and the branching of the nerves afford an unexpected wealth to the organism. Each observation is valuable, but let us be very careful in generalizing. ... Truly, knowledge has taught Us caution in expressing it. Every neophyte rushes to shout about and proclaim whatever he has heard, not caring about the consequences. However, with knowledge also comes co-measurement."

If you will read all the accessible writings about the centers, you will see how diversely their names are given and also how the faculties are revealed in man at the time of the opening of any of the centers.

Thus, the solar plexus was often identified with the Kundalini (but not the *Muladhara*) and the *Manipura* chakra with the Chalice, or the "Celestial Axis."

In remote antiquity, the *Sahasrara* center was identified with 666 petals and not with 960 or 1,000

Likewise, the center of the throat is located, not in the thyroid gland, but nearby. The centers are not located in the glands. They are near them, and they coordinate the work of the glands.

There are a multitude of the finest branchings of the centers, but one need not think that the centers occupy much space.

The *Svadhishthana* center is located in the pelvic region and is actually connected with the sexual functions. During the process of spiritual development this center is subordinated to and controlled by the center of the solar plexus.

* * *

In the book *Agni Yoga* that paragraph which describes empty tombs should be understood literally. Indeed, there are empty tombs. For, at the completion of a mission, and as the date approached for the departure of an Adept who had been living among people, a make-believe funeral was often held for him so that he could join the Stronghold in the *physical* body. Sometimes the body would be taken away after the funeral, because it was in a state of catalepsy, as in were. In some cases, a substitute would be buried, as it was, for instance, at the departure of Master R. But cases of dematerialization of the physical body are extremely rare. Even the mortal remains of Buddha were cremated.

Indeed, Christ did not dematerialize his body during the Transfiguration, but appeared to his disciples in a subtle body. Likewise His Resurrection took place precisely in the subtle body. Remember how He would not allow Mary Magdalene to touch Him, for touching a High Spirit appearing in a subtle body may cause death because of the difference in vibrations.

* * *

High beings create through psychic energy, the power of which is dependent on the kindling of the fires of the heart. The Chalice is the source of creativeness, but psychic energy gives a concrete form to creative ideas.

* * *

The pains may be very great and torturous. When the center of the lungs is kindled, one is not able to move without involuntarily crying out. One is compelled to sit without changing the position, and the breathing is strongly impeded. And certainly all these conditions are repetitious. The nagging sensation and burning in the extremities are equally painful. Also very unpleasant are the tension and stirring in the solar plexus, which are accompanied by excessive discharge of saliva and nausea. Bicarbonate of soda taken internally considerably relieves this condition. The kidneys become very sensitive. Tension in the centers of the head, particularly at the back of the head, is also torturous. Of course, all the painful symptoms in the course of time become weaker and weaker. Now and then, not a little time is required for the opening of this or that center. Moreover, their fiery transmutation is needed, which is still more painful and is full of dangers.

* * *

One must remember that certain manual labor can be so fatiguing that the psychic energy may become suppressed. During psychic sendings the physical body should usually be in repose. It is dangerous to send the energy when one feels tired.

* * *

What is a moderator? During fiery transmutation, it is beneficial to cover up the centers a bit, in order to prevent conflagration. This covering is sometimes effected by the so-called "psychic slip cover" created out of a condensed envelope of psychic energy. But all of this will sound like *abracadabra* to the average reader, therefore it is wiser to avoid such details.

In conclusion, one may add that all the descriptions of the attainment of higher abilities through the opening of the centers may appear easy on paper, but in reality there is nothing more difficult. Many lives may pass in a constant unbreakable striving for the broadening of consciousness and the refinement of receptivity prior, not to just the partial opening of this or that center, but to their work on all the seven circles and planes. No mechanical exercises will lead to anything high. For not the physical irritation, and not even the partial opening of one of the centers is needed, but the fiery transmutation of all centers, which can be achieved only through the complete purification of thinking and the kindling of the fires of the heart.

Therefore, blessed is he who in previous lives was already striving along the path of broadening of the consciousness and purification of the heart.

Observe events. Remember that patience is the highest achievement; co-measurement, the highest wisdom; and knowledge of dates, the highest knowledge.

24

11 September 1937

I was very glad to have your avowal that you are not in the least interested in the so-called *siddhis*. This is the most correct approach for their awakening. It does sound paradoxical, but it is precisely the ability to contain opposites that is the touchstone, or evidence, of the presence of spirituality in us. All ancient Teachings, as well as the Teaching of Christ, indicate the necessity of comprising antitheses, for life itself is woven from such seeming contradictions. But this fundamental truth is forgotten at present just as is forgotten and eliminated from daily life the moral perfectment and refining of all our senses, so essential for the perception of Bliss, which is sent to us from Above. Only when the inner man is purified can our psychic energy enter into constant cooperation with the higher energy.

Yes, that man who lives with his heart and who constantly dwells on the idea of being of service to the welfare of humanity, that man is in complete harmony with his higher Self. You are profoundly right when you say, "The thought that high contact can be achieved through the path of physical exercises seems to me not only crude but entirely unworthy of a spiritual thinker." Indeed, the misfortune of modern pseudo-occultists is that they ignore all the higher qualities of the human soul and its moral purity, the main and most essential condition for all true spiritual achievements. They rush to the easily accessible physical exercises, which either completely ruin their health or, when they fail, make disappointed and embittered unbelievers out of them. But it is still worse when the physical exercises are performed by natural mediums, because they develop rather quickly a certain ability to communicate with the nether world, and, being often of doubtful morality, as well as ignorant and unexperienced in discerning these communions, they fall prey to the dwellers of the spheres nearest Earth, which often results in criminal obsession. Unfortunately, contemporary physicians do not believe in this scourge of our cruel and licentious age. Therefore so many miserable victims cannot be cured; whereas suggestion and command issued by a pure heart could eject the criminal entity dwelling within.

In the process of purification of the heart the highest *siddhis* open up in us, namely the ability to help our fellow men in spirit and to cure spiritual and physical ailments. The man who is pure in heart is often a healer and a protector of the whole district from various epidemics and even catastrophes. The legend about a whole city being spared because of one saint who lived in it has deep significance. This legend, too, came to us from the East. In our region there is a strong belief in the benevolent influence of the emanations of a pure person over the whole district. A pure heart is a panacea for everything and everybody.

I also understand that you adhere to a chosen method of preparing yourself for meditation. Everything spiritual is so individual that everyone should sense precisely with his heart what is particularly close to him and follow this path. I am so fond of a statement in the *Bhagavad Gita*, this finest pearl of the Eastern writings, that I never tire of repeating it, and so I shall quote it to you as well. "Man comes to Me by various paths, but by whatever path man comes to Me, on that path I welcome him, for all paths are Mine." It is impossible to indicate better and more precisely that the form is of no importance; only the idea itself is essential. But people cling to forms most of all, thus losing any understanding of the thought behind them.

Permit me to send you as a present the book by Origen, *De Principiis*. I must confess that my heart aches when I think of the stagnation and inertia of our Russian Orthodox Church. At the same time that the Western clergy is harkening to the spiritual evolution and has ordained the study of the works of Origen, our Russian Orthodox clergy still continues to consider him a heretic! At times I feel that the obvious concealment, during the pre-revolutionary period, of the attainments of our greatest guardian and defender of the Russian nation, St. Sergius of Radonega, had a reason, in that to some eyes he may have appeared to be a heretic because of crossing himself with only two fingers. But when the Greatest Name is ignored and secondrate names are extolled, it is a sign of loss of co-measurement, which is tantamount to the downfall of spirituality.

Certainly, the reading of *The Secret Doctrine* is not easy. The scope of this work is too grandiose. One should get acquainted with the Eastern Teachings and with the general idea of the evolution of thought in order to be able to better assimilate it. Undoubtedly, with your background for such reading the difficulty will not be great.

I am always glad to hear from you, and I do hope that we

shall have many points of contact in our consciousnesses. On the basis of a united consciousness many useful things can be created. I would like so very much to clarify certain touchy problems and remove the ugly excrescences that have piled up in the course of many centuries, and have obscured the purity, the lofty simplicity, and the beauty of the fundamental aspects of the spiritual teachings of all times and nations.

25

23 September 1937

Each individual, or isolated human ability has not an absolute, but a relative significance. Intellect without the enlightenment that comes from the fires of the heart and also the heart that is not supported by intellect are ugly manifestations. Balance is essential in everything. The goal of evolution is the attainment of the balance, or harmony of all human abilities and feelings. The tragedy of our age is indeed in the existence of the terrible conflict between the intellect and the heart. If Infinity lies before us, then surely all our abilities can develop infinitely. But here again their correct development will depend upon the equilibrium, or harmonious unfoldment, of all the potential forces that are stored in man. Synthesis is the highest harmony.

* * *

Each planetary cycle, or Round, has its limit for the development of the human organism, and with each new cycle the degree of achievement rises. Thus, Manas, or the highest intelligence on our Earth will receive its full development in the Fifth Round and in its Fifth Race. Meanwhile, we are still in the Fourth Round and in the time of the consummation of its Fifth Race; hence, for our Round, Manas has already reached the apogee of its development. And with the birth of the Sixth Race, or rather, with its confirmation, because there are quite a few people who already belong to the Sixth Race, we shall enter the epoch of the development of spiritual consciousness, whose foundation lies in the heart.

* * *

Assuredly, any contact with the dark ones inevitably brings its consequences in one form or another. Hence, discrimination of people is of paramount importance, so that we may know how to protect ourselves from these wolves in sheeps' clothing.

All sorts of "phobias" and "isms" are equally unjust when they are spread over an entire nation. Each nation has its positive and negative characteristics. And nowadays many nations display their least attractive qualities.

Any aggression of a usurping and malicious nature has no place in evolution. And the destiny of such nations is already weighed on the scale of justice, but, of course, the final blow for each country is destined to come at a preordained date. Sometimes, if poison is eradicated too quickly from the organism, the balance may be disturbed and occasion a premature collapse. Similarly, in both the organism of the planet and its population it is necessary to suffer the poisonous areas, precisely in order not to disturb the balance, for otherwise somewhere a very useful process, or growth of new power, will be cut short.

26

1 October 1937

There are quite a few people who approach the Teaching with covetous aims, and when their hopes fail to be fulfilled, they become fierce enemies of the Teaching. We have examples of such lamentable occurrences. Therefore, all the newcomers should be warned that they should not hope to acquire some special privileges or earthly goods. The karma accumulated by them will go on, but undoubtedly it will be eased in proportion to the purification of their hearts, the broadening of their consciousnesses and their ability to apply in life the Advices given in the Teaching. Do not tire of repeating to people that all our happiness lies in spiritual joy, in the broadening of consciousness, in the refinement of our feelings, and in spiritual giving. Whosoever knows these spiritual joys, whosoever has become affirmed in them, about him it may be said that he has found the kingdom of heaven within himself.

I deeply rejoice at your remark that it is hardly possible to expect an especial feeling toward us from those who approach us. Besides, there is far more joy in giving than in receiving. During these days of incredible world tension, when the spatial currents are so mixed and are refracted against chaotic whirls, one cannot demand serenity from those who surround us. We must be lenient to others and avoid agitating, or rather irritating questions. I may say that I am extremely cautious in dealing with the weak points of my correspondents, and with rare exceptions I avoid so-called personal instructions. Indeed, the books of the Teaching deal so completely with all the essential foundations that are necessary for the regeneration of consciousness that I rather prefer to give explanations of those passages that are difficult to understand. I am always glad to give spiritual support, but I avoid giving written instructions to people with already molded characters. People nowadays have become particularly sensitive and, therefore, not only the least disapproval of their conduct or actions but even giving simple advice (unless it corresponds with their desires) evokes offense. Personal presence is necessary for a strong influence. The person whom you have mentioned undoubtedly has some latent clairvoyant abilities, but like all beginners he loves to exaggerate, attributing them to the greatest manifestations. Indeed, the majority think that all they have to do is to show some interest in the books of the Teaching, and their centers will open! So few are ready to understand that for this there is needed primarily an inner purification and an achievement of the heart. Moreover, ordinary mediumistic manifestations are often mistaken for the opening of the centers. I know that my explanations of some psychic visions (of course, with the aid of the Teacher) were often considered unsatisfactory and even caused offense. Human conceit is the most terrible and the most common obstacle to spiritual progress. One must know how to fight this foe unremittingly. Humility is ordained to us and is expressed first of all by self-renunciation, or rejection of egoism.

I shall quote for you a Discourse which is most timely:

"We always remain physicians in all actuality. We must treat people with a medicinal purpose in mind. We constantly meet sick people, and must first of all be mindful of equilibrium. People particularly seek Us when misfortune is already staring them in the face. Measures must be taken not only to enlighten the consciousness but also to cure sicknesses. People do not understand that We have to treat them like dangerously ill patients.

"When We advise you to be cautious, it does not mean that We consider you careless, on the contrary, We only consider the fact that someone is going through an unheard-of tension, and that there is a need for special caution. If you will put yourself in the place of a physician, you will come closer to the goal. At present people are especially tense and require a wise influence. One may often have to agree with them in details in order to safeguard the most essential. To bring relief from fear, one may have to give encouragement. Thus, the entire method of a wise physician must be adopted by a teacher of life. Often an obvious sickness may be arrested by a simple word of encouragement. Let us not analyze where and when the illness began. Primarily, a physician does not condemn, but anticipates a better method of stopping decay. In every illness there is evidence of decomposition. Thus, also with human errors, curative remedies must be applied.

"You heard recently about obsession—an almost hopeless case because the sick woman was too tired to struggle and became subject to the obsessor. One may be able to check the growth of terror through personal magnetism, but it is not possible to exercise influence in writing. In like manner, the people around the sick person accelerate the illness. Usually such obsessed people must first of all be transferred to a new place, and everything around them must be renewed. People fail to understand to what an extent the surroundings contribute to the development of certain diseases. Thus, one should become used to the role of a physician. Our inner life is full of medicinal activities."

* * *

Advise your friends to find time to gather in small groups at a definite hour and send their best aspirations to the Teacher. Such messages will fuse with the primary energy that is sent forth by the Great White Brotherhood—thus, much benefit will be achieved. Indeed, a heart's striving toward the Teacher will create powerful discharges for the purification of the turbulent atmosphere in space. You should advise them to strive in the simplest possible way, holding in their hearts the Image of the Teacher, or aspiring toward him through a silver thread which issues from the heart.

Here is another discourse which indicates the benefit and necessity of actions:

"Learn to discern the veils of Maya. If we speak about veils, it means there is something concealed. Thus, the Primary Energy is concealed. Wise is he who can perceive in different creations where lies the eternal, indestructible base. Without this discernment all will appear as Maya and as a baseless mirage. One cannot live only among phantoms. The very basis of eternal life demands realization of where that stability exists upon which a tired traveler can lean. Inevitably man will come to seek an eternal foundation. Thought about immutability can inspire man to action. This striving toward action is a healthy sign.

"We may be asked, 'What are the conditions in which it is easier for Us to help people?' Of course—in action. We can say to those who ask for help—Act! In such a state it is easier for Us to help you. Even an action of little success is better than inaction. We can add Our energy to the energy shown by you. It is no wonder that a homogeneous substance blends more easily with a similar one. Thus, if We wish to apply Our energy, We seek the most useful application of it. We send the energy, not for the awakening of man, but for the strengthening of a force that is already tensed. A man who is suddenly awakened from sleep can perform most senseless actions. One should not suddenly disturb those who sleep; but when a man is in a conscious waking state We can help him.

"Likewise, you will now be asked, 'What must one do' Answer, 'Act, and in such motion Our help will come.' When We and Our Brothers ask you to act, growth is needed, refinement of the psychic energy is needed, otherwise the veils of Maya will tightly seal all approaches.

"We advise action often enough. When you write to friends, advise them to act. At present the forces of nature are intensified. He who runs away will be knocked over, but he who resists will find new strength. We help the daring ones, and there is action in Our Ashram. New tension will not be fatigue, but renewal."

And so, action in everything and always. Verily, only action will protect us from the perilous Maya. Indeed, each one of us knows how we are often afraid to start an action because Maya has already woven its yarn out of all kinds of fears and prejudices. But if we could find enough courage within ourselves and would act in spite of all evidence, all our fears would prove to be just a mirage—or simply a scarecrow. A few days ago one of our co-workers wrote and confessed that in spite of the advice which was given him to visit someone who could be very helpful, he could not do so because he was sure that only great unpleasantness would result from this meeting. Finally, after almost two years had elapsed, he decided to take this, as he thought, risky step, and the results were, of course, entirely inverse to his pessimistic expectation; thus two years were lost for useful construction. Fear to approach people and preconceived judgments can greatly impede any construction, for, verily, God helps the brave.

And now I shall answer your questions.

1. *Ketub* is one of the names for psychic energy.

2. *Asuras*—exoterically speaking are the fallen or evil gods, but esoterically, the reverse. Thus in the *Rig-Veda* this term is used to designate the Supreme Spirit. Asu means breath, and Prajapati (Brahma) from out of his breath created the *Asuras*. Only in later times when the initial "A" was used as a negative prefix did the term *Asuras* signify "*no-gods*," and only the term *sura* remained connected with the divine element. But in the Vedas precisely the *Suras* have always been connected with the sun and were regarded as lesser deities. You will find the details about the *Asuras* in *The Secret Doctrine*.

3. "The Plan of the Luminous City" is the name of the ordained new city, the city of the Sixth Race.

4. *Dorje*, has the same significance as the swastika.

5. "The edges bent toward the sun" signify a forward movement, whereas the edges bent in the opposite direction signify retardation, the latter symbol is accepted by the Shamans. The Druids had a ritual in which all those who were present had to move around the sacrificial place or altar, exactly in the direction of the sun, whereas the Hierophant himself was moving against the sun, thus symbolizing his superior knowledge. Truly, only a Hierophant can resist the great force, and only such tension can bestow the sparks of the highest knowledge. As you can see, all the meanings of symbols have become mixed and interlaced.

6. "For Seven Purposes" means that each advice should be applied as broadly as possible and on various occasions in life.

7. "The Ray of Venus" can be beneficial if the brown gas which envelops our planet does not impede it. (See *On Eastern Crossroads*.)

8. The Uighurs are a Turki Tribe in Central Asia.

As for the photographing of emanations, it seems to me it would be advisable to try various films. Some are able to get good results using the most ordinary films, even without any particular preparation, and in daylight. Of course, as in everything else, patience and discipline are to be applied. The best way is to take photographs in a room saturated with the aura of the photographed person. Sometimes even the introduction of some new object into the room will disturb the experiment. Furthermore, the auras of both the photographer and the one photographed should be in full harmony. (See paragraph 465 in *Heart*.)

* * *

Let us rejoice that the seeds which were sown are giving good crops. Likewise, our great country is purifying itself and is growing. Many touching manifestations are noticeable among the young people. Verily, the hundreds of thousands of Ivans have risen in defense of their country and will be able to build the Fiery Chariot, which will carry them across all abysses. And so, in spite of all the terrors in the world, there are also reasons for rejoicing. Realizing that all the events will only benefit the New Country, may we be ready for an attainment of the heart.

27

23 October 1937

There exists a remarkable formula, "All that lives comes from life." For our purpose we may paraphrase it and say, "All that is new comes from the new and is for the new," therefore the New Teaching is also for the New World. Dying consciousnesses are unable to assimilate either of these—never will they be able to understand the meaning of events. It is amazing to observe this complete inability to adjust to the new conditions and to the new psychology of the masses—this is already a kind of ossification.

And yet, it would be wrong to think that at present there are not many seekers; on the contrary, there are many more than ever before, but they are scattered in the most unexpected places and sections of the population. Also, it cannot be denied that many are frightened by the very mention of occultism. Indeed, during the last decades, there appeared so many occult organizations full of trappings that every earnest seeker now tries to stay away from everything that bears the label of occultism. Nowadays, we are in need of new definitions that will meet the requirements of the modern terminology accepted by science, which, in its recent discoveries, has come so close to the subtlest energies and the subtle realm. You know how I dislike the word *occultism* and all pompous references to the initiated and initiations, because there immediately come to my mind all the props and paraphernalia of the pseudo-occult organizations.

I advise you to begin to seriously study the actions of psychic energy. In the books of the Teaching many hints are given about the most interesting experiments. By the way, a woman friend of ours, a psychiatrist, performed a series of experiments with psychic energy and with the power of thought. With the assistance of apparatus that could register the slightest pulsation of the heart she was able to prove that various qualities of thought correspondingly heighten or lower the tension of the vibrations that are recorded on the apparatus. These experiments were performed upon a few people individually and later upon several participants at one time. It was discovered that thoughts of high quality sharply raised the vibrations. Also, concentration of several people on one thought produced an amazing intensification of vibrations. I consider such experiments most significant. In this way one should approach the study of the inner man.

Other experiments of this psychiatrist along the lines of automatic writing were equally interesting. By studying the automatic writings of nervous and unbalanced individuals she often was able to establish the origin of their illness. The following case is particularly instructive. One young man committed a grave crime and when arrested he could recall neither his name nor his address, and his entire past disappeared from his memory. Of course, the local authorities did everything they could to identify him, but all their efforts were fruitless. Our friend was approached and asked to render her services. She applied her method and awakened in the young man the ability to write automatically. Within a very short time he developed this ability and wrote down his complete autobiography. Further investigation confirmed the correctness of his testimony thus acquired.

It should be noted that during the process of such writing, our friend compels the one who writes to read aloud so that his physical consciousness will not participate in the least in this process of the expression of the subconscious. Undoubtedly, automatic writing in cases of certain abnormalities and hidden illness can open up new possibilities. But, of course, not everyone can awaken this ability in man. Our friend obviously possess in a great degree the ability to awaken mediumistic powers in her patients. In addition, acting consciously, she is able to direct this power of theirs in the desired direction. Such experiments are full of interest, but certainly great caution is needed, and any hasty conclusions are not desirable. In such phenomena as automatic writing many factors have to be considered, the decisive one being the moral level of the personality of the investigator, or conductor, of such experiments. Certainly one should not expect that the patient will always reveal his own forgotten experiences or his true trend of thought; often, some obsessors from the other world may try to take possession of the nerve centers of the patient. Well and good if the experimenter is able to prevent the entrance of base visitors, but there may be unexpected appearances of the darkest forces. Therefore, the aura of the investigator should serve as a sort of shield. It is gratifying to note that in the young countries much interest is shown in many manifestations which but recently were relegated to the realm of crude superstition and charlatanism.

The New Epoch is marked by the sign of Aquarius, and its ruler is Uranus. You probably know that the affirmation of the power of the rays of Uranus always coincides with new trends in the whole life of our planet. It is also significant that the co-ruler with Uranus is Saturn, this symbol of the dark forces. Thus, all great epochs were marked by these two opposites, this struggle of the Forces of Light with the forces of darkness. The tension of one side correspondingly intensifies the opposite side. Victory in this battle is on the side of Uranus.

We read in one of the Russian newspapers that scientists who were observing the special transit of Mercury near the sun, which happens only once in a thousand years, found that although the atmosphere of this planet does not presuppose any signs of life, it is not improbable that there is a possibility of the existence on it of some forms of life that do not correspond to our earthly conditions. Such an admission is already a great step forward in the thinking of the scientists. One could have told them that the present condition of Mercury is very grievous, because it is undergoing a state of obscuration; the elements on Mercury are in a state of tremendous tension and are battling, as it were. Therefore, there is actually no life there now as we understand it here on Earth. The new cycle on Mercury will be higher than the present cycle on Earth. But the nearness of the planet to the sun does not necessarily signify its higher development.

* * *

And now regarding your young friend who is so anxious to go to India. India is beautiful, and I thoroughly understand his yearning. But to find a true Teacher even in this country is very difficult nowadays. Perhaps he will be able to find a few learned Sadhus. Among the followers of Ramakrishna and Vivekananda there are some fine individuals, but the disciples who personally knew these teachers have almost all passed into the Subtle World. Furthermore, I doubt that even some of the high Sadhus could transmit to him the real Raja Yoga. Many years of preparations and other conditions as well are required in order to fit oneself for this most difficult achievement.

Undoubtedly, your friend will also come across a few fakirs—we call them mediums. Europeans confuse the phenomena of the fakirs with the high achievements of Raja Yoga. Every now and then one learns of one or another yogi, but after due investigation one finds that these yogis have most peculiar habits. For instance, in the recently published book, *A Search in Secret India*, the author (an Englishman, Paul Brunton) described the yogi Vishudhananda of Bengal, who demonstrated to him an experiment based on the transference of the life principle. The "yogi" ordered that a sparrow be caught and strangled. When all those present were convinced that the bird was dead, the "Yogi," after many manipulations, concentrated upon the dead sparrow. After awhile this concentration turned into a trance. Within a short time the bird began to tremble and finally it flapped its wings and came to life. But when the "yogi" came to himself, the bird died again. Certainly, no true Raja Yogi would ever allow a bird to be killed for such an experiment; precisely this fact indicates that the author of this book was dealing with a fakir.

Recently one of the best Sanskritists, who are now rarely met in India, visited us and stayed for a while. We discussed with him the state of ancient knowledge in his country, and this scientist, being a Buddhist, was quite outspoken and confirmed that it is now extremely difficult to find a pundit who is well versed in the esoteric traditions, and what is more important, who can well grasp the meaning of them. At present, this Sanskritist is on his way to Tibet in search of ancient manuscripts.

A tibetan lama also visited us. He had thoroughly studied theoretically and, to some extent practically, certain systems for the development of the *siddhis*. He, too, regretted the decline of knowledge and confirmed the fact that illumined lamas are very rare exceptions among the present-day lamas. In the monasteries, under cover of the Teaching of Light, black magic is often practiced. He also told us that all systems of the forced development of the *siddhis* often bring very sad results. But if an aspirant is found to possess a strong will and a pure heart, his achievements may be quite significant. Particular attention is paid to the development of concentrated thinking, and complete concentration of thought upon a chosen object. Such concentration and meditations constitute the most important part of spiritual upbringing. He asserted that during the state of a certain kind of meditation, which turns into a trance, such successful pupils go through the whole process of dying and then returning to life. All of them describe this process, and particularly, after darkness and a red sphere, crossing into a sphere of white light, as a state of indescribable ecstasy. There is a detailed description of the successive transference of consciousness through these spheres, with all the accompanying sensations. Of course, there is always some danger that one may not come back to life at all. To achieve such a degree of meditation years and years of practice are needed, and, as the lamas state, it is necessary to kindle the fires of the heart, which, in itself, is already a great achievement.

Let us hope that your friend will be exceptionally lucky and will not be disappointed. With the increase of European travelers who are in search of Mahatmas and Yogis, one may meet among the vagrant *sadhus* not a few disguised policemen, swindlers, and even murderers. I can testify to this based on personal experience.

Therefore, I do not advise your friend to go to India only in search of Teacher, for he will merely waste a great amount of strength and time, which will not be justified by the results. Knowledge can be acquired in any country, just as the Teacher invariably appears when the disciple is ready. This law is immutable.

However, if the heart resounds to the lofty beauties of nature, then our majestic Himalayas and that peculiarly saturated spiritual atmosphere, which has been accumulated around them during thousands of years, owing to the presence there of the Abode of the Mahatmas and of the blessed Rishis—all this will undoubtedly leave an indelible impression for the rest of the life.

By the way, I love to recall a passage from the *Dobrotolubye*: St. Anthony, while dwelling in the desert, during the period when he was a hermit, begged the Lord to indicate to him a Teacher who could instruct him in the highest knowledge and every virtue. He was then directed to the nearest town to a certain cobbler.

* * *

My answer to your question about the significance of concentration upon the little finger was confirmed by the Teacher. Not wishing to give an incorrect interpretation I always verify my answers. To me personally it is entirely of no importance on what to concentrate in order to obtain certain results. Believe me, my dear friend, the entire pharmacy mentioned in many occult books is very harmful, because the development of each person is entirely individual. Even in the practice of medicine patent remedies are regarded by enlightened physicians as quite dangerous. In America frequent cases of dangerous poisoning from patent medicines have been disclosed. So much the more is caution needed in those methods which apply in dealing with the subtlest energies. But the coarseness of contemporary consciousness is amazing, and people attempt to approach the most subtle manifestations with an axe.

Also, you must bear in mind that when the need for unity is mentioned in the books of Living Ethics, it is not outward unity which is meant, but the unity, or harmonization of consciousnesses that does not come in one hour. Such unity requires a mutual foundation of high morality and complete recognition of the oneness of the Hierarchic Principle, consequently, an absolute devotion that teaches us discrimination first of all. But the chaotic mixing of the most varied elements only because they have fastened the label of *occultism* upon themselves is impermissible. One can and should treat tolerantly and magnanimously the rare groups of fine quality, but why must one go so far as to eat with them at the same table! Why create artificial explosions by combining uncombinable elements? One should not bring together the sheep and the wolves, one should not gather all into one heap. Is a formless pile the goal of the given Teaching? Nature is our best teacher, and therefore we should observe more attentively how, while containing all, at the same time she harmoniously and goal-fittingly chooses neighbors in all her kingdoms. There are plants that will never be able to grow together, and yet each one of them is useful in its own place or soil; whereas were they forcibly planted in close proximity, they would lose their usefulness and degenerate. One should beware of degeneration through the admittance of poisonous neighbors.

You are interested to know whether every belief is based upon an occult foundation or is just an empty superstition, and you quote a popular saying, widely spread in Serbia, "If, while laying the foundation of a house, the masons immure the shadow of a man who stands before the house, all sorts of misfortunes and failures will descend upon him."

There is no doubt that each belief is based on some forgotten truths and teachings, which, in the course of thousands of years, were distorted and became unrecognizable. Many similar concepts, belonging to different planes of existence and therefore differing in their qualities, have been piled upon each other and eventually woven into one web of popular beliefs, at times reaching such a state that it is utterly impossible to separate them and to arrive at their origin. We see the very same thing regarding the concept of the shadow of which different nations frequently have opposite interpretations.

And so the shadow, being the opposite of light, was always considered by the peoples of the East to be a concept of darkness and therefore hostile. Hence came the idea that absolute spirituality has no shadow. Among many tribes of Asia there exists a belief that the Devas do not cast a shadow, therefore, a holy man should not have one either. The foundation of this belief should be sought in the teaching that deals with the first ethereal races of humanity and the subtle spheres, since the high substance of the Subtle World, being itself a source of light, cannot cast a shadow.

In India, even up to now, it is considered a great misfortune if, during the marriage ceremony or some other festivity, the shadow of a passer-by falls upon the exposed dishes of food or gifts. The reason for this belief is that the shadow of a passer-by will not only arrest the beneficial rays of the sun for some time, but, besides, it will imprint upon these objects the influence of his personal karma. In connection with this I shall quote a remarkable passage from *The Secret Doctrine*: "A shadow never falls upon a wall without leaving thereupon a permanent trace which might be made visible by resorting to proper processes. ... The portraits of our friends or landscape-views may be hidden on the sensitive surface from the eye, but they are ready to make their appearance as soon as proper developers are resorted to. A spectre is concealed on a silver or glassy surface, until, by our necromancy, we make it come forth into the visible world. Upon the walls of our most private apartments, where we think the eye of intrusion is altogether shut out and our retirement can never be profaned, there exist the vestiges of all our acts, silhouettes of whatever we have done." [Op. cit.]

Thus the personal chronicle is not a fantastic dream, for we come across similar chronicles in the world of gross matter. According to the ancient Teaching each particle of existing matter must serve as a record of all that has taken place.

But in European traditions we come across the opposite interpretation of the shadow. Thus, in the old German legends a loss of the shadow was considered to be the sign of a soul sold to the devil. But even in this interpretation we can trace the distorted reverberations of the most ancient Eastern traditions, for the devil, or the Prince of Darkness, is their evil spirit—Mara, the symbol of destruction and death. Hence, a person who has lost his shadow already belongs to death.

Man dies when his astral double, or shadow, leaves him.

From what is said above it is obvious that one may find in the custom that you related a trace of a remote truth about the unbreakable and unalterable link between man and his shadow, or the astral double. But, nowadays, this knowledge has become distorted and has degenerated into the crudest superstition.

In the case that you have mentioned, of course it is not the immured shadow itself which is of significance, but the idea and belief that underlie this action. The thoughts of such a "victim" impress images of terror upon his aura and thus paralyze his psychic energy, making him open, or extra sensitive to all hazards. But were he to believe that the immuring of his shadow would bring only benefit to him and a special protection to his physical body, his well-being and his health would undoubtedly improve in proportion to his belief. As to the ceremony itself, namely, that of putting a gold coin in a pot of butter and burying it in the foundation of the house in order to ward off the calamities which the immured shadow might bring, at present I cannot find any explanation for this, except one—that the gold coin in some mysterious way is acquired by the prescriber of all these manipulations. Of course, the tenacity of this or that belief or superstition is based, first of all, or ignorance and autosuggestion.

It is obvious from the above how important and urgent it is to study from every angle the qualities and actions of psychic energy, with which each human is endowed.

The Teaching of the East affirms that balanced and developed psychic energy consciously or even unconsciously (to us) becomes our best Guiding Star.

* * *

You ask how is one to understand that "Teros and Tamas must work like brothers," (*Illumination*, 168). Teros is synonymous with spirit, motion, or light. Tamas is synonymous with matter, inertia, or ignorance. The life of the Cosmos is composed of the equilibrium of these two elements. The predominance in nature or in a human being of one of these elements leads to decomposition and final destruction. The necessity for equilibrium of these elements can be seen in all of life. Thus, today we can see most clearly in the life of entire countries and nations what comes of violation of equilibrium. People think that they have advanced in many ways, and they proudly point to their mechanical achievements. But they are very little advanced in the knowledge of spiritual and ethical foundations. Man has perfected himself in ways and means of fratricide, but he has lost the ability to think about the foundations of existence. Indeed, those problems which could improve life remain neglected. Try to question the world at large and you will behold a shameful spectacle. Only a minority will manifest some striving toward the foundations mentioned above, and even this minority will timidly whisper about the Subtle World, about the continuity of life, about the significance of thought and the need for ethical concepts. Acceleration of mechanical discoveries does not lead to concentration of thought. If we were to write the history of knowledge concerning these foundations, it would speak clearly about the immobility of consciousness. Therefore, if humanity wishes to flourish, it should think of the foundations, and it should speedily intensify the actions of Teros, even at the expense of those of Tamas, for otherwise it is impossible to re-establish the lost equilibrium.

And so, self-perfectment requires the balancing of these two principles within oneself—Teros and Tamas. All the teachings of antiquity speak with unanimity about the concept of a Golden, or Middle Path, about the Harmony which is understood as the equilibrium between spirit and matter. Thus, Teros and Tamas should work as brothers.

What is "Marakara"? (*Heart, 307*) Marakara is the abode of the spirits of darkness. Mara is the prince of Darkness. He is also called a destroyer and death (of the soul). There is no lower and more oppressive sphere in the Subtle World than Marakara.

* * *

What is meant by the "vibrations of the Silver Bridge"? (*Heart, 357*) This is the name of the vibration that is sent by the Teacher to the disciple for the strengthening of the tired heart. This vibration strengthens the bond between the disciple and the Teacher. This silver Ray can be seen by the spiritual eye.

28

14 January 1937

So much harm has been caused by the premature disclosure of information! But this can be understood only by those who have well assimilated the law of causes and effects and who therefore are able to realize what effects can be engendered by this or that cause. This is the reason why I also have to restrict myself and leave part of your questions unanswered. In this time of general confusion and intensified assaults by the dark forces, which we are now experiencing, it would be inadmissible to entrust something secret or holy to paper, which passes through so many hands. Much would be distorted and harmfully interpreted.

In great antiquity when the Teachings of Light were transmitted orally or in veiled symbols, there was great goal-fitness, or co-measurement in this. But nowadays, are there many who comprehend the meaning of even simple words? A vivid example of such lack of understanding and even of malicious interpretation is displayed in the review which I received dealing with one of the books of Living Ethics. While reading it, I was amazed! I certainly do not intend to enter into any polemics, but I must say, to my regret, that the injudicious thoughts expressed therein are not only simply primitive but already border on the self-delusion of malicious ignorance.

Thus, this objector does not understand that the Teaching of the Spirit, or of Living Ethics, is the best armor for the body. Yet even contemporary physicians, such, for example, as the French physicist and biologist, Georges Lakhovsky, in his work *How to Achieve Immortality* comes scientifically to the conclusion that all moral teachings have, first of all, a purely biological foundation. Hence, his advice, "Do not become angry, do not be jealous, do not be envious, do not become irritable, but be kind and optimistic, and you will live to a very old age." If I shall find a spare moment, I shall give you a brief outline of this most interesting work, which so closely touches upon the significant influence of psychism and psychic energy upon man's entire life.

It is amusing to read how this objector repeatedly attempts to justify certain small sins, throwing the whole responsibility for them upon the devil.

Likewise, he is obviously very much attached to his astral body, and the idea of parting with it grieves him. However, one must always bear in mind that the astral body is necessary for life on the physical plane because it serves as a connecting bridge; but after crossing into a higher state, the astral body, just as the discarded physical body, is looked upon as litter. The physical body is necessary to us, but in the further evolution it will be replaced by the densified astral body. The astral body is likewise necessary for certain tasks connected with the physical world, therefore some of the Great Teachers preserve this body.

But actually the Great Teachers have every reason to consider the astral body as unnecessary litter. Indeed, we should try with all our might in our physical life to restrain the astral body and to concentrate our attention upon the development of the mental body. The Great Teachers value the actions of their disciples performed, not in the coarse astral body, but in a more subtle body. It is also said in the Teaching that with the spiritual growth of man, his sojourn in the astral world can be limited to forty days.

Our opponent does not agree that "The path of the world evolution ... progresses not by the way of the lower strata ... but through cooperation with the Higher Planes." Thus, he obviously denies the Leading Principle in the Cosmos. One may ask, How, then, does he understand the idea of Christ or the "All-forgiving" Lord God? Is not the concept of Christ in itself a cooperation with the Highest Planes?

To his conceited concluding words that "M. should give not only the leaves from his garden but also good fruit trees with succulent fruit on them," we may remind him that already in the first book the Teacher gives him an answer:

> "Wherefore O Lord, dost Thou not trust me to gather the fruits of Thy Garden?
> But where are thy baskets?
> Why, O Lord, dost Thou not pour upon me the streams of Thy Bliss?
> But where are thy pitchers?
> O Lord, why dost Thou whisper and not proclaim Thy Truth in thunder?
> But where are thy ears? It were better, moreover, to hearken to the thunder amidst the mountains." (par. 296)

We may as well finish on that.

29

1937

I am returning to you the list of your questions and my answers to them.

1. Our forces grow from our contact with people. Each exchange of thoughts, each collaboration enriches our consciousness, and confrontations and comparisons also teach us and at the same time strengthen our self-confidence.

2. Everything earthly, all earthly circumstances stand in the way of all that is High, but striving hearts soar above obstacles.

3. Unfortunately, the human spirit in most cases resists the divine element in itself and in everything.

4. *Tshur* is here meant in the sense of survivals or of the old outworn consciousness. *Tshur* could also mean a hobgoblin, hence, all kinds of superstitions and prejudices. The meaning of this is that it is impossible to assimilate the coming New

World with an old consciousness, old ignorance and all its manifestations.

5. "The canon, 'By thy God' is the higher." This means that this canon is higher (wiser) than the affirmation "By my God." In the first statement there is tolerance and understanding, whereas in the second is hidden the embryo of exclusion and fanaticism.

6. The term *Skandha* is used in the Buddhist philosophy. Literally, *Skandhas* means groups of qualities which constitute the personality of man. Exoterically they are divided into five groups:

1. Form or body;
2. Sensation;
3. Consciousness;
4. Motives (karma);
5. Knowledge.

Bear in mind that not only each of our actions but each of our thoughts creates a vibration, and precisely these vibrations are the *Skandhas*. Thus, the *Skandhas* make up the sum total of the subjective and objective man. The *Skandhas* generated by man are his inalienable possession (karmic) which actually follows him in his new earthly incarnation. Karmic results of the past life follow man, and in his next life he will gather all the *Skandhas*, or vibrations which were imprinted by him on the astral, for nothing can come from nothing—therefore, there is a link between lives, and the new *Skandhas* are born from the previous ones or from their propagators. Thus, *Skandhas* build our karma, or inversely, karma is built out of *Skandhas*. Remember what is said in the Teaching about the Chalice of accumulations.

7. Phenomena, performed by mediums or black magicians who do not take into consideration the atmospheric and other conditions often produce a reaction which, owing to the forced extraction of energies and their combinations from space, could be compared in its destructive force with an explosion. This violation, as explained, causes the execrable atmosphere of agitated electrons. This seems to be clear.

* * *

Now about the Pact and Banner of Peace. Could there be such individuals, who, though regarding themselves as educated and even spiritual, do not understand the most fundamental and important significance of the Pact and Banner of Peace? They seem not to understand that the significance of the Banner of Peace lies, first of all, in the fact that by safe-guarding human creativeness there is implanted in the consciousness of the masses and of the growing generations reverence precisely for the spiritual values, which gave life to mankind. After all we cannot consider the magnificent cathedrals, libraries, and museums as material values! Is a degree of ignorance possible that would attribute these symbols of spiritual creativeness to material values?

* * *

Certainly, initiative should be encouraged, in principle. But bear in mind that initiative is often confused with manifestations of selfhood. Besides, without evidencing austere discipline of the spirit, initiative will result in wavering and spasmodic attempts which lead nowhere. For everything that is spasmodic is doomed to destruction, since it is impossible to build on convulsions. Not in vain was discipline or obedience placed at the basis of all ancient Teachings. And in the Teaching that is given to us the necessity of such discipline is stressed a great deal. What is Hierarchy if not discipline? In all ancient religions and philosophical schools there existed a general teaching and also the teaching for the devotees. And precisely in this teaching for the devotees discipline of spirit was taught, and obedience was the first step toward it. Every leader must first of all learn to obey, otherwise how will he know what is a command and what its fulfillment?

You quote a line from The Call, "All is revealed; all is attainable.:" This is said in relation to the Cosmos. Indeed, the whole Cosmos is open for our perception. But the mysteries of Cosmos are revealed only in complete correspondence with the consciousness and heart of the questioner; and so it is in the Teaching. Hence, always remember about the golden equilibrium between mind and heart. Without this equilibrium there is no true progress, and all mysteries remain closed and inaccessible. Therefore, let us manifest both mind and heart in all our actions.

30

19 November 1937

I was much saddened to learn that though you started affirming and strengthening your health by means of psychic energy, suddenly you began to doubt and gave up this very useful practice. Only an iron will and iron steadfastness, or rhythm, can bring one to the goal. Certainly, it is impossible to expect that through a simple affirmation of health extracted teeth will suddenly start growing again. (Such attainments are still in the distant future.) However, constant autosuggestion undoubtedly would have brought an improvement in the general condition of your health. Therefore, I greatly regret that you gave up this useful, strengthening practice. None of our efforts are ever wasted, and if not in this incarnation, such strengthening of the will would bring good results in the next one.

And so, my assertion that theoretically all yogic achievements may seem easy, but in practice there is nothing more difficult, brought disappointment to you instead of a new influx of encouragement and perseverance. Now you will understand why I always regret that such writers as Ramacharaka, while giving not a bad exposition of some systems of Indian Yoga, at the same time speak with the light-mindedness of a dilettante about the ease of mastery of the highest achievements of the Raja Yogis. The beginners who read this take his word on faith and start with all their zeal to practice the prescribed exercises. Later, when their expectations are not fulfilled, they become very disappointed and turn into fervent deniers and even enemies. Nobody wishes to think that if one wants to become an outstanding artist, painter, or a scientist in any sphere of knowledge, not only many accumulations in this direction in past lives are needed but, in addition, years of stubborn and constant labor in this life. How much the more then must one persistently strive toward broadening and disciplining one's own consciousness, which alone can aid the refinement and fiery transmutation of our nerve-receptors, or centers. Indeed, spiritual achievements, being connected with the growth of consciousness, are the most difficult ones.

A striking example of this difficulty is now presented by our healthy humanity, which, after many millions of years of existence and incalculable bitter lessons, is now about ready not only to exterminate the whole human race but also to explode its own planet.

It is not fitting for the followers of the Teaching of Life to give way to depression and to weaken themselves by doubt. The followers of the Teaching of Life live for the future in the realization of Infinity, and therefore they know that no striving, no rhythmical, or continuous, effort *will* remain without results. They realize that actually only the striving and efforts applied by them in each labor are the basis of all achievements. The crystal of psychic energy, this philosophers' stone, is accumulated through the unceasing striving and efforts of many centuries.

* * *

Work for the unification of co-workers! We were given a Covenant—unity, courage and achievement. With these fiery qualities the New World is built and the right to enter the Stronghold of Great Knowledge is earned.

31

23 November 1937

We hold to the opinion that extreme caution should be practiced in accepting members, and especially so when we grant them the right to vote. We all have a responsibility to guard that which is Entrusted. In the very first volume of the Teaching it is said: "Do not destroy people by confiding too much unto them. Often the burden of the load presents only a view of the back." Therefore, we advised that only well tested friends be admitted to the meetings of the Board and given the right to vote; the active members should have the right to vote, whereas the probationary members should not have this right. Out of consideration for people, especially for the youth, we have first of all to give them an opportunity to know themselves. They must realize that entering upon the preparatory path of service is not like joining some sort of club where entering and leaving is of no consequence. They must realize that the Teaching of Life to which they have listened puts a certain spiritual obligation upon them, even if they are not yet able or willing to realize it. Therefore, before they bind themselves still more, they should thoroughly check their intentions and strivings in order that they may avoid becoming apostates by departing later on. There are quite a few betrayals, conscious and unconscious, but our sacred duty is to try by all means to guard the structure of Light against them. I can go even further and say that no heroic achievement is possible without betrayal, but nevertheless we must do everything in our power to perfect that which has been entrusted to us.

And now to your questions. Undoubtedly, many co-workers are helping the Forces of Light in the Subtle World. At present, the battle there is even stronger than it is on Earth. Therefore, it is advisable to have this in mind and not to avoid sleep, for some zealous co-workers attempt to reduce their hours of night's rest. Often the work in the Subtle World is even more productive than earthly work. Do tell this to your nearest friends and ask them to write down their nightly experiences. Gradually they will learn to discriminate among the complicated symbols and to discern in the impression received a certain confusion, which occurs because of insufficient discipline and lack of clarity of consciousness. But with the right striving, clarity will come. Let them fall asleep with the thought of flying to help, wherever the Great Teachers may send them.

I have read the page in the book you mentioned. I quite understand that by the words "to exclude the action of the mind" the author means that one should stop the disorderly flood of thoughts which prevents us from grasping the sendings issued by the Great Source and assimilated through our higher centers. This is easier to achieve at the borderland of sleep, because then a natural quieting of disorderly thinking takes place. Therefore it is indicated that one should learn to catch the sendings precisely on the threshold of sleep or at the moment of awakening. Hence it is necessary to develop in oneself a special constant watchfulness of the heart. When the thinking is sufficiently disciplined and our consciousness has mastered that aspiring watchfulness, then one may hear the Voice of the Teacher. Not only in the moments of concentrating upon his Image but even when the mind works with clarity on some definite problem. And so, in everything there should first be discipline, clarity, and rhythm. But the fleas or bunny rabbits of thought deprive us of any possibility of higher perception.

Also, it is incorrect to say that one must dispassionately repeat an already worked out formula many a time. I quite agree that physical effort alone will only impede, but striving of the heart is essential for success; verily the unutterable striving of the heart is the key to all locks. Such striving has nothing to do with either dead apathy or physical effort, known as so-called tension of the will. Blessed is he who is able to feel the burning and striving of this fiery energy.

Regarding paragraph 552 in *Aum*. Undoubtedly, there is interdependence of action, and the clearer the character of the incarnating individuality, the more marked are its manifestations in the desires of the expectant mother.

In my answers to the paragraphs indicated by you I shall preserve the numbers of the paragraphs in *Fiery World III* so that it will be easier for you to check them.

62. Of course the Subtle World is the astral world with all its subdivisions into lower and higher spheres; then comes the Fiery World, and, finally, the Higher World.

82. The Guiding Star of man is the emanation of the seed of his spirit, or accumulated straight-knowledge, which propels him toward Light. And this Guiding Star burns brightly after the hardships of life. Only in highest tension can our energies be refined and transmuted into higher strivings. Indeed, strivings mold the character, or karma, of man. It is necessary to firmly remember that karma is built primarily out of the motives, strivings, and thoughts of man, whereas actions are only secondary factors.

Thus, the good accumulations of many lives mold karma, which is directed by the *Guiding Star of straight-knowledge.*

86. Fiery Baptism means the spiritual transfiguration or assimilation of the pure Fire of Space. During Fiery Baptism the opening of certain nerve centers takes place.

The accumulation of the fiery, or primary, energy makes it possible for man to ascend into the higher spheres when crossing into the Subtle World. The more we have of this energy, the higher it will carry us. This energy is accumulated by way of unwavering striving toward self-perfectment, work, and complete devotion to the chosen Teacher.

97. When the physician sees that the death of a patient is inevitable, an artificial attempt to prolong his life may cause severe suffering to the departing one and might even seriously harm his subtle body. That is why one should show attention and solicitude for the departing ones.

158. Numerous cosmic energies are evoked from the Subtle World and act invisibly on our physical plane. Not to mention the unprecedented pressure of the electrophorous manifestation, radio waves, and other invisible rays which are now being used by humanity, each earthquake, each commotion, each explosion, and all the horrors of war bring the lowest strata of the Subtle World and the physical plane closer together. Wars and revolutions are the most dreadful, the most powerful evocations of the lower energies from the Subtle World. The lower entities are nourished by the emanations of blood and decomposition. One can well imagine what kind of entities fill the atmosphere around destructive actions. Only strong spirits who are shielded by a firm protective net of psychic energy can resist this infection. Indeed, there are also not a few who practice necromancy in small inadmissible forms.

165. The Jinn are the elemental spirits. In all the Eastern, and especially Arabian tales, the Jinn served the magicians who knew how to control them. Thus, according to a legend, Solomon's temple was built by Jinn. Each legend has a certain particle of truth in it; in life also, the enemies, or the servants of darkness, help to raise an illumined undertaking. Laws are similar everywhere. Darkness emphasizes Light. Evil elevates the concept of Good, etc.

170. Actually, the spatial battles take place throughout the entire expanse of the manifested Cosmos, but their manifestations are of various degrees. The Fire of Space is the binding element between all the worlds in the entire manifested Space; therefore, each manifestation, each battle, regardless of where it takes place, in one way or another affects all the worlds, or all Space. It is said in the Teaching, "A feather falling from the wing of a small bird produces a thunderclap in the far-off worlds." Thus is indicated the unbreakable bond which exists between all manifestations.

175. Every planet passes repeatedly through various cycles. Likewise, fiery destructions and constructions have already visited out planet as well as others, but the degree of their intensity differs in conformity with the spiritual state of the inhabitants. All reactions may be beneficial during the high state of a planet and its population. Lemuria perished from fire.

595. The oil of wormwood, when rubbed in, is beneficial for swollen glands. Also in Switzerland the physicians give a very

light brew of wormwood to patients who suffer from swollen glands.

The Northern Lights that you observed were noted as especially bright in Dvinsk. The reddish light is a very characteristic feature of the Northern Lights. The vivid Northern Lights glow with all the colors of the rainbow.

And now a few lines from the Teaching:

"If we picture the greatest Spiritual Toiler on Earth, he will naturally represent an incomparable power in the Subtle World. The contact with purified Fire of Space will propel Him into the Fiery World. There is no boundary that would impede the ascent of a spirit not harboring doubt. Doubt is like a tear in a balloon. Thus, in Infinity all is borne in motion. I say this to remind that the natural position of man is upright. Doubt is nothing but pockets full of holes—no diamonds can be kept in them. Doubt does not dwell in Our Ashram—the upward current is great. Many efforts are needed not to break away from Earth. The earthly chains are put on willingly and consciously. Sacrifice is molded out of love, and the experiences of former lives bestow love for sufferers. Experience will either kindle love or sharpen hatred. But who will be the first one to sit down upon the stake of hatred? Perhaps the hater himself. Love should be wise and active. In trying to understand this, it is easy to stumble or become sanctimonious. Only labor for the benefit of the world will produce balance. Labor gives joy and the understanding of Infinity. It also gives realization of the motion of the worlds.

"One will ask, In what lies the best pranayama? Through what is a better rhythm developed? By what is the worm of despondency conquered? Through labor. Only in labor is the enchantment of perfectment formed. And in labor the Fiery Baptism will come."

* * *

Let us strive into the future. At present we are experiencing grave days. The terrible deeds will bring their grievous karma. Today's giant may become a dwarf tomorrow. Thus, amidst storms and commotions karma is built and dates are fufilled. The events of the world reveal a mosaic that can only be perceived from the mountain tops.

32

27 November 1937

I could not answer your letter sooner because I felt distressed. Great is the tension of the atmosphere. The madness of nations reaches its limit and the cosmic currents are raging. The pundits in our area predict terrible earthquakes, and people are now afraid to sleep in their houses. Lately, in Northern India earth-tremors of various intensities are felt practically everywhere; there is destruction and loss of life, but in spite of all fears, our valley remains intact. Three dates in November are marked astrologically by the most sinister omens. Likewise, the solar eclipse, which is expected in the beginning of December, will not result in anything good. It is interesting to observe that during eclipses the activity of psychic energy is greatly decreased, and at the very moment of the full eclipse, it almost ceases.

And now I shall attend to your questions. I shall also try to explain once more my point of view regarding the place in the Gospel of St. John that seems to puzzle you: "Destroy this temple and in three days I will raise it up." (2:19) We know what significance was attributed by the followers of Christ to the possibility of his resurrection on the third day; and they were quite right since one of the tasks of Christ was to prove to his disciples the survival of the soul and the immortality of the spirit. No one will deny that precisely the repeated posthumous appearances of Christ were a great factor in strengthening and spreading his Teaching. In Gnostic literature significant details may be found about these manifestations.

And so, after attentively rereading the indicated chapter, I must once more say that I could not find anything illogical either in the answer of Christ or in the interpretation of these words by the Evangelist. I cannot accept the thought that Christ could offer such a crude proof or experiment to affirm his right or authority. Never would any Great Teacher resort to miracles in order to assert his power,. All the miracles that They have performed always had in view the selfless goal of helping sufferers and the poor. Those who questioned Him were thinking in accordance with earthly standards. But the Great Teachers always apply high measures everywhere and in everything, thus uplifting the consciousness of their disciples.

And if we were to suppose that Christ had in mind the destruction and restoration of a stone temple, we could as well ask. Why did He need a period of exactly three days for this purpose?

We know that so-called miracles can be performed only when the necessary cosmic conditions are present, but we also know what an enormous amount of Primary Energy is wasted for the performance of a comparatively minor manifestation or miracle. Therefore, the restoration of the whole temple would have required an enormous expenditure of energy, which could have resulted in some catastrophe. The Teaching states that each forced manifestation brings forth a heavy atmosphere of agitated electrons. And awareness of the latter condition compels the Great Teacher to avoid so-called miracles, or, in other words, to make cautious use of the Cosmic Forces. Higher knowledge imposes a duty to practice the highest caution.

You write, "It is said that the worlds were created by the Word and the Will of the Highest One. Why then should the words of Christ not be understood literally—in line with the conversation which took place?" But who would take literally the first statement you have mentioned? The Word of the Highest should be understood as a vibration or motion of Divine Energy, and the Will is the impulse of attraction or repulsion generated by the bipolarity of the Elements. But who can calculate how many aeons were necessary for the formation of our tiny Earth alone? Would not this "Word of God" stretch out for millions of aeons for the formation of our planet alone?

Perhaps now you can sense why the thought about the restoration of a stone temple by Christ as a proof of his power is linked with difficulty with the Great Image, whose consciousness contained the synthesis of the three worlds.

And as for the supposition that people will be resurrected in their physical bodies, it seems to me that only total ignoramuses can think such things. Besides, the Scriptures repeatedly say that "neither doth corruption inherit incorruption."

Furthermore, the physical body alone cannot be looked upon as the temple of the spirit, but it is actually the subtle, or spiritual, body that is the true carrier of the immortal spirit.

Further on you put a question. Which moment of the crossing from the physical world into the Subtle should be considered as a resurrection, since the Arhats pass on without losing consciousness?

When talking about his resurrection, Christ did not have in

mind his conscious passing into the Subtle World, but actually his appearance in a subtle body amidst physical conditions. Of course, such an appearance of the physically dead person in the materialized subtle body was striking proof of His resurrection and thus strengthened the disciples; faith in His Teaching.

To base the resurrection of Christ solely on the disappearance of his body from the tomb would indeed be more than absurd.

Likewise, I protest with all the strength of my spirit against the supposition that "Christ could have secretly given an order to remove his body and then to declare that he was alive, or resurrected." Such an act would have been unworthy of the Highest Spirit. We must understand that the Great Teachers of humanity never mislead anyone, and each deed of theirs is in strict harmony with all their statements. According to the testimony of his disciples, Christ repeatedly told them that he would be betrayed into the hands of men and would be raised again on the third day—those who have ears, may they hear!

You quite correctly state that the Gospels were written considerably later than the time of Christ, and even after the time of his nearest disciples. Besides, we must take into consideration the censorship of many zealous church fathers. Merezhkovski, in his books *Jesus, the Unknown* and *The Blessed Augustine*, gives much valuable information regarding the "authenticity" of the Gospels. The episode mentioned by H.P. Blavatsky in connection with the choice and confirmation of the authentic Gospels by the spiritual Fathers was found by me in a brochure by H. S. Olcott. Unfortunately, I hid it too well, and I wanted to translate it for you. I shall attempt to find it.

Please do not think that I want to overpersuade you. Not at all, I simply express my sentiments and understanding, and, partially, the knowledge regarding these questions. Only our heart can lead us when we try to follow these paths, therefore, follow your own conviction.

I am not at all surprised that *The Secret Doctrine* distressed you. It is not an easy book, and one must be well acquainted with Eastern philosophical thought in order not to be lost among the many terns and names, which often mean one and the same thing. The vastness of the task on one side, and a certain unavoidable reticence on the other, make the book still more difficult to understand. I advise making extracts or notes while reading, this would help very much. Likewise, bear in mind that the Sons of Flame, Sons of Reason, Sons of Brahma, the Solar Ancestors, the Great Kumaras, Manu, the first Teachers and Kings, the Founders of religions, leaders and philosophers etc.—all of them are the same Seven Greatest Individualities, who manifest in their various aspects on our Earth, and today, They actually form the Kernel of the White Brotherhood.

I shall now clarify the meaning of the paragraphs from the books of the Teaching which are mentioned by you.

Agni Yoga, 315. The summit that is mentioned here is Mt. Everest, or, as it is called in Tibetan, Jemo-Kang-Kar, She who Rules the White Snow. The highest point on Earth and also both earthly poles have a tremendous significance, because of the reservoir of electromagnetic forces which is collected upon them. When the crucial moment shall come that will decide whether or not our Earth will continue to exist, these points will play the decisive role in the salvation of our planet. As you know, all the attempts to reach the top of Mt. Everest, so far were not successful and caused the loss of many lives.

Aum, 122. Here a purely physical lubrication of the respiratory channels is spoken about. One is advised to lubricate the nasal passages (the nose) nightly with a preparation of vaseline and menthol. This excellent disinfectant refreshes the breath and prevents colds.

Aum, 129. About the triple sign. When the trinity, or triunity, of all Existence is realized, when all the three substances—physical, astral, and mental—are fully formed and thus are able to manifest in a clear-cut separation, then it is most edifying to study such an organism.

Aum, 250. Here is discussed a special kind of clairvoyance, when you look at a person sitting before you in full light and are able to evoke his former images. N. K. and I performed such experiments, but the strain on the physical eyes was too great, because the subtlest energies become visible, and thus painfully reacting upon the eyes and greatly weakening them. It is rather difficult to explain this process of clairvoyance, but the results were remarkable. Similarly, I have seen many incarnations of my own family, of people close to me, and even of people whom I knew but slightly. In all those cases the psychic energy was given a certain direction, and then it began to act independently. All so-called miracles are performed through psychic energy.

* * *

And now abut the Prince of the World. Certainly the battle with the Forces of Light fills him with despair. He knows that he is unable to win and therefore he prefers to explode the planet so that he may remain for some time yet in the atmosphere of the explosion. Near the fragments (of course, not the physical ones) of an exploded planet, its atmosphere is preserved for a lengthy period, which would enable the Prince of the World to remain in it. In fact, the higher layers of space are not accessible to him, and therefore he has either to float amidst the fragments and their surrounding atmosphere or go to Saturn. But the conditions on Saturn are very oppressive, and how many aeons would have to pass before our planet would again reach a state that would be favorable for the development of fully conscious life!

You write that you "understand the uselessness of the struggle against the Divine Principle of Good," and that you are amazed that such a great spirit as the Prince of the World could oppose the immutable law. Yet even four-fifths of the two billion human beings do not understand this. Besides, what an incredible power of spirit must be possessed in order to be able to admit one's error and begin a new path overburdened by aeons of terrible karma.

We know about the limitlessness of self-perfectment, therefore the spirit who has fallen to the level of the Prince of Darkness could hardly have had all the needed qualifications for perfection. When a spirit attains the realization of the potentiality of his limitless power and immutability, when he masters many cosmic mysteries and forces and knows that he can become a creator of this or that world, when he realizes the ignorance of the masses that surround him, then, indeed, a tremendous power of the heart is required to resist many temptations, and, first of all—pride of spirit. One should always remember that not a single human feeling disappears; on the contrary, all feelings grow without end, and must therefore be transmuted into higher perceptions of good or they may become more refined in evil. Why is it so difficult to recognize that the Prince of the World, being the Host of our Earth by cosmic right, could not overcome a feeling of pride and jealousy toward other Spirits of Light? According to the esoteric data, at the time when the Great

Brothers of Lucifer, the archangels of the Christian Church who came with him to our Earth, built the eternal movement; at the time when They said, Why be limited to Earth alone when all worlds are destined, thus creating the right path for humanity and establishing a real exchange through broad cooperation with the far-off worlds; Lucufer preferred to segregate himself from his neighbors. But in the unity of Be-ness, through the law of interchange, any kind of isolation leads to disintegration or death. Therefore, Lucifer was able only to complicate the flow of life, but he could not stop it. His Brothers, who are perpetually on Guard and who are at the top of Jacob's Ladder, are the true Saviors of mankind.

Not from the writings of Kryjanovsky, but from the Gnostic writings can one get the idea of Lucifer as a bearer of sacrifice for the development in man of the knowledge of good and evil. Much confusion exists around this legend. One should attentively read *The Secret Doctrine* and then light will dawn.

And so, let us not create a poetic image of the Prince of the World. Perhaps after aeons and aeons his redemption will begin, but at present he has reached the apogee of hatred for humanity, and is about ready to display the apotheosis of his reign of destruction.

* * *

The manifested world is based upon the bipolarity of all that exists and therefore it is but natural that limited human thought, in searching for the reasons for the existence of opposites and in picturing the Divine Origin only in its positive aspect, inevitably had to come to the conclusion that two Elements exist, perpetually fighting against each other—God and Devil. And so, the Planetary Spirit, the Prince of the World, became the personification of all evil, of all the imperfection which exists in nature.

But the lofty thought of the East long ago solved the problem of the existence of evil. The One Element, the One Divine Principle, or the Absolute, which contains the potentiality of all Being, therefore all the opposites as well, also bears in Itself the eternal process of unfoldment, or perfectment. Upon this process or motion are based all manifestations and the entire evolution. Motion, or evolution creates the *relativity* of all concepts, out of which arise the opposites. Only through perpetual change and comparison of pairs of opposites can reality be comprehended.

33
30 November 1937

The lack of information and discipline manifested by "a certain representative of the White Brotherhood" mentioned by you makes me doubt his identity. Indeed, only in actions of earthly people can we observe such lack of stability, giving up one work in order to grasp at something else, in short, a pitiful instability and chaotic disorder. But all actions and indications that come from the Great Brotherhood are distinguished by their austere harmony and consistency. And even among the earthly co-workers of the White Brotherhood no one would attempt to infringe upon the benevolent work, particularly if he knows that this work is related in some way to the missions of the White Brotherhood.

Lately, there have appeared a great many of all kinds of representatives, messengers, and teachers who claim to belong to the Solar Hierarchy (?!) and even to the White Brothers themselves! All these impostors cause nothing but confusion and corruption among the ignorant and naive seekers of cheap sensations.

But each true messenger or teacher, and each teaching, can be based only on Truth and on their personal merits and worth. There is no other criterion on Earth. Truth does not sink in water or perish in fire. The world has witnessed more than once the slandering of the Highest and lauding of false values, but the survival of the latter was of short duration.

To all those who mock at the Great Truths we can say once again: "Did you not crucify Christ? Did you not mock Him when He was suffering on the Cross? Did you not burn and persecute His followers? Did you not torture thousands and thousands of the best minds, who brought you the light of knowledge? Did you not arrest the evolution of human thought, and thus cast humanity into the madness of self-destruction? Is it not said about you, 'You have changed your garments, but you can be recognized by your deeds'?"

By the way, not a bad book came out recently n English, *God Is My Adventure* by Landau, a Polish writer. In it the author describes his meetings with all the known spiritual leaders of today. It is useful to read this book, for it gives an idea of what kind of spirituality is in demand today by the masses of the West and of America. Especially popular is a certain former clergyman, Dr. Buchman, who states that God is a millionaire, and therefore one should not avoid costly gatherings in fashionable hotels and equally costly automobile trips, etc. The rich and bored idle people are very glad that there is someone who cares about them and designs the whole program of their day, at the same time assuring them that their comfortable and pleasant life is of extreme importance and usefulness. Especially popular are the public confessions introduced by Dr. Buchman, in which it is customary to confess all one's sins against the established code of morals.

Since this book came out some more new spiritual leaders have arisen. They appear on the platform in sumptuous dressed, adorned with precious stones, and preach something like this, "Drink and be merry, and thus you will be pleasing to God." There is no doubt that these are signs of the dark times when the forces of darkness are marching in close ranks to destroy all good undertakings and all lukewarm and spiritually unstable people.

* * *

You should not think that your particular karma causes you to lose your friends. Devoted friends are the most rare manifestation. Who had them? Let us recollect all the historical examples. Nowadays, the absence of true friends is a general karma. The madness of malice, hatred, and, of course, ignorance—the root of all abomination—have destroyed all vestiges of humaneness. Therefore, let us rejoice together in the knowledge of having well tested friends.

I am especially pleased to read about your vigor. Preserve it, and whenever possible let it change into solemnity. Indeed, the Karma of many nations is coming to a climax, and we are witnessing a grave hour. Verily, solemnity befits such a time. Besides, solemnity is the best bridge to the White Brotherhood.

"Not many can understand the power of such a shield. Amidst the raging currents, the rock of invincible solemnity stands adamant. Every force that surrounds man can be scientifically explored. He himself can generate any force within himself and can forge an impenetrable armor from it. Likewise, one must realize that solemnity is the best bridge to Us. Our help flies swiftly through the channel of solemnity and slowest of all through the channel of fear and despondency. One must know that We send the blue rays of help in the hour of danger."

Preserve in your heart the Image of your best Friend, the Great Teacher, and all joy will be yours.

34

3 December 1937

Intimate discussions in front of works of art are very beneficial, the vibrations of harmonious tonal combinations create a special atmosphere. The reaction of visitors to a museum unerringly reveals their essence.

It is also certain that works of art possess a healing quality. Some physicians have hung the paintings of N. K. in their sanitariums for the treatment of mentally sick people.

Great is the power of art! This truth slowly, but surely wins its own way. If leaders of governments fully realized the great pedagogical significance of art, they would apply all their efforts and means to awaken the creative fire in nations, and they would nourish it with sound, color, and beautiful forms. No revolutions, no aggressive wars would find a response in a refined consciousness that responds to the higher vibrations. Coarse spirits like wrestling and boxing and the crudest games deprived of beauty, such as football, etc., only add to the coarsening of mores. The beauty of the subtle power of thought and creativeness is forgotten, and what is left is only the thundering, roaring victory of crude force.

And now your questions:

1. "Is the kernel of the spirit, the Divine element, eternally unchangeable, or does it remain so for one cycle only?"

Answer: In each physical cell there is an embryo and a kernel which correspond in man to the fiery seed and the kernel of the spirit. Thus, the fiery seed in man, being the essence of the pure Divine Origin, remains unchangeable and indestructible throughout eternity.

The kernel of the spirit, or the higher Ego in man, grows and changes infinitely, provided that it receives normal nourishment from all the centers; that is, if the psychic energy brings into action the higher nerve centers of man. And if man, who is the bearer of the kernel of the spirit, succeeds here on Earth in spiritualizing his essence through the opening of his higher centers toward the end of the Cycle, or the Fourth Round of our planet, he will find himself in full consciousness in the sphere which corresponds with him and with all this accumulated energies, or abilities. If, in successive Rounds, man manifests the same unremitting striving toward perfectment, he will likewise preserve his immortality for the next interplanetary period, and so into Infinity. However, one must remember that changes in the kernel of the spirit can take place on the way to ascent as well as on the way to descent. But after a prolonged downfall the ascent will be extremely difficult.

2. "It cannot be that God unconditionally allowed some other power—Satan—to exist. Satan is man, with his base aspirations—nothing more."

Answer: In understanding the existence of evil together with the Element of Good the whole difficulty lies in that having humanized the Unutterable Divine Origin, and, at the same time, seeing the many imperfections of the manifested world, people are justly perplexed but the idea that a benevolent and all-merciful God could allow the destructive cosmic cataclysms and all the horrors and sufferings that people undergo in their struggle for existence. And so, limited thinking begins to create the image of just as powerful a force of evil, represented by the antagonist of God, or Satan. But if we cast away the limitation or humanization of the Unutterable Power and accept the majestic pantheism of the ancients, the echo of which we find in the Testaments of all the great Teachers, in the Old Testament, and in the Gospels, then everything will fall into place.

God, in his aspect of the Absolute, contains the potentiality of *all that exists*. In the Absolute, or in the World of the Highest Reality or Be-ness, of course there is no *evil, as such*. But in the manifested world, which is the result of differentiation, all the opposites are present, i.e.—light and darkness, spirit and matter, the opposite polarities, good and evil, etc. I strongly advise you to assimilate the primary foundations of the Eastern philosophy—*the existence of the One, Absolute, Transcendental Reality, its dual Aspect* in the conditioned Universe, and the illusion, or *relativity*, of whatever is manifested.

Only through comparison of this duality, or pairs of opposites, are the sparks of knowledge struck, and perfectment, or evolution, becomes possible. Eternal motion, or evolution, creates the *relativity* of all concepts. Thus, perception of reality can be achieved only through perpetual change and the comparison of pairs of opposites.

The action of opposites creates harmony similar to centrifugal and centripetal forces, which, being interdependent, are necessary for each other in order that *both of them may exist. If one were to cease to exist, the action of the other would immediately become destructive.* Precisely, the manifested world *is kept in balance by the opposing forces.* These counterforces, or pairs of opposites, acquire this or that color, or quality, in our consciousness, in other words, they become either good or evil. On each plane of manifestation the degree of evil and good is determined by the consciousness of man, in accordance with the degree of his development. What is good on the lower plane may appear as evil on a higher one and vice versa. Hence, the *relativity* of all concepts in the manifested world.

Thus, when we shall realize that the concepts of evil and good in their cosmic aspect are relative, then, of course the existence of Satan as the focus of self-sufficient evil on a cosmic scale will fall by itself, or be overthrown.

But it is equally certain that the image of Satan as a fallen angel and the Host of our Earth (therefore of human substance) does exist, to the misfortune of our planet, and, alas, he is very active.

In the esoteric Teachings of the East it is indicated that Lucifer came to our Earth together with the other High Spirits who sacrificed themselves for the acceleration of the evolution of the planet and its humanity. But Lucifer was not the highest among his Brethren, and when the time came for him to take on the earthly and dense sheaths, his spirit could not remain on its former height. Beginning with the early times of Atlantis his downfall had already started. And in all the following ages we see him as the fierce antagonist of his great Brothers, who were continuously ascending in the glory of Light. The Hindu epics immortalized the Fallen One in many images, the best known among these being that of King Ravana of the island of Lanka (Ceylon), who was the adversary of the godlike King Rama; and the abductor of his wife, Sita. The very fact that the spirit of the Fallen Angel in the potential of the kernel of the spirit bore energies that are akin to our Earth was actually fatal for him, for through this he was particularly attached to Earth. We know that each immersion, or incarnation, in a dense sheath inevitably obscures the knowledge of the spirit. How much more intensified was such obscuration, due to the imperfection of these sheaths during the final days of Atlantis when the full involution of the spirit into matter was completed! Only the Highest Spirits who came from the higher planets and whose spiritual potentiality is subject to the higher attraction have preserved their Light unobscured during their entire earthly path. Now you will understand the dimensions of the Great Sacrifice that was, and is still being made by these true Saviors of humanity. They swore to undergo the battle with the hierophant of evil and to remain with suffering humanity on Earth to the very end of its existence. Do reread *On Eastern Crossroads* and everything that I have already written you about Lucifer.

Lucifer is now at the head of the Black Brotherhood, which is very powerful, for it has co-workers among the masses over the entire span of the planet. Indeed, the dark forces always act through masses; in single combat they are not strong. Likewise, they are distinguished by greater unity than the co-workers of the Forces of Light, for the realization of danger is at times the best unifier. Unfortunately, many "glow-worms" do not believe in the forces of darkness and present a sad spectacle of disjointed units and lukewarm ones about whom the Apocalypse speaks so sternly. Yes, not numerous are the armies of Light on Earth, but in spite of that, with the help of the Higher Knowledge of the Hierarchy of Light, the final victory will always be on the side of the Forces of Good.

Thus, the ignoramuses laugh at the existence of Satan and, by that very fact, they confirm the correctness of the words of one subtle thinker, "The victory of the devil lies in his ability to convince people that he does not exist."

Certainly, when we do not believe in or deny something, we cease to be wary of it and easily fall into the snares set by the numerous agents of darkness. It is indeed very sad that during long centuries the most ignorant and extremely dangerous belief was inrooted that Satan ruined humanity by giving it the knowledge of good and evil. People habitually repeat this shocking absurdity and do not care to ponder at all what kind of man would be one who did not know the difference between good and evil. Would he not simply remain an irresponsible animal? What human being would agree to revert to such an animal-like existence, even if it were in the garden of paradise? The great gift of discrimination, and therefore of free will, is a divine gift, and only by possessing it can man become the image of God. Therefore, such a gift *could not* be brought by the forces of darkness, but was a sacrificial offering to man by the Forces of Light. That explains the original name of this Messenger, which was Lucifer, the Light-Bringer. But during the ages the great meaning of this legend was lost in the West, and remained only in the Sacred Teachings of the East.

In the Sacred Teaching there is an explanation clarifying this meaning. "Thus 'SATAN,' once he ceases to be viewed in the superstitious, dogmatic, unphilosophical spirit of the Churches, grows into the grandiose image of one who made of *terrestrial* a divine MAN; who gave him, throughout the long cycle of Mahakalpa, the law of the Spirit of Life, and made him free from the Sin of Ignorance, hence of death."

Actually, such a "Satan," as you already know, is the *combination* of those High Spirits, who, together with the Fallen Angel brought to humanity the light of intelligence and the great gift of immortality. Therefore, it is precisely They who should have been called the "Light-Bringers," or Lucifers. The Fallen Angel *lost his right to this name.*

Here are a few remarks about the life after death, which will answer your question.

To those who claim that "No one ever came from the other world and that nobody is able to look in there," one should answer that this statement is not correct, for it *does not* correspond to truth.

Using the language of a good Christian one could tell such an objector that by his statement he actually denies the testimony of Christ himself. Indeed, Christianity was confirmed chiefly by the posthumous appearances of Christ to his disciples.

Not a single intelligent or enlightened persona nowadays would doubt that Christ was resurrected, not in his physical body, but in the subtle body, or the body of Light. Does not the Apostle Paul confirm this by his numerous statements that "this corruptible must put on incorruption," or we do not die but change, etc. Also it is emphasized in the Gospels that Christ during his appearances after his death on the Cross and his resurrection would usually become suddenly visible and just as suddenly disappear. Precisely, these sudden appearances and disappearances (which are now scientifically established) are so characteristic of the temporary materialization of the subtle body. In the Gnostic literature one comes across indications that precisely during such appearances Christ transmitted to his disciples the mysteries of the other world.

We can advise all those who wish to come nearer to the supermundane manifestations to get acquainted with the vast literature of all centuries and nations in which the world beyond is discussed. Indeed, the majority of people do not even suspect what an enormous quantity of works on these subjects is in the world! The world was never without those who were able to see, who, having a more perfected organism, were able to perceive what is concealed from the gross physical eye. Who would dare to declare today that, only because he does not see the X- or Y-rays or does not hear the sounds which fill space, let us say, radio waves, all this does not exist? Who would care to put upon himself a label of ignorance by such statements? Science has already discovered rays that can make the physical man invisible. Who would want to assert that in the future it would not be possible to discover an apparatus that would help to look into the world beyond just as simply as we see and hear a man on television, even thought he is separated from us by thousands of miles? Why are people so anxious to limit all possibilities and, above all, themselves? If already today some children are born who can see through the densest matter with their physical sight (which has been proven many times), why, then, should we not believe those who are also able to see the Subtle World with their physical sight? This limitation of the admissible, or lack of imagination, must be outlived, for otherwise *no advance in knowledge is possible.*

And now, returning to the good Christians, one has to say again that there are the ones who should be particularly careful in denying the existence of a world beyond. Are not the lives of the revered saints full of descriptions of all kinds of manifestations and visitations by the denizens of the Subtle World, or the World of Light?

It is most comforting that nowadays in all the civilized countries there is so much interest in the study of questions linked with so-called "supernatural" manifestations. England, America, France, Sweden have established at the universities chairs for research in psychic manifestations. Many scientists pay the most serious attention to these questions. Indeed, in almost all countries of Europe and America Societies for Psychic Research were established long ago, and the results achieved by them show a great scientific interest. Even in Italy, this citadel of Catholicism, such research is now permitted. Thus, the most popular newspaper in Bologna dedicates a daily column to acquainting its readers with activities and successes in the study of all possible parapsychic and posthumous manifestations. In the same newspaper Dr. Stopolini relates his talk with an eminent representative of the Catholic Church, regarding the attitude of the Church toward such types of research and spiritualism, which is widespread in the West. The clergyman said that the Catholic Church is a zealous guardian of its great traditions, but by no means does it forbid certain experiments when they are performed by educated and competent persons for the purpose of research; however it systematically forbids them when participated in by ignorant and irresponsible people who care only to satisfy their curiosity and are not able to discriminate in the *quality* of such manifestations.

We must admit that the remark of this clergyman is most sensible, and one can only wish that the rest of his colleagues would join him in his broad outlook with regard to these questions.

And as for reincarnation, there are sufficient indications about it in the Gospel. They are well chosen by Annie Besant in her book *Esoteric Christianity*. The law of reincarnation is the foundation of all true teachings. If we reject it, the whole sense of our earthly existence will fall away of its own accord. Besides, who can explain satisfactorily all the cruel injustice of the fact that one is born handsome, rich, and happy, whereas another must drag through a pitiful life, often as a cripple, or struggle all this life against the most cruel injustices and calamities? Today, the newspapers and magazines, especially those in English, are filled with all kinds of cases from the realm of the so-called supernatural, or the other world. It is rare when a newspaper does not mention one or another remarkable case, which is substantiated by plenty of witnesses.

And so, we may affirm that when so many scientists are now taking serious interest in everything connected with the realm of psychic manifestations, we may witness great discoveries in the nearest future. Thus, in America alone there are about forty professors who are occupied at present with the study of telepathy. Yet quite recently the initiator of these experiments, Prof. McDougall, was ridiculed by his colleagues and even deprived of his chair at the university.

The irrefragable proofs of the actuality of the other world and the life in it exists in great quantities and are available to many, but the trouble is that the broad masses are very badly informed about this. Besides, the atavism of the Middle Ages still makes many people fear the horns of the devil in every manifestation that is not understandable to them. Likewise, the fires of the Inquisition are still very fresh in the memory of many who suffered from them. Hence, there may be fear in connection with these matters.

I am enclosing a translation of a curious article from an English newspaper of January 15th in Lahore: 'An account was recently made public by the Commission that was appointed by the Archbishop of Canterbury and York in 1922 for the discussion of the Christian doctrine. Its purpose was to find out to what an extent the representatives of the Church of England are in agreement with each other, and also to study what could be done to lessen or eliminate some of the disagreements.

"The Commission is against some of the points concerning traditional beliefs and rejects the infallibility of the Bible, claiming that its authority must not be used to prejudge investigations in any sphere.

"The Commission considers the historical statement regarding the Immaculate Conception to be unconvincing, and declares that belief in the physical resurrection of the dead must be discarded.

"On the other hand, the Commission declares that the resurrection of Christ was just as real and concrete an event as was his crucifixion. [?!]

"The Commission is divided in its opinion on the possibility of miracles, but it agrees that God can perform miracles if he chooses to do so.

"Likewise, it affirms that there can be no opposition to the theory of evolution, which can be based upon the theory of the creation of the world as expounded in the Book of Genesis. All educated Christians agree that these statements must be looked upon as mythological in their origin, and therefore their significance for us is symbolical rather than historical." As you can see, the logic of these resolutions is most unusual.

I hope that you will be able to utilize something from the above. It really is difficult even to imagine the torrent of books dealing with life in the Subtle World that inundates the book markets in England and America.

In England, books on this subject written by the clergyman, G. Vale Owen, were very popular. These books were dictated by the spirits. Two or three volumes of this series of communications, "Life Beyond the Veil," are in my possession, and I must say that they deserve attention. There is no doubt that these books were given under the supervision of the White Brotherhood. The Great Teachers use many methods for awakening the consciousness of humanity. Every group receives, according to its consciousness, what it can assimilate and what is closest to it.

35

11 December 1937

With pain in my heart I read the sad news about the accident of your friend. Verily, such a death is dreadful for the family. However, it may even have been a blessing for him. Especially illumined souls who become victims of any accident pass into the Subtle World with unusual ease. The Guardians of Light put them into a revivifying sleep so that the subtle body may have time to recover from injuries; and by the time they wake up they find themselves already cared for by friends.

As for the malicious and ignorant gossip that will no doubt take place because of this case, it seems to me that this circumstance should not disturb anyone who is devoted to the Teaching of Life. Many dreadful and unfortunate accidents also happen to slanderers and their kind. How do these evil-minded, blind people explain them?

Indeed, to all those who rise and blaspheme against the purification of the foundations of the one Teaching of Light, it should be said again and again: "Did you not crucify Christ? Did you not mock Him when He brought you the Light of Truth? Did you not persecute and burn His followers? Did you not torture tens of thousands of the best minds which were bearers of the light of knowledge? Did you not arrest the evolution of human thought, and thus cast humanity into the madness of self destruction? Did you not rise in the time of Christ as you also do now, purportedly defending the distorted foundations of the one Teaching of Light? You have changed your garments, but you can be recognized by your deeds!"

At last I found the brochure written by H.S. Olcott in which he discusses the means that were used by the representatives of the Church for choosing and affirming the canonical Gospels.

While analyzing the legendary character of the biographies of all the great Teachers and Reformers, Olcott proves that all these biographies were built according to one most ancient pattern. As an example, he cites the myths that illustrate the life of Christ and also the means by which these myths were asserted in the Christian church. Of course, the thought expressed by him is not new, for many of the most eminent historians were of the same opinion. We find the very same statements in the *Secret Doctrine*.

Here is a quotation for you: "The life of Christ had reached the apogee of a myth toward the time of the Nicean Council, which was convoked to solve the arguments amongst some bishops, and to examine, with the idea of canonizing, three hundred more or less apocryphal Gospels which were being read in the churches as revelation, or inspired Scriptures.

"We can see samples of some of these in the existing apocryphal New Testament, but the majority of them have disappeared by now. Whatever is preserved of the true cannon, undoubtedly can be considered as the least prejudiced. However, even such a conclusion must not be accepted hastily, since, as you may know, Sabinus, the bishop of Heraclea, (who personally appeared at the Council of Nicea), affirms that 'except Constantine ... and Eusebius Pamphilus, these bishops were a set illiterate, simple creatures that understood nothing'; which is equivalent to saying that they were a set of fools. ... Pappus tells us of the bit of magic resorted to decide which were the true gospels. In his *Synodicon* to that Council Pappas says 'having promiscuously put all the books that were referred to the Council for determination under a communion-table in a church, they (the bishops) besought the Lord that the inspired writings might get upon the table, while the spurious ones remained underneath, and it happened accordingly.'"

I am including a Discourse dedicated to the Day of the Universal Festival. Please read it to the nearest friends.

"You know how We appreciate the feeling of solemnity. Indeed, solemnity creates constancy in upward striving. And this feeling flourishes especially during the days commemorating the Great Heroes. It is especially significant that humanity reveres Our Brothers under different names. Many books may be found dedicated to the reverence of Our Brotherhood. Yet people think that their heroes have nothing in common with Us. But the most revered ones, those who were practically deified as giants of humanity, were not They the actual founders of Our Brotherhood? Let us not forget that They appeared on Earth under a special Ray, and that is why Their birth was associated with certain legends. We should not obliterate these narratives, for they heighten solemnity and help to assimilate the Great Images. We do not correct the dates which were established conditionally. As for ourselves, We send benevolent thoughts for the Festival of Humanity. Solemnity should not be violated when we know what great achievement is connected with this Memorial Day.

"People do not know even one hundredth part of the significance of the deeds of the Great Teachers. People have reduced the most beautiful sacrifices to something common and self-seeking. But even while belittling, people preserve a fraction of solemnity. Let us, with utmost patience, help to maintain at least the embryo of the beautiful feeling of solemnity. This feeling transforms life and produces heroes. Thus, let us accompany the memorial days with some unusual achievement. Service is expressed in a great deed which can be performed in any human state. The manifestation of an achievement is a joy to Us. We indicate the path, but one must walk by human feet—such is the law, which was given by the Great Savior.

"The manifested achievement is sealed in our Treasuries. The ignorant attempt to turn reality into mirage, but fortunately we preserve the proofs of Great Achievements. Thus, let us dedicate the Great Day to an unusual achievements."

36

1937

It is right to be aware of actions, for in every action there is a foundation for a new possibility. The proverb, "Water does not flow underneath an immovable stone" well expresses the occult truth, "Motion is life; its cessation, death." Psychic, or life-giving energy develops and grows only through being constantly and rhythmically applied, but spasmodic manifestations of it lead nowhere and can even be injurious. That explains why busy and active people are so enduring and long-lived. Therefore, we should not be afraid of being over-burdened but, rather, we should try to maintain a certain rhythm and acquire calmness in all our actions. Cooperation will considerably lighten the accepted load. You know in what progression the strength of harmonious energies increases. *Brotherhood* just came out. May this book, which speaks about lofty brotherly unity, not remain on the shelf as a dead load. When the inevitable meeting with the Great Teacher takes place, shall we be able to look into his eyes if we fail to fulfill the fundamental covenant regarding Unity?

We know that the non-fulfillment of the Teacher's Counsels acts as a reverse blow. This blow cannot be immediately felt, because the results of great actions are not at once evident. In ancient times this law of karma was well understood, but nowadays the majority are deaf and blind to all cosmic laws.

I would also ask you to collect all the most valuable data on psychic energy, that are so generously strewn in the books of the Teaching. Indeed, the realization of psychic energy should build a powerful step in the evolution of the world. It is actually psychic energy, which, under different names, knocks at all gates. Psychic energy creates the New Epoch, and already many of the best scientists confirm what has been said in the books of the Teaching. At the moment I have before me a review of a most interesting work in French, *How to Achieve Immortality* by the biologist and physicist, Georges Lakhovsky. This book so fully conforms to all that is said in the books of Living Ethics that I would like to quote for you a few extracts from this scientific work. Thus, Mr. Lakhovsky indicates that for the achievement of immortality three rules should be observed: (1) one must believe in longevity, that is believe in the possibility of reaching a great age; (2) one should avoid anger, malice, envy, jealousy, and irritability, and on the other hand one should develop kindly feelings and a good disposition, which is necessary to sustain not only moral but also physical equilibrium; (3) one must not fear death, but believe in immortality. Fear of death shortens our life. Our existence depends on the circulation of the blood, which enables the various areas of our body to receive the necessary materials, especially oxygen. It is known that many blood vessels may contract under the influence of purely psychic experiences, as a result of which the circulation is disturbed and the blood rushes toward some parts of the body and flows away from others. A person who is given to feelings of anger, jealousy and envy constantly disturbs his circulation, which in time produces strong changes in the organism leading to disease and death. Indeed, during a powerful psychic reaction the delicate blood vessels may burst, which might result in dangerous and even deadly hemorrhages. Hence his advice—do not be angry, do not be jealous, do not be envious, but be good and OPTIMISTIC, and then you will live to a very old age.

After expounding the physiology of anger he describes remarkably well *the electrical manifestations in the organism, which are its life-givers.* During anger and other negative emotions, which not only cause the contraction of the blood vessels but also paralysis of the individual nerves, these electric currents (psychic energy), which flow through them form the sympathetic nervous system, break, and thus "the electric nourishment" of the glands producing the internal secretions (on whose normal activity depends the life of the organism) ceases, and the latter fail to work as is necessary for our health.

In our cellular substance that surrounds the nucleus, there are chromosomes and so-called chondriosomes. These elements are, according to their properties, the receptors of various electric waves, as it were, which come partly from the depths of Cosmic Space and, of course, they vibrate mainly upon our psychic energy. The whole life of the organism, according to Lakhovsky, depends upon the vibrations of these chromosomes and chondriosomes, the receivers of the electric waves. The retardation or cessation of the electric vibrations that go through them signifies disease and death.

Thus, *the moral Teachings acquire a completely unexpected biological foundation.* And the significance of psychic energy, which is basically Fohatic, is thus affirmed. Fohat, as we know, is cosmic electricity, or the Primary Energy, which reveals itself in various stages on the plane of manifestation. Now you will also understand how beneficial are the vibrations that are sent by the Great Teacher during an illness. There is hardly a night when I do not experience these healing vibrations of various degrees of tension and duration.

Lately, science has very closely approached the most profound occult discoveries in the realm of subtle energies. Therefore you may declare firmly and calmly before everyone your knowledge of the reactions of psychic energy, which so obviously manifests itself in the transmission of thought at a distance and also in the increase of the vibrations that can be recorded by a very sensitive apparatus during intensive mental work. We are studying psychic and parapsychic manifestations in which all the best and foremost scientists are at present interested. We can also assert our knowledge of the existence of the Stronghold of Knowledge, or the Brotherhood of the Mahatmas—these Elder Brothers of humanity, who have dedicated themselves to the great knowledge in the name of the Common Good, and who watch the evolution of the world. All the great discoveries, all the great ideas invariably issued, and are issuing from this Source of Knowledge and Light. Professor Hurley says, "There must exist advanced Beings in the Cosmos, whose minds are just as superior to ours as ours are superior to the intelligence of an ordinary beetle. These Beings take an active part in governing the evolutionary processes of nature."

Thus, if someone is ignorant of the existence of this Beacon Light of humanity, we can only feel sorry for him and advise him to become acquainted as quickly as possible with the enormous literary material encompassing thousands of years, in which are recorded innumerable facts and proofs about this Stronghold of Knowledge, not beyond the clouds but here on our Earth.

Therefore, if some ignoramus is proud that he is not receiving indications "from beyond the clouds," this does not mean that the loftiest, the most valuable indications are not transmitted by a method as yet inaccessible to such a representative of the limited consciousness. As a matter of fact, the sacred scriptures of all peoples present us with indisputable facts indicating that all the religions, not excluding the latest one—Christianity—were founded precisely on a Revelation which came "from beyond the clouds." All these inert, haughty people should be advised to increase their knowledge. We completely believe, or rather, know about the means of communicating with the supermundane world, yet we also emphasize the possibility of receiving indications, not "from beyond the clouds" from some sort of heaven-dwellers, but precisely from the Mahatmas, the Great Teachers, who are in physical bodies and have a definite place on Earth. That is why we are so interested in all the experiments with thought-transmission at a distance, which occupy about forty professors, headed by Professor Rhine, in America alone, not to mention other, European scientists. The great Plato said, "Thoughts rule the world."

Our contemporary, Professor Compton, expressing the hypothesis that there must be an active intelligent force behind each phenomenon of nature, and that thought influences matter, concludes one of his books with the following remarkable words, "It is possible that the thoughts of man are the most important factor in the world."

And, thus, starting with the influence of the ideology of thought, we arrive at the understanding of the mechanics of thought. Therefore, do collect wherever possible facts and scientific proofs relating to the psychic realm and to the ever-growing interest in this subject.

There is at present a little girl in Latvia who is under observation by a committee composed of several physicians. This girl can read the thoughts not only of her mother but also of strangers. Friends have sent me a book about this phenomenon written in German by one of the physicians who is observing this girl. We are interested in all the results achieved by individual scientists, as well as by the societies for the study of parapsychic manifestations in America and Europe. The experiments of European physicians with radioesthesia are also quite interesting.

In this age of the expansion of thought and of new amazing discoveries bordering on the world of nuomena and of ever-increasing speed in the transmission of communications it is preposterous to hear about negation and limitation of the possibilities hidden in the Infinite.

Part IV

1938

1

25 January 1938

You probably already know that I do not like the word *occultism*. This word is stigmatized by the narrow-minded attitude toward it and sets one's teeth on edge, so to say. I realize that it is difficult to withdraw it everywhere, but wherever possible I would try to avoid this term of yesterday. Secret Teaching, Sacred Knowledge, or even Secret Knowledge already sounds better. Actually, the present task is to propel the consciousness of people toward new approaches, toward a new horizon, to the future with its new discoveries, which also demand new designations. Therefore I would like to emphasize still more strongly that the path of self-denying, active achievement will consist in adhering to the cognition of the secrets of nature, which are primarily contained in man himself, who is a synthesis of all its kingdoms. This cognition will inevitably lead to a new attitude toward the whole order of life, toward all being. And the covenants of all the Teachings of Life, or Living Ethics, will acquire an invincible value.

Likewise, is it not better, wherever the form of exposition permits, to bring in a more generalized understanding of the Divine Origin? I would have preferred to avoid ecclesiastical expressions wherever the Great Principle is meant. Concepts of will and covenant are always linked with personality and, therefore, not to be connected with the presentation of the All-inclusive Principle. It seems to me that it would be far better to replace these concepts with *cosmic law*.

I have read the chapters about the church councils. Apparently I am quite dull, because I cannot understand why the word *consubstantial* seemed to be less acceptable than "the only begotten"? If the second term is accepted, so much the more should the first one be. Each son is consubstantial with his father. Apparently, the Greek equivalent of this word has still another special meaning. But indeed I do not consider myself sufficiently competent to be discussing all these puzzles of the theologians. I believe it to be a useless waste of time. The Covenants of Christ have a far greater significance than His origin.

Did you get the book by White *The Warfare of Science with Theology*? Although it was published in a greatly abridged fashion, nevertheless it contains most valuable material, which is more convincing than theological controversies.

Here I will quote to you from *Dobrotolubye*, Volume I the prognosis of Anthony the Great about the state of monasticism in the not too distant future.

"26. At another time St. Anthony disclosed to his disciples that because of the lessening of zeal, monasticism will become weakened and its glory will grow dim. Some of his disciples seeing a great number of monks in the desert, adorned with many virtues and zealously advising the emulation of the holy life in a hermitage, asked St. Anthony, 'Father, how long will this zeal and fervor last, and this love for seclusion, poverty, humility, abstinence, and all other virtues for which this multitude of monks are so assiduously striving?' The man of God answered with sighs and tears: 'The time is coming, my beloved children, when the monks will leave the deserts and will begin to flow into rich cities, where, instead of these desert caves and narrow cells, they will erect proud structures that could vie with the palaces of kings; together with this will grow love for the accumulation of riches; humility will be replaced by pride; many of them will take pride in their knowledge, but an empty one, alien to good deeds, which alone accompany true knowledge; love will grow cold; instead of abstinence gluttony will increase, and many of them will care for sumptuous foods no less than the laymen, from whom monks will no longer differ either in garb or in headgear; and although they will live a worldly life, they will call themselves hermits.' (A monk is actually one living in solitude.) 'Besides, they will call themselves by patronymic names, stating, "I am of Paul; and I of Apollos" (I Corinthians 1:12), as if the power of their monasticism were in the merit of their forefathers; they will glorify themselves through their fathers, just as the Jews do through their father Abraham. But there will also be those who will be much better and more perfect than we, for he is blessed who could transgress and did not, could do evil and did not, rather than he who is attracted to the good by the multitude of zealots aspiring toward it. This is why Noah, Abraham, and Lot, who led such exemplary lives amidst evil people, are so justly glorified in the Scriptures.'"

Yes, the most difficult is to wash clean the body of Christ. And the most senseless and corrupt manifestation is contained in the affirmation of certain representatives of the Church that "they are not terrified by the deniers of truth, but by the Theosophists and any occultists who wish to present Christ in their own way. And they will fight them with any and all means, until death." You sense what is hidden under this affirmation. One is frightened at this revival of medieval intolerance. At its basis lie chiefly the very same motives which created the Inquisition, this apotheosis of human ignorance and greed.

At the same time, we read in the American papers that due to the Christmas holidays, the American judicial authorities decreed that forty clergymen, who were in jail for various misdemeanors, were permitted to go home for twenty-four hours to spend the holiday with their families. Only one clergyman, who was accused of a grave crime, was not granted this permission.

There are not a few criminals among the clergymen the world over. And how many take on the office of priest only for the sake of providing a secure livelihood!

But a new consciousness is coming to replace the old one, and it will accept the Covenants of Christ and all His Great Brothers in the light of a new understanding.

The New world carries on its banner—Knowledge, Tolerance, and Cooperation.

2

29 January 1938

In attempting to expound the foundations of the Universe, we should remember the limitlessness of knowledge and, consequently, the mystery that upholds the world. Therefore, as you probably have already noticed, I am always trying to somewhat soften assertions which are too categorical when they touch upon the most mystical and profound bases of Being.

When speaking about the Universe, it is customary to oppose spirit to matter, as such. But basically such contradistinctions are incorrect and appear as a sort of Maya or Illusion. We know of One Element, which is called Spirit-Matter. Eastern philosophy asserts that Parabrahman has no manifestation outside of the veil of Mulaprakriti, or that Spirit without matter is naught. An example of a piece of ice (dense matter) which dissolves into water (a fine state of matter) and which finally is converted into steam (spirit) illustrates excellently the correlation of spirit and matter. Therefore I would say that all that exists is composed of various combinations of differentiations of the One element—Spirit-Matter. Thus, Spirit is above, and under it are all degrees of matter. Verily, spirit is the consummation of Matter.

Therefore, one should have in mind that there is no matter which does not have the presence of spirit in it in some qualifying manifestation. For, wherever there is any manifestation, there is life, or spirit. I know that it is usually customary to define matter as passive, chaotic, and inanimate, but all of these definitions are not explicit.

Primary Matter or *Materia Matrix*, which lies at the foundation of the Universe, being the primordial conductor, or carrier, of spirit, cannot be chaotic or inanimate; only its lower stages acquire the quality of a chaotic state.

Materia Lucida, one of the successive stages of matter more or less known to us, is resplendently beautiful and possesses the property of plasticity to a high degree.

Also, one should not call Spirit, Absolute Mind, regarding it in contradistinction to Matter, because only by crystallizing into matter or flowing into it does the spirit reveal its potentiality and accumulate reason through contact with the world of forms. Spirit is consciousness, but Cosmic Mind is the collective reason of the entire manifested Universe. We have the Crown of the Cosmic Mind in the Hierarchy of Light, or in the Logoi.

The Element—Spirit-Matter—actually contains the entire manifested Universe, therefore one should not say that on one side is spirit and on the other, primary matter. Verily, they are one, and only various degrees of the differentiation of this Element in its combinations can, and do give all the diversity of the manifest and visible Cosmos.

I realize that it is impossible to altogether avoid opposites, because the coarse physical manifestations are so immeasurably removed from their origins. Besides, precisely while comparing pairs of opposites, we lay the first steps of knowledge; and upon the next steps we already learn to combine these opposites.

Are you surprised by the expression "negative abstraction"? But if we would remember that the Mahatmas called spirit without the veil of matter, *nihil*, or that the Vedantists, in defining the Primary Cause of Being found nothing but negation and called it Causeless Cause, or Rootless Root, or simply

Neti, Neti (not That, not That), then the term "negative abstraction" will be acceptable.

There is no Divinity outside the Universe. Therefore the expression "the aspect of Divinity and Universe" may cause confusion.

In your quotation from a lecture on *The Secret Doctrine* there is an inaccuracy. The lecturer may not have been aware of it. Thus, he says that "the atoms are qualitatively alike and have no individuality." This is not quite so, the essence of the atoms is one, but they differ qualitatively. This difference can be noted in their vibrations. Every atom responds to the vibration akin to it. Since each of them has its own definite vibration, *it means that they do* possess an embryo of individuality.

* * *

Our solar system is composed of a greater number of planets than is now known to science. It is true, several of them are still in the process of formation. Although Uranus and Neptune belong to the higher attractions, yet one should regard them as members of our solar system; and these two planets have tremendous influence upon our planet and, indeed, upon the entire solar system. The influence of Uranus will be manifested with particular vividness in the coming era.

Human evolution is regarded as the crown of the Universe, but we know that the earthly man is still very crude in his form and tissues when compared with, let us say, the dwellers of Jupiter and Venus.

* * *

The full annihilation of personality alone is possible, but not of the individuality that partially manifests as this personality. At the completion of one of the Manvantaras, during the scrutiny of the Book of Lives of each individuality, there will be absent from such books whole pages (earthly incarnation) in which the individuality could not, through its partial manifestation as a personality, gather the harvest of the higher energies which nurture it.

* * *

I understand the despair that grips one during the reading of *The Secret Doctrine*. Yet this stage of facing the Greatness of

Cosmos is unavoidable. The time will come when despair will be replaced by joy in contemplation of the majestic and eternal phantasmagoria of Infinite Be-ness.

For facilitation I would strongly advise you to copy from *The Secret Doctrine* only those places that contain the occult, or sacred Teaching. You will see that a great deal will become clear. The profusion of diverse material, collected for confirmation of this or that proposition, sometimes obscures the basic thought. Try at first to underscore only such places.

One must also understand that Space presents in itself an ocean of Fire, and its fiery sparks form numberless monads.

3

11 February 1938

To be able to find joy in thinking about the dear one who has crossed into the better world is in itself a big spiritual attainment. Verily, one may rejoice when the spirit passes over into the Subtle World having become cognizant beforehand of the striving toward the Hierarchy of Light. Such a spirit receives support from the Great Teacher, continues his study and associates himself with that work which is closest to his spirit. All earthly bonds, spiritual and of the heart are not only preserved in the Subtle World, but even grow more and become more refined. And your calmness and joy, in a large measure, arise because during the night hours your spirit dwells in full communion with the one dear to you. Luminous, joyous striving thoughts do not burden the one who crossed over, but, on the contrary, such fluids strengthen him and his striving toward the Common Good. Therefore, rejoice at the possibilities opened before O. V., and grow your own wings so that your crossing can be equally joyous and beautiful. If people knew the truth, if they could convince themselves that the moment of death is a moment of greatest bliss for a luminous and striving spirit, the fear of death would forever leave them.

Also, do not be disturbed because you have to work a great deal in order to support yourself materially. But one should not get over-tired, therefore I strongly advise you to avoid especially heavy work. Devote the hours of rest to the Teaching, and whenever possible attempt to sow good seeds, always speaking on the level of your companion's consciousness and not forgetting the canon "By thy God." It will be excellent for you to extract themes from the Teaching, but do it meticulously, without omissions, out of all the books, *in strict sequence*. I can also offer you one more task, extremely useful. It is absolutely essential to compile a complete index, or as it is called, a concordance of all the books of the Teaching. Indeed, this is a self-denying labor, demanding a great deal of patience and exactness, and it seems to me you could carry it out excellently. I was informed that one of the members of the Society has made an index to the books of the Teaching, but I do not know if it was done for all the books; besides, I do not know whether that index compiled by him was all-encompassing and whether it represented what is called a concordance. Precisely, when not only one word alone is mentioned that is to be found on certain pages but also all its combinations, i.e. the two or three words following it indicating a new combination. Ponder on this dedicated labor and acquaint yourself with the technique of such work. Of course, this work can be shared by several co-workers.

I am also very glad to hear that you have taken upon yourself the duty of attendance of a day at the Museum. One could invite groups from the educational institutions and schools, and give them brief explanations and biographical data about the artist and about the significance of art as the most powerful factor in the spiritual development of mankind.

We were informed that soon a Women's Section will start its activities at the society. Of course, I realize that if you have not familiarized yourself with the local language, your direct activity will have to be somewhat limited. But you can give useful advice or support a desirable measure. Therefore, observe this section, but if you see that it is difficult for you or does not respond to your inclination, do not force yourself. Choose what is closer to you. But visit the society often. I value a great deal the fact that you like our R. Y., the presence of a friendly aura in the society is especially beneficial. We greatly strive to establish unity among all co-workers, and value most of all those who understand the significance of this lofty covenant, the one and only bulwark of every structure, particularly a spiritual one. Often, those who have read all the books of the Teaching, nevertheless cannot realize that without an understanding of sustaining unity among members no spiritual progress is possible. Many understand unity as acceptance by all co-workers of their opinion only, and cannot find enough generosity within themselves to make a concession. Yes, nothing is more difficult to learn than cooperation. And yet, the new step of evolution insistently demands the establishment of such cooperation. All fields of science, all kinds of labor, owing to their ever-growing complexity, have already passed the bounds of single efforts, and the cooperation of many workers is needed in order to achieve new and urgent tasks. Therefore I offer you one more highly useful activity which you can practice precisely in daily life. Support cooperation and instill peace.

* * *

Combine physical labor in full measure with spiritual labor, and your spiritual joy will multiply.

All Great Teachers labored much, and physical labor was not alien to them. Remember St. Sergius. Christ also labored much; He earned his living by carpentry and pottery. This side of the life of the Great Teacher is practically unnoted in the authorized Scriptures, but it has been preserved in the Apocrypha and, of course, in the esoteric records. Eventually there will be found more Apocrypha closer to His time.

Thus, labor, but do not overtire yourself. All Great Teachers spoke similarly about the Middle Path. All extremes, which react harmfully upon our health, must be abandoned. We must safeguard our instrument, because its condition is reflected upon our spirit and can considerably suppress its manifestations. We can ascend only with an unburdened spirit. Therefore be careful and forgo such heavy work as shoveling snow, etc.

And now I wish to say to you—have faith in the New World. A powerful rock is rising amidst chaos. The Forces of Light are guarding it. But people who see from a narrow-minded point of view, who cannot leave off the rut of old thinking and therefore cannot understand the span of the current shifting, cannot understand the searchings and ponderings that now fill the best hearts. Ivan, in hundreds of thousands, has awakened, the shifting of the consciousness of the people is vast, and in spite of all difficulties the country of the future is growing and beginning to understand its destiny.

I have faith in our motherland, and I not only believe but know that the achievement facing us is difficult, yet it is joyous to realize that we can sow seeds which will give the richest harvest. At present the whole world is passing through thrice difficult days, and it was indicated to read in the Apocalypse the first verse, chapter 21—"And I saw a new heaven and a new earth." So it is, and with the old consciousness one cannot enter the New World.

If you have questions, I will be glad to discuss them with you.

The dark forces proceed in a united front, hounded by fear of their approaching weakening. The year 1942 marks the end of the Black Age; our planet will enter a new, better epoch. Although the effects of the Black Age will still tag along, the bright sowings already begin to produce sprouts under the beneficial rays of new combinations of the luminaries; and the sowers of darkness will begin to suffer defeat. At present, these sowers are reinforced by heavy cosmic currents throughout the whole world. This is why it is so essential for all those who know about the extraordinary moment to guard unity, because it will defend them from many attacks. Unity is the best shield for the health.

Accept with your heart my best wishes and preserve the joy of the possibility of spiritual and physical work.

4

8 March 1938

Trust is one of the rare qualities, and it lies in the foundation of every construction. Without trust there can be no progress or development. Therefore, you are blessed if this rare quality has already become your possession. Guard it and deepen it through your heart's discernment.

I read with interest about the preparatory path which brought you to the acceptance of the Teaching of Life. It is truly good to pass through the preparatory classes and convince oneself of the extent to which the evolution of thought and the complexities of life have outrun the congealed formulas of our established church dogma.

Now to your questions. You write that in the *Chalice of the East* one is advised not to risk one's life for the salvation of one's neighbor. To my regret I cannot now find this place, but apparently this assertion was made in connection with some specific case.

On the basis of the Teaching of Life given to us, I will say that in everything co-measurement must be shown, in other words, goal-fitness, which reigns in the entire Universe. Everything should be adopted from the point of view of the Common Good, or benefit for all humanity.

Let us imagine that a man who bears the responsibility for the destiny of an entire country and nation (the ruler or a commander-in-chief) rushes to save a man (often unworthy) and thus perishes himself. Will such an act be commensurate or goal-fitting? Could one put on the scale the destiny of a whole country against the life of one man, or even of many? Yet the sentimentality that never sacrifices itself will indeed be the first to shout that in any and all cases man must, without any deliberation, sacrifice himself.

I recall a case told to me: In an American school a teacher suggested discussing the following topic: A factory owner—a great benefactor—walked on a road; in front of him walked, reeling, a drunken beggar; suddenly, from around a corner came a car and ran over the drunkard. The question was, Should the factory owner have rushed to save the beggar and risked his own life, or was he right to hold back from the possibility of being killed? The teacher—an American—insisted that the factory owner, who carried a responsibility for the lives of many workers, acted correctly in preserving his life. But a storm of indignation arose, and public opinion insisted that a man should not reason, but is obliged to sacrifice himself for the sake of his neighbor (forgetting that they themselves daily crucify their neighbors in every way). Truly, such consciousnesses have not yet left the first grade and cannot understand that each sacrifice must be sensible, otherwise only evil will result. Often, so-called good deeds appear unjust when viewed from a higher plane. Even folk wisdom decrees, "Some goodness is worse than theft." Does it not happen that in our ignorance we are often ready to load the wrong people with benefits, at the expense of the more worthy ones? Are not the best cultural works subject to ridicule and slander? Are not the best deeds cast aside by people? And yet, these very same people are moved to compassion by a saved drunkard, forgetting that the price paid for it could have benefited an entire country, or even countries.

Therefore let us say that man should, wherever possible, help his fellow man, but he can only risk his life in a case where he does not bear great responsibility. It would be a tremendous lack of co-measurement and a heavy loss for all humanity if people who benefit all mankind were to senselessly risk their lives. But if we talk to the masses, we must say that man should always and in everything hasten to help his fellow man. Verily, that man is a hero who risks his life for the salvation of his fellow man. But there are different kinds of risks and sacrifices. How important is the sacrifice of a physician or a research scientist, who works self-sacrificingly with terrible destructive substances in order to discover a remedy for pernicious ailments! But these conscious martyrs and benefactors of humanity are seldom remembered.

Thus says the Great Teacher: "Everyone who enters the Path of Service, sooner or later must seal such service of Light with a personal achievement. This service will not be realized if there is no cognition of goal-fitness. And this concept will be assimilated if the spirit knows its designation. Courage and wisdom issue from one and the same concept of Good. Man carries within himself the measure of the essence of his deeds. It is impossible to tell how and when the decisive hour arrives, but we know in our heart the time of the fulfillment of the date. Thus, wisdom and courage help us to understand the entire responsibility for the benefit of all mankind."

* * *

Now, the next question: What kind of death should be recognized as natural? Of course, the most natural death is from old age. At times one must also recognize as natural the death caused by illness, because from his birth man usually carries within himself the germ of illness. In the ugly, abnormal conditions of life, created by depraved humanity, practically all types of deaths may be considered not natural.

Often an illness helps the subtle body to cleanse itself from many abominations, therefore a lengthy illness frequently assists a better crossing. Of course, almost all the so-called accidents are the result of karma.

Your third question is about the One Path. Strictly speaking, there exists only one, leading Path, truly the path of evolution, but numerous and varied are the pathways attendant to this Path. Verily, the One Revelation, brought in all ages by the Great Teachers of humanity, is that one royal Path. However, the sects and the distortions of the Teaching engendered by their followers become the numerous, multiform, and often hard pathways along which the masses of mankind crawl. Every Teacher stresses that detail of the One Revelation that is most needed at a certain stage of consciousness.

When the consciousness has assimilated the foundations of the Teaching of Life, all that takes place with us and around us inevitably takes on another meaning. The broadened consciousness carries over the starting point of the thinking into the supermundane plane and unites with the consciousness of the Elder Brothers of our humanity. Such a consciousness learns to live in its true home and knows in spirit and heart its Friends and Helpers. Their Help comes when needed and useful, therefore let us perform our life's mission in patience, giving an example of courage and devotion to those who surround us. For encouragement let me give you a page from the Teaching of Life.

"You know that phenomenal actions cannot always take place. In addition to cosmic causes and the intrusion of negative forces from the Subtle World, there may be reactions due to so-called lack of faith. It is difficult to draw a boundary between lack of faith and doubt, both vipers are from the same nest. The Great Wayfarer often taught that as is the faith, so is it given. Let us not forget that Christ could not perform miracles because of lack of faith, one can find some references to it. Nowadays the scientists would replace *lack of faith* with *denial of authority*. It is of no importance which expression is used, the meaning is the same. The break in the current of energy interrupts even the most powerful sendings. One can observe this physical manifestation, beginning with the most commonplace situations.

"When We warn against doubt, We speak about a physical law. People may reject the most powerful help, because free will can destroy the healthiest conditions. A man may become irate and repulse the Hand holding him back from a fall. The Teacher must warn against the harm of doubt.

"One may recall how the disciples doubted the power of the Teacher and at once received a blow, which they called destiny. But this definition is not correct. What sort of destiny is it when a man severs the salutary link? It is right to evaluate the foundations of faith as a vital cause of advance."

Also: "You know how unexpectedly the mosaic of life is molded. But this unexpectedness is only on the earthly plane. A man often speaks or writes with one purpose, but he is directed by the Higher Forces to quite a different goal. A man thinks that he has achieved success in a direction desired by him, when in reality he has attained a far greater success in an unexpected field. He writes to a certain person, but the results come from an unexpected quarter. Often We deduced multiform results from one action. If We were to enumerate all consequences, man would become confused. He would attempt to diminish his psychic energy and thus weaken it. Only through the broadening of consciousness can one acquire a broad horizon. The Great Wayfarer taught the broadening of consciousness. He repeated, 'Open your eyes and ears.' Indeed, He suggested opening the ears not only to His instruction, but He also pointed out that true depth of reasoning can be acquired with the broadening of consciousness. But one cannot thread a rope through the eye of a needle. A great messenger is not absorbed by a narrow ear. One can imagine how many of His Teachings did not enter the ears of His listeners! Some were remembered fragmentarily. The connection was lost, and thus was lost the original meaning. I will not say that the meaning became wrong, but the beauty of the word was erased. Thus, many Great Teachers suffered distortion of their thoughts. In the spatial records the thoughts of the Teachers are better preserved. As a beneficent dew they descend to those who can receive them. Knowing this, the Teachers are not disturbed by earthly distortions. The predestined will reach, and an open heart will accept. Human thoughts also grow in space. Every heroic, self-denying thought is already a seed for the future world. Not only the Great Teachers but every thinker may become a builder of Good in Cosmos. People do not wish to dwell in thought about the far-off worlds, yet these very thoughts will be a fine purifier of knowledge. There will be no envy, malice, or coarseness on the spatial pathways. The Great Teacher often directed the glance of the disciples toward the luminaries saying, 'Many homes, and everywhere there is life.' He wanted his disciples to love Infinity."

Let us always remember the salutary bond and that each event, each action has many consequences. If there is aggravation today, there will be joy tomorrow.

5

15 March 1938

I am deeply touched by your words about the joy you find in the study of the books of the Teaching of Life. Truly, is it not joyous to reflect on the brief, profoundly wise, vital formulas, so untiringly and generously strewn? The joy of the broadening of consciousness is one of the loftiest and purest joys. Indeed, only the broadened consciousness permits us, in spite of all the horrors that take place, in spite of the trampling of the most sacred concepts and foundations of human dignity, to preserve compassion and love for humanity in the heart. The heart is also nurtured by thinking.

With your entire spirit strive to the light of the future. Psychic energy, which carries us into the supermundane spheres, is accumulated here on Earth, and its best awakener and teacher is the joyous striving into the future, full of illumined labors—as on Earth, so also in the Subtle World. If people could understand that for a pure and aspiring man the very crossing into the Subtle World is the highest joy, the highest exaltation, and a full joining in the beloved labor, then many would strive to attain this joyous and broadened state through a worthy life on Earth.

Your psychic energy is at present in a fine state, and I rejoice at this. But because of the indescribably oppressive cosmic currents, which produce terrible perturbations in space, I ask you to guard your health and not to be aggravated by any lack of understanding expressed by those whom you meet. One has to speak with everyone in accordance with his level of consciousness. The entire White Brotherhood lives by this covenant. In it is contained great wisdom, goodness, and great compassion. The lot of a Teacher is identical in all ages. He must have patience and compassion to talk at his listener's level. He must touch on the same questions endlessly, and he must not vex his interrogator by reminding him that the question set was already answered long ago. Truly, one is amazed at the inexhaustible patience of the Great Teachers, who through incalculable aeons have accepted the most oppressive, the most difficult incarnations for Themselves, in order to move and raise the consciousness of ungrateful humanity, which constantly and in every way has persecuted and crucified its Liberators and Saviors. Thus it was, thus it is, but let us hope that there will be some enlightenment in the coming epoch.

6

17 March 1938

All that you write confirms the grave condition of the world in this black age of ours. Again and again the best representatives of humanity must suffer through the tragedy of an age-old battle of all that is progressive and vital against the outworn and deadening concepts with which the consciousness of the majority is filled. As we see, this battle has already taken on a planetary scope, and is carried on in all realms and in all fields of life; yet the adherents of Light and progress are multiplying, and each new idea or discovery is more readily recognized then at those times when because of ignorance the discoveries most essential for humanity were postponed, sometimes for hundreds of years.

The path of the benefactors, or enlighteners of humanity is thorny, and this must not be forgotten. Therefore, it is so important, beginning with the school bench, to acquaint children with the Golgotha of all the martyrs of science and thought, and chiefly, with those grave consequences which humanity reaped because of the refusal to accept at the proper time this or that scientific discovery, this or that expansion of the mental horizon. Solicitude about the expansion of consciousness and the corresponding horizon must become the care and goal of education, otherwise humanity will not emerge from the zone of self-extermination, destructive uprisings and wars.

A broad, all-embracing mind follows the rhythm of cosmic necessity, in other words, that of evolution, therefore it welcomes each new milestone that is revealed in one or another domain in the life of a country. It will not pass by, because it knows that each milestone may reveal new horizons of the great Knowledge which reigns supreme in the whole Universe.

Thus, let us welcome and follow evolution which, in its wonderful sequence, discloses to us all the new facets of limitless Knowledge.

7

5 April 1938

I rejoiced at the themes of your lectures and at the fact that they are accepted with such interest by your listeners. You are doing important work. The education and upbringing of people is the most important, most essential, and urgent task of each country. One must have it constantly in mind. No ruinous revolutions, no excesses are possible where the people have realized their destiny in the Universe and their responsibility, and when they can clearly perceive the significance of their achievement in life. Only an expanded horizon can exclude not only self-destructive stagnation but also every fanaticism, be it religious or revolutionary, and can indicate the orderly path of evolution.

Remember that Christ also taught the broadening of consciousness. "He repeated, 'Open your eyes and ears.' Indeed, He suggested opening the ears not only to His instruction, but He also pointed out that true depth of reasoning can be acquired with the broadening of consciousness. But one cannot thread a rope through the eye of a needle. A great message is not absorbed by a narrow ear."

Labor in joy, sow benevolent seeds.

Someone is disturbed because the books of the Teaching of Life speak in one place about the benefit of sleep, and in another about the harm of drowsiness. Indeed, these concepts differ greatly. A healthy sleep of from six to eight hours (in a city) is not only beneficial but absolutely necessary, because during these hours our subtle body receives its much needed nurture from the Subtle World. On the other hand, drowsiness may occur due to several reasons, and one should discern them. Drowsiness often occurs because of cosmic causes, and also because of a contact with a sick, vampiric aura, which can suck out energy even to complete exhaustion of strength. Also, there are frequent cases when our psychic energy is suddenly needed by someone close to us, and, because of the law of the spiritual magnet, our energy hastens to help immediately; and, indeed, during its outflow we feel drowsiness, or even dizziness, and, as it were, a temporary, brief absentation.

Drowsiness is harmful for people of a lazy nature and for those who hardly trouble themselves with thinking, because it may become a chronic condition with them. Such a person becomes open to all kinds of external conditions, including obsession. He is easily subject to any contagion, and in case of a dangerous illness has no strength to fight it because his psychic energy is in an embryonic state. Well developed and balanced psychic energy is a source of longevity. Psychic energy is the elixir of life.

Now about manifestations from the Subtle World. In the sacred scriptures of all nations there are indications about posthumous appearances and communion with the Higher Forces, at times through teraphim, and these may be quite diverse. In the bible there are also indications such as, for instance, King Saul's vision of the prophet Samuel, if I am not mistaken. Also, from all the descriptions of the posthumous appearances of Christ, it is clear that they took place in the subtle body. Pay attention to the sudden appearances within the closed doors of a chamber and the way they are stressed, and likewise the disappearances. Also, for some reason the disciples did not at once recognize Him during these appearances, and when their eyes were opened and they knew Him, He vanished out of their sight. All this definitely points to the resurrection of Christ, precisely in the subtle body. All those who have been witnesses to similar manifestations from the Subtle World in our time can also confirm this customary suddenness of appearances and also disappearances. Only the blind, or absolute ignoramuses can accept the physical resurrection of the Great Teacher.

Moreover, does it not seem to you that the appearance in a subtle body from another world is a far greater miracle than that of resurrection in the physical body? The time will come, and it is not far off, when physicians shall resurrect the dead, if the subtle body has not yet become separated from its dense envelope or, as it is said in the East, until the silver thread, that links the subtle body with the physical, breaks. It is possible that people will attain such skill in black magic that, after the egress of the subtle body, the remaining physical sheath could be taken by another dweller from the Subtle World. In Tibet these manifestations can be observed, and the body which remains is, in many cases, taken over by an abominable elemental or the spirit of an animal; and such a corpse, upon becoming alive, usually attacks the people nearby and often chews them to death. True, such possession of the body is possible only if it belonged to a very base man. But in India even now one can witness the phenomenon of a transfer of the life principle. Thus, a fakir, before the eyes of a few Europeans, revived a sparrow which had just been strangled. He himself fell into a trance, and while he was in that state, the sparrow became alive and even started to fly, but as soon as the fakir came to, the sparrow again expired.

There is an excellent book by the famous French astronomer,

C. Flammarion, in which he collected over one thousand recorded appearances from the Subtle World, and all kinds of manifestations of psychic energy. In its time the book was translated into Russian. It would be good to find it.

As to the question of the condition of our planet prior to the fall of Lucifer—according to Eastern writings and *The Secret Doctrine*, we know how advanced and beautiful was the civilization of the Third Race when it was guided and acclaimed by the Great Spirits from the higher worlds. The final fall of Lucifer took place in the Fourth Race, but his departure from the path of Light was already marked at an earlier time. When the human substance in him outweighed the divine, he became jealous and started the disastrous battle against the Great Brothers, which has now reached its limit. Remarkable is the fact that in order to achieve his goal of becoming the full and only ruler of Earth, his chief efforts were directed toward the humiliation of woman. He knew that with the demeaning of woman the coarsening and degeneration of humanity was unavoidable. There exists a most ancient saying, "Where women are revered and safeguarded, prosperity reigns and the gods rejoice." The New Epoch under the rays of Uranus will bring the renaissance of woman. The Epoch of Maitreya is the Epoch of the Mother of the World. It is remarkable to observe the rapid rise of the women of India. There one can see women occupying the posts of ministers and other responsible positions. Many women of India are excellent speakers. The Indians readily elect women, because they have faith in the common sense of their wives. But, of course, there are also opponents of the liberation of woman. In certain dominions in India where women are at the head of the government one sees many innovations, the temples are open for the lower castes, universities are founded and also museums, laboratories, hospitals are patterned after European lines.

8

19 April 1938

Of course, I fully trust your heart, and your aura is the guarantee of the best possibilities. You write that you are a novice in public life, but this is not to be feared, since experience comes with work; but the most important lies in the spiritual accumulation, in the quality of psychic energy, and no experience can replace the essence of this beautiful energy. Therefore in the basis of everything let us place precisely this gauge.

I rejoice that you are paying attention to children. Indeed, the most urgent, the most essential task is the education of children and youth. In all countries very little and extremely poor attention at that is given to this question on which depends the entire welfare and strength of a people and a country. It is usually customary to confuse education with upbringing, but it is time to understand that school education, as it is established in most cases, not only does not contribute to the moral upbringing of youth, but acts inversely. In the Anglo-Saxon countries the schools are occupied mainly with the physical development of youth to the detriment of their mental development. But the excessive enthusiasm for sports leads to the coarsening of character, to mental degeneration, and to new diseases. True, not much better is the situation in home education under the conditions of the modern family. Therefore, it is time to pay most serious attention to the grave and derelict situation of children and youth from the moral point of view. Many lofty concepts are completely out of habitual use, having been replaced by everyday formulas for the easy achievement of the most vulgar comforts and status.

Without delay one should set up an organization of kindergartens and clubs, or communities, where children of different ages can gather in groups and be given the spiritual food which is lacking in schools and families. We learned recently that in California and elsewhere in America an organization dedicated to Prof. Roerich began its activities. The young people, members of this organization, call themselves "Torchbearers." A torch is for them a symbol of knowledge transmitted by great men and women of the past and present. Young Torchbearers choose from these heroes and heroines the image closest to them and strive to emulate it in their life. Their goal is to carry this torch of wisdom and achievement into the future, for the benefit of coming generations. Acquaintance with the self-sacrificing lives of all ages and nations helps the children to realize the grandeur of human dignity and destiny, and teaches them to love self-sacrificing attainment. From history we know that each great epoch was marked by the influx of a powerful wave of reverence for heroism in all its manifestations. The Ordainment of the Great Brotherhood is—create heroes.

If one were to impart to children lessons of high morals from the lives of the heroes of all ages and all peoples, the sacred laws of existence could thus be imparted in the form of attractive narratives and examples from the life of all kingdoms of nature. The accumulated wisdom of the ages can be presented in the simplest forms, and thus many new vistas will be revealed. Actually, such lessons are remembered even better when they are presented to children, as you are doing, in short plays, with the children acting the parts of the heroes. Therefore I highly approve of your program. In their gatherings the children could use the name of their chosen hero.

Also useful are studies of the arts and of the most prosaic handicrafts, as nothing awakens the latent abilities so well as the possibility of a direct personal accomplishment. Good are choral singing, folk dances, and all those studies which demand unified rhythm. And one should especially encourage children to express their opinions about all they have read, heard and seen; such discussions will lay the foundation for thinking. It is equally important to conduct attractive studies and games that demand especial attentiveness. After all, memory is primarily attentiveness. In the senior groups, the keeping of diaries could be introduced so that all the good that has been done during the day and all the acknowledged errors could be written down. And in beginning a new day, a resolution could be made not to allow certain conduct to take place during that day, such as irritation, rudeness, or lies, and, on the contrary to stress special attentiveness, politeness, solicitude for those around, etc. Keeping such a diary, for the purpose of self-analysis, will help considerably in eradicating undesirable habits and affirming new and useful ones. Habits form qualities. Let us also not forget useful excursions for the children in order to become acquainted with various branches of labor, science, and art. It is absolutely essential to teach the children love for nature in all its manifestations. In this respect, all kinds of picnics and walks are useful for assembling botanical, entomological, and mineralogical collections. All in all, assembling various collections greatly assists the acquirement of useful knowledge.

You are right in attempting to get acquainted with different pedagogical and educational systems; thus, one can choose out of each day the very best and animate it with the synthesis of the Teaching of New Life, or the Teaching of Living Ethics. By the way, did you collect in a separate notebook all indications about upbringing and schools from the books of the Teaching?

With the help of the parents one could also organize a cooperative library for children and youth. The significance and influence of the book upon the young consciousnesses cannot be measured, because it is unlimited. This domain must become the subject of special exclusive care of the state. Often, the books read first give an impetus and direction to the further development of thinking. How many mutilated lives, how many crimes committed by minors, if one were to analyze the thinking of these criminals, will prove to be but the results of the books read by them, or plays and crimes seen in the cinema!

I shall read your essay with great joy. The program of education is as broad as life itself. The possibilities for improvement are inexhaustible. Do you not think that we are on the eve of a new approach to and reconstruction of the entire school education? The quantity and speed of new discoveries in all domains of science grow so rapidly that soon contemporary school education will not be able to walk in step with and respond to the new attainments and demands of the time; new methods in the entire system of education will have to be devised. Precisely training in synthesized thinking will become an urgent necessity.

In conclusion I shall quote for you one discourse: "You know to what an extent a word enters into a child's heart. Especially up to seven years of age one may recall memories of the Subtle World. Children feel how they sensed that special life. It is useful to ask children whether they remember some particular thing. Such touches are called the opening of memory. Even if with years the memory of the past again becomes dim, nevertheless there will remain a spark of beautiful existence. The Great Teacher loved to uncover the memory. He brought the children close to Him and not only asked them questions but also touched them with His hand, thus increasing the vividness of recollection. He not only loved children but also saw in them the advance of humanity. He was right in treating them as grownups, for when the remote past or the Subtle world is recalled, the mind becomes that of a grownup. Children will never forget the one who approached them as an equal. They will retain this memory for their whole life. Maybe the children remembered the Teacher better than did those who were healed by him. Thus, one should remember that the minors will be the continuers of life, and everyone must impart to them his experience. But it will be wiser to awaken in them the memories of the Subtle World. The most profound spiritual life will be molded where the spark of the existence of the Subtle World began to glow, and where communion with the Invisible World was facilitated. The appearances of the Teacher in a subtle body strengthened the disciples in the reality of the Invisible World. Not all could be receptive to the substance of this World, but, nevertheless, the window was set ajar."

Thus, through cautious touches this knowledge will enter the consciousness of the growing generation. Truly, the work for the expansion of consciousness is without end. It is joyous to see how many hearts already respond to the forgotten truths.

9

23 April 1938

I hasten to fulfill your request and to give my opinion regarding the Call to the Women of the Whole World. I do not see why you cannot put this thought into practice. Each reminder about woman's dignity and the importance of women in constructing new forms of life is highly useful and timely.

The advancement of women in governmental circles and their successful execution of various public duties in may countries have so strongly affirmed the recognition of their equal abilities that only very backward consciousnesses can raise objections in principle to this statement and to the admittance of women to the most responsible positions.

Your young country, now living in its springtime and aspiring toward the welfare and renascence of its people, of course can but harken to the steps of evolution; therefore it should rejoice at the possibility of strengthening its spiritual and intellectual power by elevating the level of consciousness and dignity of its women. "It is not possible for the bird of humanity to fly on only one wing."

Woman's mind is not inferior to man's, because the higher qualities of this faculty derive from the spirit, which is sexless. Intellectuality is acquired through education and training; therefore, place woman in the necessary conditions and the results will be obvious. True, the main stimulus for the liberation of woman's consciousness and from her subjugated position will come from the new education. From early years it will create an understanding of the foundations of existence, of the destiny and role of man in the Universe, and thus will give a new trend to the entire thinking, the result of which will be a broadening of the horizon on all walks of life. And only then can one expect the eradication of many most harmful prejudices and habits which have become customs, and of the most vulgar aims and occupations, which are the main evil and causes of the present corruption and madness. I regard as the most frightful manifestations the universal infatuation with luxury and the monstrous growth of its inseparable companion—vulgarity, which has adorned itself with every kind of "royal" diadem. The worm of vulgarity is dangerous because of its vacuity; easily and imperceptibly penetrating everywhere, it quickly multiplies and engulfs even a healthy tissue. The honor of engendering this most odious worm belongs, as in everything, to both Origins.

* * *

Someone speaks about the illogical and absolutely false formula, "Let him who desires peace, prepare for war." This formula, by the way was translated in a slightly changed way, "If you desire peace, be ready for war." There is not much difference, and yet there is a shade. I agree, that the understanding of this formula in a narrow, one-sided, practical application as an increased manufacture of destructive weapons of war and dangerous poisons, etc., will, of course, lead to catastrophe in one form or another; but a true and spiritual understanding of it becomes an essential step for man's new realization of his destination in the Universe.

Verily, man is summoned to world construction amidst chaos, and he should train himself for the courage of eternal vigilance and for participation in the cosmic battle that incessantly takes place around him. If he does not wish to be engulfed by the waves of chaos, he must be ever ready to oppose all evil. We cannot be non-resistant to evil without becoming at the same time traitors to all humanity. The duty of every spiritually developed consciousness is to be ever on guard, and with all one's might to put an end to evil.

It was said by a Great Teacher: "Every man participates incessantly in three battles. Man may imagine himself to be in complete repose, but in reality he is taking part simultaneously in three battles. The first one will be between the free will and karma. Nothing can liberate man from participation in the conflict of these two elements. The second battle rages around man between the disincarnate entities of good and evil. Thus man becomes the prey of one of these. It is difficult to picture the fury of the dark ones who attempt to possess man. The third battle roars in Infinity, in Space, between the subtle energies and the waves of chaos. It is not possible for human imagination to encompass these battles in Infinity. The human mind understands earthly conflicts, but cannot, looking up into a blue sky, imagine that powerful forces and whirls are raging there. Only after mastering earthly feelings can man ponder about the invisible worlds. One should become accustomed to such thoughts. Only they will make man a conscious participant of the infinite forces.

"Ponder about being constantly present before the image of Infinity. The most lofty words cannot express the Supreme, and only during brief moments can the heart become atremor with the transport of cognition. Learn to remember these moments, for they will be the key to the future. It is impossible to accept all the innumerable worlds as being filled, yet the Teacher directs us to this. Learn to honor Him with trust; without this bridge you cannot cross."

And so, there is no falsehood in the correct understanding of the foregoing formula. Therefore one should not compare or liken it to the formula, "If you wish for good, do evil, etc.," because "be ready for war" does not mean—start war. For a correct comparison one should have said, "If you wish for good, be ready to repulse evil." This is the very thought that passes like a red thread through all spiritual teachings. Therefore the images of Bodhisattvas and our Archistrategists are accompanied with swords and spears as symbols of their ceaseless battle with chaos and evil.

I also wish to ask a question, What formula can be regarded as absolute or, as someone said, absolutely just in our manifested world, the world of differentiations and relativity? Even such a seemingly undisputed formula as "Thou shalt not kill" is not always applicable. Also another one "love thy neighbor as thyself:" may bring sorrow to a close one instead of benefaction. Because, truly, love of self may be closer to madness or to hellish intent. If such a man applies his own measures to his neighbors, they may become disastrous for the latter. Only in the light of the spirit can one look for a true interpretation and application. *Evolution presupposes the relativity of each concept.* This is why all Teachings insist upon the development and accumulation of straight-knowledge, which alone can apply each concept with *co-measurement* and *goal-fitness* upon every step of life.

The tension in the world is constantly increasing. Events are hastened, but the Forces of Light will steer all into proper channels. Learn to find joy in labor and in endless knowledge during the most difficult days.

10

23 April 1938

You bewail your indisposition, however I think that a considerable share of all painful manifestations must be attributed to the unusually heavy and complex cosmic currents. On certain days our community feels the very same painful symptoms, some more strongly and others more weakly. On one day there is noticeable in everyone a weakening of the eyesight or an irritation of the mucous membranes; on another day, a peculiar stuffed feeling of the organism, such as distension of and heaviness in the stomach; at times, peculiar pains in the heart or an unusual weight and pain in the back of or the crown of the head are felt; there may be frequent flows of blood to the head and a special dry heat in the entire body; pains are frequent and a sort of rotation or stirring in the solar plexus; and particularly painful at night are a burning in the extremities and a pulling sensation in them.

Usually these sensations occur about two or three days before an earthquake or some particular storms and other calamities. It is hard to enumerate all the unexpected pains and sensations, and they pass as quickly as they suddenly appear.

You fret at the impossibility of doing more work for the Common Good than you are now doing, but how can it be measured? Often people very active on the physical plane manifest themselves weakly in the Subtle World and vice versa; and people who, in comparison, are manifesting less, perform vast work on the spiritual plane. It is not for us to judge who does more and who does less. Chiefly, all efforts should be applied for the best execution of that work which is given to us, and in those conditions in which we are placed by karma,. A conscientious attitude toward everything will push apart the boundaries and bring better possibilities. Therefore, blessing to you if you love plain people and regard helping them as your calling. The greatest privilege consists in the possibility of rendering many-sided help.

Therefore, rejoice in that you can help physically and spiritually—the physician of the body must be also the healer of the spirit. And what a vast quantity of wondrous fire is hidden in the contact with simple people.

And now to answer about the paragraphs from *Brotherhood* indicated by you.

318. "How to develop ability to work in the Subtle World?" First of all, one should start by continually feeling himself to be living in two worlds. This is not difficult at all because we cross each night into the Subtle World, where, if our subtle body has been sufficiently developed, we can apply our subtle energies with good benefit. When we go to sleep not thinking of rest, but striving to the Hierarchy of Light with a thought of useful labor, we thus direct our energies to active help where it is most needed. Consciously sending oneself into the Subtle World can be increased to such an extent that we begin to remember clearly our many-sided work at night and our visits for the purpose of rendering help to people often quite unknown to us. The next stage will be to cognize such a sending in the waking state and even during one's usual occupation. At first, such a sending will flash out in the consciousness through a sensation of a sort of momentary absence, and later there will remain an impression of having visited someone, or even of having heard two or three words; at times there will be sensed the characteristic odor of a definite locality known to us, or a glimmer of people or a place will pass by—then we shall know that our detached energy is working in that direction. These manifestations occur daily, but for this some solitude is needed. They are more vivid and frequent in the evening, and before going to sleep, and are especially intensified at dawn.

Where there is a high degree of spirituality, the divisibility of spirit is so great that the detached particles of psychic energy work unceasingly in full harmony with like particles of energy sent by kindred souls. In fact, the purified energy will participate in the most urgent tasks for the benefit of all humanity. Therefore, one should think more often of and feel a desire to take part in this enlightened work. As you already know, all ancient Teachings affirm that the emanations of a Yogi, or even of a pure man, render the atmosphere healthy over a wide area, and even arrest epidemics, destructive earthquakes, and other calamities. Such a bearer of Light himself feels only fatigue after an extremely salutary application of his emanations.

I am adding here the explanation of other paragraphs indicated by you from *Brotherhood*.

56. Patience is in itself great knowledge or, rather, great knowledge is born out of great patience. The wise one knows that all comes at an appointed date, cosmic combinations cannot be hastened. It was said long ago that the greatest man is he who is most patient. Thinking more often about Infinity we learn to understand the great patience which must lie in the foundation of each structure.

Besides, having before one's eyes the heroic example of the inexhaustible patience of the Great Teachers, who, during incalculable millennia, labor for the benefit and salvation of humanity, which in its ignorance impedes and destroys in every way Their labors, it becomes easier to endure our misfortunes and difficulties.

228. It seems to me that it is truly joyous to realize that solitude does not exist, and that each one of us is surrounded by loving souls on this or another plane. With such sendings these loving souls endeavor to create around us a benevolent atmosphere, but it is necessary to realize this, to open our heart to their calls and sendings, and not to obstruct them by dark emanations issuing from oppressive thoughts colored by doubt and often by an absolutely unsubstantiated offense. Dark emanations are impenetrable for subtle energies.

323. Indeed, Kriya-shakti is thought-energy. In order to create in the subtle spheres, an accumulated, highly developed psychic energy is needed, together with imagination and a faculty of clear ideation. Therefore, work in the arts is so necessary.

328. The lightning of thought mentioned in this paragraph was sent by the Teacher to strengthen my eyesight, which was

considerably weakened after work with small print. I saw this lightning with my physical eyesight, or rather, with open eyes—it unfolded itself rather slowly before my eyes, as if touching them with a broad, very long fiery strip of a pinkish-lilac color. Afterwards, my eyesight became considerably stronger. Of course, this lightning was saturated with a special property of healing energy.

You ask, Could people have lightning-thoughts? Undoubtedly so, because each clear-cut and intensified thought gives off a fiery flash, which means that during spiritual growth and a necessary tension of psychic energy, fiery flashes could become lightnings. But for this spirituality must be high.

329. You ask what to do in order that subtle work might become manifest each instant. The answer is given in paragraph 318 and in this very same paragraph—329. One should realize and feel to such an extent that we are living in two worlds that this realization would never leave us; and this is not difficult, for we are consciously aware that we live on the physical plane, yet this realization does not at all impede any of our mental work, in spite of the fact that the process of thinking is already at work on a subtle plane, because the mind belongs to the fourth dimension, or the realm of metaphysics. And for the facilitation and greater fruitfulness of such work in the Subtle World it is essential to love it. Where there is love there is a better performance, and, consequently, a mutually better result.

373. Indeed, knowledge of astrology will considerably facilitate healing through the rays of the luminaries. A horoscope, cast correctly, will indicate which rays of the luminaries and which combinations of them are most beneficial for the said individual. I also advise you to study so-called medical astrology, it can offer most interesting suggestions. When the means of admitting and condensing the rays of the luminaries shall be found, then, indeed medicine and science will occupy themselves with the study of their useful application. But at present we already know to what an extent man's health is improved when the luminary favorable to him according to the horoscope is found in congenial combinations. Therefore, he who knows about the position of a luminary favorable to him can while gazing at it consciously absorb its strengthening force. The most important reaction takes place through cognition. If a man who does not react to a lofty work of art stands before it in the dark, as it were,

then, similarly, the man through whose nerve centers pass healing rays will remain insensible to their influence unless he has trained his consciousness in that direction. However, if one were to let pass through him rays of such strength that they would forcibly open his centers, the latter would be reduced to ashes under such a full impact. Reciprocal action and conformity are absolute conditions in everything.

377. Undoubtedly, rhythm adds to the working ability, and each work demands its own rhythm. It is very desirable that this rhythm should be refined in quality and should respond as closely as possible to the individual rhythm of the worker. Some rhythms, in the course of time, not only completely suppress in man receptivity to more refined vibrations but even incite very low and coarse manifestations in him. I have often pondered over that question. It seemed to me that our modern technocracy with its ominous, monotonous, and inexorably dead rhythm of the machines must react destructively upon the psyche of the workmen, entirely stifling their receptivity to the subtlest rhythms in nature and the manifestations of the human soul. Eventually they turn into actual robots, able to react only to the habitual and crudest rhythms. But a man who loses the ability to receive the higher vibrations unavoidably turns into an animal, or speaking more correctly, into a beast. Therefore, I greatly welcome shortening the hours of machine labor and also decreasing the quantity of workers in the factories and mills. The machines, in their present applications and usage, are monsters, and veritable weapons of hell. They will remain such until their proper significance shall be rightly understood and measures are taken to paralyze the harm inflicted by them. This paragraph quoted by you was given for the affirmation of my thought.

422. You ask what kind of vibrations could avert a strong attack of pain. Vibrations as yet unknown to science which are sent by the Teachers. The case described in this paragraph relates to my own experience. In dream I saw the condition of my heart and sketched the pattern of its contractions. The next day I experienced these painful contractions, they were quite strong. At that time I heard the call and indication to lie down in a certain way, and immediately the help was sent through rays or vibrations which continued for twenty minutes; afterward I got up as if risen from the dead. I frequently feel the vibrations

which restore my heart action; at times, this occurs daily, lasting for quite a lengthy period. The vibrations that are sent differ greatly in their intensity and rhythm and also in the quality of the sensations and, of course, in reaction. They also are sent to various nerve centers in turn, at times concentrating on one, at other times upon two or more centers. It happens that special rays, that have definite terms in the White Brotherhood, are being circulated through my organism; each of these differs according to the sensations experienced and the results. At times my iron camp bed shakes and hums from the ray which runs through. My experiences are written down in several scores of notebooks, and at that I could not always write down everything.

The condition described by you could have taken place because of similarly healing vibrations, but if they reacted painfully upon the heart, then, maybe, these were cosmic currents, absorbed by the sensitive organism.

464. "Why does much of that which has been gathered into the Chalice remain concealed for entire lives?" This happens due to several reasons, mostly karmic ones. A man must redeem or learn something, and therefore he is born in conditions inapplicable for revealing his acquired abilities (which perhaps had been the cause of this downfall), and thus he must develop new and often contrasting qualities within himself. Or a man may receive a special mission, for which a too strong manifestation of a certain ability acquired in the past would only impede or even disturb the fulfillment of the said mission, since it could entice him into another direction. Also, frequently a man, bound by strong karmic ties, is born into a definite family which cannot give him an organism befitting all his accumulations. You know that the image of man is created by the energy of all humanity. The atavism inherited from ancestors is not always easy to surmount. Therefore, lofty spirits, with great accumulations, are at times not able to receive an organism which suits them in every way. A noticeable lack of balance or so-called idiosyncrasies are often a result of nonconformity between the spiritual accumulations and the acquired instrument. A musical virtuoso receives a violin made of tin instead of a Stadivarius.

483. Yes, each one entering upon the Path of Service for the Common Good is unavoidably subjected to all kinds of tests, which are the results of his increased spiritual and mental work, and also of the hastening of the karma that is being outlived by

him. Each thought process changes something in our karma; therefore, if it is directed toward benevolent construction, a corresponding purification takes place, but these purifications may be painful. It is good if we learn to love difficulties, because only personal experience, personal trials and sufferings teach us great patience and compassion, those qualities which lie at the basis of all achievements.

* * *

Why think that women have in general less psychic energy than men? This is a great error. In the determination of the quantity of psychic energy sex is of no importance. Indeed, there may be greater or lesser bearers of psychic energy, but its possession is given equally to both Origins. The Holy spirit, the Hindu Shakti, or energy, is feminine in origin. Woman is not deprived by nature of anything, the more so in spiritual abilities. Spirit has no sex. At present woman's thinking ability may be developed in general complexity on the whole in a somewhat lesser degree than man's, but by no means is this shown in isolated, individual manifestations. Besides, if this reduction of mental ability is somewhere noticeable, then it is only due to the fact that the conditions and surroundings of the woman's life, created by centuries-old oppressions, contributed toward it. Lock up an infant in an empty room and in complete solitude, and even if he be a genius at birth he will grow up an idiot. No matter how great may be the past accumulations, to manifest them, not only a suitable instrument is needed by also *suitable conditions*. The French proverb says, "Circumstances make a great man." Woman, in all countries, and in all classes of society was for countless ages in almost full subjugation and under the guardianship of a family. In the last century she was still deprived of the right not only to a higher education but even her schooling was adapted to a state of feeble-mindedness, as it were. During centuries, with very rare exceptions, woman's merits were not only passed over in silence but it was publicly censured if these merits exceeded the usual boundaries of the narrow field of household activities. Yet the woman gave, and all was accepted from her, though mention of her name was carefully avoided. A great deal of injustice was done, and still is, in relation to woman. Therefore, at the coming of the New Epoch, woman herself must realize that she is in no way below man, that she is not definitely ill-favored by nature. It is especially painful to hear women themselves affirm their lower state, so to speak, even in cosmic creativity and in the cosmic plan. What a destructive fallacy! Let us realize with all our being the great destiny of woman, the Mother, giving life, and directing and inspiring humanity on the path of evolution. Thus, Asanga, the great teacher of Buddhism, desiring to give the highest definition to the qualities of Buddhas and Bodhisattvas, calls them "Mothers of humanity."

Indeed, there are not a few intellects deprived of the power of psychic energy, and their thought remains sterile, because it is bereft of the magnet, akin to psychic energy, which collects similar energies around it, for life in space as well as in earthly constructions. Verily, sterile is the thought not imbued with psychic energy, and especially impoverished is such a mind in the Subtle World. Let us also not forget that there exist many kinds, or rather qualities of this primary energy, and therefore let us strive to its highest manifestations in the self-sacrifice of an aspiring heart.

* * *

We shall be glad to receive the clipping with the snapshots of young people. Where there is the greatest denial, God's harvest is near. The pendulum, powerfully propelled to one side, swings with the very same brandish to the other. Not a display of piousness is needed, but a cognition of the spiritual principle.

* * *

True, musk acts differently upon people. It is said that from the best curative remedy some people draw its highest qualities, whereas others get only the very lowest. All is individual. There are people who cannot stand either musk or valerian. Of course, musk primarily increases the psychic energy and thus raises the vitality of the entire organism. Psychic energy, as the primary energy, is the very elixir of life.

* * *

The year 1942, according to all the most ancient writings, is considered to the end of Kali Yuga and the beginning of the new, beautiful cycle. However, this does not mean that the heavens will open and at once paradise will come on Earth. No, the consequences engendered by the end of Kali Yuga will still be felt, and with even greater force on certain parts of the planet, but on the other parts new construction will begin.

11

29 April 1938

I have a great request to make of you, to check and test the consciousness of those approaching the Teaching of Living Ethics with regard to their containment of opposites. As a rule, such containment is acquired with difficulty. And for many it becomes an unconquerable stumbling block. The Lord Buddha insisted first of all on such containment, and if he noticed that a disciple could not master this foundation which supports the entire structure, cosmic, as well as mundane—that of daily life— he did not admit such a disciple to further learning. People of small consciousness cannot at all understand that all their life they just adapt themselves to the containment of counterpositions more or less successfully for themselves or beneficently for the General Good. But if you point this out to them, they will vehemently deny it and become indignant. Containment of a pair of opposites takes on in their consciousness a mask of hypocrisy, yet even in the Teaching they find contradictions and, at best, inconsistencies. They read the Teaching with a dead spirit and accept each affirmation only in one exclusive application. The complex pattern of life is not assimilated by, and escapes from a limited consciousness.

There are very few who understand that goal-fitness, issuing as a result of counterpositions, prevails in the entire Universe. There are also those who even see in the carrying out of goal-fitness an analogy with the Jesuit formula—the end justifies the means. These consciousnesses are most dangerous, and often they are almost hopeless. They cannot understand that in all things and everywhere there is one measure—the Common Good, or purity of motive; only a pure heart can prompt the correct understanding of the application of cosmic laws and the formulas of the Teaching. There are not a few of those, who, hearing about the covenant of non-violence, will admit, in their deadening and one-sided conception of it, the invasion of chaos and thus will become the destroyers of many lives. It is interesting to verify how the statement is understood that "Jinn build the temples." Likewise, no one will ponder that the most sublime Teachings, by which the world's balance is still upheld, were the causes of the greatest bloodshed. The most High, in ignorant and evil hands, becomes a weapon of cruel persecution and violence.

It would be good to prepare discourses about containment, and the application of goalfitness. At first, they could be held individually, but with sufficiently advanced consciousnesses, and later one could gradually enlarge the number of participants. Let the participants in these discourses bring their own example of most varied cases in life, in order to show how well they understand the application of the guiding law of goal-fitness, which may also be called the law of Great Equilibrium.

12

7 May 1938

It is excellent that you are showing so much discrimination in admitting newcomers. We rejoice, not at the quantity, but only at the quality. All members must firstly, secondly, and thirdly, perfect themselves in the qualities pointed out in the books of Living Ethics. This should be the main and urgent goal of everyone who approaches. And this task is so immense that more than one life will be needed to acquire at least a few of those qualities. One of the primary and basic qualities will be knowledge of how to safeguard that which is entrusted. If such knowledge is present, it will in itself testify to considerable past accumulations.

Those who approach for the first time must fully realize that drawing near to the forces of Light is dangerous if it is done only out of curiosity and light-mindedness, or conceit. The responsibility of those who have contacted the Light is great, and nowhere can one escape from it. Therefore we should realize that we must decide for ourselves, Can we rise in spirit or is there danger for us, in that because of spiritual weakness we may retreat and thus condemn ourselves? Why fill up the legion of Judases, which, as it is, has grown to monstrous proportions?

Frightful is the fall of human dignity in the world! But such is the end of Kali Yuga. Only the rarest individuals can rise above the plane of our visible reality and understand those laws which move events and consequently people. Great knowledge is not forgiven and always evokes the malicious antagonism of crowds and average people. Therefore, Great Teachers, in all ages, ordained speaking according to the level of the consciousness of the listeners. Deviation from this wise counsel always resulted in the collapse of many enlightened undertakings and human lives. In the books of Living Ethics it is said, "A Yogi can do everything. Yet all is not permitted the Yogi." Do many understand the profound meaning of this statement?

Likewise in *Agni Yoga*, paragraph 50 it is said: "When will people understand the significance of thought and word? Still do people lend greater importance to the spilling of a sack of worthless seeds than to the spilling of destructive words. Any rodent may pick up the seeds, but even an Arhat may not annihilate the consequences of thought and word" and in *New Era Community*, paragraph 126 a warning is given: "In connection with the evening gatherings, it is ingenious to note unusual contents of speech or a very strange expression. But reflect—does there not hang on each letter of this expression a great number of lives?" Truly, who can say how often a work spoken carelessly became the cause of the downfall of one man, and even of many? And the downfall must be understood not only in the physical but also in the spiritual sense.

You have probably noticed that on the first steps of the discipleship, all are possessed, as it were, by a mania for teaching, and such "teachers," while not having as yet sufficiently assimilated any one book of the Teaching, begin to cast into space formulas distortedly understood by them, thus causing mental confusion and creating new enemies for themselves and for the Teaching.

Verily, to all those who wish to boast of their great knowledge one should recall the words of the Teaching, "Only the ignorant try to spread the dry twigs of pompousness on the window sills. He whose house is filled with knowledge does not fear to carve a slice of thought." Precisely, he who knows will discern when and where and what can be disclosed by him. The governing principle for him will be the ordainment—to speak according to the level of the consciousness of the listener.

My heart trusts your heart and knows that you will find the most necessary words for a clouded consciousness and for all those who need a timely, heartfelt reminder about great caution. Let each heart sense the unutterable tension that the Hierarchy of Light is undergoing in holding back the assaults of chaos evoked by the forces of darkness. The previously mentioned bloody sweat of these self-sacrificing Guardians is not a metaphor or hyperbole, but stern reality. Therefore, we must apply all our knowledge, in order not to immeasurably overload the Burden of Him who stands on unrelieved Watch.

The heart truly aches when one realizes the extent of irreparable harm inflicted by the hands of those to whom was shown much warmth of the heart and visible and invisible care. How greatly overloaded is the age-old labor of the Great Hierarchy, because not one of the Earth-dwellers can and does wish to imagine the gigantic scope of the raging Armageddon! Verily, the visible and invisible worlds participate in this cosmic battle. Yet the ignorant blaspheme and deride the lofty concepts that could have served as a steadfast anchor amidst the raging stormy elements. Humanity is like a ship in a storm whose captain and crew have become raving mad.

In conclusion I would like to give you some more paragraphs from a new book: "You know with what difficulty harmony of consciousness is achieved. We do not speak about the leveling of consciousnesses, because, owing to the generosity in the Universe, equality does not exist. Yet, since nothing is repeated, the harmony of all parts is nevertheless required. It is the more difficult to imagine with what complex means one can assist the equalization of consciousnesses. One man is already on his way to the summit, but the other one has not as yet approached the base, and they do not have a common ground for thinking. If you give them equal knowledge, for one it will be insufficient, whereas for the other it will cram his thinking and bring in confusion, which may end in treason. Many a time the Teacher must measure what can be actually assimilated without harm. Better not to say everything than to overfill and cause betrayal. The essence of wisdom is in the understanding of all variations fit for harmony. Thus one can see that the Teacher at times hastens, but at other times restrains. One should realize that at such times the Teacher observes a whole procession of travelers and evens up their steps.

"It should not be forgotten that while on his path man cannot see much of that which is created. Also, one should not be astonished when the Teacher sets milestones covering a distance far ahead. The Teacher points out different milestones, which sometimes seem insignificant when regarded from the earthly plane, but they may be symbols of great significance. Moreover, one should not wonder why such milestones are given for long periods. Let us not forget that the problem of time does not exist in the Subtle World, and signs flash out according to their significance, but not in the earthly sense. The Thinker said, 'Who can know the measures that exist in space? We may harken, but one should not apply the measures of dwarfs to giants.'"

Thus, let us surround ourselves with vigilance and wisely discern the scope of the consciousnesses of those who approach us, but let us not cram them. One should not bring in confusion, which may become greatly destructive. Let us have constantly in mind the closeness of curious ears, and let us not repeat what is greedily caught, interpreted willfully, and carried into the enemy's camp. This is an Advice. Likewise, frequent mentioning of cosmic upheavals are undesirable. Nothing infuriates small consciousnesses so much as foreseeing and forewarning of a possible calamity for them. All faint-hearted people expect an immediate easing up of all earthly burdens and, later, the coming of the Golden Age, just for them and definitely in their own understanding. Therefore, one should not confuse, and arouse in these consciousnesses apprehension and fear, which often in the final analysis give birth to treason.

We should think more about self-perfectment and about helping one's fellow men, according to one's strength and abilities. Therein lies the whole vast task of man, the entire meaning of Existence.

* * *

Because of the grave times, one should speak about the need for joy and of the terrible harm of any and all depression. Therefore I am quoting here a Discourse, useful for the entire group. "Even during the difficult days you know that strength issues from joy. I said long ago that 'joy is a special wisdom.' Verily so, because joy must be observed, discerned, and realized. Depressed people carry a cloud of miseries and woes. In this dark covering they cannot perceive joy. Because of this pall of sorrow people become blind and lose strength. They cannot help themselves. They do not admit Our Help, because depression and irritation are impenetrable. As if no one ever told people about the harm of depression!

"Depressed people are said to be deprived of their share. Ponder these words. Who has deprived them of their inherent share? First of all they deprived themselves of any possibilities. They began their own destruction long ago. Discontent, malice, irritation cut off the path to joy. Dark thoughts deprived them of the source of strength. Selfhood prevented the discernment of joy. Egoism whispered, Joy lies only in personal gain. Thus the most fruitful joy was hidden behind ugly piles of depression. Those blinded by depression are the most pitiful of bipeds.

"Man possesses the highest gift—to know joy. The lofty brow is given in order to perceive the Highest. From the far-off worlds to the tiniest flower everything offers joy to people. A new store of strength flows at each joy, because therefrom issues tension, which opens one more gate.

"Who gave to people the right to imagine that they are forever deprived of their own share? This lie was shouted by ignorance. But a wise hero, even at the hour of persecution, knows that the path to joy is not closed. People forget a simple truth, that all is in flux, sorrow is forgotten; but the sparks of joy glow forever. Through Our long lives We can confirm that joy is unforgettable and serves as an influx of strength. Happy are those in the Subtle World who can affirm joy. When We say, 'Joy is hastening,' it is verily near. But people often do not wish to notice it, for they have bound themselves by a predetermined sending. And so, joy may remain behind, without the desired effect. Look around broadly and gather all the flames of joy."

And now I shall give the answers to your questions.

1. The metalization of plants should be used with great caution. In fact, specialized knowledge and facilities for laboratory research are needed. You have probably heard that certain supposedly harmless chemicals, broadly accepted by American farmers for use on vegetables and fruits, have brought considerable suffering to the population. In America, many people have begun to cultivate their own vegetable gardens fearing such chemically "harmless" produce. Therefore, the metalization and the use of solutions for spraying plants, for example, one of iron, must be handled with full knowledge and caution.

2. True, certain already tested inoculations against infectious diseases, such a smallpox, are permissible, and in some loca-

lities where smallpox is particularly raging these inoculations are as yet the only means of combating this contagious disease. Other inoculations have not yet been sufficiently investigated and, indeed, they may be dangerous. However, where there is a good store of psychic energy, no contagion is to be feared. But do we often meet such people? The crystal of psychic energy gives immunity from all sicknesses and is a true elixir of life. Therefore, scientists and doctors should direct all their attention to the study of, and research on psychic energy.

3. In some specific cases of illnesses, of course the physician has the right to use narcotics. They are harmful for people with open centers and particularly at the time when any one center is in a state of inflammation. But it is regrettable that an overwhelming majority of physicians do not know anything about such inflammations, therefore, much harm will be continually done through incorrect diagnoses. One could tell them: "People used to arm themselves against the known plagues, but at present neither the black death nor cholera are terrifying, and not even cancer or meningitis, but new types of so-called neuralgia are coming into being, which may become fully epidemic. We could call these illnesses sufferings of psychic energy, and, at the same time, there may be signs of infection. But it will be some time still before physicians will pay attention to these new forms of illnesses. They may be called fiery fever, but the name is of no importance, for it is more important to understand the cause. Let us not lull ourselves with the thought that the change of races unavoidably brings with it many disturbances. Everyone who ponders over psychic energy understands that it must be kept pure. One should understand that a sullied energy will produce terrible spatial manifestations. ... No one has the right to sully the cosmic current, it will multiply the sufferings of many and, first of all, one's own."

Therefore, let us value those physicians who possess a goodly store of psychic energy and whose experience has taught them that the best healer is he who does not violate the natural process of an illness, but only watches and helps the organism with the simplest remedies in its battle with illness.

If one were to follow the latest attainments in medicine and science, one could find almost every year a declaration of the discovery of new methods of curing the diseases mentioned by you. However, the fact is that each patient requires an individual approach and method of cure. Thus, we know that in one case an external cancer was cured by an abundant sprinkling of soda on the afflicted place. In another case some unknown small root helped. The wife of an employee of ours was cured by some local remedy of a cancer of the breast that was in a greatly advanced and neglected state. And it is of interest that she took that same medicine for a long time, but with no results while she lived down in the valley, but as soon as she moved to our mountains this remedy brought beneficial effects. It is without doubt that a stay in the mountains reacts favorably upon people ill with cancer, perhaps owing to the fact that heights affect the blood. Blood changes on heights, becoming more abundant in red corpuscles and thicker.

Soda is a preventive against cancer, but some people cannot take it; also, I heard from one physician that soda does not seem to be good for gastric catarrh. There is here a remedy that local inhabitants take against cholera, as a specially powerful disinfectant. This is a plant which has been used for ages for cleaning the teeth—probably this is why they have such excellent teeth. It is said that a minimal dose of it, two or three drops diluted in a glass of water, is a preventive against many stomach and intestinal ailments, cancer among them. This remedy possesses a special penetrative property, and it destroys all intestinal bacteria. It can therefore serve as a prophylactic; when rinsing the mouth after meals, one may swallow one or two drops of this water.

* * *

For tuberculosis a decoction of the flower and even the leaves of the aloe with milk and honey is very good. Strange as it may seem, a brew of barley is also useful. Equally good is the concentration of the sun's rays upon the afflicted parts by means of a round magnifying glass, performing a sort of rotating massage around the sick spot. Sometimes one may even permit a light burn. But certainly, all these methods should be applied only under the supervision of a physician. Any ignorant use of them will bring undesirable results. Wonderful cures are now achieved in India through the use of sun baths, which are taken precisely at early sunrise. According to all sacred teachings, at sunrise the rays of the sun are especially powerful in their healing properties.

Thus, the best healers are the rays of the rising sun, pure mountain prana, and especially, pure thoughts and aspiration of the heart toward high, altruistic tasks. The most enlightened physicians and scientists are gradually beginning to pay attention to thought, and are already performing remarkable tests; and the greatly ridiculed Christian Science begins to draw merited attention.

13

5 July 1938

It is incorrect to surmise that "beyond the threshold of death we leave our grievances, rancor, and all kinds of offenses, debts and debtors, hate and hostility" and that "we are reborn on Earth again and again without these qualities, pure, illumined worthy to enter the eternal kingdom."

In reality, beyond the threshold of death we leave nothing out of he baggage enumerated by you, and we acquire still more besides. Man crosses into the Subtle World with all his vices and virtues, he indeed preserves his character in full. "Ulcers of the spirit are carried over into the Subtle World if they are not gotten rid of on Earth." Also, was it not said that "the sower is here, and the reaper is there" in the Subtle World? Moreover, all of our properties and qualities are refined or strengthened there, hence, those who are malicious here become still more furious there, and vice versa. Furthermore, we are not reborn such little angels as is usually imagined. Often, very real little devils are hiding under these innocent, on the surface, infants. Each Ego, at each new rebirth, preserves and brings along its entire baggage of the past. Where else can the entire accumulated experience be taken? After all, not only each of our actions but also each thought creates a vibration, and precisely these vibrations are the energies that enter the structure of the whole man, objective as well as subjective. Indeed, these energies engendered by man are his inseparable property (karmic), which follows him also in his new earthly life. The karmic consequences of the past life follow man; and he, in his next life, will collect the energies or vibrations impressed by him on the astral, because nothing can issue from nothing; therefore the link exists between lives, and the new, fine envelope is molded out of the former one. The aura of the newly born is white or colorless, because the consciousness has not yet colored it. But at the first glimmer of consciousness, the aura becomes tinged with its corresponding color.

And so, we truly bring along our old baggage, though not all acquired abilities can be manifested in one earthly life, the reason for this being again a karmic one (personal karma and the karma of entire humanity); the physical instrument is not yet adapted to the manifestation of the diverse accumulations of our individuality. Similarly, spiritual synthesis, in its cosmic range, reveals itself only at the completion of the earthly journey. Therefore, there are so few individuals who possess this highest gift.

* * *

It is futile to think that Christ, when bringing Judas closer to him, did not know where the free will of this disciple would bring him. Definitely, He did know. He also knew His end, because it was not the first time that Judas had come near Him. Christ knew who was hiding behind the image of Judas. Judas was a traitor of long standing, and not just once did he betray Christ. Yet it was said long ago that precisely the Jinn build temples. Through the crucifixion of Christ Judas gave to the world a new God.

Likewise, other high Spirits knew when this or that traitor approached them. The laws of karma are complex, and often a traitor approaches, not because of our personal karma, but because of the karma of a group or even of a nation. Each betrayal is a luminous ascent for the betrayed one, but an abysmal horror for the traitor and for those who abet him.

Truly, people who never heard about the law of karma or those who do know about it yet never penetrated into the most complex entwinements of this law that catches in its plaiting masses of participants, and even entire nations, will never understand how the immutable law acts. They will also not understand the statement that Jinn build temples. They will not comprehend that, due to humanity's imperfection, precisely such a paradox takes place.

Only a naive average man thinks that friends alone help to uplift a man, and that where Light is nothing evil can approach. Such a man will never rise to the realization that only antipodes uplift each other. Lukewarm followers, like an amorphous mass, remain with nothing and recalling to mind the apocalyptic statement, they are truly spewed out of the mouth of time.

It is difficult for an average man to attain the understanding that we grow only through obstacles.

* * *

Of course, no one can assert the omniscience of Christ during his earthly sojourn. But there is no doubt that He knew the main stages of his Path and also the nature of the people who approached Him. Much lesser personalities know this unerringly through their accumulated straight-knowledge. Karma brings upon their path certain people with whom they are destined to build. The moral state of mankind makes this choice weighty and difficult. However, the dates of some events are coming close, and one must choose from a limited number. Moreover, the choice is often dependent upon the participation of other co-workers. These are very few who reflect upon the frightful moral condition of humanity; furthermore, there are people, good and pleasing, who are absolutely incapable of accepting the burden of an active achievement, or even assisting with it. Fear, and apprehension of appearing ridiculous paralyze their best intentions. There are many who are vehement in evil, but very few who are vehement in Good. And those good, but by nature cowardly people increase the ranks of those who are non-resistant to evil; by leaving the best possibilities to the Jinn, they increase the calamities and sufferings of humanity. Still, for every attainment courage is needed, but a courage combining wise solicitude and caution.

Likewise, there can be no nebulous prophecies coming from the Highest Source. Reread paragraph 24 and 25 in *New Era Community*. The destined executors of prophecies know their meaning and significance. Therefore, let us not think that Christ, this Great Spirit, did not know what was destined for him. To each bearer of the achievement a full chalice is offered, and he himself chooses whether he wishes to accept it in its entirety or only a portion of it. According to the law of antithesis, the worst brings the best. Who, therefore, of the valiant toilers of the spirit, will not accept the full chalice? In the Teaching acceptance of the full chalice is also advised, and we shall not deviate from this Advice.

To all vilifiers we shall say in the words of a great Thinker, "He who takes into consideration the opinions of multitudes will never rise above the crowd." I do not know a worse lot than to remain amidst crowds! Therefore, we look upon all evil commentators with calmness. There are people who strive for golden crowns, but there are others who direct their entire aspiration toward the attainment of a crown not made with human hands and therefore eternal.

* * *

I am quoting here from a Discourse. "Precisely crowds, with their shouts, were leading the Great Teacher to special sufferings. Crowds, these very same crowds, shouted about a kingdom, and they also hastened the execution. Thus they singularly aided the fulfillment of the prophecies. It is impossible to imagine the karma that was cast upon the masses of madmen! Many can recall at present the events which fell upon the shoulders of many subsequent generations. When I advise refraining from senseless words and thoughts, I ask you thus to think about the future. The Teacher could have walked on the Path of Achievement without the roars of crowds, but precisely those who had been healed by him filled space with threats and maledictions. Such a manifestation of free will could be called by many names, nevertheless it will remain free will. It is correct to regard free will as the highest gift, but how wisely one should use this precious treasure!"

A careless word, even in itself good, but spoken not at the right moment and not according to the level of the consciousness of one's listeners, increases the ranks of the enemies. Therefore it is so important to refrain from giving out that which is secret. Verily, he who knows and understands the full significance of words is able to safeguard that which is entrusted.

14

12 July 1938

Of course, now you will have to acknowledge that I was right in advising you not to discuss the Teaching amidst obviously hostile surroundings. Likewise, you will now be convinced that my first letter remains in full force, for it contains answers to almost all the questions again put before me. You write that someone asks by whom and in what way is the Teaching given. The answer to the first question is given in the Teaching, and its Author gives his name in several of the books. The answer to the second question is also given in the many pages of those same books. All such questions reveal how superficially the books are fathomed by these questioners.

As to those who worry about whether any distortions have crept into the Teaching, one may ask them, Did they not realize that it is just as easy for the Teacher to point out this or that mistake which slipped in as to give the next page? Yet, the rhythm of the Teaching is continuously increasing. But regrettably, mistakes by the printer and the copyist are unavoidable. However, they were corrected as far as possible. I do not know any book that does not have some misprints, and especially in our time of loss of quality in everything.

I am also sufficiently acquainted with the gift of human nature or consciousness, and I know that no assurances can ever convince anyone. Only our personal, inner conviction, which has its root in the accumulations of our past lives, can help in discerning the truth. Therefore my affirmations also will never be accepted by the doubting ones. I beg of you, be assured that we do not attempt either to persuade or dissuade anyone, and we rise up with all the power of our spirit against any forcing of the books of Living Ethics on anyone, and more so any kind of authorities. Each one must follow his path. Only he can deeply feel the truth of the Teaching and become aflame in his heart to the Call of the Teacher, who has in his former lives already approached the Teaching and the Great Teachers. Among those who approach for the first time there are always many waverings and doubts. But where doubt has made its nest, the fires of the heart cannot be kindled. Doubt is the most frightful poison. Nothing can be attained in any field of endeavor where there is evidence of doubt. No discovery could have been made if the searcher doubted the correctness of his theory; the proverb "Faith moves mountains" has a profound meaning. Man does not realize that throughout his entire life he does things he believes. Precisely what to believe and how to believe comprises the solution of the problems of being. Man's free will or free choice molds his destiny.

Those who wish to follow Christ exclusively should follow him. But let them clearly define which Christ they wish to serve, the evangelical Christ or the Christ of the later-day churchmen. In this realization there will already be a shifting of consciousness. None of the Great Teachers will ever demean any one of the Great Founders of ancient or later religions, because, verily, the very same Ego has many a time reincarnated in some of them.

And to widely proclaim the hierarchical succession of Great Teachers was never permitted. A thinking disciple fully realizes the harm of such untimely announcements in doubting or hostile hands. Only novices, who do not understand that on each carelessly spoken word may hang the destiny and life of many people, ask questions the answers to which were given in remote antiquity during the highest initiations. Human consciousness has hardly changed since that time, and many ways, alas, has become even coarser.

You write that there are those who are indignant at the admonition encountered in the first book—"love Me"—and consider it a sort of importunity. To this I say, Apparently the hearts of these people have become petrified, and they do not know what is the fire of the heart, what is the flaming love of the disciple for the Teacher, and what joy these words of the Teacher awaken in the flaming heart of the disciple. For by this very declaration the Teacher not only accepts the love of the disciple but also brings him nearer and encourages him to follow this, the shortest and royal path. Subtle are the strings of the heart, and only when they are tempered by its fires, which are kindled by contact with the furnace of life, can they transmit to us the secretly resounding mysteries of man's being. Nothing coarse, nothing demanding, doubting, denying, deriding will find a key to any mystery of the higher Be-ness. Hence, this hatred by the desiccated hearts of all Light, of all joy filled with the higher beauty of devotion and love for Hierarchy.

I regret it if my opinion about certain books has deeply hurt a good man, but I cannot take it back. It would be dishonest for me to praise what I know to be a distortion of truth. Likewise, someone wrongfully insists about our seeming unfriendliness toward Theosophists, because this is untrue. Our attitude toward Theosophists was always most friendly, and we have quite a few friends among them. Many Theosophists in different countries read and love the books of the Teaching. There are numerous Theosophical groups which often practically exclude each other.

Truly, it is sad that there are people who speak negatively about the books of the Teaching and yet have not read any of them. And of those who regard themselves as respectable and educated men, who would renounce and speak disparagingly about that which he does not know at all or with which he has only a superficial acquaintance? Will such criticism be based on truth? Have not readers the right to demand at least a primitive honesty from the critics?

But it is said that no Teaching was ever extolled by friends; always and in everything the fury of enemies helps. The Jinn build the temples. A sign from heaven was demanded even from Christ, and he was accused of ejecting the devils through the diabolical power of the prince of the devils. Read again the Gospel of St. Luke 11:15. Remarkable is the answer of Christ to these casuists, in the same chapter. Strange as it seems, those who attack the books of the Teaching and loudly denounce them are precisely those who do not know them, just as they do not know their own Scriptures.

As to those who refuse to read the books of Living Ethics out of personal offense at my opinion about certain books, it remains but to pity them. We never refuse to read any book offered to us, in order not to somehow pass by a precious pearl. However, discrimination was placed in the foundation of discipleship, always and in all Teachings. H. P. B. especially insisted on discrimination, which is contained in the fires of the heart, in straight-knowledge—this eye of Dangma. And so, I will say once again that whatever is linked directly with H. P. B. is deeply revered by us. One may again regret that, apparently, some foreign and Russian Theosophists not only do not know the entire collection of H. P. B.'s works but are not even cognizant of the whole history of the Theosophical movement. A great deal of light could be shed if such books as the big volume of around 500 pages of *The Mahatma Letters to A. P. Sinnett* and a similar volume of *The Letters of H. P. Blavatsky to A. P. Sinnett* should become accessible to those readers who do not know English.

Regarding the accusation of my being intolerant toward the Theosophical Society, this accusation is obviously laying the fault at another man's door. Long before the appearance in the magazine *Occultism and Yoga* of the excerpts from my letter to Dr. Asejev, in which I speak about my attitude toward certain books of L.,, I had written proofs sent to me by friends, about some

Theosophical authorities who spoke against the books of Agni Yoga and forbade their followers to read them. Is it possible that they would deny their own words? One wishes to say to all—be more kind and much will become easier.

The Teaching speaks about the canon "By thy God." Therefore, tell those who, though accepting the Teaching, cannot accept its Source or those through whom it is transmitted, that they should not be disturbed by these questions. For them, let there be neither the Source nor the intermediaries. Let the Teaching speak for itself.

Indeed, I agree with you that the refusal to accept the Source deprives the words of the Teaching of the highest magnet of the heart and of the higher beauty. But the refusal to accept the intermediaries *cannot* diminish the Teaching. Therefore, I beg you to assure everybody that I do not pretend to any authority and ask them to forget about my existence.

Once again, I must say that to all questions and objections brought by you from the listeners and participants of the Agni Yoga group there are exact answers in the books of the Teaching. Having read the objections and questions, it becomes clear that no one troubled himself to get thoroughly acquainted with all fourteen books of the Teaching published to date.

The Brotherhood of Light is based upon unity, and therefore all its participants are united in the one Stronghold., One could have answered these inquirers with the following words, "And Jesus knew their thoughts, and said unto them, Every kingdom divided against itself is brought to desolation; and every city or house divided against itself shall not stand."

Grievous is the atmosphere of disunity and blasphemy. I do not know any worse one; the greatest harm, including pernicious ailments, can be the result of it. Contemporary medical scientists assert that all moral principles have a purely biological foundation.

If the Teaching is close to you, you will not carry it to the bazaar. From all my heart I wish that you may soon get out of the poisoned atmosphere.

All light to you.

Have just looked through the copy of my letter to the person mentioned by you, and notice that I write about straight-knowledge, the accumulation of which gives us the possibility of penetrating into the very essence of things. Precisely, straight-knowledge is the sole criterion in all judgments. But nowhere did I liken straight-knowledge to inspiration or Hiero-inspiration. However, there is no doubt that only an accumulation of straight knowledge gives the possibility of direct and constant communion with the Teachers, and thus being able to receive, not fragmentary information, but the entire Ocean of the Teaching. I am quoting here an excerpt from this letter: "Indeed, the only true Teacher is the 'Invisible' Teacher (the Teacher of the Great Brotherhood). But are there many who can have direct access to such a Teacher? This does not mean that the Teacher is inaccessible, no, verily, he is the closest. But this closeness cannot be endured by all. It is revealed without harm only to him who has carried the Image of the Teacher for many centuries in the innermost recesses of his heart. Without this age-old accumulation and the established magnetic link, it is difficult to absorb the rays that are sent by the 'Invisible' Teacher, they may destroy the unprepared recipient. Even in the case of age-old tests and approaches, the new earthly envelope, or recipient, must become accustomed to this receptivity over many years. The invisible rays are very powerful and sometimes act more strongly than radium."

In view of having written previously to my correspondents about the acceptance of disciples and about the earthly teacher, to ease up my work I am enclosing here the existing copies of those pages. But now I will answer concerning your doubt regarding straight-knowledge. Indeed, it is difficult to develop or awaken straight-knowledge in oneself, yet there is no other criterion. Full discrimination comes only in this way. And the main difficulty is that straight-knowledge is not awakened in us while the feelings of selfhood, conceit, hypocrisy, or insincerity predominate in our heart. Only when these vipers are ejected does the voice of the heart take their place, and straight-knowledge becomes clear and infallible. Believe me, if someone is striving sincerely, he shall meet his earthly teacher and recognize him. But very, very rarely do these occurrences take place on our Earth. Let us recall the insignificant number of disciples that even the Great Teachers had during their earthly lives. Since those times humanity has not improved, and crucifixion and betrayal of the earthly Bearers of Light still continues. And the very same traitors, having only put on new masks, are contriving still more subtle methods of inquisition.

Yes, it is most difficult for people to comprehend the law of Hierarchy. Yet, at the same time, precisely those who vociferate most of all against this cosmic law, are nevertheless blindly submissive to any hierarchy, beginning with standardized conditions, customs, and style, and ending with even accepting the hierarchy of evil in its hidden multiformity. After all, the hierarchy of evil is much closer to the earthly spheres, and its numerous followers, the inhabitants of the lower spheres of the Subtle World take delight in instilling in people the most abominable thoughts and in pushing them to the most fratricidal disunity and actions. During the days of Armageddon the forces of evil have become stronger, therefore it is so essential to cognize the Hierarchy of Light, and to strive upon this Path with one's whole heart. Of course, as it always was and will be, darkness itself will devour darkness. But how many "lukewarm" ones will perish, who could have been saved if they had realized the danger in time and had taken strong hold of the Hand of Help stretched out to them.

15

6 August 1938

Indeed, if the author of *Cosmosophia* narrates with such convincingness and vividness the sojourn of the soul of a sinner in the astral spheres, then he holds all the cards. The astral world is primarily a subjective world, therefore, if the author of this book so vividly describes certain conditions in the astral world, he probably has already experienced them himself or is going to experience them. It is indicated in all teachings that our most clear and considered thought and most keen feeling will give direction to our entire sojourn and state in the spheres of the supermundane world; in the same way, the very last thought has a deciding significance in the power of sending the spirit into the subtle spheres. In *The Mahatma Letters to A. P. Sinnett* there is a place in which Master K. H. points out the significance of the last thought before death. An example of an executed criminal is cited, how this murderer, as in a nightmare, will again and again experience in the Subtle World his crime and the full horror of his execution until the energy become exhausted. Our state in the Subtle World is molded out of our subjective moods, thoughts, and motives, in as much as our feelings become more acute. Somnolent and idle people will drag out there a still more wearisome existence deprived of their accustomed physical, external stimuli. Therefore it is so important to develop in oneself the ability to think and to direct thoughts toward creative labor, because creative thought has unlimited application in the Subtle World. But I would not advise anyone to dwell upon the horrors of the lower astral planes.

Verily, human imagination is lacking to describe all the multiformity of existence on either side. There is no doubt that the lower entities of the supermundane world are nourished by the emanations of decomposition, and are especially attracted by the magnetism of decomposed blood. Hence, there are all kinds of larvae near cemeteries, stockyards, on battlefields, in taverns, etc. They actually attach themselves to drunkards, and to gluttons who are eating meat. On the earthly plane many people already bear such vampires upon themselves.

If, in the lowest strata of the Subtle World, base human entities suffer from these larvae, they suffer no less when contacting the higher dwellers of the Subtle World. Just the approach to them of a higher spirit causes painful burns, and the astral tissue of their bodies begins to decompose.

In nature everything is mutually nurtured, and, of course, of the remains of decomposition nurture the larvae of the lower spheres, then according to analogy, the emanations of the higher spirits nurture the higher and middle spheres. True, in India, alongside the unsurpassed height of philosophical thought and spiritual purity, one may encounter the most disgusting expressions of various demoniac cults and animalistic obsessions, including the most abominable necromancy. There exists a sect, the followers of which feed on the brains of corpses. One may meet them in the cemeteries on a moonlit night occupied with their abominable task; where the Light is brightest, darkness is blackest.

There are villages here whose inhabitants at a definite time of the year meet at night in a forest glade, which is strictly guarded. Here the priests, in order to appease the evil spirits, evoke the lower entities. For this they perform a plentiful slaughter of animals, and with a certain rhythm of drums they bring those present into a particular state in which the lower entities, attracted by the emanations of freshly shed blood, obsess some bodies with greater ease. Such obsessed ones become infuriated and attack mostly women and children. Often these obsessing entities chew their victims to death.

You are right in regarding the descriptions of astral horrors with disgust. Every Teaching of Light must primarily direct to wisdom, to joy of labor, to perfectment, and to highest beauty, while only indicating the unavoidable sufferings in the Subtle World of those who have offended the law of Equilibrium, or harmony. Knowing the significance and power of thought, one may not pause long upon the images of terror and darkness without grave consequences.

We have already heard about the attack mentioned by you. All this reveals to you the local level of consciousness. The withdrawal of the article by M. L. is understandable. People do not like it when the nail is hit on the head. Several countries are occupied at present with the problem of indoctrination. Do you not think that this indoctrination of man will not be far removed from the creation of a kind of comprachicos? But I advise attacking the new country less. It enters the period of rebirth, and one should safeguard and sustain it in every way upon this path. "He who thinks of the past, loses his sight."

"Masses of people have shifted in urgent searchings, and they cannot reconcile material progress with the higher spiritual foundations. The present era is reminiscent of a certain period in Atlantis. At that time they could not find equilibrium; however, though one is now aware of a like nonconformity, some, more vitally alive nations, may find the necessary concordance. We see where the inception of synthesis may be realized. It will not be where the pendulum of life is inert, but where it is swinging to the utmost. There the significance of the Common Good is understood; there it is known that it can originate only with the Common Good. The formula is not yet pronounced; however, it already ripens in the depth of consciousness. ... Service, above all, discloses the path of realization of the Common Good. Not finery or rituals, but service to mankind. For many centuries words about cooperation have been uttered. Frequently, ideas were in advance of material possibilities, but at present people have found a multitude of useful adaptations, and the time has come when it will be necessary to remember about the Common

Good." Thus, look to where the pendulum is swinging to the utmost.

Now I shall answer your letter of July 4th. Verily, soon I shall have to put upon myself a vow of silence, because I see that my letters do not transmit what is in my thoughts. Different meaning, different shading is given to my words, and you know that precisely the tone makes the music. But apparently this shading of expressions is not grasped by people.

I advise you to curtail your correspondence as much as possible. Take time for a serious study of the works of H. P. B. and of the Teaching of Living Ethics, and to become acquainted with the newest scientific discoveries, and attainments in the field of medicine. Avoid all kinds of "esoterics," not they will build the new world, but the spiritual toilers who give their souls for the Common Good. The revaluation of values will touch upon many things. It is astonishing to see how, in time, many terms lose their meaning and become completely unacceptable. Prepare for a new step, which is being laid broadly and powerfully.

16

13 August 1938

I agree with you that what has been already published cannot be regarded as something subject to concealment. And yet, sensitiveness or co-measurement should prompt where and when it is fitting to use one or the other—speech or silence. Much depends upon how to transmit, how to clarify, and under what circumstances to allude to or advance one or another concept. Sometimes, even the mere mention of the higher worlds or a spirit will be unfitting and will only cause blasphemy and terrible antagonism. Therefore I cannot agree with the opinion expressed that excessive caution is just as harmful as excessive talkativeness. I will say that if excessive caution is to be judged, talkativeness is already condemned. It is always better not to complete than to alter. Remember how often the Teaching speaks about the harm of that which is told not at the right time. "Even an Arhat may not annihilate the consequences of thought and word." How often a human life hangs upon such a word!

So much is distortedly refracted in limited consciousnesses, and the resulting harm is enormous. Only the rarest of individuals can rise above the plane of our reality (to use a better word, evidence) and understand those lows that govern events and consequently people. Alas, great knowledge is not forgiven and evokes the angry antagonism of the crowd and of mediocrities. Therefore, in all ages Great Teachers ordained speaking according to the level of the consciousness of the listeners and in co-measurement with circumstances. Deviation from this wise covenant usually ended in the destruction of many enlightened undertakings and the loss of human lives.

If someone is in a quandary saying, "In what way were many more mistakes made since the time of Christ—in superfluous speech or in superfluous silence?" I shall answer that in everything related to Christ and his Teaching, not that which was superfluously said or left unsaid brought much harm, but precisely the ignorant distortion of his simple statements and covenants for the sake of greed. Of great benefit would be the work of clarifying the New Testament in the light of a synthesis of all the existing spiritual Teachings. Indeed, very fitting are the parallels quoted by you between the Teachings. Certainly, not a few of these are also in Buddhism. At present, a minister, Arthur Massey, is occupied with this task and is writing about it in a small local magazine "Vision."

* * *

Verily, representatives of the Sixth Race will have to work not a little on themselves spiritually in order to open up the nerve centers. But at the next stage of refinement of the organism, this process will be considerably eased and hastened. Nevertheless, without discipline, efforts and labor, nothing can be achieved.

Wherever possible, one should replace the words *Lord, God, Creator* by *Divine Principle*, for the anthropomorphic concept linked with the word God has become too strongly enrooted in the consciousness of the masses. It is desirable to somewhat advance the thinking of the people toward the realization of the magnitude and infinitude of the Principle of all Being, and of understanding their responsibility as the bearers of this Principle. People read in their sacred scriptures and speak about the Unutterable, Incomprehensible, and Invisible God, yet at the same time they endow this Incomprehensibility with all the anthropomorphic qualities, feelings, and actions!

You write that you "often hear remonstrances against the Teaching of the East because it lacks the teaching of love, such as is to be found in the Gospel." This reproach is extremely unjust, and those who remonstrate disclose their ignorance. Precisely the greatest cult of Love exists in the East. All their spiritual teachings, all their mythology, all their epics, all their poetry and folklore extol this lofty feeling, through which all is created, all lives and moves. Indeed, nowhere is Love so sung about as in the East, in all its subtlest nuances and qualities. All Yogas have as their basis love of or devotion to the chosen Ideal. The highest form of Yoga is called the Yoga of Love. In this Yoga the Divine Principle takes on the aspect of the Beloved One (be it he or she) for the most powerful form of love is expressed in the love of the Two Origins. Verily, the entire poetry of the East is one hymn of love for the Divine Principle in all its aspects, from the Unfathomable and Unutterable to the image of a personal God, Guru, Mother, Beloved. Thus, the Teaching of Living Ethics is also a call to Love, to Service for the Common Good, which is the highest form of love, because it is devoid of selfhood. Love for humanity demands complete self-abnegation and self-sacrifice. For if the love for the Beloved brings an answer from the Beloved, the love for humanity is crowned with a wreath of thorns.

To facilitate attainment for the Common Good, all Teachings of the East indicate to us the awakening of our love for the Hierarchy of Light, for the chosen Guru, for striving toward the Great Service. The Teachings of the East, just as the Teaching of Living Ethics, affirm the education of the heart for the assimilation of the highest form of love. Love for humanity is an active attainment of love. Love for Hierarchy is the greatest joy and rapture of the spirit. But one form of love without the other is imperfect; therefore, blessing to him who can contain them both in his heart.

Now, about the engenderment of humanity on our planet. First of all, it is essential to understand that the lunar evolution was considerably lower than the earthly one, and the dwellers of the moon did not possess mind, or so-called intellect. At their termination of the lunar evolution, their minds did not exceed the instinct of animals. However, there are now also not a few Earth-dwellers whose minds are not far removed from the instinct of animals! In fact, many people still live by instinct. Therefore, the lunar monads, for that reason, had to start their new evolution on Earth with the vegetable and animal kingdoms in order to adapt themselves to the conditions of the new planet. The Barhishads mentioned in *The Secret Doctrine* belong to an evolution of other, much higher worlds, also far from being perfect. True, among them were monads of various degrees of development. They aided in the investiture of the lunar monads with human sheaths. In connection with this read page 86, "Supplementary Notes" in *The Mahatma Letters*. Precisely the Barhishads founded the first race of men on our Earth. But all they could do was to provide the astral covering only, with its animal instincts. Therefore, for the speedier awakening of the embryos of the mind, it was necessary to receive an impulse, or spark, either from those Spirits who already were endowed with higher understanding and with a fully formed mental body, or from the *Agnishavattas, Kumaras,* Archangels, and so forth, as they are called in various religions.

The variety of nature's species depends precisely on the spirits that are attracted from other worlds, and even systems. For, during the explosions of this or that world, its astral sphere is sometimes attracted to the orbit of a planet which belongs to another system.

Thus, the poets, whose imagination drew for them beautiful aerial images of the lunar-dwellers, would have shuddered at sight of some of the real lunar inhabitants, covered with hair and possessing other peculiarities. At that, their inner structure deferred from ours, as did their vision also, they could see in front and in back. We must get used to thoughts about an *endless variety* of creations and about *the lingering* of evolution upon the first steps. Only with the inception of the mind does evolution enter into the speeded-up process of development, and this mind, when in harmony with the Guiding Forces, can raise the planet to a great flowering or, adversely it will hasten its disintegration or downfall.

Thus, one should always remember, firstly, the entire multiformity of evolution on Infinity, and, secondly, the basic scheme. Actually, the lower entities pass through the lower kingdoms of the planet in order to adapt themselves to its conditions and to develop the lower envelopes. But when completion in the highest animal type is reached and a possibility arrives of so-called human intelligent evolution, the Builders, or the Hierarchy of the Spirits of higher evolutions from other worlds, sacrifice their essence to array the monads in a human envelope, and even they themselves reincarnate in these envelopes, during different periods. Human evolution proceeds on three planes; physical, psychic, and spiritual.

I think that should our planet happily complete its ordained cycle the spirits of earthly humanity could fulfill the role of the *Barhishads* on a new planet, and the highest monads among them could even become the awakeners of the fire of the mind; for, was it not said in *The Secret Doctrine* that in the Seventh Race many men will become sons of immaculate parents and will be Buddhas. But if our planet does not endure, and explodes before the date, then the majority of our humanity may definitely find itself on a lower planet and will again have to pass through its lower kingdoms. Great conformity and goal-fitness rule in Cosmos.

It is said that on the higher planets there are fewer animals, and they are far more perfect. Thus there are no insects and beasts of prey on Venus. There exists a veritable kingdom of flights. People fly, birds fly, and even fish. And the birds understand human speech. The colors of fishes and of birds' feathers attain amazing combinations and beauty.

I shall quote here a useful Discourse: "You know how difficult it is for people to accept the multiformity of evolution. First of all, they will talk about the one law. Each one will bring up those fragments about the Universe which he chanced to learn. There will be found many conflicting facts, and people will not be remiss in reproving someone for inaccuracy. Disputes and perplexities arise mostly from an inability to comprehend Infinity. An earthly mind with difficulty pictures a scheme that will remain inviolate. It is equally difficult to imagine all the branches of the very same law, nevertheless, one should become accustomed to the cosmic multiformity. Our planet, with its subtle spheres, can experience the most unexpected influences from the far-off worlds. One should not think that our solar system presents something isolated; on the contrary, all the worlds are in the most subtle reciprocity. Thus, the basic law is immutable, yet each heavenly body can create individual features around itself.

"The representatives of the most remote evolutions can get along on Earth with the people of the Sixth Race. One may also observe that the conception of the world fluctuates from primitive to enlightened realization. However, irreconcilable extremes are not only noticed amidst manifestations of nature, they are still more startling in the Subtle World. One may visualize how the reactions of the most remote systems can intrude. Such reactions can be likened to explosions and tornadoes. They bring in a sort of revolution, therefore one should not picture the Subtle World as something subject to the dead-letter of the law. Even in the higher spheres conflicts of psychic forces can occur, and one should get used to these concepts.

"Only a clear realization of the great diversity can safeguard from harmful limitation. At first one should try to sense oneself as living in Infinity, and later one can become strengthened by the realization of the far-off world. Thus, one will arrive at the thought of the diversity of evolution."

Now, about purgatory, or the middle spheres of the Subtle World. The lower strata are quite close to the description of hell. In fact, it depends upon man himself how best to make use, for himself and others, of his stay in the middle spheres. The higher spheres become accessible to us in accordance with the measure of our purification, and before our immersion in the state of Devachan we cast off the already outworn astral envelope; the purer it is, the more quickly it decomposes. The astral envelope of the higher spirits, after being utilized, is given over to the Spatial Fire with the help of the Teacher. However, not all spirits immerse themselves in Devachan; there are strong spirits who do not need this stopover and who hasten to continue their earthly path. If, in the Subtle World, man would strive to realize his errors, the entire evolution would be considerably hastened. But the difficulty lies in that average people—not good and not bad, but without strivings and clearly expressed abilities—when entering the indifferent and grey sphere of the Subtle World that is compatible with them, usually drag out in it the very same burdensome and depressed existence. Their small consciousness and undeveloped thinking do not permit them to rise in spirit and ascend into the higher spheres where creativity of thought reigns. Tepidity, indifference, and laziness are our most frightful executioners. They are the devourers of psychic energy, which alone makes us conscious possessors of the Chalice of Amrita—Immortality.

It is impossible to outlive vices in the Subtle World; they must be outlived on Earth. Because only on Earth can we receive new impulses of energy and regenerate or transmute these into their higher manifestations. But in the Subtle world with the help of Guides one can realize the harmfulness of passions not yet outlived and can impress this knowledge upon the subtle centers to such an extent that in the new earthly rebirth it will be easier to conquer the attraction to this or that vice. If we could get rid of our vices in the Subtle World, of what use would be the earthly incarnations? And so, for the transmutation and sublimation of our energies—passions—we need our earthly, physical laboratory, in which are united and transmuted the elements of all worlds.

The most beautiful sojourn in the Subtle world is enjoyed by the souls of the great workers of thought and creativeness who gave their labor for the good of mankind. There they will find unlimited possibilities for applying all their abilities and strivings. One may envy the existence of Marconi and Flammarion in the subtle spheres.

Powerful, evil-minded souls, and souls who lived only for sensual pleasures suffer greatly, because of their inability to gratify their malice and passions. They virtually burn in the flame of their passions. Actually, for the most part they become obsessors and whisperers at night. They cannot ascend into the higher spheres, for the mere approach of a dweller of those spheres brings sufferings upon them, and their tissues begin to decompose in contact with the purer fluids. The torture from such burns of the subtle body surpasses bodily sufferings. The horrors of the lower strata of the Subtle World defy description, and it is better not to pause upon them in order not to increase them and so burden oneself with such thought-images.

* * *

I laughed a great deal at the practical wisdom in interpreting the words of the prayer, "And lead us not into temptation. ..." But it seems to me that if the Lord were always solicitous not to lead us into temptation, we would not learn anything. Our spirit is tempered by trials, and the essence of man is cognized only through temptations. Verbal instructions and warnings are of no avail; man is known according to his deeds. Picturing God in the role of a tempter of course does not befit the majestic Divine Principle, therefore it remains to suppose that in the words of this higher Self that He or it should hold him back from offense. But I prefer to say, "Blessed be the obstacles, through them we grow." True, one should not deduce from this that a bicycle can be left on the street without supervision or a safe can be left open. All is well in its place.

Thank you for the book, I have not as yet succeeded in reading it to the end. Many things are curious in it. But I believe that it was quoted "dressed up" already in another country, therefore there is included in it much that could not have been uttered under the conditions in which the dispute took place; and of course this greatly weakens its interest. Besides, the explanations of mysteries and the affirmation of the resurrection of people in the physical body are not very convincing and only turn back the thinking to age-old errors. Also unjust are the attacks on certain Socialist writers and thinkers. Thus the author in vain attacks Gorky, whose words he quotes: "I see spread before me a grandiose panorama of Earth, like a giant emerald, exquisitely faceted by the labor of free humanity. All people are intelligent, and it is natural for each one to accept the feeling of personal responsibility for everything that is created by him and around him. Everywhere are cities, gardens, imposing buildings, everywhere the forces of nature work for man, mastered and organized by his mind, and finally he himself becomes verily the ruler of the elements. His physical energy is no longer wasted on coarse, dirty work; it is transformed into a spiritual one and all its force is directed toward the investigation of those basic questions of Existence, for whose solution human thought has been unsuccessfully struggling since remote times."

Having read these beautiful lines, I can only say that every intelligent person who strives toward progress, toward the Common Good, undoubtedly shares these hopes of the great writer. Note how the defender of God and spirit ridicules the statement of Gorky that the forces of nature will be mastered and organized by the mind of man, and *physical energy* itself will be transformed into a *spiritual one*. It seems absurd to this reader that one can direct energy toward the investigation of questions of Existence! He regrets that "Gorky, in spite of all the wealth of his phantasy, could not invent any other work for people than occupation with theological investigation"?! But does not the investigation of the problems and laws of Being constitute the subject of utmost importance in science? Does not this research disclose before us ever new laws and mysteries of nature—visible and invisible—of the far-off worlds and of the entire Universe? To condemn Gorky for poverty of imagination is unfitting. The picture drawn by Gorky is the dream of every thinking man, and many understand that its realization is possible only in a very remote future. For are there at present many intelligent people who understand their responsibility for all that is created by them and around them? And of those whose physical energy has been transmuted into a spiritual one there are probably still less. What do you think?

* * *

Only a petrified heart will not aspire toward the Common Good, but will think only about the salvation of its own soul and about its resurrection in a physical body! One should think not about one's own salvation, but about the offering of life's achievement for the Common Good. Many of those who thought about the Common Good and sacrificed their lives for it were closer to God than those who had his name on their lips and thought only of their own salvation. "He that loveth his life shall lose it; and he that hateth his life in this world shall keep it unto life eternal."

17

10 September 1938

I must say about Tagore that I greatly love his wonderful image as a poet; but as a reflector of the thought of Hindu religious philosophy Vivekananda is closer to me. Tagore has not that dynamic quality that is so characteristic of Vivekananda. Tagore is the personification of gentleness, and his very voice, a high tenor, presents an astonishing contrast to his patriarchal exterior. Maybe, in this can be found the key to a certain duality which is inherent in him.

I think that Tagore, being under the influence of the West, stands up for the meaning of "art for art's sake." The formula itself, "art for art's sake," is not devoid of depth, for in the end everything leads to art. After all, art is a search for and expression of perfection in everything. Therefore, each striving, each action of man, when being perfected in its expression, in this way already approaches the realm of art. Nature itself in its constant creation of new combinations is an expression of the highest art. Thus, this formula could be paraphrased—perfectment for perfectment's sake.

At the end of the last century a timely protest was raised among Western artists against the excessive dominating significance of subject matter in paintings at that time. The subject of the painting was regarded as foremost, and the purely artistic problems were relegated to a secondary place. And thus in the West a formula came into being—"art for art's sake"—and it proved to be very useful. But, as usual, this beneficial step, in the course of time also degenerated among mediocrities into the most absurd forms, even to the imagery of the so-called "abstract" paintings in which nothing could be deciphered.

But now a new step approaches, the step of synthesis, and it is necessary to know how to combine purely artistic problems with creative thought and beautiful form. Our esthetic pleasure must be correspondingly broadened, in order to absorb art in its entirety. All the Muses must be summoned to participation in a single work of art. Each creator must imbibe the fundamentals of all arts, that he may create his work through them.

Verily, art should serve to uplift the consciousness of humanity. But to limit the means of expressing it is impermissible. The concept of art, already rejects all ugliness, and therefore beauty remains its only gauge.

* * *

Now, regarding the many-faceted imagery of a poet in his concept of the Deity. A poet, turning to a Higher Being, rises in spirit toward a higher image of manifested beauty. And where to seek this beauty if not in a symbol highest for us, in the perfect Image of the Crown of Creation!

The Sublime Being differs infinitely in an Eastern consciousness from the Sublime Being as conceived by the Western consciousness. The Highest Being, in the Eastern concept is not separated from his Creation.

His Creation is He Himself. The Eastern consciousness, in contrast with that of the West, is basically synthesized and is accustomed to uniting and containing all. Therefore it reveres the Great Origin in all its Aspects, because all aspects and all paths belong to It.

It is said in the Upanishads, "The Supreme Being penetrates

everything with Itself, consequently it is the innate possession of everyone." Every Hindu imbibes this concept with his mother's milk. The Eastern consciousness, being used to regarding itself as a particle of one infinite life manifested in endless phantasmagoria of changeable worlds and creatures, easily absorbs all the forms of such manifestations. He knows that he himself is but a reflection of the Supreme Being, which is revealed in the constant process of unfolding its boundless essence.

The Rishis of India, in their deep wisdom, knew about evolution, or the unfoldment of one boundless life, and understood that human consciousness can ascend to Truth only through familiar symbols. Therefore, alongside the highest concept of the Unutterable Mystery of Be-ness they gave it a majestic range of the most beautiful Images, so as to evoke and implant in it the entire gamut of subtlest nuances, feelings, presentations, and thoughts. And so, the imaging of the Supreme Being always fully corresponds to that degree of development on which man is to be found.

Great beauty is contained in the realization of unlimited life, unlimited evolution, in the cognition of unity in the multiformity of all existence, and consequently of the basic equality of mankind. But no less beauty is contained in the realization of the unlimited power of the human mind and its thought-creativeness. The highest life is revealed in the incalculable variety of manifestations of nature, and man—its creation—in his turn is summoned to create in the images and ideas accessible to him. Therefore, a poet, a musician, and an artist, who express creative thought, must find within the depths of their being those symbols which most of all respond to their heartstrings.

The knowledge of how to reflect in one's creation the entire scale of subtlest feelings, images, and thoughts is a great containment. Therefore, let us not limit the creators, let them pour out their song in all the multiformity of the sounds and visions revealed to them.

The East proclaims: "Two types of men do not worship God as a man: A man-beast who has no religion, and a liberated soul rising above human weaknesses and transcending the boundaries of its only nature. Only then can it worship God as he is."

The Highest Being, as conceived by Tagore, comprises all the most beloved by him, all the most beautiful Images, which live in his heart of a poet. Each touch calls forth the fire of thought-creativeness, and each heartstring will resound in its own way to the depths of consciousness touched upon.

According to the quotation from the article "A Poet's Religion," Tagore stresses the boundlessness of evolution and knowledge. In reality, only one Truth exists—the Truth of the infinity of Be-ness—and consequently, of Knowledge. In the manifested world this infinity of Be-ness is expressed in an eternal motion of cycles or in changes of conditions. Each one of these shiftings, or, as they are sometimes called, Manvantaras (Manvantaras of the Universe, of the worlds, and of human life), has as its goal to reveal and to polish a new facet of the a Jewel of Limitless Knowledge.

Ponder also how manifold is the creativeness of the great Guardians of Knowledge. How many different aspects of Truth They have to *simultaneously* plant and affirm in order that humanity may advance. A too great light blinds, a too small one obscures, therefore, with cautious touches is humanity raised up into the Wondrous Palace destined for it under the All-Containing Dome. But there are periods when consciousness enters, as it were, a blind alley and cannot leave it without special help; then ensue purifications, which are manifested in revolutions, in the casting out of old dogmas and values. These periods are grave, but they do bring a healthful recovery, and further ascent becomes possible. The Great Teachers of humanity acted as Healers of spirit and body, but their followers did not understand their solicitous touches and instead of the ray of a physician, drove in a coffin nail.

Thus, let us accept all expressions of Truth, and let us evaluate them only in accordance with their beauty.

18

10 September 1938

Indeed, all great ideas were brought into the world by exceptional individuals. And if, after they were brought into life, the dark ones distorted them, nevertheless their fundamental truth was unimpaired. In fact, the dark forces in their own way help to affirm enlightened ideas in the world. The dark ones hasten every process of corruption and therein lies their particular usefulness. Without their participation it would be far more difficult for the ideas of Light to become affirmed if one takes into consideration the level of consciousness of contemporary humanity and the shocking quantity of lukewarm ones, or non-resisters, ready for any compromise so as not to disturb their usual way of life. Thus, the sufferings of the oppressed would have been dragged out into millennia, and the bacchanalia of the ruling classes would bring many countries to final dissolution and degeneration. Precisely because of the low level of humanity as a whole and also because of the often unwise leadership, one has to regard revolutions as an uprising of healthy cells for the defense of the whole organism. Remember how the Russian Revolution was hailed by many countries. To what an extent these plaudits were disinterested and sincere is another matter. In human fashion, each one considered his own temporary gain. But in any case enough was, and is, now written about the former Russian despotism, barbarism, frightful poverty, and the backwardness of our people; the latter statement regettably was not without foundation. Therefore, we should value the shifting that took place in the consciousness of the masses, because, at the cost of terrible sufferings, a new step has been achieved that will help all mankind.

From the enclosure sent by you a reader might come to the conclusion that someone is against the great ideas of liberty, equality, and brotherhood—ideas which alone keep humanity alive! But if these leading ideas were to be put aside because they seem utopian, as it were, then it would be better for humanity to cease to exist as soon as possible. Unless these ideas are carried in the heart, humanity will sink into unheard of crimes and depravity and will slowly disintegrate and perish from the calamities engendered by them.

If these ideas are utopian, then all Teachings of Life are utopian in like measure.

The French revolutionaries sought to achieve social liberty and equality, or the assertion of those principles or forms of freedom and justice that have to be laid in the foundation of every healthy state, namely, freedom of conscience and thought, freedom of choice of occupation, and the equality of all citizens, or abolition of classes (privileged castes). True, only unenlightened people understand freedom as insubordination and equality as a leveling of abilities. Nevertheless, a basic social equality must be realized. Every citizen of a country is equal before its laws, and only his abilities determine his position in the social structure and labor.

I agree with the deductions of Prof. Frank quoted by you. It is also quite true that "equality in an absolute sense cannot be realized and that the Hierarchic Principle is a natural attribute of society." Hierarchy is a cosmic law, and this very same cosmic foundation affirms the equality of each monad, as far as the growth of its individuality is concerned. Therefore, state laws, in order to serve the vital interests, should reflect cosmic laws. Thus, every born citizen of this or that country, due to his birthright becomes potentially eligible for all rights, i.e., as it is said in the United States of America, "every citizen of America may become its President." Indeed, this right must be safeguarded. But as you know, the citizens of many countries are deprived of that very kind of equality. Thus, all have an equal birthright, but all are not equal according to their abilities. And this inequality is not only goal-fitting but also just, for abilities are achieved by personal labor and personal efforts during countless millennia. And this inequality ceases to be inequality and comes under the guiding law of hierarchy. The tormenting problem of the equality and inequality of people could be solved if the law of reincarnation were to become accessible to the consciousness of the masses. An outstanding public figure, Michael Roberts, I believe, once said, "If the members of the Cabinet were convinced that after death they would be reincarnated in families that live in the poorest quarters of London, social reforms would have been initiated with astonishing haste." One may add that many other things would also have been changed.

* * *

I do not agree that "in our time only a man who is put in prison can dream about liberty." True, a prison deprives a man of freedom of locomotion and action, but how many other skillfully hidden forms of slavery still exist in all state systems! It is in vain to think that there is at present no legitimized social slavery. It may be even stronger now than ever before. And the most lamentable of these types of slavery is assuredly slavery of thought and slavery of woman. It is unbelievable to imagine that in this, our age, when even the most backward consciousnesses have accepted the law of evolution, there can still exist dead dogmas, or that the subjugated position of woman, mother of humanity, is tolerated! Indeed, this subjugated position of woman is a most shameful madness and is the cause of the degeneration of humanity. Soon this truth also will become obvious. But at present, alas, even among the acknowledged "outstanding" minds, one may hear the opinion expressed that women should not be given equal education with men, and also that women should not aspire to the professions and positions occupied by men. The latter circumstance is of course the most important. What abysmal egoism rings out in this statement!

Nevertheless, we shall ask, Exactly which positions or professions should be regarded as belonging exclusively to women? In enumerating all those for both sexes, there will remain none for women. Could it be that the entire significance of woman is brought down only to giving birth, nursing, and to the entertainment of man? But, then, what a low opinion man has of himself if his "entertainer" has to be deprived of higher mental development. It is remarkable that the "sages" who deprive woman of higher education, at the same time proclaim hypocritically that "the destination of woman is much higher;' however, what this "much higher" is, they do not explain. Does it consist in creating unsuccessful specimens of a purely masculine mind so as to increase one's own enslavement and thus add to the degeneration of mankind? Still, psychic energy cannot be violated when it demands manifestation. Whence come this frightful spreading of psychic illnesses and the ever-growing number of the mentally deficient, now observed especially in America? Thus, according to medical statistics, one in every 20 persons is a candidate for an insane asylum at one or another period in his life. The number of weak-minded is equally shocking. Alexis Carrel gives this data in his book *Man the Unknown*. His book is interesting and gives a true picture of the crumbling of our materialistic civilization. Based upon scientific data, Carrel points out the paths for the restoration of humanity's health. However, since even a wise man stumbles, one may also find in this useful work certain peculiarities. As a matter of fact, in this book Carrel expresses the opinion mentioned above about the education of women. While adhering to the idea of evolution, at the same time he cuts it short, leaving only a limited education to women and depriving them of a place in the structure of life! But one cannot go against evolution, and we already know how high is the cost to humanity of each such resistance. Examples of this are obvious in all revolutions.

It is said in the books of the Teaching of New Life, "At the time when We speak about equal and full rights, the servants of darkness expel women from many fields, precisely where they could bring the most benefit. ... Precisely now one should think about full rights, but darkness inundates the domains that are the most strained."

* * *

Why should one think that the application of higher principles is possible only in a community? Service for the Common Good must and should be realized in all circumstances. But, truly, through conscious cooperation such service increases in an incalculable progression.

One should not frighten the readers by a desire to turn everyone back to a primitive patriarchal community. People, as a rule, picture this primitive patriarchal community quite differently. Let us not forget that the New Epoch also demands new definitions. And nothing is further removed from contemporary thinking than a patriarchal state, and a primitive one at that!

Nowhere does the Teaching of Living Ethics, or of New Life, insist upon living closely together. On the contrary, it even warns against bodily jostling. It constantly repeats that cooperation must be revealed in daily life, in all conditions in which we are placed by life. Bodily crowding and all kinds of petty things in life create a heavy atmosphere in which, instead of unity, a malicious disunity is sustained. *At all times, everywhere, and in all things* a conscious friendly cooperation is needed. But all artificial unions never brought, or will bring, any good. In the family we already have an example of communal living. And why should we think about some sort of primitive, patriarchal community and not try first of all to fulfill our responsibilities in our own family? Among solutions of the problems of communal living why not pay attention primarily to home life? Indeed, if people would realize the meaning of the communal principle, they would manifest more common sense upon entering into a marriage. They would understand the responsibility that they assume for the joining of often incompatible elements.

One can cooperate successfully while being in different cities and even in different countries. With every new scientific discovery and invention distances become of less and less consequence. And the only true unity, *unity in spirit and consciousness* becomes stronger and more powerfully asserted. Brotherhood can be realized only in unity of consciousnesses. The Teacher works for this unity of consciousness with the closest disciples, but physical unity is not taken into consideration. And even closely harmonized consciousnesses that are in comparatively close bodily proximity must part at times for the renewal of their forces and for new accumulations. Hence the instruction of Lord Buddha about the necessity of travels for the members of the community.

Consequently, one should understand community, not in the narrow sense, but in a very broad one—precisely as cooperation with all humanity, with all worlds, with all that exists. People suffer greatly from lack of a friendly attitude toward each other, therefore, to lock them up in closed communities will only strengthen their alienation from the world community, which contains all humanity and all planes of Be-ness.

Verily, *the epoch of common cooperation* is being created.

* * *

I also do not agree with the interpretation of only the positive role of the monasteries. The fact that some of them did exist for several centuries does not prove anything. Countries went through many kinds of upheavals. Rulers were replaced, also princes of the church and abbots of monasteries; yet the countries, palaces, and monastery walls continued to stand firm. But we know from history that the most venerated and outstanding saints left monasteries and founded new religious orders, often of wandering monks and nuns. The true Spiritual Toilers striving toward a change for the better, toward evolution, could not remain within dead walls, which often were more reminiscent of a prison of the spirit than a hearth of Light. With the exception of some, the monasteries when founded exerted that benevolent influence on the population which they were supposed to exert. But already in the books of *Dobrotolubye* and even earlier, one can find descriptions of terrible vices developing in the monastic communities. Not a few similar references are to be found also in Buddhist literature. Human nature is alike everywhere.

I shall quote here a timely and useful Discourse: "You know that there may be times worse than war. You well know that

We regard war as an infamy of humanity. How, then, shall We name the time that would be worse than war? Perhaps one could call it the putrefaction of humanity. Armageddon should not be understood as only a physical war. Armageddon is full of incalculable dangers. Epidemics will be the least of the calamities. The main destructive results will come from psychic perversion. People will lose confidence, they will sharpen their minds in mutual injury, they will learn to hate all that exists beyond the boundaries of their own dwellings, falling into a state of irresponsibility and sinking into depravity. To these madnesses will be added one more, the most shameful one, the revival of the battle between the Masculine and Feminine Principles.

"At the time when We speak about equal and full rights, the servants of darkness expel women from many fields precisely where they could bring the most benefit. We spoke about new fissures in the world, but the new battle between the Principles will be the most deadly one. It is impossible to imagine the destruction such a battle can bring! It will be a resistance to evolution! And you know the costliness to humanity of each such resistance. In these convulsions the young generation will be perverted.

"Plato spoke about the beauty of thinking, but what kind of beauty of thinking is possible during enmity between the Principles! Precisely now one should think about full rights, but darkness inundates the domains that are the most strained. Let us say that all attacks of the dark ones will be turned to good. Those who are humbled in Kali Yuga will be elevated in Satya Yuga. But let us not forget that these years of Armageddon will be exceedingly tense. Even health must be especially guarded. The cosmic currents may contribute to many illnesses. One should take into consideration that this is an unrepeatable time! Some people think that merely the avoidance of war alone will solve all problems. The near-sighted ones! They do not see that the worst war is inside their homes. They think that they can cheat evolution! And yet, there do exist green open spaces where evolution grows, and Our solicitude is there.

"The Thinker ordained that the gifts of all the Muses be safeguarded. Only these accumulations will help to conquer darkness."

This is probably the reason why there is so much silencing,

and opposition is shown to the Banner for safeguarding the Treasures of the Muses.

For many, the most decisive time now begins. Many will have to reveal their true passport. People cannot realize as yet that the main difficulty lying before them is their constant admittance of the most ugly lack of co-measurement. From lack of co-measurement issues all destruction. From early childhood it is necessary to ingrain the ability to discern the most important and essential, consequently, to distinguish all that is truly great from the second-rate and null.

One should reread more often about the law of co-measurement on page 122 in the second volume of *Leaves of Morya's Garden*. "From non-comeasurement results destruction, blasphemy, lie, treason, and many other ugly manifestations." The stronghold of Brotherhood is CO-MEASUREMENT.

Do not tire of insisting on the application of co-measurement in all manifestations of life. To begin with, one should try to lose the habit of humiliating others. Because we truly cannot grasp with our earthly vision the entire significance and depth of all that takes place, and also of the true essence of man.

Develop co-measurement—this basis of cooperation.

Part V

1939

1

1939

You write that someone is indignant at the fact that in the books of the Teaching of Living Ethics permission is given to eat smoked or dried meat, whereas all other Teachings altogether do not allow the use of meat. We have to answer that apparently this inquirer has not sufficiently mastered the spirit of the Teachings mentioned by him, and likewise has not become fully acquainted with all the books of Living Ethics. He looked over or did not read to the end those discourses which pertain to the problems of food. But before giving any explanations about the reason for permitting the use of smoked or dried meat, I would like to ask him if he practices the ethical rules in all his actions with the same zeal as in the question of restricting food; and then I would like to remind him that Christ said, "Hear, and understand: Not that which goeth into the mouth defileth a man; but that which cometh out of the mouth." It is also said in Buddhist texts: "If one could attain perfection only through the renunciation of eating meat, then a horse or a cow would have reached it long since." Asceticism has no value as a means of liberation of the mind from earthly bonds: "It is far more difficult to find a patient man than one who subsists on air and roots." Yes, it is most difficult for people to comprehend that the principal purification lies in the purification of thoughts and motives, and in the broadening of consciousness, because karma is primarily created by thoughts. When a man is lofty in spirit, when the fiery transmutation of the centers has taken place, he can render the most harmful substances harmless upon his inner fire; his powerfully discharged psychic energy purifies and transmutes everything. One should remind many of those who adhere strictly to vegetarian food and at the same time do not miss an opportunity for slander, of the forgoing statements by the greatest Teachers of humanity.

Let us also remind this inquirer that localities exist in Tibet and Mongolia where it is practically impossible to obtain vegetables, because they either do not grow there or cannot ripen. The Buddhist monks are compelled to live solely on barley and mutton and yak's meat, nevertheless, there are among them very worthy souls.

And now I will remind you of a few paragraphs in the books

of Living Ethics that apparently have not been read to the end by some inquirers. In *Aum* at the end of paragraph 227 it is said: "Likewise, when I indicate a vegetable diet, I am guarding against nourishing the subtle body with blood. The essence of blood thoroughly permeates the body and even the subtle body. Blood is so undesirable in the diet that only in extreme cases do We permit the use of meat which has been dried in the sun. It is also possible to use those parts of the animal where the blood substance has been thoroughly transmuted. Thus, vegetable food also has a significance for life in the Subtle World."

Moreover, a seeming follower of the Teaching of Living Ethics wrote me that it is regrettable that in the books of the Teaching abstention from alcohol is nowhere pointed out! And yet, in the second part of *Leaves of Morya's Garden* it is said that "the use of wine ... [and] narcotics takes away three quarters of ... [man's] vitality." and in *New Era Community* it is stated that "drunkenness is the enemy of psychomechanics"—an enemy of psychic energy, which is the basis of our existence. It would seem that this could hardly be stated more strongly, but people who do not take the trouble to fully acquaint themselves with the Teaching begin to lie and to vilify. They do not even understand that when the Teaching speaks of self discipline, about mental and physical purification, this means of course, abstinence from all kinds of excesses, no matter what they may be, and from substances and habits harmful for the organism.

Brotherhood, 21. "Any food containing blood is harmful for the development of subtle energy. If humanity would only refrain from devouring dead bodies, then evolution could be accelerated. Meat lovers have tried to remove the blood, but they have not been able to obtain the desired results. Meat, even with the blood removed, cannot be fully freed from the emanations of this powerful substance. The sun's rays to a certain extent remove these emanations, but their dispersion into space also causes not small harm. Try to carry out a psychic energy experiment near a slaughterhouse and you will receive signs of acute madness, not to mention the entities which attach themselves to the exposed blood. Not without foundation has blood been called sacred.

"There can thus be observed different kinds of people. It is possible to convince oneself particularly as to how strong atavism is. The desire for food containing blood is augmented by atavism, because the many preceding generations were saturated with blood. Unfortunately, governments pay no attention to improving the health of the population. State medicine and hygiene stand at a low level ... on the path to Brotherhood there should be no slaughterhouses."

Brotherhood, 22. "Yet there are people who speak much against bloodshed but are themselves not averse to eating meat. There are many contradictions contained in man. Only the perfecting of psychic energy can promote the harmonization of life. Contradiction is nothing but disorder. Different strata have corresponding contents. But a tempest can stir up waves, and not quickly thereafter is the right current again established."

There is a Discourse on this subject also in *Supermundane*. "Not a few terrible results occur owing to opposition to Our Indications. Some people oppose most useful advices, others fulfill them outwardly, but inwardly oppose. One should pay special attention to the latter circumstance.

"If people could understand of what small value are their external, pretended smiles!... The most useful advice loses its significance when it is inwardly rejected; then only the outer shell remains. One should also remember how many useful indications are distorted. As an example, let us take the problem of food. We are decidedly against eating meat. It has sufficiently impeded evolution. Still, there may be a famine, and then dried and smoked meat may be permitted as an extreme measure. We are decidedly against wine, it is just as impermissible as is narcosis, yet there are illnesses where alcohol is needed. We are decidedly against all narcotics, but there are cases of such unbearable sufferings that a physician has no other way but to resort to them.

"It will also be argued, Why not use suggestion against any pain? Indeed, one could, but it is not easy to find a person who possesses a sufficient power of suggestion. It would seem that these Indications of Ours are clear enough, but there are people who will stir up confusion and do harm. The whisperers will affirm that We allow the use of wine, narcotics, and meat. They will demand absolute forbiddance; but should they become hungry or ill, they will be the first to reproach the Teacher who left them with no alternative.

"In addition to sanctimoniousness one may expect all kinds of cunning. People will deceive themselves if they can only vindicate their weaknesses. Yet they will not ponder what danger they are creating. They seemingly wish to become Our co-workers, but where is the solicitude that lies at the base of each cooperation?

"The Thinker used to say, 'Beware of all assurances of love, the great foundation of the world needs not assurances, but actions'."

It seems to me that the Discourses quoted here fully clarify the attitude of the Teaching of Living Ethics toward the problems of food and the use of alcohol.

2

1939

In one of my letters I already wrote that I consider marriage a sacred concept, and also that I will never cast a stone at a woman who, because of self-sacrificing love, ignored the established conventions, providing, however, that she does not build her happiness on the misfortune of others. It seems to me that this is spoken broadly enough, and I would not want to enter into further explanations regarding all cases when it is permissible to break the conventions. After all, every sensible human being well understands the significance of the inviolability of marriage and of the harmony of the family for the growing generation and in the structure of the state. It is said in the Teaching that the family is the prototype of the state. The welfare and the well-being of the state rest upon the firm foundations of the family.

If, however, one were to cite the most immutable cosmic truths that establish the inviolability of marriage, the majority would undoubtedly use these proclaimed truths to vindicate the violation of it. Thus, if one were to affirm to them that the sacredness and inviolability of marriage has as its basis the great truth about twin-souls, with an eased conscience they will at once start to look for that half which belongs to them, and without fail will find it at someone else's fireside. There are not a few who explain all their infatuations as cosmic attractions. Is it possible to explain to these people that precisely the purity of their married life will bring them faster and closer to finding the kindred soul? If one were to tell them that during moral licentiousness twin-souls feel an especially sharp antagonism toward each other, they would not believe it and would become indignant. Whereas, only where there is purity of feeling are the most beautiful unions and best possibilities attainable. Owing to the moral degradation of contemporary humanity, a harmonious union is rarest of all, yet only then are the greatest achievements possible in all worlds.

It is shocking to observe how light-mindedly people approach the Teaching, which demands from them the most serious, the most penetrating attitude toward all vital questions together with a realization of one's full responsibility not only for each action but also for each thought. The Living Ethics, though primarily setting forth the moral foundations, also demands a full realization of responsibility, fulfillment of one's duty and all accepted obligations, and honesty in everything and toward all. Each lie, each deceit, each hypocrisy is severely condemned. A man who has entered the path of the Teaching of Living Ethics must account for all his deeds and should know that his violation of the moral foundations will entail redoubled consequences for him, for he cannot say that he acted because of ignorance.

Thus, purity in married life is an absolute condition for all true disciples. How can one approach the Covenants of Light if the soul is full of unbridled feelings? One of the Teachers says that "In ancient times the master who purified silver had to sit before the crucible in which was the melted mass of metal until he could see his face reflected in the purified metal. The improvement of the human essence—the law of evolution—refines crude forms of life in accordance with a perfect pattern and must bring these forms to that point of development where this pattern shall be reflected in each organic cell of these forms, in all conditions and states—physical, mental, and spiritual; and fire, i.e., pressure, tension, and sufferings are the only levers by which the mass—the human race—can be raised from the crucible. The physical substance must be raised into the light of the substance of higher mentality, where the renunciation of any attachment to the lower conditions of the substance—*the passions*—will make possible the manifestation of more refined and perfected spiritual forms. . . .

"Any sensible man cannot fail to see the great necessity of changing the methods of instituting marriages and of certain stipulations in existing marriage laws if we wish to see a better race of human beings, which is on the way to replace ours. But the rejection of the present marriage laws, a conscious lowering of ideals, and the acceptance of a lawlessness that was dominant in antediluvian times, can only have one result—*degeneration*. Humanity will not acquire strength and knowledge through regression deep into past centuries; only a purifying, progressive motion creates evolution. Therefore, education and upbringing should be directed toward finding a true union of both sides in marriage, and monogamy must be established instead of the existing disorderly mixing of sexes. . . .

"A good gardener, desiring to cultivate a beautiful flower of a certain family, collects seeds or takes a graft from the best sample of the chosen species and combines it with another sample of the same family; and when he receives in this manner a perfected variety he will try not to mix its seeds with the lower specimens of the same family. The same laws are also applicable to the human race. Therefore, no refutation can make out of that which is usually called 'sexual freedom' anything but freedom for the satisfaction of lower desires . . .

"In the future more perfected race true marriages will be just as common as they are rare at present. . . .

"Of course, it is unthinkable to insist on the continuity of marriage bonds between people who are antagonistic, faithless, and cruel to each other, for this would be the worst kind of tyranny, but it is essential to institute a careful choice, and to use natural means for establishing a wise combination. A wrong or unfavorable aspect of the planets, covetous considerations, or an abnormal sexual attraction approaching an unhealthy state are responsible for the majority of unhappy and unnatural marriages at present.

"Humanity is now developing under a different aspect of the universal law from the one that ruled the birth and evolution of man during the early centuries of this Cycle. The law of differentiation—disunity—ruled in the far-off past, whereas now, primarily, the law of unity acts, and those who, because of egoistical desires, attempt to oppose the preordained Divine Plan exclude themselves from the evolutionary current . . ."

In conclusion, I will give one more quotation: "Woman of the present race approaches the highest point in the coming Cycle, and every woman who can save man from his lower 'ego'—in that she herself does not succumb to the temptations that her lower nature places also on her path, thus affirming the existence of a higher phase of life—this woman, in the coming Cycle, will do more for the salvation of the race to which they both belong than any man, no matter how great he may be. The coming epoch is the epoch of woman, and therefore, in the end precisely woman, far more than man, will be summoned to the austere responsibility for the immorality of our age. The coming time affords a great possibility for woman, therefore I again appeal to you, daughters of Light, pray that God who is within you may help you to preserve purity..."

3

26 January 1939

All the symptoms described by you of imbalance in your system are more than understandable. Who can remain indifferent toward the unheard-of counter-currents in the rhythm of the cosmic currents during the days of Armageddon, which react upon everything that exists? Precisely, Armageddon is not only terrifying because of the unbridling of the dark forces but also because of that disharmony of currents, which primarily reflects heavily upon especially sensitive organisms and thus temporarily throws out of line the bold fighters against the inundating waves of the raging chaos. Only a strong, disciplined will, knowledge, and firm striving on the indicated path of Light can safeguard from the grave consequences of these cosmic disturbances. During such days one should constantly remember that the hour of testing of our forces has come, and the least deviation or weakening of the will can carry us away into the path of calamities. Blessing to him who can be imbued with solemnity during the days of he most profound significance.

The entire moral level of man is like a barometer, it either rises or falls, as Pirogoff* says, and of special danger are those fluctuations which are brought about, not by ideas, but by instincts and lower psychism. During fatal and unavoidable periods when morality is at a particularly low ebb, it is essential to direct all the forces of spirit toward self-perfectment. Therefore you are right in asking how to acquire patience, for without this quality it is impossible to begin self-perfectment. Patience lies at the core of all achievements, therefore it is the greatest

---

* A great Russian scientist.

quality. It is easiest of all to acquire patience through love for service and for the Great Teacher. Of course, it is also affirmed in us during straight-knowledge, or in better words, when being spiritually enlightened by the lofty meaning of this particular concept—patience—but such attainment is far more difficult. As in everything, the path of love is the shortest and the most beautiful, and for him who knows what love is, it is also the easiest. Thus, my advice to you who have felt the fiery burning of the heart toward the Teaching will be to strengthen yourself in patience through love. Each irritation restrained, each manifestation of tolerance will be like a flower offering for the Teaching.

One can also help oneself considerably through the development of constant recollection of this quality in all circumstances of life. Indeed, it is necessary to attain such recollection that independent of all else it will remain constantly vigilant in your consciousness, ready each minute to remind you of itself. An ancient mantram had also in mind the strengthening of this recollection. Precisely, recollection helps self-discipline, which is quite difficult. Many years pass by before we succeed in bridling our feelings, which are ever ready to reflect their least and unexpected stimulation. Indeed, patience is one of the most difficult qualities; not in vain is it said that the truly great man is he who is great in patience. However, that which is difficult is truly valuable, therefore it is right to apply all one's forces to the mastery of this treasure.

You ask, "In what cases should one apply the canon, 'By thy God,' and when is it our duty to demonstrate resistance to evil?" As an example, you quote Christ's prayer about forgiveness of those who persecuted him because "they know not what they do." And here you make the deduction that "If actions are to be vindicated because of the level of the consciousness of the person who acts, but who does not know that his actions are caused by darkness, then one may surmise that it seems that one should not resist such evil, as was done by Christ."

To this I will answer that the canon "By thy God" and non-resistance to evil, are two completely different concepts. The canon, "By thy God," means, in other words, containment, and at the same time, co-measurement; precisely co-measurement does not admit sufferance of evil. The canon "By thy God" is applicable where there is evidence of good, even if it be narrowly understood. But the application of this canon in regard to evil as non-resistance to it will be not only an act of sufferance, but even cooperation in evil. Non-resistance to evil is admittance of the invasion of chaos, as a result of which occur all possible calamities and the downfall of multitudes.

It is regrettable that it is customary to regard the Teaching of Christ as the teaching of non-resistance to evil. This is the most appalling error. Indeed, Christ severely condemned all evil, all hypocrisy and a negligent attitude toward good. But one should learn to discriminate where non-resistance to evil can be used, and which measures are applicable in each case; a senseless choice of these can lead to a still greater calamity or dissolution. One should also know that every spiritual Teacher takes an oath not to strike at those who make attempts on his life. Thus, Christ also could not resist the crude force directed against Him. But He resisted evil in His every word, His every action when it did not concern Him personally. His mission was to accomplish His path by human feet and hands, and to reveal to people that one can sacrifice oneself in the greatest love for mankind and suffer the most cruel tortures because of the desire to bring to people the Light of the truths continually forgotten by them. The prayer of Christ for his torturers is full of compassion, and even justice, for, truly, what could hired executioners know and understand of the greatness of Him whom they tortured? Whom they were COMMANDED to torture! Verily, not the hired torturers, but their instigators took upon themselves the most *bitter* karma. Similarly, Pilate, who washed his hands and showed NON-RESISTANCE to the greatest evil when it was in his power to arrest it, prepared for himself the hardest destiny.

It is correct that an evil action is co-measured karmically with the consciousness that perpetrated it. All that is meditated in malice colors our aura especially strongly and weighs heavily upon the consciousness. And, at the same time, the man who creates evil while being but dimly aware of what he does prolongs and hardens his path immeasurably because he may begin to improve his destiny only after realizing the depth of evil created by him. One may, indeed, pray for those who do not understand the significance of their actions, for grievous is the destiny of such an animal-like state of mind. Thus, Lord Buddha said, "Of two people who have committed the same error, he is worse off who does not realize it. ... For one cannot expect a man who does not consider himself guilty to manifest effort for the cessation of his erring. In order to cure oneself, one has to know one's ailment, but the realization of it does not give health; for that, the necessary condition is a manifestation of will." Karma is created by thoughts, therefore, likewise "There is no merit for the one who gives gold, thinking he gives a stone." The happiness of humanity lies in the hastening of evolution, and one can imagine how the low consciousness of the majority holds back evolution.

You assume that "the dark doers of harm are confident that it is they who do good." But I do not agree with this assumption. All conscious doers of harm, in the depths of their consciousness know full well the covetous cause of their actions. Even the so-called unconscious ill-doers, for some reason, are always trying not to suffer personal harm and chiefly, not to their pockets. The degrees of consciousnesses are without end, and we can still see not a few animal-like consciousnesses. Verily, there is not greater misfortune than ignorance.

However, the canon "By thy God" must be applied in life, practically on every step. During each conversation, when there is no unity of consciousnesses, our first duty is not to infuriate our companion by contradiction and censure of his convictions, but, starting with his best possibilities and considering the level of his consciousness, we should gradually and patiently broaden his horizon. Thus, speaking with a Moslem, you will not begin by praising Lord Buddha or demeaning Mohammed, but you will interchange with him all that is beautiful in his religion, and when opportunity arises, you will explain more deeply and broadly the meaning of some sayings of Mohammed that have entered the treasury of world wisdom. Thus you will also do in any other situations in life. You will not speak with an avid chauvinist against his country, but you will discover the best expressions and qualities of his nation, and you will point out to him new ways for developing its particular qualifications. Your breadth of understanding of national beliefs will smooth over the factor of chauvinism and, unexpectedly for him, his limited consciousness will begin to respond to the note of containment. And so, one should learn to carry on timely conversations without animosity but evaluating your companion with friendliness. Precisely, carry them on with PATIENCE and respect for your adversary, not permitting irritation, derision, and other unworthy means. And in each conversation one should know how to sacrifice one's self, one's knowledge, and not to boast of one's enlightenment. Remember that it is said in the Teaching that only a pompous ignorance loves to spread on window sills the dry, small twigs of its knowledge, but he who truly knows does not fear to snip off a piece of his knowledge when it can oppress and humiliate his companion. In this manner, the canon "By thy God" is merely a manifestation of selflessness, without which nothing can be achieved. It is a great error to liken it to non-resistance to evil. If you wish, accept this canon as a manifestation of mercy. And so, the canon "By thy God" is fully compatible precisely with resistance to evil. One can put a stop to evil by various means, and straight-knowledge should prompt the *limits* of possibilities when applying the given canon.

And paragraph 378 from *Hierarchy* must definitely be remembered, because every one of us should strive to extinguish and arrest evil, primarily, of course, in oneself and in one's own surroundings. Verily, with all our being, with all the forces of the soul let us uphold good and fight evil; fight that evil which is on the outside of us as well as that which nestles within us. Evil is always evil, irrespective of its location. Let us remember that it is a severe battle for his beloved striving for truth and perfection which the human spirit is destined to carry on. As Pirogoff says, "One should pay more vital attention to upbringing than to education," and he is quite right in this. But in daily life the word *upbringing* has taken on the most ugly connotation, as an understanding of acquiring good manners and training in sport. Practically no one ponders that education primarily concerns the whole inner substance of man and his entire character, and that it is the instilling of the foundations of ethics into the child's consciousness from the earliest possible years. But, alas! At best, we are being taught the ethics of prize-fighters.

And now, something else. The rumors related by you, which are spread by vindictive people, are so characteristic of ignorant elements. As usual, unenlightened people of little culture everywhere and in everything are apt to judge everyone in accordance with their own secret cravings, and, of course, the question of material welfare occupies the foremost and most honored position with them. Therefore, all their suspicions are usually directed to this angle.

Are we not used to hearing from the average citizen of any

country in the world that his government thinks only of its own welfare, that all its officials are corrupt or venal, etc. Likewise, where such citizens see evidences of activities that are beyond their consciousness, or expenditures for works of art, which they in their ignorance have not yet learned to value, their dull malice and envy begin first of all to weave the very same patterns about some mysterious sources of means, of hidden schemes, etc. Through all ages the real good was persecuted, only the tinsel of pseudo-truths is dear to the average man's heart. Why think that in our age of violence, of the right of crude might, the consciousness of the majority would be different? Actually, in accordance with the rumors and opinions cited by you, one can judge the degree of moral and cultural development of such thinking.

Indeed, this consciousness will not be far removed from the consciousness of the peasants who, during the cholera epidemic, killed the doctors, accusing them of poisoning the wells. One has to attribute all such carping to the very same source of all ills and calamities, namely *ignorance*. Yes, education may be attainable, but upbringing is far more difficult, and as for a state of culture, this is an exception, because it is the sign of true aristocracy—aristocracy of spirit and soul.

You are right—*to enter into polemics with an ignorant opponent is senseless.* The columns of newspapers, in most cases, are at present filled with such calumny, coarseness, and vulgarity that there is even a joke that although it was in the papers it proved to be true. The printed word has lost its one-time unfailing authority and the high significance of bringing light to broad masses. There are not a few newspapers at present which are not the disseminators of enlightenment, but are, alas, hotbeds of all kinds of deception, to put it mildly. The worthiest thoughts, the constructive tasks and views of outstanding people find no place, even on the last pages of these informers of the masses.

Besides, in order that a retraction may be effective it is necessary that it be printed in the same paper in which appeared the article that one protests against.

To the contemporary Cicero who exclaims, "O Catalina, when wilt thou cease persecuting us!" I would answer, "I hope, never, because the end of persecution would mean the beginning of decomposition." There is an earthly law, according to which, from the moment persecution ceases and general acclaim is achieved, decomposition sets in. Struggle is the basis of existence and progress, therefore, without it man turns into a nonentity and toward license. In our days the battle has indeed become stronger and broader, for today one cannot name even one field of life in which there does not occur a clash of different principles. Therefore the Teaching says, "*Love the battle.*" But we must strive to transfer this battle to a loftier plane, and for this it is essential to develop and affirm one's own inner truth by means of penetrating deeper into the Teaching, into oneself, and into a harsh battle with self. Thus we will elevate ourselves and all those who come in contact with us. Again we have returned to the lofty concept of upbringing and of self education. On that I will end.

I am sending you courage to acquire patience and solemnity during the grave days of Armageddon. During especially hard moments compare yourself with the millions of unfortunate ones, and you will attain peace. Comparisons are useful.

All light to you!

CONTENTS

Part I
1935

1 – *16 July 1935*	7
2 – *22 July 1935*	12
3 – *30 July 1935*	16
4 – *30 August 1935*	17
5 – *3 September 1935*	19
6 – *5 September 1935*	21
7 – *24 September 1935*	27
8 – *1 October 1935*	31
9 – *1 October 1935*	32
10 – *1 October 1935*	33
11 – *8 October 1935*	35
12 – *11 October 1935*	39
13 – *15 October 1935*	43
14 – *7 October 1935*	51
15 – *4 November 1935*	56
16 – *16 November 1935*	61
17 – *18 November 1935*	70
18 – *26 November 1935*	75
19 – *7 December 1935*	76
20 – *7 December 1935*	80
21 – *9 December 1935*	86
22 – *12 December 1935*	88
23 – *14 December 1935*	90
24 – *17 December 1935*	91
25 – *18 December 1935*	92

Part II
1936

1 – *11 January 1936*	97
2 – *17 January 1936*	99
3 – *18 January 1936*	104
4 – *21 January 1936*	109
5 – *25 January 1936*	112
6 – *4 February 1936*	115
7 – *18 February 1936*	118
8 – *7 February 1936*	122
9 – *18 February 1936*	124
10 – *22 February 1936*	126
11 – *17 March 1936*	131
12 – *19 March 1936*	135
13 – *30 March 1936*	145
14 – *30 March 1936*	149
15 – *15 April 1936*	154
16 – *16 April 1936*	159
17 – *17 April 1936*	161
18 – *2 April 1936*	166
19 – *24 April 1936*	169
20 – *29 May 1936*	171
21 – *14 May 1936*	172
22 – *24 May 1936*	176
23 – *25 May 1936*	184
24 – *26 May 1936*	188
25 – *8 June 1936*	190
26 – *15 June 1936*	197
27 – *18 June 1936*	198
28 – *22 June 1936*	202
29 – *25 June 1936*	205
30 – *23 July 1936*	209

31 – *3 August 1936*	213
32 – *14 August 1936*	216
33 – *24 August 1936*	221
34 – *31 August 1936*	225
35 – *5 October 1936*	228
36 – *23 October 1936*	230
37 – *25 October 1936*	232
38 – *9 December 1936*	237
39 – *10 December 1936*	239
40 – *17 December 1936*	242

Part III
1937

1 – *1937*	249
2 – *7 January 1937*	250
3 – *14 January 1937*	256
4 – *27 January 1937*	258
5 – *19 February 1937*	260
6 – *9 March 1937*	266
7 – *1 April 1937*	266
8 – *6 May 1937*	267
9 – *14 May 1937*	270
10 – *17 May 1937*	275
11 – *17 May 1937*	278
12 – *28 May 1937*	284
13 – *4 June 1937*	292
14 – *11 June 1937*	302
15 – *19 June 1937*	306
16 – *2 July 1937*	310
17 – *6 July 1937*	311
18 – *19 July 1937*	313
19 – *31 July 1937*	316

20 – *9 August 1937*	324
21 – *16 August 1937*	328
22 – *19 August 1937*	332
23 – *2 September 1937*	336
24 – *11 September 1937*	342
25 – *23 September 1937*	344
26 – *1 October 1937*	345
27 – *23 October 1937*	350
28 – *14 January 1937*	359
29 – *1937*	361
30 – *19 November 1937*	364
31 – *23 November 1937*	365
32 – *27 November 1937*	370
33 – *30 November 1937*	376
34 – *3 December 1937*	378
35 – *11 December 1937*	386
36 – *1937*	389

Part IV
1938

1 – *25 January 1938*	395
2 – *29 January 1938*	397
3 – *11 February 1938*	400
4 – *8 March 1938*	403
5 – *15 March 1938*	408
6 – *17 March 1938*	409
7 – *5 April 1938*	409
8 – *19 April 1938*	412
9 – *23 April 1938*	416
10 – *23 April 1938*	419
11 – *29 April 1938*	427
12 – *7 May 1938*	428

13 – *5 July 1938*	435
14 – *12 July 1938*	438
15 – *6 August 1938*	444
16 – *13 August 1938*	447
17 – *10 September 1938*	455
18 – *10 September 1938*	458

Part V
1939

1 – *1939*	469
2 – *1939*	472
3 – *26 January 1939*	475

AGNI YOGA SERIES

LEAVES OF MORYA'S GARDEN I (THE CALL)	1924
LEAVES OF MORYA'S GARDEN II (ILLUMINATION)	1925
NEW ERA COMMUNITY	1926
Signs of Agni Yoga	
AGNI YOGA	1929
INFINITY I	1930
INFINITY II	1930
HIERARCHY	1931
HEART	1932
FIERY WORLD I	1933
FIERY WORLD II	1934
FIERY WORLD III	1935
AUM	1936
BROTHERHOOD	1937
SUPERMUNDANE (IN 3 VOLUMES)	1938
LETTERS OF HELENA ROERICH, Vol. I	1929-1935
LETTERS OF HELENA ROERICH, Vol. II	1935-1939

AGNI YOGA SOCIETY
www.agniyoga.org

www.ingramcontent.com/pod-product-compliance
Lightning Source LLC
Chambersburg PA
CBHW071552080526
44588CB00010B/884